h/o

PS 571
S8

THE LITERATURE

OF

SOUTH DAKOTA

Edited, with Commentaries by

JOHN R. MILTON

Dakota Press

1976

The University of South Dakota, Vermillion, South Dakota 57069

CONTENTS

Acknowledgements

From *Journals of Lewis and Clark:* A New Selection with an Introduction by John Bakeless. Copyright © 1964 by John Bakeless. Reprinted by permission of The New American Library, New York.

From *Roads from the Fort,* copyright, 1954, by Arvid Shulenberger. Reprinted by permission of Harcourt Brace Jovanovich, Inc.

The Song of the Messiah by John G. Neihardt, copyright 1953. Permission to reprint granted by Hilda N. Petri.

"Storm and Stampede" from *Dakota Cowboy* by Ike Blasingame, copyright 1958 by Ike Blasingame. Reprinted by permission of Jack Blasingame.

"Toward the Sunset" in *Giants in the Earth* by O. E. Rölvaag. Copyright, 1927 by Harper & Row, Publishers, Inc.; renewed, 1955 by Jennie Marie Berdahl Rölvaag. Courtesy of Harper & Row, Publishers, Inc.

PREFACE

That South Dakota has a literature of its own, and an interesting literature, is attested to by the bibliographical sources such as J. Leonard Jennewein's *Black Hills Booktrails* and the State Library Commission's pamphlet, *A South Dakota Bibliography*. However, there has never been a reasonably definitive collection of this literature. O. W. Coursey's books—variously called *Literature of South Dakota* and *Dakota Literature*—were published in the 1920's and included a smattering of biographical material and verses representing South Dakota writers of that time. These books are useful in their way, but they are neither discriminating nor complete.

Any collection of the literature of South Dakota must include at least some of the writing done by visitors or passers-through. For almost a century and a half the main impressions of South Dakota came from explorers, fur traders, military men, gold seekers, foreign travelers, Eastern journalists and even some professional writers who spent a little time in the Territory or the State. The purpose of this anthology—the first of its kind—is to portray South Dakota through the literature which has been produced by a variety of writers who at one time or another were in South Dakota. In later years, largely since World War II, the emphasis shifts a little to writers who actually lived in the state or were born here. In the past fifteen years local writers have developed at a rapid rate, for the simple reason that some of the energy which once had to be put entirely into survival can now be directed into the arts, into the cultural creativity which is eventually necessary to the spirit.

A thorough collection of the literature of South Dakota would demand a large and expensive book—probably several books. The selection for this anthology has taken into account literary value as well as general cultural values and has included most of those writers who are well known both in South Dakota and elsewhere. Much good material was regrettably omitted because it did not deal specifically with South Dakota even though the writers lived here. Some readers will wonder why Laura Ingalls Wilder is not included, especially since there has been a popular revival of her work in the 1970's, partly caused by the television series. One could argue that her stories were intended for young people and that they would seem out of place in this otherwise adult collection. Perhaps a better reason is that the Wilder books are easily available and can be read separately. Finally, of course, the simple matter of space dictated that only a certain number of writers should be represented. The choice of writers is the editor's painful task and his responsibility.

Concerning the order in which the materials appear, it seemed more appropriate to arrange the pieces according to the chronology of the subject matter than to arrange the writers by the chronology of their birth dates. Since many of the earlier pieces are some kind of personal reporting, the two orders actually coincide, with the notable exceptions being Frederick Manfred and Arvid Shulenberger. In the latter part of the book, the contemporary pieces are only partly arranged by authors' ages; an attempt was made to provide a measure of continuity according to subject, theme, and treatment.

It is my hope that the book may be read as a continuing story of South Dakota, a portrait from the time of Lewis and Clark to the present.

Several years ago a much smaller version of this anthology was tried out in a class in South Dakota literature at Vermillion High School. The course proved popular, and I wish to thank the teachers who taught the course, used the hastily-assembled book, and encouraged me to continue my efforts to provide a better and more comprehensive book.

The Northwest Area Foundation (formerly the Hill Family Foundation of St. Paul) has given both encouragement and financial help. Without either, the book could not have been born. Further indispensable help has come from the National Endowment for the Arts, and I wish to thank the Endowment's Director of the Literature Program, Len Randolph. He and John Taylor of the Northwest Area Foundation have kept me going through their personal interest.

I wish also to thank Charlotte Carver of the South Dakota Arts Council for helping with a grant application; Suzanne Miller for assistance in gathering the often-elusive biographical information, so that all of the writers in the book may be identified as fully as possible; and Sharon Jensen, to whom I owe much, and without whom neither I nor Dakota Press would function properly.

J. R. M.

INTRODUCTION

The first "literature" of South Dakota was the journal of exploration, followed by the travel narrative, these appearing long before South Dakota became a state.

The journal of exploration was not intended to be literary, but today we can read these journals for their mixture of realism and romanticism, for their descriptions of the land before it was subjected to civilization, and for the "story" of each journal, sometimes as exciting as the narratives of modern times. The realistic detail was the result of gathering information about a new land; the romantic response to the land was partly in keeping with the literary tendencies of the time—early 19th century—and partly a result of the overwhelming landscape which often evoked a sense of awe in the first explorers.

The first of the journals was written by a Frenchman, Francois La Verendrye. He and his brother Louis-Joseph, with two companions, were possibly the first white men to explore in what is now South Dakota, arriving at the present site of Fort Pierre early in 1743, claiming the region for New France (Canada), and leaving their father's name on the site in lasting tribute. The journal was written in French, in the form of a letter to Marquis de Beauharnois, Governor of New France. A few other journals in French, most of them very brief, exist from later in the 18th century.

The first journal written in the English language in South Dakota seems to be that of a Scot, James Mackay, who entered this region from Canada also, in the 1790's. But the first widely-read journal in English, and the first by white Americans, was the record of the Lewis and Clark expedition, 1804-1806, with the two men taking turns writing the account of the long trip across the continent. The journey was one of the great odysseys of the world, and the journal is a remarkable document, even though Lewis and Clark were not famous for their spelling ability. Because they travelled across the entire state, from south to north, following the Missouri River, their document is properly the first South Dakota literature.

The travel narrative became popular when the steamboat "Yellowstone" made its first trip to Fort Union in 1832, opening this part of the country to what we would now call tourists. The travel narrative is more often a result of curiosity, or sightseeing, than of exploration as such. And usually the narrative was revised and rewritten, polished and made more literary, after the traveller returned home. Such well-known people as George Catlin and Audubon left commentaries on their Missouri River trips, both in writing and in painting. Dignitaries from Europe, such as Paul Wilhelm, Duke of Wuerttemberg, wrote books after visiting the region.

Between the 1830's and the discovery of gold in the Black Hills in the 1870's, geological and military expeditions were common in the western half of the state, each expedition filing a report which was both official and personal, so that parts of these documents may almost be treated as literature. Some of the more enduring reports came from John Evans, F. V. Hayden, Lt. G. K. Warren, Eugene Bandel, and Gen. W. F. Raynolds.

With the coming of Lt. Col. George Custer, the discovery of gold, and the Battle of the Little Big Horn, events were reported by military men, including Custer, by gold seekers, by opportunists and newspaper men, and eventually, in retrospect, by dozens of 20th-century novelists who found drama in the struggle for the Black Hills. For accounts by the people who were there, a good source is *Black Hills Booktrails*, by J. Leonard Jennewein. Historical novels, written later, abound. Some of them are literary in the best sense; others are more properly called popular. Many have been made into motion pictures. Not only Custer's military exploits (or lack of them) became the subject of historical novels, but also the Lewis and Clark expedition, the lives of mountain men in the 1820's and 1830's, and the many engagements between the military and the Sioux over several decades. The Lewis and Clark expedition is the subject of *Tale of Valor,* by Vardis Fisher, *The Conquest,* by Eva Emery Dye, *No Other White Men,* by Julia Davis, *Westward the Course,* by Hildegarde Hawthorne, *Star of the West,* by Ethel Hueston, *The Magnificent Adventure,* by Emerson Hough, *Hobnailed Boots,* by Jeannette C. Nolan, *Forward the Nation,* by Donald Culross Peattie, and *In the Gates of the Mountains,* by Will Henry. Some of the better novels about Custer are *The Dice of God,* by Hoffman Birney, *Montana Road,* by Harry Sinclair Drago, *Yellow Hair,* by Clay Fisher, *Broken Lance,* by Frank Gruber, *Bugles in the Afternoon,* by Ernest Haycox, *No Survivors,* by Will Henry, and *Red Mother,* by Frank B. Linderman. Not all of these novels take place in South Dakota, however, since Custer was stationed in North Dakota just before the losing battle which occurred in Montana. But the list of historical novels at least touching on South Dakota or events which themselves touched on the state is almost endless.

In the early part of the 20th century, when settlement was progressing at a rapid rate, the state had its first "boom" of home-grown literature. In fiction, the cowboy and Indian were popular as subjects. Kate and Virgil Boyles, of Yankton, and Will Lillibridge of Sioux Falls, each published a number of novels and each had one best seller of over 100,000 copies, a remarkable feat for the time. Over a period of years, settling in Dakota was dramatized in fiction by Hamlin Garland, O. E. Rölvaag, W. Hyatt Downing, Laura Ingalls Wilder, and many other writers. Garland tended to be gloomy and to see the harshness of the land, Rolvaag showed Norwegian immigrants isolated far from home in a sea of grass as they attempted to make new homes and survive the winters, Wilder somewhat romanticized or sentimentalized the hardships and created happy endings, and other writers found their niches somewhere between the two extremes.

At the same time, poetry flourished through the founding of *Pasque Petals* magazine in the 1920's and through the cowboy verses of Badger Clark. By and large, however, the chief staple of South Dakota literature for many years was fiction. Most of the verse written during the earlier periods was religious in a sentimental vein, and the dust bowl of the 1930's was better and more realistically dealt with in fiction. Borghild Dahl wrote of education during the depression in *This Precious Year.* William Cameron Johnston's *Bathroom's Down the Hall* was set in a boarding house during the years of drouth. The depression could also be used as a test of character, as indicated in the title, *Out of This Nettle,* a novel by Mary Gates. And long-range wisdom and the discovery of identity with the land emerged from Frederick Manfred's *The Golden Bowl,* along with a recognition of the life forces which had existed on the land long before the advent of man.

In addition to the literature *about* South Dakota, whether written by natives of the state or by visitors, several books by South Dakotans who left the state before they became famous achieved national or international recognition. L. Frank Baum, who edited an Aberdeen newspaper for several years, wrote *The Wizard of Oz,* which became a classic and prompted fourteen books about Oz. Cameron Hawley, whose *Executive Suite, Cash McCall,* and *The Lincoln Lords* were best-selling novels, was born in Howard. And in a less literary field, Dale Carnegie, who worked in Pierre at one time, made a fortune from his practical book, *How to Win Friends and Influence People.*

Since 1960, or thereabouts, regional literature has blossomed again, different this time because of changing modes and attitudes. Although the low population of the state determines that there will be a relatively small number of writers, several circumstances have furthered the literary progress of the state beyond that which might be expected. *Pasque Petals* still has its versifiers and its audience after forty years. The Black Hills Writers Group is active. In 1963 the founding of the *South Dakota Review,* a literary review which has achieved national prominence, offered a local outlet for fiction and poetry meeting high standards. A more recent publication, *Sunday Clothes,* has provided an additional outlet. The poets-in-the-schools program, sponsored by the National Endowment for the Arts, has made young people more aware of the experience of poetry. And disgust with life in the large metropolitan areas has brought a number of fine writers into the rural and small town environments of South Dakota.

Even though South Dakota has never been completely barren, as some uninformed outsiders have thought, either in landscape or in literature, it seems that with the problems of settlement and survival disappearing into the past, and with the new concern for the arts, literature will flourish.

J.R.M.

I

WILLIAM CLARK

Born in Virginia on August 1, 1770, Clark moved with his family to Kentucky when he was fourteen, learning the tactics of Indian warfare at an early age. By the time he was nineteen he was serving in the army, but seven years later poor health forced him to resign. In 1803, when the famous Louisiana Purchase added to the United States what is now approximately the northwest one-third of the nation, Clark was once again in the army, as a lieutenant, joining Meriwether Lewis in command of an expedition to explore the new territory. Lewis, more formally educated, and in President Jefferson's favor, was put in first command and promoted to captain. However, Lewis considered Clark a good friend and also recognized his ability to act quickly in time of decision, and so during the expedition he constantly referred to Clark as captain also.

The journey, with a complement of men ranging in numbers from about twenty to over forty, was a memorable one which now ranks with the two or three most important and daring travels in world history. Largely following the course of the Missouri River, the expedition went from St. Louis to the Pacific Ocean, by boat and on foot, and returned safely, having lost only one man (Sergeant Floyd) on the entire trip of thousands of miles through unknown territory.

During the expedition, 1804-1806, both Lewis and Clark kept journals. (Sergeant Gass also kept a shorter one.) Neither of the men was expert at writing, or spelling, and the original journals are often difficult to read. The first publication of the journals, in 1814, was not complete and was extensively rewritten in a more "literary" style of the time. The later Thwaites edition preserved the original spelling, punctuation, and notations. The edition used here is a new one, edited by John Bakeless, with some attention to grammar but with no basic changes in style.

The selections are from Clark's portion of the journal and cover a period of time during which the expedition was in South Dakota, outward bound.

Following the expedition Clark served as governor of Louisiana, as general in charge of the territorial militia, as Indian agent, and as territorial governor of Missouri. In 1822 he was appointed superintendent of Indian affairs at St. Louis by President Monroe, an office he held until his death on September 1, 1838.

THE JOURNALS OF LEWIS AND CLARK
(From Sioux City to Yankton)

19th August, 1804

A fine morning. Wind from the S.E. Prepared a small present for the chiefs and warriors present. The main chief breakfasted with us and begged for a sun glass. Those people are all naked, covered only with breechclouts, blankets, or buffalo robes—the flesh side painted with different colors and figures. At ten o'clock we assembled the chiefs and warriors, nine in number, under an awning, and Captain Lewis and I explained the speech sent to the nation from the Council Bluffs by Mr. Faufon. The three chiefs and all the men or warriors made short speeches approving the advice and council their Great Father had sent them, and concluded by giving themselves some credit for their acts.

We then brought out the presents and exchanged The Big Horse's medal and gave him one equal to the one sent to the Little Thief, and gave all some small articles and eight carrots of tobacco. We gave one small medal to one of the chiefs and a certificate to the others, of their good intentions.

Names	Great chiefs I have mentioned before.
The Little Thief	Karkapaha—Missouri
The Big Horse	Nenasawa— "
Crows Head, or	Sarnanono—Oto
Black Cat, or	Neeswarunja—"
Iron Eyes, or	Stargeahunja—"
Big Ax (Ox), or	Warsarshaco
Big Blue Eyes	
Brave Man, or	

One of those Indians, after receiving his certificate, delivered it again to me—The Big Blue Eyes. The chief petitioned for the certificate again. We would not give the certificate, but rebuked them very roughly for having in object goods and not peace with their neighbors. This language they did not like at first, but at length all petitioned for us to give back the certificate to The Big Blue Eyes. He came forward and made a plausible excuse. I then gave the certificate to the great chief to bestow it to the most worthy. They gave it to him. We then gave them a dram and broke up the council.

The chiefs requested we would not leave them this evening. We determined to set out early in the morning. We showed them many curiosities, and the air gun, which they were much astonished at. Those people begged much for whiskey. Sergeant Floyd is taken very bad all at once with a bilious colic. We attempt to relieve him without success as yet. He gets worse and we are much alarmed at his situation. All attention to him.

20th August, Monday, 1804

Sergeant Floyd much weaker and no better. Made Mr. Faufon, the interpreter, a few presents and the Indians a canister of whiskey. We set out under a gentle breeze from the S.E., and proceeded on very well. Sergeant Floyd as bad as he can be, no pulse, and nothing will stay a moment on his stomach or bowels. Passed two islands on the S.S. Sergeant Floyd died with a great deal of composure. Before his death, he said to me, "I am going away— I want you to write me a letter." We buried him on the top of the bluff a half mile below a small river to which we gave his name. He was buried with the honors of war, much lamented. A cedar post with the name:

Sergeant C. Floyd
died here
20th of August
1804

was fixed at the head of his grave. This man at all times gave us proof of his firmness, and determined resolution to do service to his country, and honor to himself. After paying all the honor to our deceased brother, we camped in the mouth of Floyd's River, about 30 yards wide. A beautiful evening.

22nd August, 1804

Set out early. Wind from the south. At three miles, we landed at a bluff where the two men sent with the horses were waiting with two deer. By examination, this bluff contained alum, copperas, cobalt, pyrites; an alum rock, soft and sand stone. Captain Lewis, in proving the quality of those minerals, was near poisoning himself by the fumes and taste of the cobalt, which had the appearance of soft isinglass. Copperas and alum are very poisonous. Above this bluff a small creek comes in from the L.S., passing under the cliff for several miles.

Captain Lewis took a dose of salts to work off the effects of the arsenic. We camped on the S.S. Sailed the greater part of this day with a hard wind from the S.E. Great deal of elk sign and great appearance of wind from the N.W.

Ordered a vote for a sergeant to choose one of three which may be the highest number. The highest numbers are P. Glass (had 19 votes), Bratton, and Gibson.

23rd August, 1804

Set out this morning very early. The two men with the horses did not come up last night. I walked on shore and killed a fat buck. J. Fields sent out to hunt; came to the boat and informed that he had killed a buffalo in the plain ahead. Captain Lewis took twelve men and had the buffalo brought to the boat. In the next bend to the S.S., two elk swam the river, and were fired at from the boat. R. Fields came up with the horses and brought two deer. One deer killed from the boat. Several prairie wolves seen today. Saw elk standing on the sand bar. The wind blew hard and raised the sands off the bar in such clouds that we could scarcely see. This sand, being fine and very light, stuck to everything it touched, and in the plain for half a mile—the distance I was out—every spire of grass was covered with sand or dirt.

24th August, 1804

Some rain last night. A continuation this morning. We set out at the usual time and proceeded on the course of last night, to the commencement of a blue clay bluff 180 or 190 feet high on the L.S. Those bluffs appear to have been latterly on fire and at this time are too hot for a man to bear his hand in the earth at any depth. Great appearance of coal. An immense quantity of cobalt, or a crystalized substance which answers its description, is on the face of the bluff.

Great quantities of a kind of berry resembling a currant, except double the size, and grows on a bush like a privet, and the size of a damson, deliciously flavored, and makes delightful tarts. This fruit is now ripe. I took my servant and a French boy and walked on shore. Killed two buck elks and a fawn, and intercepted the boat, and had all the meat butchered and in by sunset, at which time it began to rain and rained hard. Captain Lewis and myself walked out and got very wet. A cloudy, rainy night. In my absence, the boat passed a small river, called by the Indians Whitestone River. This river is about 30 yards wide, and runs through a plain or prairie in its whole course.

In a northerly direction from the mouth of this creek, in an immense plain, a high hill is situated, and appears of a conic form, and by the different nations of Indians in this quarter, is supposed to be the residence of devils: that they are in human form with remarkable large heads, and about 18 inches high, that they are very watchful, and are armed with sharp arrows with which they can kill at a great distance. They are said to kill all persons who are so hardy as to attempt to approach the hill. They state that tradition informs them that many Indians have suffered by those little people, and, among others, three Maha men fell a sacrifice to their merciless fury not many years since.

So much do the Maha, Sioux, Otos, and other neighboring nations, believe this fable, that no consideration is sufficient to induce them to approach the hill.

25th August, 1804

A cloudy morning. Captain Lewis and myself concluded to go and see the mound which was viewed with such terror by all the different nations in this quarter. We selected Shields, J. Fields, W. Bratton, Sergeant Ordway, J. Colter, Carr, and Corporal Warfington and Frazer, also G. Drouilliard, and dropped down to the mouth of the Whitestone River, where we left the pirogue with two men; and, at 200 yards, we ascended a rising ground of about 60 feet. From the top of this high land, the country is level and open as far as can be seen, except some few rises at a great distance, and the mound which the Indians call "Mountain of little people, or spirits." This mound appears of a conic form, and is N. 20 W. from the mouth of the creek. We left the river at 8 o'clock. At r miles we crossed the creek, 23 yards wide, in an extensive valley, and continued on two miles further.

Our dog was so heated and fatigued, we were obliged to send him back to the creek. At 12 o'clock we arrived at the hill. Captain Lewis much fatigued from heat—the day, it being very hot, and he being in a debilitated state from the precautions he was obliged to take, to prevent the effects of the cobalt and mineral substance which had like to have poisoned him two days ago. His want of water, and several men complaining of great thirst, determined us to make for the first water, which was the creek in a bend N.E. from the mound, about three miles. After a delay of about one hour and a half to recruit our party, we set out on our return down the creek through the bottom, of about one mile in width, crossed the creek three times to the place we first struck it, where we gathered some delicious fruit, such as grapes, plums, and blue currants. After a delay of an hour, we set out on our back trail, and arrived at the pirogue at sunset. We proceeded on to the place we camped last night, and stayed all night.

This mound is situated on an elevated plain in a level and extensive prairie, bearing N. 20 W. from the mouth of Whitestone Creek nine miles. The base of the mound is a regular parallelogram, the long side of which is about 300 yards in length, the shorter 60 or 70 yards. From the longer side of the base, it rises from the north and south, with a steep ascent to the height of 65 or 70 feet, leaving a level plain on the top 12 feet in width and 90 in length. The north and south parts of this mound are joined by two regular rises, each in oval forms of half its height, forming three regular rises from the plain. The ascent of each elevated

8

part is as sudden as the principal mound at the narrower sides of its base.

The regular form of this hill would in some measure justify a belief that it owed its origin to the hand of man; but as the earth and loose pebbles and other substances of which it was composed bore an exact resemblance to the steep ground which borders on the creek, in its neighborhood, we concluded it was most probably the production of nature.

The only remarkable characteristic of this hill, admitting it to be a natural production, is that it is insulated or separated a considerable distance from any other, which is very unusual in the natural order or disposition of the hills.

The surrounding plains are open, void of timber, and level to a great extent; hence the wind, from whatever quarter it may blow, drives with unusual force over the naked plains and against this hill. The insects of various kinds are thus involuntarily driven to the mound by the force of the wind, or fly to its leeward side for shelter. The small birds, whose food they are, consequently resort in great numbers to this place in search of them—particularly the small brown martin, of which we saw a vast number hovering on the leeward side of the hill, when we approached it in the act of catching those insects. They were so gentle that they did not quit the place until we had arrived within a few feet of them.

One evidence which the Indians give for believing this place to be the residence of some unusual spirits is that they frequently discover a large assemblage of birds about this mound. This is, in my opinion, a sufficient proof to produce in the savage mind a confident belief of all the properties which they ascribe to it.

From the top of this mound, we beheld a most beautiful landscape. Numerous herds of buffalo were seen feeding in various directions. The plain to north, northwest, and northeast extends without interruption as far as can be seen.

25th August

The boat under the command of Sergeant Pryor proceeded on in our absence (after jerking the elk I killed yesterday) six miles, and camped on the larboard side. R. Fields brought in five deer. George Shannon killed an elk buck. Some rain this evening.

We set the prairies on fire as a signal for the Sioux to come to the river.

27th August, 1804

This morning the star called the morning star much larger than common. G. Drouilliard came up and informed that he could neither find Shannon nor horses. We sent Shields and J. Fields back to hunt Shannon and the horses, with directions to keep on the hills to the Grand Calumet above, on Riviere qui Court.

We set sail under a gentle breeze from the S.E. At seven miles, passed a white clay marl or chalk bluff. Under this bluff, which is extensive, I discovered large stone much like lime, encrusted with a clear substance which I believe to be cobalt; also ore is embedded in the dark earth resembling slate, but much softer. Above this bluff, we had the prairie set on fire to let the Sioux see that we were on the river, and as a signal for them to come to it.

At 2 o'clock, passed the mouth of river Jacques. One Indian at the mouth of this river swam to the pirogue. We landed and two others came to us. Those Indians informed that a large camp of Sioux were on the River Jacques, near the mouth. We sent Sergeant Pryor and a Frenchman with Mr. Dorion, the Sioux interpreter, to the camp with directions to invite the principal chiefs to council with us at a bluff above, called the Calumet. Two of those Indians accompanied them, and the third continued in the boat showing an inclination to continue. This boy is a Maha, and informs that his nation were gone to the Pawnees to make a peace with that nation.

28th August, 1804

Set out under a stiff breeze from the south, and proceeded on past a willow island at two miles. Several sand bars. The river wide and shallow. At four miles passed a short white bluff of about 70 or 80 feet high. Below this bluff the prairie rises gradually from the water, back to the height of the bluff, which is on the starboard side. Here the Indian who was in the boat returned to the Sioux camp on the river Jacques. Captain Lewis and myself much indisposed owing to some cause for which we cannot account. One of the pirogues ran a snag through her and was near sinking, in the opinions of the crew. We came to below the Calumet bluff and formed a camp in a beautiful plain near the foot of the high land, which rises with a gradual ascent near this bluff. I observe more timber in the valleys and on the points than usual. The pirogue which was injured, I had unloaded, and the loading put into the other pirogue, which we intended to send back, and changed the crew. After examining her and finding that she was unfit for service, determined to send her back by the party. Some load which was in the pirogue much injured.

The wind blew hard this afternoon from the south. J. Shields and J. Field, who were sent back to look for Shannon and the horses, joined us and informed that Shannon had the horses ahead and that they could not overtake him. This man not being a first-rate hunter, we determined to send one man in pursuit of him, with some provisions.

Orders, August 28th, 1804

The commanding officers direct that the two messes who form the crews of the pirogues shall select each one man from their mess for the purpose of cooking, and that these cooks, as well as those previously appointed to the messes of the barge crew, shall in future be exempted from mounting guard, or any detail for that duty. They are therefore no longer to be held on the roster.

M. Lewis   Captain
1st U.S. Regiment Infantry
Wm. Clark   Captain &c.

(at Gavins Point Dam)   29th August, 1804

Some rain last night and this morning. Sent on Colter with provisions in pursuit of Shannon. Had a tow rope made of elk-skin. I am much engaged in writing. At four o'clock, P.M., Sergeant Pryor and Mr. Dorion, with five chiefs and about 70 men and boys, arrived on the opposite side. We sent over a pirogue, and Mr. Dorion and his son, who was trading with the Indians, came over with Sergeant Pryor, and informed us that the chiefs were there. We sent Sergeant Pryor and young Mr. Dorion with some tobacco, corn, and a few kettles for them to cook in, with directions to inform the chiefs that we would speak to them tomorrow.

Those Indians brought with them, for their own use, 2 elk and 6 deer, which the young men killed on the way from their camp, twelve miles distant.

Sergeant Pryor informs me that when they came near the Indian camp, they were met by men with a buffalo robe to carry them. Mr. Dorion informed they were not the owners of the boats and did not wish to be carried. The Sioux's camps are handsome—of a conic form, covered with buffalo robes painted different colors, and all compact and handsomely arranged, covered all around. An open part in the center for the fire, with buffalo robes. Each lodge has a place for cooking, detached. The lodges contain from ten to fifteen persons. A fat dog was presented as a mark of their respect for the party, of which they partook heartily, and thought it good and well flavored.

30th of August, 1804

A very thick fog this morning. After preparing some presents for the chiefs, which we intended to make by giving medals, and finishing a speech which we intended to give them, we sent Mr.

11

Dorion in a pirogue for the chiefs and warriors, to a council under an oak tree, near where we had a flag flying on a high flagstaff. At 12 o'clock we met, and Captain Lewis delivered the speech; and then made one great chief by giving him a medal and some clothes; one second chief and three third chiefs, in the same way. They received those things with the goods and tobacco with pleasure. To the grand chief we gave a flag, and the parole and wampum with a hat and chief's coat. We smoked out of the pipe of peace, and the chiefs retired to a bower, made of bushes by their young men, to divide their presents, and smoke, eat, and council. Captain Lewis and myself retired to dinner, and to consult about other measures. Mr. Dorion is much displeased that we did not invite him to dine with us—which he was sorry for afterward. The Sioux are a stout, bold-looking people; the young men handsome and well made. The greater part of them make use of bows and arrows. Some few fusees I observe among them, notwithstanding they live by the bow and arrow. They do not shoot so well as the northern Indians. The warriors are very much decorated with paint, porcupine quills and feathers, large leggings and moccasins—all with buffalo robes of different colors. The squaws wore petticoats and a white buffalo robe with the black hair turned back over their necks and shoulders.

31st of August, 1804

After the Indians got their breakfast, the chiefs met and arranged themselves in a row, with elegant pipes of peace all pointing to our seats. We came forward, and took our seats. The great chief, The Shake Hand, rose, and spoke at some length approving what we had said, and promising to pursue the advice.

Martoree, second chief (White Crane) rose and made a short speech, and referred to the great chief, Parnarnearparbe (Struck by the Pawnees). Third chief rose and made a short speech, Areawecharche (The Half Man). Third chief rose and spoke at some length to the same purpose. The other chief said but little. One of the warriors spoke, after all were done, and promised to support the chiefs. They promised to go and see their Great Father in the spring with Mr. Dorion, and to do all things we advised them to do. All then concluded by telling the distresses of their nation by not having traders, and wished us to take pity on them. They wanted powder, ball, and a little milk. (rum)

Last night the Indians danced until late in their dances. We gave them some knives, tobacco, and bells, tape, and binding, with which they were satisfied.

We gave a certificate to two men of war, attendants on the chief. Gave to all the chiefs a carrot of tobacco. Had a talk with

Mr. Dorion, who agreed to stay and collect the chiefs from as many bands of Sioux as he could this fall, and bring about a peace between the Sioux and their neighbors, &c.

After dinner, we gave Mr. Peter Dorion a commission to act with a flag and some clothes and provisions and instructions to bring about a peace with the Sioux, Mahas, Pawnees, Poncas, Otos, and Missouris, and to employ any trader to take some of the chiefs of each, or as many of those nations as he could, particularly the Sioux, down to Washington. I took a vocabulary of the Sioux language, and the answer to a few queries such as referred to their situation, trade, number, war, &c. This nation is divided into twenty tribes, possessing separate interests. Collectively, they are numerous—say from two to three thousand men. Their interests are so unconnected that some bands are at war with nations with which other bands are on the most friendly terms.

This great nation, whom the French have given the nickname of Sioux, call themselves Dakota—Darcotar. Their language is not peculiarly their own, they speak a great number of words which are the same in every respect with the Maha, Ponca, Osage, and Kansas, which clearly proves that those nations, at some period not more than a century or two past, are of the same nation. Those Darcotars, or Sioux, inhabit or rove over the country on the Red River of Lake Winnepeg, St. Peters, and the west of the Mississippi, above Prairie du Chien, head of River Des Moines, and the Missouri and in waters on the N. side for a great extent. They are only at peace with eight nations, and, agreeable to their calculation, at war with twenty-odd. Their trade comes from the British, except this band and one on Des Moines who trade with the traders of St. Louis. The Sioux rove and follow the buffalo, raise no corn or anything else, the woods and prairies affording a sufficiency. They eat meat, and substitute the ground potato, which grows in the plains, for bread.

In the evening, late, we gave Mr. Dorion a bottle of whiskey, and he, with the chiefs, and his son, crossed the river and camped on the opposite bank. Soon after night, a violent wind from the N.W. with rain. The rain continued the greater part of the night. The river a-rising a little.

II

FREDERICK MANFRED

As the Lewis and Clark expedition "opened up" the huge northwest territory, trappers and mountain men came into the area to collect furs, to explore, and to trade with the Indians. One such man was Hugh Glass, of somewhat vague origins, who as a member of General Ashley's expedition in 1823-1824 separated himself from the group and was attacked and nearly killed by a grizzly. Left for dead by three friends, he survived, crawling, stumbling, walking, and rafting his way back to "civilization," all the time vowing revenge on his friends for having deserted him.

The story is true, but Manfred has dramatized it (especially the revenge motive) in his 1954 novel, *Lord Grizzly*. The section reprinted here is from the middle of the novel as Hugh Glass struggles to reach Fort Kiowa. The action occurs in what is now South Dakota, mostly in the northwest and central part.

Manfred was born Frederick Feikema, of Frisian descent, on January 6, 1912, in Northwest Iowa. He graduated from Calvin College in Grand Rapids, Michigan and then traveled back and forth across the country during the depression years, working at a variety of jobs including semi-professional basketball (Manfred is six feet nine inches tall). Eventually he settled in Minneapolis and began writing under the name Feike Feikema. His first novel, *The Golden Bowl*, was set in South Dakota. Shortly before the publication of *Lord Grizzly* (his seventh novel) he changed his name to Manfred. Since then he has continued to write novels and short stories, has had one volume of poems published, and has served as writer-in-residence at the University of South Dakota. He lives in Luverne, Minnesota.

LORD GRIZZLY

A cool evening breeze woke him.

Opening slow eyes, Hugh rose out of rolling dreamland into a land of ragged ocher gullies and bald gravelhead bluffs and wind-streaked skies.

One long look at the ragged gullies and Hugh let himself sink back into torpor. Why live? Ae, what was the use?

For a little while Hugh let himself drift through a fur-scented purgatory, between a state of dreamy sweet death and a state of prickly sour life.

But his stomach and blowy belly had other ideas. "First things first," it said. "Turn out, you lazy white nigger, and round us up some grub. There's work ahead. And sweet revenge after that. Turn out, old hoss!"

Hugh heard his stomach talking so clearly he was sure he was at last out of his head, had at last gone loco.

"Turn out!"

"Ae, ae, master. I heard ye the first time."

And half-smiling, half-afraid of the whimsy, Hugh threw back the heavy stiff silvertip grizzly fur and, with a groan, rolled over on his belly and rose to his hands and knee and had a look out of his hole.

The sun was almost down, sinking clear and yellow across the South Fork. That meant another striker of a cold night. It made him shiver to think about it.

He cleared his throat, hawking up balls of night spit. He stretched his limbs as much as the redgray monsters in his back and bum leg would allow.

In methodical fashion he set about getting his meal. He had himself some frost-sweetened bullberries, and wild turnip or tipsin roots, and a couple dozen white grubs, and fresh water.

He was washing up when he spotted a gopher. Like an Arab about to pray at sunset, it sat on its haunches at the edge of its hole, paws folded across its chest.

Hugh's old predatory eyes narrowed. Fresh meat. Ae. But how to catch it.

Almost immediately he had an idea. Fix a snare with deer sinew. He snapped off a couple dozen whangs or fringes from the front of his buckskin shirt, tied them together into a good sound leather string about three feet long. He made a slipknot loop at the end.

The moment he advanced, the striped yellowgray gopher vanished tail-whipping into its burrow. Hugh placed the snare carefully around the edge of the hole and then lay back, waiting, the end of the string looped around a finger.

He waited.

He watched the sun hit the horizon in a vast explosion of clear yellow light. He watched shadows race in from the bluffs across the South Fork.

After a while the gopher couldn't resist it. It had to have a look, if not a last peek, at the fading day. Its head popped out an exploratory second; popped back in. Then it popped out its head again for a longer look; then a still longer look—and that instant Hugh jerked the snare and had himself some squealing fresh meat. It had a strong wild taste, naturally salty, and he relished it.

Fortified, quickened, he began the long climb south, up, up, toward the divide on the hogback. The going was rough right from the start. The gully zigzagged sharply, sometimes cut very deep to either side into the sloping land. It was cold, bitter cold. The higher he went the thicker the prickly-pear cactus became, the more numerous the anthills. The heavy bearskin soon began to weigh like a lead sheet on his back. For every three feet he crawled forward on loose dirt, he slid one foot back. Soon too he hit gravelheads with sharp cutting little pebbles. Occasionally in the dark he rammed head-on into boulders, scaring the wits out of himself, making him think for a moment he'd run into an-other she-rip of a mother grizzly.

The higher he climbed the colder and more brisk the northwest wind became. Another frost was due as soon as the wind let up, and this time a sharp one, maybe even a good freeze. It would be a hard night on hands and knees. It would also be a hard night on a broken leg with poor circulation.

He was glad about one thing. The old she-rip fur might hang heavy on his back but it was warm. Maybe its weight did cut down his traveling time but it more than made up for it by the comfort it provided. Hugh snuggled under it as he struggled along.

The stars came out crisp white. The wind veiled black dust across his path. The gully became shallow; at last lifted up and became a low draw with thick clumps of bunch grass and occa-sional beds of prickly-pear cactus.

Gradually Old Hugh tired. His good leg trembled with quick fleeting cramps. His elbows quivered from the ache and pain of various stone bruises.

He rested, panting; slept awhile, ganting; awoke with a start, shivering; crept on, bad leg slaping behind; rested some more, puffing; slept.

He dreamt of dying alone in a gully, cold and blue and bloated with snakenecked greenblack turkey buzzards circling hungrily overhead.

He woke with a jerk; crawled a few yards; rested; slept.

He dreamt of Jim and Fitz sitting around a jumping fire and arguing about him.

Cold and shivering, he again woke with a guilty start; crept on a ways; rested; slept.

He dreamt of his two boys, the blackhead and the sunhead, dreamt of the old she-rip tearing him up and down his back.

And creeping along in the black night, he fell into a small washout. He was so exhausted when he hit bottom he didn't bother to see if his bad leg had tumbled down with him. It was too cold to bother. "I feel queersome," he murmured. He curled up as best he could, snuggled under the heavy grizzly hide, and fell asleep.

He slept through dawn and on through a sunny glinting day. Rusty dusk lay over the sloping land, and over the bald tan bluffs and small red teat mesas forming the ridge to the south, and down in the far valley of fall yellows behind him to the north, when he at last poked his head out of the small washout.

"This child's slept a hole in the day, 'pears like."

He stared at the brown evening. He blinked bloodshot eyes. His bowels rumbled with hunger. "This child needs meat." He began to puff just thinking of the work ahead. "And this child needs wadder too."

Stiff-limbed, with one of the redgray monsters raging again, the one in his back, he clambered out of the washout.

One good look around and he knew he was doomed to go without either grub or water for that day—unless he ate rusty dead bunch grass and drank his own urine. There was nothing, not a bush or a tree or a trickle of water.

Like a dog digging for gophers, he scrabbled some dirt out from under a thick clump of bunch grass. Ae. Nothing but dry hard dirt. In digging, dirt packed in under his fingernails and he sucked them clean in his mouth. The dirt had a sour flour taste.

He pinched in his brain to help quiet down his growling stomach. He worked up some saliva to wet his throat and lips. He hoped the wind would stay down during the night. Wind dried one out.

Just before black night swooped down over the long swinging land he had a last look around. From the spot where the sun had set he plotted his course for the night. The course lay between two small red crumbling mesas directly south. He saw that his climb during the night previous had lifted him fairly high out of the South Fork valley. He also saw that the rest of the way to the top of the hogback divide lay smooth and undulating ahead of him. Even the incline was much more gentle.

There was no sign of redskin or varmint in the godforsaken drygrass country. The land was clean of green grass and running red meat. The sky above was clean of flying flesh. There was nothing but himself and the twinkling stars above and the rustling dried bunch grass below. He was alone. Solitary. There was only himself to feel sorry for himself. There was only himself to tell he was himself. Only he knew that he knew. He was alone.

"These parts make this child so lonesome for company he's about ready again for huggin' with a she-grizzly."

He shivered in the cold. "But I'll say this for the frost. They won't be any more mosquitoes this fall. Or green bottleflies."

He found it in him to go on without food. Some little energy had seeped into his well during the night. For a little while there was enough to work the pump.

He laughed grimly to himself when he thought of the trail he was leaving across the country: two long tracks, a round dent, and a pair of wriggling marks—a three-legged two-tailed whang-doodle for sure. Ae, and maybe even Old Wakantanka himself at last come down to earth to play a Christ's role.

He crawled on slowly like a three-legged dog dragging a stinking gamy leg and walking on sore pads.

Thrown stars moved across the black skies.

"Wadder," Old Hugh murmured, "wadder. Got to have wadder."

He looked up at the star-flying skies. "Don't it ever rain in this godforsaken country? I'd catch me some fresh rain water in me bearskin." He wetted his cracked lips; tried to work up some saliva for his parched throat.

"Wadder," he murmured, "wadder. If I only had wadder I wouldn't mind goin' without meat."

The closer he got to the two little red teat mesas the stonier the terrain became. Bunch-grass clumps became more sparse. Even the cactus beds became rare. Rough blackred stones began to shred his bearskin elbow and knee guards. Prickly brush tore at his buckskin shirtfront as he straddled over them. Old Hugh cursed the country. Much more of it and he'd have to cut up his bear-skin for clothes and guards.

He stopped to rest on a long flat rock. Before stretching out he felt around first to make sure there weren't any rattlers around.

He panted, mouth open, beard floofing in and out of his cracked lips.

He panted. It was hard doin's, all right. Ae. And probably the death of him at last.

He thought of the gamy death smell that'd been hanging around him a bit stronger the last day. He explored his back under the bearskin. Some of the scab had come off the sinew-seamed wounds. In a couple of places he could pull out the deerskin stitches. The stitches came out easy, greasy, like old hairs pulling out of rotted follicles. He pushed his arm around farther to touch the open sore above the loose flap of flesh and bared white ribs. Still slippery with pus. He felt of it gingerly. His hand came away stinking. Bah!

He found the open wound hadn't rotted through to his lung. He was done for if it had. Ae. He'd seen men rot away into slow death once the corruption got into their bellows.

He explored it carefully again. He felt the bare bone of one of his ribs. He felt the string of a loose tendon. Or was it a blood vessel? There were also odd squirming bits in the middle of it.

Squirming? Ho-ah. Maggots, then. Ae. So he was rotting away like an old down buffalo in a wallow like he feared.

He lay down flat on his belly. Just about dead before he'd even crossed the first divide, he was. With at least one more big divide to go and a long raft ride after that down the Cheyenne and then the great Missouri itself—and the raft ride probably the toughest part of the trip.

Why live? Ae, what was the use?

He wept.

He dipped into sleep and dreamt of campfires. There were many of them and they all were one. Around the jumping flames sat Jim and Fitz still arguing about him. He himself lay stretched out on his belly, his back blooming with little bloody plum trees. But once again he couldn't make out what Jim and Fitz were saying.

He called out, "Jim? Fitz? Where be ye? Come clost so I can hear ee."

The roar of his own voice woke him from the flame-jumping nightmare.

His head buzzed. A terrible headache cracked in his skull. When he looked up at the stars, they became streaks of light rushing from east to west, and when he looked ahead, the pair of red mesas blurred off into a dancing mountain range.

He dipped into sleep and dreamt again. This time he was back in Lancaster. Back with his white wife Mabel and his two sons, blackhead and sunhead. There was a final supper of some sort, a supper which for once had begun with jolly joshing, with the boys happy that Pap and Ma for once were getting along a little. It was the night he'd come home with a new hunting rifle, a Lancaster model, instead of coming home drunk as he usually did. The food was good, though somewhat skimpy. The talk was pleasant, though somewhat chaffy. Hugh was glad Mabel was smiling some again. He liked seeing his boys happy. And Hugh had just begun to think maybe Mabel was actually having a change of heart, giving up her notion that he should get a better job, accepting his notion that they should move farther west so he could hunt for a living, giving up her airish notion of rising in the world—when somehow, he didn't know just how, somehow it happened that he dropped a family heirloom of her mother's, a prize hand-painted bowl, breaking it to a thousand smithereens.

That set it off. To the sad horror of the lads, he and Mabel were at it again. She threw things at him: mops, pails, pestle, bread-board, coffee grinder. He might have accepted all that, but she spotted his new Lancaster gun. She picked it up by the barrel end and rushed toward him, intent on smashing its butt over his head. That was too much for Hugh. Let her break his new gun over his own noggin? Never. Not on your life. He jumped up and wrestled it from her. Enraged that he should dare show physical resistance, she slugged him. In a flash Hugh balled his own fist and hauled off and hit her smack in the face, hit her so hard she spun across the room and landed in the woodbox. There was a terrible silence. And in that silence it came to Hugh at last, finally, that he could never live with that she-rip of a woman. She was just too much for a man. There'd never be a living with her, of any kind, no matter how much he loved his lads, Blackie and Sunny. So he deserted. Deserted the lads even though he heard them calling after him, lonesomely, "Pap! Pap! where are you going, Pap?" But Hugh hardened his heart; pretended he didn't hear them. "Pap! Pap!"

Their shrill boyish voices calling him woke him with a start from his dream. He looked around wildly as if half-expecting to see the lads themselves.

Again his head buzzed with a terrible cracking headache.

He shuddered. What awful dreams he was having lately.

He lay flat on his belly, possessed by the after depression of the nightmarish dream, lay possessed by a dark sense of guilt, so dark he shuddered again involuntarily.

Deserted them, that's what he'd done. What a miserable coward he was. Maybe Mabel was a rakehellion she-rip, ae, but the boys were still his boys, of his own flesh and blood, that's a fact, and good boys too, boys who deserved to have a father. It hadn't been their fault that he and their she-rip of a mother hadn't been able to get along. Not at all.

Deserted them. Ae. Too cussed independent he was.

He said it aloud the first time. "Maybe that's how come it's this child's turn to be deserted. Bein' paid back in kind, he is."

The saying of it aloud startled him.

Deserted? He deserted in turn? The lads Jim and Fitz desert him? Impossible. Not his lads. Impossible.

He turned his head over and rested on the other cheek. He pushed the thought angrily from his mind.

He lay puffing.

The dark aftereffects of the dream persisted. It weighed down on him. It haunted him.

He couldn't get rid of the idea that maybe he'd been deserted

20

after all. Thinking on it, a man could see how it explained every-thing—no dead bodies around, no horses, no gun or possibles, no hunter's or trapper's truck about.

Oh, but the lads wouldn't've left him behind to die the hard way. Impossible. He put it from his mind. There was work to do.

Crumbling with weakness, parched and cracking with thirst, cells sucking with hunger, somehow he found it in him to rise to his elbows and one good knee and crawl on.

Crawl on. Creep on. Nose on. Past stones. Around boulders. Through rocky defiles. Over cutting jagged outcroppings.

He stopped to rest. He lay puffing, ganting.

Deserted? could his companyeros Jim and Fitz have deserted him?

He considered the two lads, each in turn.

Jim now. Jim was too goodhearted to pull a stunt like that on his Old Hugh. Jim had good upbringing. Not Jim. No.

He puffed; rested.

And Fitz? Fitz, well, Fitz was a horse of another color all right. Fitz was hard, practical, cautious. There was no room for pee-doodles in him. Fitz never laughed. Something wrong with a man who never laughed. And then all that book learning of his. Any-body knew that reading made a puffball lighter in the head. Read-ing filled the head with excuses on how not to be a man in a fix. On how not to be a brave buck. In a fix a bookman sat down and told over all his ideas afore he got to work and shot his way out of a fix. In a fix a man hadn't ought to have but one idea—and that was how to get out of a pretty fix pronto. Concluded to charge—did so. That was what true mountain men did.

Fitz? Yes, Fitz might think on it in a close fix.

He crawled on, crept on, nosed on.

Twice he scared up mule-eared jack rabbits. Another time he flushed up a herd of fleeing flagging white-tailed antelope.

Once he almost had a jack rabbit. The jack cowered until he was on top of him. In the starlit quartermoon-lit night Hugh saw it first as a round gray stone. Its roundness in the midst of the tumbled coarse jagged rock attracted his feeler hand as something to rest on in relief. He put his hand on it. There was a giving of soft fur and flesh. And a startled squeal. And then before it oc-curred to him it might be meat to eat, before his hand could instinc-tively close on it, the jack rabbit squirted to one side and, in a huge shrilling bound, was gone.

"Meat," he muttered, smelling his hand and recognizing the warm milklike rotted-clover smell of the creature, "meat."

He rested, puffing, cheek resting on a hard cold rock.

The dark thought wouldn't leave him alone. The tougher and

grimmer the crawl up the hogback became, the more he became convinced, even possessed, with the idea that his lads Jim and Fitz had deserted him, that Fitz had somehow talked Jim into it.

Deserted. The lads had deserted him. That Irisher Fitz had done it.

Damned Irish. Never was any good for anything except run away from a fix. A fighting Irishman usually meant an Irishman afraid of being called a coward. They could talk forward faster and walk backward faster than any other dummed two-legged creature on earth. He'd sensed it in Fitzgerald from the first. Too practical, too cautious. Hard front and soft back. And the boy Jim, though a Scotchman like himself, too young to know better. Damned Irish. That's what a man got for learning life out of books.

Deserted.

A wave of hate swept over him. If there was one thing Old Hugh hated, it was cowardly deserters. Amongst mountain men alone in a far wild country full of enemy varmint there just wasn't room for cowards, deserters, or they would all go under. In red-devil country mountain men had to stick together. It was the code. He himself had often risked his topknot to save some comrade left behind in battle. Many a time. He didn't deserve to have this happen to him. Especially not at the hands of his own lads, Jim and Fitz. Not after the way he'd saved their skin from the major's wrath.

How could his own lads have come to it?

He crawled on. Nosed on. Crept on.

But the dark thought was back again the next time he lay flat on his belly to rest.

Could they really have deserted him? His lads?

He couldn't shake the notion. He remembered too well how the lads had let him cover up their sleeping on guard, remembered how they had not talked up like men to say they were guilty of negligence, that they had indirectly caused the death of Augie Neill and Jim Anderson. If they could be cautious once, they could be cautious twice.

Cautious. Ae. Too cautious. "Ae, and you can lay your pile on it that it was Fitz's idee too. He talked Jim into it. Poor lad."

But Jim was a coward to let Fitz talk him into it. The black-hearted bugger. Leaving him to die the hard way.

"If this child ever gets out of this alive, the first thing he's gonna do is track them cowardly cautious devils down and kill 'em. Inch by inch. Slow torture 'em. Skin 'em alive. Fry 'em alive. Punch pine needles and pine slivers in 'em like the Pawnees did to Old Clint and make torches out of 'em. At the same time, so they can watch each other go up in smoke." Hugh ground his teeth; clenched and unclenched his fists.

Another wave of hate passed over him. The cowardly snakes. The cowardly squaws. Leaving him to die the hard way. Alone.

"Oily cowards. Someday this old coon will have a showdown with ee, lads."

Those two devils who called themselves mountain men had a code all right. Deserter code. Ae.

Well, he had a code too. A code which said a man had a right to kill deserters. It was a crime before God and man both to desert a man in a wilderness full of howling red devils, taking his possibles away from him, leaving him without food, with nothing but his naked hands left to fight off the varmints. Leaving him without a last bullet to kill himself with in case of unbearable pain. Or in case of capture by red devils. The lads knew a hunter always saved one last ball for himself in case of a pinch. If he could help it, a hunter did all he could to avoid torture by Indians—like Old Clint suffered at the hands of the Pawnees.

Leaving him with a ripped-up back and a broken leg. Ae, he had a code too, and it said to kill deserters on sight.

Waves of hate flushed over him. He ground sand in his clenching fists.

"Them oily cowards. If it's the last thing I ever do, I'm gonna live long enough to kill the both of 'em. The major is gonna know too. They're maybe laughin' to themselves right now, thinkin' they got away from it, not buryin' me, playin' me for a sucker, and runnin' off with the best rifle this side of the Ohio. But they'll have another think comin' someday."

He got to his hands and knee and crept on. He crept until he couldn't anymore.

He stopped. He lay ganting in a long crack in the rocks. He watched the quartermoon sink orange then slow red into the gold-dusted black rim of earth.

"Meat," he said, "gotta have meat. Or there'll be no sweet revenge for this child."

The long crack in the rocks reminded him of the grave the lads had dug for him back in the gully.

He lay puzzling about the sandy grave. If he was dead, why hadn't the lads buried him? And if he wasn't dead, why had they dug it at all?

Open grave. His grave. Place for his old bones to molder in.

While they were at it, why hadn't they dug it at least a decent six feet deep? They didn't have the excuse that the ground was too hard or too stony. The sand was soft and deep.

The more he thought on it, the more he became absolutely convinced he'd been deserted. The lads probably began to dig his grave; saw he wasn't going to die after all; were in a hurry to catch up with the major; took to their heels. Ae. Took to their heels, grabbing his gun and possibles. The very lads he'd befriended and protected. Fitz and Jim. Lads he'd come to love. Lads he'd always chosen as his hunting companyeros. He could have chosen Augie Neill and Jim Anderson, but he had chosen Fitz and Jim. Jim had asked special for the privilege the first time and he had agreed. Augie and Jim Anderson didn't care. They were too full of fun.

Fitz and Jim. Why should they desert him when he'd never done them any harm? He'd never deserted them.

Lying in the long crack in the rocks, the rock edges cutting into him cruelly in the long lonely dark night, Hugh brooded on their ungratefulness. He turned it over in his mind. It burned in him. Seared. Ungrateful devils. And that after he'd stuck his own neck out for them.

He'd get them if it was the last thing he ever did. If the Lord didn't get them first.

He got up on his hands and one knee and crawled out of the long crack in the rocks and nosed on into the darkness ahead.

He crept on until he couldn't anymore; stopped.

He let his head hang heavy from his bulky shoulders, too exhausted and too tired to slip forward on his belly, too weak to weep.

When he found it in him again to look up, he discovered dawn was just beginning to gray the east. He also discovered that in the dark, while he'd been busy with dark deserter thoughts, he had crawled between and beyond the pair of teat mesas. Ho-ah! That meant he was over the divide, that he had nothing but downhill going until he hit the Moreau.

Something in the sloping and far resloped landscape caught his eye. It was the silhouette of a great butte. It came up out of the tar-dark earth and reared over the graying horizon and against the sky like some altar of sacrifice. Its flat top glowed faintly pink where the first shafts of predawn red caught the dark red rock. It glowed a little as if the coals and bones of some sacrifice were still glowing on its flat place of fire.

Hugh's old bleary eyes stared at it. Where had he seen it before? He was sure he'd seen it before. Sartain sure. Ae. The red dark reality of its rearing up before him and the vague red dark memory of it in his mind kept changing places, swinging around like a double-arrowed weather vane on a single pole.

Thunder Butte. Ae, that was it! Thunder Butte. Thunder Butte. Ae. He was seeing the back side of it. On the way up from

24

Ft. Kiowa with Major Henry and the lads he'd seen the front side of it.

The seeing of it overjoyed him. The seeing of it brought Ft. Kiowa closer. What with downhill going ahead and good old Thunder Butte at last in sight, he was sure to make it now. Because once he'd crawled far enough to leave Thunder Butte out of sight behind him, he'd be on the Cheyenne and floating down on river currents.

He sighted down the long slope below him. The channel of a creek or a river angled off in front of him toward the southeast, angled just to the right and south of Thunder Butte. Was that the Moreau at last?

He looked beyond the angling zigzagging channel. Far over a low sloping he saw another channel. The second channel was deeper and wider, more pronounced, with a still further hogback ridge beyond it.

Hugh nodded. Ae. The first was probably only a good-sized creek and the second the Moreau itself. The creek probably joined the Moreau on the other side of Thunder Butte.

Hugh mapped out his trail. He'd take that gullyhead off to the left there and follow it down to the creek. The Thunder Butte creek would have water and wild roots and berries. Once on the creek, he'd cross it and follow it a ways until he got to that pass just south of the Thunder Butte, then crawl over the creek ridge to the Moreau. And at the Moreau he was sure to find a lot of water and good grub.

Dawn came up fast. It burst over the east rim of the earth in a vast racing explosion of pink then saffron then white clear light. The detail of the valleys stood out clearly in the strange zigzagging streaks of light and dark.

Hugh examined the rocky plateau around him. Nothing. Not a spear of grass. Not a stir of life. He'd have to go on without food again.

He found a hollow in the rocks and curled up under his silvertip bearskin.

His last thought was the hope that a rattler might crawl in with him. A rattler was dangerous, ae, but a rattler was meat. Sweet meat.

He woke by midafternoon in blinding sunlight. His first thought was of Fitz and Jim and of how sweet revenge would be.

His next thought was of his belly and of how hungry he was. "This child could right now eat the wild hairs out of a bear, he could. A she-rip at that. Gladly."

And his next thought was of how refreshed he felt after the sleep. It amazed him that his old creaking beat-up body could come back like a young man's after a good sleep. "This child's been in many a tough fix, with his body all in one piece and no bones broke, and it carried him out on two legs. But I'll be dog if this don't beat all the way it's carryin' me out this time."

To quiet his belly he jammed a piece off his buckskin shirt; pummeled the piece to shreds; chewed it until leathery juices revived his saliva buds. " 'Tain't exactly buffler boudins but it'll do until I catch me some."

He made a final sighting down the long undulating rock-cropped slope toward the creek ahead with Thunder Butte as the mark to go by.

Compared with the day before, the going was wondrous easy. There were still many sharp stones and rockjuts the first ways, but it was all downhill, and most places he could slide and coast.

The gullyhead widened into a ragged irregular gash. Volcanic ash showed black ribs in the pinkyellow clay cuts. Soon clumps of rusty red bunch grass began to appear; then cactus beds; and then anthills again. He had himself a few geranium-flavored acrid cactus ears, munching and chewing them thoroughly to get every last drop of moisture and sustenance. He thought of having another but was afraid of getting the misery skitters. The misery skitters could weaken a man faster than a double dose of galloping consumption.

He crawled along steadily.

He was halfway down toward Thunder Butte creek when night began to race in a dooming black from the east. The sun went down in a brilliant throw of colors, an explosion of yellows and whites and peony-pink glories, limning the whole irregular, jagged, scissored horizon from far southwest to high west to low northwest with a glowing white-hot gold.

Despite his terrible hunger, his emaciation, his parched throat, the nauseating pervading stench of his rotting back, Hugh couldn't help but marvel at all the spectacular colorings. "With a little salt and some pepper to flavor it, a man might almost make a feast on it."

He hurried on, every now and then looking out at it, and finding himself strangely exalted by the swift transformations of the marching, retreating, rioting glories, by the violent struggle between the shafts of light and the clouds of darkness.

At last darkness won out, absolutely, except for twinkling stars and a lazy recumbent quartermoon in the west.

With darkness, too, came easier terrain. Keeping well away from the gully and taking the ridges along the falling sloping draw, Hugh found the ground smooth again and easy to crawl on. If it weren't for badly shredded knee and elbow guards, a stranger

26

might think him out on some picnic lark, part of some three-legged sack race.

He crawled steadily all night long. Carefully he nursed what little strength he had. He stopped to rest and puff; once slipped off into a restless nap; crept on, slid on.

It was almost dawn when he hit the creek. For once he didn't bother to make sure no Indians or she-grizzlies lurked in the brush along the creek banks. He plowed straight through the yellowing bullberry bushes and down into the little stream of running water, wading out into the middle of it, bad leg and all, and gulped water and splashed his face, all the while murmuring little talk to himself in his feverish joy at finding water, hinnying like an old boar happy to be at his favorite trough again.

Hugh drank until his belly hurt him.

He ate frost-ripened bullberries, and wild onion roots, and a few white grubs.

The sun was just up when he slid under low plum bushes in a short receding draw away from the creek.

A good day's run. Almost ten miles. He was moving at last.

Again he woke in midafternoon, in brilliant lemon September sunlight.

This time, however, even though he'd had something to eat the night before, and had water and food again on rising, he didn't feel refreshed. Going without food on the first hogback was finally catching up with him.

There was something else too. His back stunk worse; his brow felt feverish. And no matter how much he drank, the dry fur lining in his mouth wouldn't wash away.

He checked over his bearskin elbow and knee guards; found he needed a complete new set. With a crude stone chisel he jammed out three new pads and bound them on.

He checked his bum leg; discovered the cords binding his splint were slack. Ho-ah. The cracked bone was knitting then and the swelling was going down. Or could it be he was generally getting thin from lack of meat?

Rusty sunset had just fallen when he set out on the next lap home. He crossed to the right side of the creek and followed it down, always holding the black silhouette of Thunder Butte in sight dead ahead in the southeast.

The bronze quartermoon had just set when he ran into the remains of a Sioux warrior. Sewed up in a skin bundle, lying out full length, some six feet above the ground on a scaffold of dry saplings, it swayed slack and lonely on four upright posts, black against the star-pricked sky. The tattered edge of skin snapped in

27

the slow night breeze. Little rawhide memento bags tolled in the slow breeze too.

Looking up at it, Old Hugh found himself suddenly lonesome for Bending Reed and the rites of her tribe, found himself lonesome even for the old days on the Platte with the Pawnees. The decaying leathery remains of the unknown warrior brought tears to his eyes. The white man might sometimes bury his dead kin six feet under, as deep as he made his privies, but the red devil placed his dead six feet above ground for all men to see, out of reach of varmint, as high as he would carry his head in the happy hunting grounds of afterlife. Ae, there swayed the honorable end of a free brave's life on Mother Earth, reared up out in the open so that his gross dark ignorant body could be given back to the powers of heaven and to the four quarters of the universe and to all the rains and to the wingeds of the air and to the little people of the earth. Ae, the red devil still knew the old and true religion. He still walked with Grandfather Wakantanka on the bosom of Grandmother Earth.

Looking up at the swaying recumbent reposing body, watching the little memento bags belling in the breeze, and imagining the penny-skinned hawknose face composed in stoic calm and peace, Old Hugh found himself hating cautious Fitz and the boy Jim with redoubled fury. Even in the midst of the most precarious existence, the Sioux tribes had time to give their fallen warrior a decent and an honorable burial. But his two friends had not only deserted him, they had left him unburied.

"If I ever lay hands on those two low-lived snakes, them oily cowards, not even their bitch of a mother is gonna recognize 'em after I get through with 'em. I'll tear 'em limb from limb, and then feed 'em hunk for hunk and rib for rib to the coyotes and turkey buzzards, and then collect their bones and burn 'em and dump the ashes in a whorehouse privy. I will. If it's the last thing I ever do. And may God forget to have mercy on their souls."

Looking up at the peaceful body of the Sioux brave withering away in the slow cool night wind, Hugh vowed he'd at least live long enough to exact his sacred vengeance.

"And when I've finished with 'em, I'm quittin' white-man diggin's. I'll join up with Reed and her tribe, beargrease or no, like I've always had a hankerin' to. I'll make the Ree my true enemy, not just a low-lived red varmint like I've always said. The red devil has a code. We ain't."

He nubbed on, hand for hand, one good knee and one bum leg sliding along.

From the dead Sioux brave on, he didn't see one solitary tree or bush. There was nothing but raw clay cuts, and rough stones, and wide islands of floury sand. There wasn't even cactus.

All night long, with hovering Thunder Butte's silhouette black against the northeast horizon, he kept thinking of Moses and his anger at the Israelites in the wilderness at the foot of Mount Sinai, kept thinking of Job and his tribulations in the wilderness at the foot of the treeless mountains of Arabia.

In the fury of his hating he got good mileage out of his torn old hulk of a body, some eight, nine miles across wicked terrain, until he hit a small spring coming down out of the rugged hills on the right.

The little spring had fresh cool water and a cluster of willows and plums. He drank the water; ate a few bitter willow twig tips; finished off with the hated plums. Then at dawn slept the dead-sleep of the dead.

There was more brilliant lemon September sunlight in the afternoon when he awoke. Along with it came a wailing jerking wind that eddied sand around his body and half-buried his bum leg and made his eyeballs grind gritty in their sockets.

The first thing he saw on looking around was towering altarlike Thunder Butte hovering high in the southeast skies. He thought he could make out a pair of eagles circling it. The whole jagged toss-ing country seemed pegged down and held in place by the massive redstone butte.

He drank morning cool water; ate a few bitter willow twig tips; munched down a dozen ripe plums.

He felt burnt out when he began to crawl again.

"Meat," he murmured, "meat. Gotta have meat soon or this hoss can fold up his wings and call it a day."

Why live? Ae, what was the use?

" 'Cept that if I let myself go under, cautious Fitz and that boy Jim'll get away with lettin' me die the hard way. Desertin' me. Them low-lived cold-bellied snakes. If it's the last thing I do, I'm gonna ring their necks and hang 'em out to dry for turkey-buzzard bait in the winter."

His burning hate finally revived him enough to get him going for the night's crawl ahead.

The bed of the creek straightened and widened, and every quarter mile it became easier going for him across the soft fanning silt aprons. The creek continued shallow and aggrading, playing from side to side in the gorge, building layer of sand and silt upon sand and silt, alluvial fan upon alluvial fan.

Hugh stopped for a sip from the creek now and then. Gradually it turned bitter to the taste, became sharp with wild salt and alkali.

"This child's gotta have meat soon," he murmured, "meat."

But watch and prey as he might, he found nothing, found noth-

29

ing, neither night mouse nor coiled rattler nor vested vulture.

It wasn't until dawn that he hit another spring trickling out of the hills to the right of the stream. A few yellowed bullberry bushes grew along its cut. He drank greedily of the cool fresh water; ate greedily of the half-dried half-rotten bullberries.

He had a last look around before crawling off to sleep. Thunder Butte loomed high over him, a massive red altar of sacrifice waiting a little off to the north of him, east by north. At least so it seemed. He had looked at it so often and so long, had dreamt about it in nightmare so often, he wasn't sure any more of his sense of direction, or his sense of size, or his sense of distance.

The dry fur lining his mouth and covering his tongue felt thicker.

"What this child wouldn't give for a peaceful pipe of 'bacca to improve the taste in the mouth ain't fit for sayin'."

But the fury of his hate had carried him another eight, nine miles closer to Ft. Kiowa and Bending Reed.

He slept the sleep of the unborn child.

When sleep receded and his old gray eyes uncracked, he found the wind down and the blue skies streaked with faint white mare's tail.

He also found that it was the misery skitters which had awakened him. Plums and the half-rotted bullberries. Or maybe the wild salt and alkali at last.

He groaned out of the midst of his miseries.

Why live? Ae, what was the use?

"Dig out the grave again, lads, this child's headin' that way, he is. His hash is settled at last."

Seven times the misery fits convulsed and possessed him. Seven times he was sure he was dying on the spot. Miserably. Head low. A gut-shot skittering coyote. And yet seven times he revived enough to think of going on to get his revenge.

Up on one knee, bad leg trailing in the willow-twig slape, hanging onto the brittle limb of a dead willow, he had a look down the creek to the east.

"Gettin' a little too clost to Thunder Butte and parts east to suit me, lads. Any closer to the Missouri and I'm liable to stumble onto a nest of Rees."

He surveyed the rise of tan bluffs to the south. The little spring led up a gully, and the gully in turn led up toward the pass low over the hogback, the same pass he'd spotted way back on the first divide.

"It'll be hard doin's again climbin' that, even if it is a low one." Hugh shook his old matted grizzly head. "But what's to be done is gotta be done, skitters or no. This child don't dare go any farther east. It's sail south or nothing."

He had a good drink and started in.

Twilight came red; night came rusty with halfmoon illumination.

Up. Up. And the misery fits seven times seven.

The trials and tribulations of an old broken man swollen with pus and hate.

"Job and his boils had nothin' on this child and his sores."

Powerful weak.

Meat. Meat. Meat.

Where did his old beat-up body get the guts to go on?

"A whangdoodle at that. Only a whangdoodle could make a go of it off a nest a maggots in his back and rot in the blood."

A ravening gut worming its way across a tan wilderness.

"My bowels boiled, and rested not: the days of affliction prevented me. I went mourning without the sun: I stood up, and cried in the wilderness. I am a brother to dragons, and a companion to owls. My skin is black upon me, and my bones are burned with heat."

He looked back over his shoulder. Thunder Butte loomed high, flat top first wavering close, then far, then close.

Up. Up. And the crest in the low pass gained at last. And dawn a lovely wildrose blossom.

"Meat. Meat. Gotta have—"

Ho-ah. What was that circling wheeling in the dawn-pinkened valley below? beside the twinkling Moreau? Not turkey buzzards?

He peered down the falling tan slopes.

Yes, buzzards. And this time it wasn't his meat they were celebrating. It was some downed critter's meat.

A surge of final ultimate energy sent him skedaddling down toward the meandering silvering Moreau River.

He scrabbled downhill until he came to the last drop-off. Cautiously, head raised like a grizzy predator, he peered past a final rock.

A dozen greennecked buzzards circled and squawked just out of reach of a dozen white wolves. The white wolves were working on a red four-legged critter down on a sand bar, their tails whisking about lively as they struggled with each other for the spoils. Around them in a ring, waiting their turn, sat a dozen impatient howling dun-gray coyotes.

"Buffler! A down young bull calf! Maybe the one I missed back in the hills!" Hugh cried. "Meat."

With a roar and a rush, silvertip grizzly bearskin lifting a little from the speed of his rush, dried grizzly paws bangling from his neck, willow slape careening on stones and loose gravel, gravel avalanches rushing ahead of his running elbows, Hugh charged through the ring of coyotes and into the boiling mass of snarling white wolves. "Whaugh!" he roared. "Whaugh! Hrrrach! Get! Getouttahere!"

At the roar and rush the bloody-mouthed white wolves leaped back. One look at Old Hugh's grizzly head and grizzly covering and they fled the sand bar, the coyotes slinking away with them. But fear a grizzly as they might, they didn't run far. They turned at the edge of the sand bar and sat down on their haunches. They watched him. They whined and got up and sat down. They licked blood off their snouts and paws, licked them slick and clean. They howled outraged at the intrusion. The vultures overhead retreated too, raising their wavering crying circles a rung or two.

With barred teeth and clawing fingers, Hugh tore at the raw red partly mutilated flesh, pulling fleece away from the underbelly, ripping off strips of soft veal from the hindquarters, sucking up dripping still-warm blood. With a gnawed-off leg bone he broke out a few ribs. With a stone chisel he jammed off a slice of fatty hump. He also had himself a couple of coils of boudin.

He'd become so thin, his teeth hurt at the least bit. Bits of raw flesh got caught between his incisors in the sunken gums.

He ate until he couldn't any more. He drank deep of the shimmering silvering Moreau, drank until his guts ached.

He ate and drank and slept all through the day. He ate and drank and slept all through the night. He slept on the sand bar, one arm laid protectively over the half-eaten red bull calf. When the wolves and coyotes and the vultures threatened, he fought them off, roaring and gesticulating wildly. Sometimes hunger woke him. Sometimes slavering snarling wolves woke him. A full belly always put him back to sleep.

III

GEORGE CATLIN

Catlin, born 1796, died 1872, was an artist and a student of the American Indian. In 1832 he was a passenger on the steamboat *Yellowstone* as it made its first trip far up the Missouri River to Fort Union near the mouth of the Yellowstone River. Later he lived among the Indians for several years, sketching, making notes, observing and collecting artifacts. While he was not an exceptional artist, his book published in 1841 made him famous: *North American Indians, Being Letters and Notes on Their Manners, Customs, and Conditions, Written During Eight Years' Travel Amongst the Wildest Tribes of Indians in North America, 1832-1839.*

His observations of the Missouri River in the following selection were made in the spring of 1832.

UP THE MISSOURI BY STEAMBOAT

The Missouri is, perhaps, different in appearance and character from all other rivers in the world; there is a terror in its manner which is sensibly felt, the moment we enter its muddy waters from the Mississippi. From the mouth of the Yellow Stone River, which is the place from which I am now writing, to its junction with the Mississippi, a distance of 2000 miles, the Missouri, with its boiling, turbid waters, sweeps off, in one unceasing current; and in the whole distance there is scarcely an eddy or resting-place for a canoe. Owing to the continual falling in of its rich alluvial banks, its water is always turbid and opaque; having at all seasons of the year, the colour of a cup of chocolate or coffee, with sugar and cream stirred into it. To give a better definition of its density and opacity, I have tried a number of simple experiments with it at this place, and at other points below, at the results of which I was exceedingly surprised. By placing a piece of silver (and afterwards a piece of shell, which is a much whiter substance) in a tumbler of this water, and looking through the side of the glass, I ascertained that those substances could not be seen through the eighth part of an inch; this, however, is in the spring of the year, when the freshet is upon the river, rendering the water, undoubtedly, much more turbid than it would be at other seasons; though it is always muddy and yellow, and from its boiling and wild character and uncommon colour, a stranger would think, even in its lowest state, that there was a freshet upon it.

For the distance of 1000 miles above St. Louis, the shores of this river (and, in many places, the whole bed of the stream) are filled with snags and raft, formed of trees of the largest size, which have been undermined by the falling banks and cast into the stream; their roots becoming fastened in the bottom of the river, with their tops floating on the surface of the water, and pointing down the stream, forming the most frightful and discouraging prospect for the adventurous voyageur.

Almost every island and sand-bar is covered with huge piles of these floating trees, and when the river is flooded, its surface is almost literally covered with floating raft and drift wood; which bids positive defiance to keel-boats and steamers, on their way up the river.

With what propriety this "Hell of waters" might be denominated the "River Styx," I will not undertake to decide; but nothing could be more appropriate or innocent than to call it the *River of Sticks*.

The scene is not, however, all so dreary; there is a redeeming beauty in the green and carpeted shores, which hem in this huge and terrible deformity of waters. There is much of the way though, where the mighty forests of stately cotton wood stand, and frown in horrid dark and coolness over the filthy abyss below; into which they are ready to plunge headlong, when the mud and soil in which they were germed and reared has been washed out from underneath them, and with the rolling current are mixed, and on their way to the ocean.

The greater part of the shores of this river, however, are without timber, where the eye is delightfully relieved by wandering over the beautiful prairies; most of the way gracefully sloping down to the water's edge, carpeted with the deepest green, and, in distance, softening into velvet of the richest hues, entirely beyond the reach of the artist's pencil. Such is the character of the upper part of the river especially; and as one advances towards its source, and through its upper half, it becomes more pleasing to the eye, for snags and raft are no longer to be seen, yet the current holds its stiff and onward, turbid character.

It has been, heretofore, very erroneously represented to the world, that the scenery on this river was monotonous, and wanting in picturesque beauty. This intelligence is surely incorrect, and that because it has been brought perhaps, by men who are not the best judges in the world of Nature's beautiful works; and if they were, they always pass them by, in pain or desperate distress, in toil and trembling fear for the safety of their furs and peltries, or for their lives, which are at the mercy of the yelling savages who inhabit this delightful country.

One thousand miles or more, of the upper part of the river, was, to my eye, like fairy-land; and during our transit through that part of our voyage, I was most of the time rivetted to the deck of the boat, indulging my eyes in the boundless and tireless pleasure of roaming over the thousand hills, and bluffs, and dales, and ravines; where the astonished herds of buffaloes, of elks, and antelopes, and sneaking wolves, and mountain-goats, were to be seen bounding up and down over the green fields; each one and each tribe, band, and gang, taking their own way, and using their own means to the greatest advantage possible, to leave the sight and sound of the the puffing of our boat, which was for the first time, saluting the green and wild shores of the Missouri with the din of mighty steam.

From St. Louis to the falls of the Missouri, a distance of 2600 miles, is one continued prairie; with the exception of a few of the bottoms formed along the bank of the river, and the streams which are falling into it, which are often covered with the most luxuriant growth of forest timber.

The summit level of the great prairies stretching off to the west and the east from the river, to an almost boundless extent, is from two to three hundred feet above the level of the river; which has formed a bed or valley for its course, varying in width from two to twenty miles. This channel or valley has been evidently produced by the force of the current, which has gradually excavated, in its floods and gorges, this immense space, and sent its debris into the ocean. By the continual overflowing of the river, its deposits have been lodged and left with a horizontal surface, spreading the deepest and richest alluvion over the surface of its meadows on either side; through which the river winds its serpentine course, alternately running from one bluff to the other; which present themselves to its shores in all the most picturesque and beautiful shapes and colours imaginable—some with their green sides gracefully slope down in the most lovely groups to the water's edge; whilst others, divested of their verdure, present themselves in immense masses of clay of different colours, which arrest the eye of the traveller, with the most curious views in the world.

These strange and picturesque appearances have been produced by the rains and frosts, which are continually changing the dimensions, and varying the thousand shapes of these denuded hills, by washing down their sides and carrying them into the river.

IV

JOSEPH NICOLLET

Born July 24, 1786, in France, Nicollet spent his early years as a herds-man in the Alps. A priest who recognized his intellectual potential secured a scholarship for him at the College of Cluses, and at the age of nineteen Nicollet was teaching at Chambéry. He later became secretary and librarian at the Observatory in Paris, then taught mathematics for a number of years, and left France for the United States in 1832.

Between 1836 and 1839 Nicollet made two expeditions up the Missouri River and one up the Mississippi in search of their sources. Perhaps his main contribution was the mapping of these areas. He died in Washington, D.C. on September 11, 1843.

The following selection is from his *Report Intended to Illustrate a Map of the Hydrographical Basin of the Upper Mississippi,* 1843, and describes the area north of Pierre, South Dakota, in July, 1839. The *Tchan-sansan,* or river Jacques, is the James River.

FROM FORT PIERRE

I supplied myself at Fort Pierre with all I could desire in the way of horses, vehicles, munitions, and provisions; but, in respect to men, the post was at that time itself in want, so that it could spare me only six. I had brought up with me from St. Louis only five men, who, for my purposes, were certainly worth ten. Four among them had proved themselves by numerous journeys across the prairies, as well as voyages over the Rocky mountains. One of them was Etienne Provost, known as *l'homme des montagnes—* the man of the mountains. I may remark here, that these western voyageurs are distinguished from the same set of men who do ser-vice on the northern lakes, by their never singing, and, although apparently sullen and discontented, are most faithful, cautious, and courageous in the midst of all dangers. The fifth man was Louis Zindel, who had belonged to the Prussian artillery, and, though totally inexperienced as a traveller in the Indian country, possessed otherwise many qualifications that rendered him most useful to me. He was a capital maker of rockets and fire-works, which proved very servicable to me both for defense and for signal.

Being at Fort Pierre, I met with a Mr. May, of Kentucky, and a young man from Pembina, who expressed a desire to join my party, as they were on their way to the British colony situated on Red river of the North. The accession of their company, and the great acquaintance possessed by the former with all things relating to the west, made me rather anxious than otherwise to have them among us. I had previously engaged William Dixon as a guide and interpreter, when we stopped at the Huppan-Kutey prairie. I now thought it advisable to engage, in the same capacity, Louison Fréniere, and the son of Baptiste Dorion, the interpreter at the post. Both Dixon and Fréniere had the reputation throughout the country of being the most adventurous and successful hunters, as well as the most experienced guides.

On the 1st of July, Provost, whom I had promoted to the rank of headman, came to announce that all our equipment was in readiness; at the same time Louis Zindel reported that he had prepared his rockets and other defensive missiles; which being duly inspected I gave orders to have the whole transported to the left bank of the Missouri. The roll being called, it was found that, including Mr. Fremont, Mr. Geyer, and myself, we mustered in all a force of nineteen strong. It was but a small one; but, relying on the pyrotechnics of Louis Zindel, the expectation of meeting with our reinforcement from Lac-qui-parle, our own good arms, and an abundance of ammunition, we shouted our huzza of departure, and got under way; not, however, without encountering some difficulties during two days, that I will now relate.

For the previous two weeks the waters of the Missouri had considerably swollen, so that the breadth of the river, at the place where we were to cross it, was a mile and a half: the current was very strong, and our passage could not be effected, notwithstanding all the activity and experience of my men, in less than a day and a half,—the afternoon of the 1st. and the whole of the 2d. of July. Mr. Fremont, Mr. Geyer, and myself, took advantage of this delay to close our scientific labors on the spot, and to post up our journals and field-books.

*　　*　　*　　*　　*

On the 2d day of July, at 4 o'clock, p.m., there remained to effect the passage of seventeen horses across the river. But the bark which had been procured was too small and too feeble to support more than the men. It became necessary to urge the horses to swim across—each man of the party taking charge of one horse. It may be well supposed that there was no lack of confusion during this truly perilous ferry; and, to this day, I thank God that men, horses, and baggage were not buried under the slime of the Missouri. The night was passed at the foot of the hills opposite Fort Pierre; and the next morning, the whole caravan (consisting of nineteen persons, ten cars, and thirty horses) were under way, ascending the hill to the Coteau du Missouri above.

The plateau that crowns the hills just referred to, has an elevation of not more than 500 feet above the waters of the Missouri; but its slope on the river side is very steep; so that, referring to the map along its whole length from the *Ni-obrarah* river, it will be seen to drain nothing but short creeks. Hence it was with great difficulty, and not until after a lapse of three hours, that we succeeded in reaching the open and unbroken country. In the meanwhile, the scouters had fallen upon a small herd of buffaloes, from which they obtained a very acceptable mess of fresh meat, of which we had been deprived for some time. This circumstance, together with the necessity of making sundry repairs to our vehicles, induced me to order a halt, after a less number of hours than is usual; for we were not more than eight miles to the NE. of Fort Pierre. It will be seen, however, that, from this spot, our journeys assumed a regularity that will dispense with the necessity of my giving any detailed accounts of them.

On reaching the Coteau du Missouri, there are no further apparent traces of the cretaceous formation. It is a rolling prairie, the soil of which is a mixture of fine sand and gravel; but still, it is partly covered by a short, sweet-scented, and grateful verdure. An inspection of the gullies shows that the basis of this soil is the erratic deposite previously described. The silicious particles of the soil are blackened by the smoke of the vernal and autumnal fires of the prairies; and as the growth is too scant to prevent the dust from being raised by the almost incessant winds that blow over them, the traveler is very much inconvenienced. There are no springs to quench the thirst; and it is only at wide distances apart that small pools are met with, bordered by aquatic plants towards which the experience of his guide is necessary to bring him to his bivouac, where he must needs have recourse to the dried dung of the buffalo for fuel. It was in the hope of extricating ourselves from difficulties of this kind that we made an examination of the forks of the East Medicine river, which empties into the Missouri about fifteen miles below Fort Pierre.

This last-mentioned river derives its name from a beautiful hill on its right bank, called by the Sioux *Pahah wakan*— translated by the voyageurs "Butte de Medicine," and in English, Medicine Hillock, or knoll. It is to be remarked, in fact, of the prairies of this region, that they present such low insulated hillocks, to which the Sioux apply the somewhat generic name of *ré* or *pahah,* according as they are more or less elevated above the surrounding plain. The affix *wakan* indicates that the locality is to them peculiarly remarkable, or even sacred, and a spot which they select in preference for some of their ceremonies.

We ascended to the top of the *Pahah-wakan* to enjoy the view over the vast prairie before us, where we could discern herds of buffalo as far as the eye could reach. This was, to say the least of it, a very consoling prospect.

Before quitting the forks of East Medicine river, we had made an ample supply of water and wood; a necessary precaution, for soon every appearance of running water disappeared. The green plains regain their uniformity, bounded only by the horizon, and presenting a smooth surface, without one sprig of grass higher than another. The deep furrows made by the buffaloes in their migrating excursions from north to south, and south to north, are the only irregularities of the surface. However, as the direction of our route is towards the eastern border of the plateau we could not help remarking, that there the undulations of the prairie are shorter, their intervals deeper, and, finally swell into hills of 80 to 100 feet in elevation. We had then reached the dividing ridge between the waters that empty into the Missouri, and those that flow into the river Jacques. The mean elevation of this ridge above the sea is 2,100 feet, and goes to 2,200 feet, if the mean height of the hillocks formed of the erratic deposite be taken into the estimate. One of the points of this ridge is indicated upon the map as my astronomical station of the 6th of July, on the route taken by us over these regions; which route is also laid down. Five or six miles from this station we reached the extreme verge of the eastern limits of the Coteau du Missouri, whence a most magnificent spectacle presents itself, extending over the immense hydrographical basin of the *Tchan-sansan,* or river Jacques.

Dixon, in truth, had been managing a surprise for us; he had been leading me through ravines and over hills, until we gained the spot upon which he wished to place me. Noticing my admiration, he characteristically exclaimed "well, come now, you want geography: look! there's geography for you."

Soon after we commenced to descend the eastern slope of the plateau, and came upon an encampment of Yanktons whom we had previously met on the *Huppan-kutey* prairie, and to whom we had communicated the plan of our itinerary. They were friends or connections of Dixon and Fréniere, whom we were glad to overtake. The encampment consisted of eleven lodges, containing about one hundred and ten persons; and as they were abundantly supplied with provisions, they were enjoying themselves in the fullness of their heart.

We pitched our own tents upon the same prairie, and I had an opportunity to enter into a long conversation with the chief of the party, (the Eagle,) one of the most intelligent and brave Indians with whom I ever became acquainted. He gave me some very important information in reference to the conduct of our expedition across the prairies, so as to avoid any unpleasant rencounter with the warlike parties that meet here during the hunting season. Perceiving that I had but a few men with me, he kindly offered an additional escort of his men; which offer I thought proper to decline, for two reasons: first, because I was unwilling to deprive his party of an assistance and protection that it might itself want on some emergency; and next, for the more prudential consideration of preserving an absolute neutrality. For, in case of meeting with any hostile parties, an attack might be commenced, the baggage robbed, and the horses stolen, before having time to reconcile matters by a friendly intercourse.

Early the next morning, having distributed our presents to the Yanktons, we continued our descent of the Coteau du Missouri along the *Wamdushka,* or Snake River, that takes its rise on the plateau, which we had just left, to empty itself into the *Tchan-sansan.* Thence we proceeded to lake *Tchan-ra-ra-chedan,* or lake of the "scattered small wood," the aspect of which is grateful to the traveller, but from the impurity of its water, affords him but little relief; and then, fifteen to eighteen miles farther, we reached the river Jacques, at a very celebrated spot, called by the Sioux *Otuhu-oju*—meaning, literally, the place "where the oaks spring up," but which I have designated on my map as the "Oakwood Settlement."

Otuhu oju (or, as the French call it, *Talle de Chénes*) was the place of rendesvous which I had assigned to the reinforcement that was to meet me from Lac qui-parle. It had been for the 8th to the 12th of July, and we reached it on the 10th— with laudable exhilaration, it may be believed, after one year's appointment, made in defiance of all unforseeable accidents. The estimate which I have made of the distance between this place and Fort Pierre is about 110 miles; its actual elevation above the sea is about 1,340 feet, and the descent from the Coteau du Missouri to the river Jacques not less than 750 feet. The last 50 miles, by our route, belong to the east slope of the Coteau du Missouri; but, as we were obliged to select our ground, allowing for this, the whole direct distance is probably 40 miles. In a similar way, estimating the distance to the head of the Coteau des Prairies, which is 30 miles to the east: the basin of the river Jacques between the two coteaux, and in the latitude of *Otuhu Oju,* may be laid down as having a breadth of 80 miles, sloping gradually down from an elevation of 700 to 750 feet. These dimensions, of course, vary in the different parts of the valley; but what I have said will convey some idea of the immense prairie watered by the *Tchan-sansan,* which has been deemed by all travellers to those distant regions perhaps the most beautiful within the territory of the United States.

I hazard, in conclusion of my remarks on the physical geography of the valley just described, the suggestion that it has been scooped out by some powerful denuding cause, and that its original geological character was such as is now observed in the Coteau du Missouri and the Coteau des Prairies, by which it is bounded.

It is only necessary to cast a glance over the map, to form an idea of the importance of *Tchan-sansan* river. It takes its rise on the Plateau of the Missouri, beyond the parallel of 47° N.; and after pursuing nearly a north-and-south course, empties into the Missouri river below 43°. It is deemed navigable with small hunting canoes for between 500 and 600 miles; but, below *Otuhu oju,* it will float much larger boats, and there are no other obstacles in its navigation than a few rafts. When we turned away from the river in latitude 47° 27′, its breadth was from 80 to 100 feet; and we could discover by the water marks on its banks, that, in the season of freshets, it widens out here to 100 yards, and south of *Otuhu Oju* to 200 yards. The shores of the river are generally tolerably well wooded, though only at intervals; the trees consisting principally of elm, ash, bar oak, poplar, and willows. Along these portions where it widens into lakes, very eligible situations for farms would be found; and if the Indian traders have hitherto selected positions south of the *Otuhu oju,* it was doubtless in consequence of its more easy navigation into the Missouri.

The most important tributary to the *Tchan-sansan,* coming into it from its right shore, is the *Pey-watpa* of the Sioux, the riviere aux Ormes of the French—Elm river; which Mr. Featherstonhaugh, relying too implicitly on the well meant information given to him by his good old guide, puts down on his map as emptying into the Missouri.

Elm river might not deserve any especial mention as a navigable stream, but is very well worthy of notice on account of the timber growing on its own banks and those of its forks. Hence it is that the Indian hunting parties, proceeding upon their winter chase across the Coteau des Prairies to the Coteau du Missouri, always take this route; not only, perhaps, for the supply of wood, but also in the expectation of meeting with game. The trading-post of Fort Pierre, occasionally sends an agent to barter with these migratory Indians. It was in this capacity of agent that Louison Fréniere spent among them the winter of 1836-'37, during which he encountered some trying difficulties. The buffaloes did not make their appearance that winter, and the small-pox spread itself among all the tribes that frequent this region, to their extermination. He was left without provisions, and with no other resource than that afforded by the roots of plants which he managed to dig up from beneath the snow. The men attached to his own service died of hunger; and when the spring came, his house was surrounded by dead bodies, alone, amidst this ravage of cold, hunger, and disease.

Ascending the shores of the *Tchan-sansan*, the bordering plains are observed to rise gradually up to the level of the Plateau du Missouri on one side, and that of the *Shayen-oju* on the other; so that the bed of this long river lies more and more deep. We left it at the spot called by the voyageurs *Butte-aux-Os*, (or bone hillock, bone hill,) in consequence of a large heap of bones of animals that the Indians have gathered up and arranged in a certain order. A few miles further we had reached the plateau of the *Shayen oju*. This table land may be considered as a continuation of the Coteau des Prairies; the head of which having yielded, to make way for the passage of the *Shayen-oju*, rises again to form the dividing ridge between the head waters of the *Tchan-sansan* and those of the Red river of the North. This extension of the Coteau des Prairies goes on blending itself with the ascending plains that rise toward the Rocky Mountains, and that divide the waters of the Missouri from those of the long river *Saskatchawan*, that empties into the great Winipik lake.

The *Shayen oju* derives its name from having been formerly occupied by a nation called the Shayens, who were driven from it and pursued beyond the Missouri, where they are still to be found. It is a river of some importance, being navigable by canoes, and its banks well wooded. The extent of its navigation is from near the *Mini-wakan*, or Devil's lake, to its confluence with the Red river of the North. Its valley possesses a fertile soil, and offers many inducements to its settlement; being, moreover, reputed as frequented by animals yielding the finest peltry, to the extent that its exploration is really dangerous, because of the rival and contending parties of Indians that one is exposed to meet with.

On reaching the plateau of the *Shayen-oju*, we were at once surprised and saddened at the sight of still interminable plains extending before us; for we had hoped that, after crossing the

43

river, some variety would present itself, to relieve the monotony of the scenery, and the listlessness consequent upon it, which seemed to be gaining upon our party. The Indians and buffaloes, that give animation to the prairies, had not made their appearance for many days; the heat was excessive; the thermometer three times had reached 93°, and we were scare of water; our horses were harassed by flies, and, worse than all, the whole party appeared to be, and were, dissatisfied. I could not but feel the responsibility of my situation, and made an effort to secure the successful result of our expedition, which for a while seemed to be endangered. A trifling incident brought about the change.

I had brought along with me in my medicine chest some *tartaric acid* and *bi-carbonate of soda,* with which I composed an effervescent draught, that was freely distributed among the party. They thus found themselves unexpectedly relieved; and, regaining new energy, we proceeded on our journey. The spirits of the party were further enlivened by falling in with a herd of buffaloes a few hours after. It was an immense herd, whose migration to the southwest obstructed our onward progress, for three days and nights. But it was necessary, for safety's sake, to get out of their path; and, besides, they might be fleeing before some hostile party of Indians; so that we preferred to take a safer position on a branch of the *Shayen oju,* laid down on my map as the *Tampah,* or Birch creek.

On the second day after reaching the latter position, Dixon and Fréniere announced some Indians, of whom three were brought into our camp, who gave information that, about eight miles off, there was an encampment of three hundred lodges, consisting of Yanktons, Sissitons, and Yanktonnans, preparing for a *"surround,"* with which it would be very dangerous to interfere. It was deemed, therefore, advisable, before advancing, to have some previous conversation with the chief of the party. Accordingly, after some necessary precautions, on the afternoon of the third day, having forced our way through the buffaloes, we met two chiefs, *Wahanantan* and *Manka-indlah,* who were advancing to meet us and invited us into their camp, where we had a most animating reception. I caused many presents to be distributed among them, which brought about talks, feasts, dances, songs, and the whole series of their usual ceremonies. This lasted twenty-four hours; after which we resumed our line of march, parting on terms of perfect amity from our new acquaintances.

V

ARVID SHULENBERGER

Born on September 9, 1918, Shulenberger was raised on a South Dakota farm and graduated from Yankton College in 1940. After teaching high school Latin and serving in World War II as a radar observer, he attended the University of Chicago, specializing in American literature and James Fenimore Cooper, and receiving the Ph.D. in 1951. He taught at the University of Kansas until he was killed in an automobile accident in 1964. *Roads From the Fort* (1954), from which the following selection is taken, was his only novel. The historical time of the action is 1857, at a point in the westward expansion when the U.S. Cavalry was increasingly active on the plains.

ROADS FROM THE FORT

Sam woke in the earliest gray-white of a frosty dawn, and looked curiously out of the tent to see whether Joe Burk was sleeping in his usual place across the fire, rolled in his blanket. He was. Burk had not returned from his upstream expedition when Sam had fallen asleep the night before, though the girl Wing had returned, from the east, the direction in which she had departed. Sam dressed himself with some clumsiness, noting with dismay how clammily stiff and cold the new deerskin trousers felt as he worked his feet down into them. Once in them, he walked to the fire while pulling his hunting shirt down over his head. He thought of Burk, happily sleeping in all his clothes inside his blanket, and wondered how long it would be before he could sleep in all his daytime clothes. By the time the shirt came down over his head and he could once more look about, Burk was looking toward him clear-eyed from where he still lay close to the fire and curved a little around the lightly smoking bed of coals.

Sam laid dry sticks on the fire, and watched them catch. Neither he nor the hunter spoke, and in a few moments Burk sat up without unwrapping the blanket from about his waist and legs.

Bell came from the tent in her squaw garments of cloth, moving sleepily and casting only a single smoky glance about before walking upstream to wash. Burk's amused glance passed from her to Sam.

"Gawd!" were his first words. "You're a pair o' young uns. Makes me feel like an ol' man to see you two wake up so early an' sleepy in the mornin'."

Sam brought a kettle of water and hung it over the rising flames. "Did you get a look at the Tetons last night?" he asked, not consciously intending anything more than an innocent question.

He was surprised to see Burk's eyes narrow and his countenance harden. The hunter looked almost suspiciously at Sam, but spoke agreeably enough at last. "Yunh. I seen 'm come an' go, two, three at a time, till late in the night. Never did see 'm all together. They wa'n't goin' to let nobody see 'm all together, jes 's I figgered."

Sam raised his eyebrows in question.

"Why," Burk said, "like I tol' yuh before, there's a lot more Teton aroun' these hills than jes' that dozen or so that come to the powwow yestiday. I know fer a Gawd's truth there's thirty, mebbe thirty-five wild Injin some'eres in these hills. Not the kind o' Injin I'd like to mix with, nuther, but I don' expect no trouble fer us if we leave 'm alone."

"You didn't see that many all at once?" Sam asked with hopeful skepticism.

"No-o-o. But I counted enough Injins two an' three at a time so that I know. Besides, there's a lot of horses. And besides, a fella tol' me over at the river, fer a fact that a whole passel of thirty Sioux with as many as fifty horses was comin' down this way. Nobody could figger much why they was comin'—but I reckon it was to catch the Yanktons movin' out o' the reservation. Injin news travels fast, mighty fast."

Sam realized at this point that Bell was standing not far behind Burk, listening to all he had said. Sam had not even seen her return from wherever she had gone upstream.

Bell leaned over now to adjust a moccasin, and then without fully straightening up or even looking again at Burk or Sam, she set off raidly toward the Yankton camp at a kind of gliding trot that carried her out of sight among the trees in a few moments.

Gabe was awaking, to judge from the grunting, thumping, and kicking to be heard from within the tent, sounds that usually accompanied his rising in the morning. Sam tightened the string belt of his pants, under the hunting shirt, and tied his moccasins, leaning over one and then the other. "Guess I'll go down to their camp too. Say good-by to them, if they're really going."

He turned and left without waiting for an answer. The frost underfoot felt cold and strange even through his moccasins and socks; he wondered if it was really the first time he had ever hiked through a new frost in moccasins, or why he should feel the cold so strongly. He walked faster, thinking of Bell's brother Deer-that-runs, and the runaway slave, and the old fellow called Prairie Dog. Like himself, they were setting out for the wilderness and freedom, leaving the safe round of a protected and official existence. He would like to see how they did it.

As he drew near the camp he could not see Bell anywhere, although nearly all the Yanktons were busily in evidence, and all their horses. The tepees were down, and the poles were tied to at least half the ponies like buggy shafts, as travoys to carry the freight of the group. Everybody looked busy except the Prairie Dog, who stood idly waiting, holding the trailrope of his pony and looking about the scene without any great show of interest or concern. When Sam stopped near him he looked at him for a moment, then spoke two English words: "Squaw . . ." he pointed southwestward over a brushy hill, "gone."

At the words, the runaway slave, The Feather, looked up from where he was rather solemnly regarding his empty two-wheeled cart, which he was apparently not going to take along after all.

"Your gal," the fugitive slave said then, "come here sayin' there is a lot of Sioux on the warpath. But I guess they ain't after us, an' we're goin' in a mighty little while. The Injin gal, though," he concluded softly, "went out to look for herself." He pointed as the older Indian had done. "She seems to be a good gal, an' I hope you treat her right. I guess she's worried about her brother."

All was in readiness for the departure; only the makeshift cart and the smoke of their last fire mounting sluggishly into the chill air marked the spot where the Yanktons had lived. The grass was too short and autumn-dry to show clearly where it had been trampled, or where it had been trampled at least by others than the deer that overran the valley.

At a grunted command from the tall Indian who was their active chief, the men and squaws clambered onto their ponies, and the half-grown boys who would have to run alongside looked to their moccasins and leggings a last time, or to the bows and arrows most of them carried. There was no shriek and cackle of squaws, and silence was the most impressive quality in the scene. The Prairie Dog, once he had sprung with surprising agility to his pony's back, turned to the fugitive slave and spoke briefly. The Feather turned to Sam again.

47

"He says to tell you sumpm else. He thinks there's mebbe more Injins out there some place waitin' for us—" The Feather gestured backward toward the northwest with a movement of his head— "but there's nothin' for 'm to do but go on." The Feather's voice dropped and he spoke as if for himself: "There's nothin' for me to do but go on, too. I can't run back to where the bills is posted for me, I don't care how many bloody Tetons is out in front of me, an' the young Injins don't want to go back. They figger they can beat any Injins that might set up to stop 'm."

Another command set the group in motion, in two or three natural and irregular columns the way a herd of animals will move. The Yanktons had only a short level stretch to cross before beginning their ascent of the first hill, the same hill from which Deer-that-runs had watched the approach of the Tetons. There seemed to Sam to be an unnatural, oppressive silence over the band, an air even of fatality in the way they advanced with only the sound of hoofs and the dragging travoys, leaving a dun track through the frost that had whitened the lower hillside. He watched them gain the crest of the hill and remain in view there some moments as if poised against the brightening sky. A slight noise at his side made him turn, to see Joe Burk, Gabe, and Wing all standing there watching as he was. He wondered for an instant where Bell was, and turned to watch the Yanktons disappear.

By ones and twos they dropped from sight, only the Prairie Dog himself waiting until they had all passed, and then looking downward for a moment to where Sam stood. He moved as if to raise his arm in farewell, then leaned forward instead, easily, far forward and down past the neck of his immobile brown pony, and picked something from the ground.

He straightened in his seat and swung his arm aloft. "Emersawn!" he said loudly, and the little cloud of dust shot upward from his hand and scattered, taking the sunlight vividly where the first direct rays had by now reached the top of the hill range. Without looking toward the four of them again, the Prairie Dog turned his pony's head after the departing Yanktons.

The four left behind looked to each other for a moment, still vaguely hearing the movement of the Yanktons' ponies in the distance, and Gabe offered a theory. "I figger he's crazy." Sam nodded without really agreeing or disagreeing.

The four of them moved as if by a common impulse to follow the Yanktons up the hill to the brow where they could watch the whole band move off into new country. A minute or two later, from the crest, they could see the Yanktons in double file, moving at a pony walk onto the first level stretch of ground. The Prairie Dog still brought up the rear, and one young brave rode ahead, thirty yards in front of the column, increasing his lead as he traveled. Sam made out with something like pride that the Indian riding on lookout was Deer-that-runs. He thought of Bell, and peered carefully at the departing squaws to be sure that she wasn't among them. He did not expect her to run off, but he wondered where she could be. He looked behind, and around over the hill slopes which he could see, to see whether she might not be approaching from somewhere.

Joe Burk moved a little farther, carefully, onto the hillcrest, and lay there peering down the far slope and across the level ground toward the Yanktons. The level stretch was a kind of valley floor, somewhat under a half-mile in width and breaking gradually at the northwest side—the far side from where they watched—into grassy ravines that led to a higher stretch of land beyond. No trees stood in those ravines, and each wide notch was whitened at the lower end with frost. The morning frost still held; on the level ground it lay only in irregular patches, for the breeze could strike most of the grass there.

The Yanktons headed for the widest and grassiest ravine mouth, the middle one of three opening off the northwest side of the little plain, directly onto the open prairie beyond. They passed the first ravine, Deer-that-runs having ridden into it a way to reconnoiter first.

Deer-that-runs had reached the wide opening of the ravine they were headed for and the Yanktons were following a hundred yards behind, near the edge of level ground. He reined in his pony.

Joe Burk jerked forward on his elbows, startling both Sam and Gabe. "Hell!" he said. "I figgered if they could make the edge of this stretch they might make it."

The attack came, announced by a massed yell and howl that was the first real Indian war-whoop Sam had ever heard. The shouts he had heard from Red Top and his three cohorts had been nothing in comparison. The whole group of Yanktons stopped in their tracks almost as if they had been waiting for the sound, and the women and children, then the men, tumbled off the ponies which stood as a kind of living breastworks about them. Even at that distance, of well over a quarter-mile, they could see the men throw their rifles forward on their arms, and see them look to their priming. What looked like all of the dozen or so Tetons they had seen at the council, came streaming out of the ravine to the west of the Yanktons, their ponies at a stretched gallop, the riders leaning forward yelling, with their short bows in their left hands.

Deer-that-runs, in his position out in front of the Yanktons, had seen the attackers hardly sooner than anyone else. At their screaming approach he reined his pony in tight, then whipped the animal forward a few paces with a rope-end. He reined in again as if changing his mind, and turned to ride back toward the besieged Yanktons. It was a worse than futile attempt; there might have been a chance of escape in riding straight on and up the ravine. Instead, he rode back toward the Yanktons; his only achievement was to become the first of the Yanktons to fall.

Four of the Tetons had already turned their course from the main line of attack, to chase the single pony that was out it front of the rest. When Deer-that-runs had turned, he whipped his pony to a gallop to meet the onrush of attackers. They rode him down, coming head-on, firing their arrows at the instant of passing. The four swung around to the main attack with hardly a look behind and certainly no pause in their race. Deer-that-runs must have been dead by the time he struck the beaten frosty ground; his own pony jumped straight over him where he lay and ran off to the south, back toward the hills, with its trailrope dragging and its head turned half sideways to keep its feet free of the rope.

Sam did not realize he was standing and yelling, until Joe Burk pulled him sharply down by one sleeve. "Don't be a damn fool," he said. "You can't do nothin'. If I figgered fer a minute that those was all the Tetons there is around, we might do sumpm about it . . . See? . . . There."

The second band of Tetons was bigger than the first and noisier, and came pouring out of one of the wooded gulches to the south, from the hill range proper, to join the first dozen running in a gradually narrowing circle around the Yanktons. Sam could have stood and yelled as much as he wanted with hardly a chance of being discovered. No yell of his could have been heard, and from where the attack was taking place he must have been standing directly in line with the sun which was at last moving high enough in a half-clouded autumn sky to throw a stream of gold light down across the furious color and movement of the battle.

It had become a battle. The cluster of Yanktons looked somber and insignificant in contrast to the Tetons screaming by them, but they were drawn into what seemed a tight defensive pattern. The crack of rifles just audible above the rest of the noise, and the drifting puffs of smoke, were signs of the Yanktons' activities, for the attacking party seemed to have only bows and arrows, though Sam was positive he had seen two or three guns among the Tetons at the council the day before. In fact the bows put the Tetons at a great advantage, beyond their advantage of numbers; the buffalo hunters could discharge between ten and twenty arrows a minute as they rode at full speed. They could shoot almost continually, and the short, three-foot, heavy bows drove the arrows hard and true.

The Tetons, when their whirling circle became discernible in detail to the watchers, showed nearly naked and not heavily painted. The color that Sam could see on many of their faces was black.

The Yanktons' defense was hopeless; even Sam could see that from the start. Without thinking, he pushed his rifle forward as if to join in the fight from where he lay, with a long shot that might bring down an attacker or a horse. He had not raised the muzzle, however, before Joe Burk's hard hand came down on the barrel, and the trapper said, "Don't do it. I don't figger they'll take after us if we don't mix in. But let'm see you shoot, an' we're goners; we wouldn't stand a chance. Not a damn chance."

Sam wanted to explain that he wasn't really going to shoot, but didn't. The fight was changing. One Teton was hit by the rifle fire. He only continued to ride, leaning farther and farther outward and falling at last, thrown by centrifugal force off the spinning wheel of horses. Another bullet struck a horse, and the animal plunged straight forward headlong creating a jam that appeared only as a brief eddy in the whirling mass. The thrown rider rolled and scrambled free of the circle, somehow missing the hoofs of the animals all about him, and the running horses swung inside the kicking dying one.

Dust was rising heavily now, despite the moisture of frost that had laid it. The yell and the steady pounding of hoofs were becoming mixed with the screams of the Yankton children and women, all plainly audible where the onlookers lay, and sounding in a kind of wild harmony. The Yankton ponies, the only shield against the attackers, were going down, and the Yanktons crouched behind them or lay behind those breastworks, dead or dying. They still fired their rifles, at almost point-blank range and oftener than Sam would have thought possible. He could make out no more than five guns still firing, or five points on the perimeter of the defense, at least, from which any fire seemed to be coming. Almost as he counted, one rifleman pitched forward across the dead horse behind which he had fought, a darkened arrow protruding from his back. The dark-looking corpse might have been the runaway slave, The Feather, but at that distance they could not be sure.

He could be sure of little else in the melee, except that Bell at least was not there. He told himself he had not thought she was, but he peered as closely as the distance would allow at the squaws' wrapped forms, and thought he could have made out Bell if he could see her at all. She had perhaps gone back to camp. The body of her brother could be seen occasionally past the dust and running horses; looking toward it again he saw one Indian, perhaps the one whose horse had been shot from under him, run toward the huddled corpse, kneel beside it, and take the scalp in the leisurely way a trapper might skin off a pelt. It was no worse than the rest of the attack, but Burk pointed toward it and grunted his surprise. "I didn't figger one band of Dakota Injins would scalp another. They sure 'nough mean business." Burk frowned and squinted, but said nothing more.

The Tetons rode close on the north side of the barricaded Yanktons, although they had not come to hand-to-hand range yet. Two more of the attackers had fallen, and another horse had been brought down. This time the horse broke free of the circling swarm and ran off at a wild tangent for perhaps fifty yards before stumbling and falling in a lather of blood and foam, throwing its rider forward onto the frosty ground. Half the Yanktons were dead—all the men apparently except three or four. Corpses of squaws and children lay in the impossible postures of violent death, about the open space in the center of the defenders' ring, and some still crouched with the stillness of trapped animals close against the bellies and sides of their own dead horses where they were half protected from the flight of arrows.

The fight moved more rapidly than Sam could follow; he lost all sense of time in watching it, and the mingled yells and screams, the steady thunder of the hoofs and intermittent crack of rifles, with the scattering dust and the shine of the running ponies, registered on his mind almost by turns. The continuous flinging of arrows which sometimes in their short flights caught the light for an instant, and the startling color of spreading patches of blood, even at that distance, made the color, noise, motion, and the bright sunlight seem a mere pageant of unlikely barbarity. Sam was aware as he lay watching, of the comfortable warmth of the sun already sinking into his shoulders through the buckskin of his shirt.

The Tetons were skillful and efficient fighters in the conventions of Indian warfare. They knew exactly at each point how the defenders stood, and almost as the last of the rifles fell muzzle downward from its owner's grasp they hauled their charging ponies to a halt. All thirty-odd of the riders slipped from their horses and ran nimbly forward. The metal of their hatchets and knives caught the sun. All was suddenly quieter, for the shooting had ended, and the Tetons' horses stood snorting and blowing just where their owners had left them. The yells of the attackers had dwindled, but rose again to a pitch that made up for the lack of hoof-beats and rifle-shots as the half-naked and sweatily gleaming Sioux charged into the quiet circle.

There was none of the excitement of war to the butchery that followed, although the Tetons kept up their yell and scramble as long as an enemy remained alive or a scalp untaken. One Yankton squaw rose suddenly from a shapeless heap on the ground, letting her blanket fall from her shoulders as she rose, and swung a full-sized woodman's ax, skillfully, in a wood-chopping stroke, at the Teton nearest her. She buried the ax-head past the eye in his naked belly, and wrenched it loose sidewise as if she were going to fell him like a tree with another stroke. Two hatchets came down on her, and she slipped down without a sound. The warrior she had killed fell with a last yell beside her.

The frost was gone from the area where the fight had occurred, and the dirt kicked up about the fallen Indians looked very dark by the patches of blood that still lay bright and red on the fallen horses and human beings alike.

"That's bad," Joe Burk said, "that little squaw butcherin' that last Injin. Lay low, they might git crazy enough to take out after anybody they see." The Tetons had apparently gone a little crazy, for one warrior hacked off the head of the fallen squaw with her own ax, and held it up, already scalped, for some moments to raise a yell among the rest of the warriors. From the watchers' distance, the object was almost too gory to be recognizable as a head at all.

From scalping the dead, the Tetons turned in a businesslike way to retrieving their arrows and scavenging through the shambles, breaking open the packs and spilling their contents over the dead owners, dragging what blankets and gear they wanted clear of the circle and piling them together.

"Hunh," Gabe said as if to himself, not far from Sam's ear, "they ain't goin' to attack nobody else. Thieves," he ended bitterly.

The Tetons moved quickly. The loot was packed on their own ponies, and their four dead also, wrapped in Yankton blankets, were laid across the backs of ponies to be carried off somewhere and buried in state atop a trestle of poles on the open plains. If the Tetons thought of the whites in the vicinity, or of anyone else, they gave no sign of it and did not look about over the hills surrounding the battleground. They hung the scalps, nearly thirty long black swatches of hair, from improvised poles, bow-ends, and odd sticks to carry on display. The scalp-locks swung to and fro as the Tetons mounted and rode one last time about the scene of the fight; they were no longer noisy.

Burk's remark that the Yanktons and Tetons were tribes of the same Dakota league stuck in Sam's thoughts. Only a desperate decision by the Tetons, to protect their buffalo land from all encroachment, could have brought on such a massacre as they had watched.

"D'you reckon," Gabe said, looking down at the Tetons, with what looked like a kind of permanent frown on his bearded countenance, "that the Yanktons thought they was headed for any such kind of trouble as all that? I guess the Tetons tol' 'em at least that they wasn't supposed to come up into their country. Didn't they figger the Tetons meant it?" Gabe spoke flatly, without looking at either Sam or Burk, as if he did not expect or even desire an answer. Sam thought of Prairie Dog, and wondered if he hadn't suspected almost what was going to happen when he made his outlandish sign and cry at the hilltop. If the Prairie Dog had known, his shout would seem at least less strange and mad.

Sam did not care at all for the wizened older Indian's ideas, and was hardly aware that the Prairie Dog was theorizing on the nature of the world and experience with his little handful of dust. In the old medicine man's farewell there had been a show of humor or mere whimsy, too, that Sam had never thought of as a part of any Indian's character—except perhaps Bell's just once in awhile. The world of abstract thought and speculation in which the Prairie Dog had moved with the pleasure of a natural philosopher was an alien world to Sam.

The war party was leaving, moving as quietly as the Yanktons themselves had an hour before. The day was turning warm, the frost was all gone and it could soon be hot down on the flat where the fight had occurred. The four of them lay quietly watching, not saying anything, perhaps not even thinking about the fight or the bloody scene before their eyes. Sam remembered what Bell had said of an old, traditional battleground to the west of the hill of the turtle, and supposed with a sense of surprise that this was it. He wondered how many scattered heaps of dead Indians and horses had lain there in the century past, and shook his head as if to clear it of a kind of thought he did not often find there.

The Tetons, with even their corpses on horseback, milled about the area for another minute, the bloody long-haired scalps dangling among them in the still valley air. Their ponies must have been used to blood, Sam thought, for though some of them still snorted and breathed heavily none of them looked chalk-eyed or skittish. In another minute the war party had lined out in a traveling column toward the northwest, moving up the very ravine the Yanktons had chosen for their own departure from the hills. They rode without looking back, and moving only at a walk they were yet out of sight beyond a shoulder of sodded hill within a few minutes.

Gabe got stiffly to his feet, and leaned over to pick up a half-dozen paper-wrapped cartridges he had laid out beside his rifle. He caught Burk's eye upon him and grinned momentarily. "For awhile there I figgered they might take out after all of us, too."

Burk nodded. "Sure. Never figgered to be dead sure an Injin ain't goin' to attact. They 'most always will if sumpm gits under their skin. Hows'ever," he added reflectively, after another moment, "no Teton is goin' outa his way to kill a white man right now this far down into army country. That 'ere ol' whitewhiskers General Harney has a pow'ful repitation all over the west-river country fer killin' Injins that has lifted white men's scalps."

They all stood up and moved about stiff-legged for a minute, stretching a little, avoiding looking down toward the piled dead, and not talking. The girl Wing turned and made off silently almost before they noticed, and Joe Burk followed, grunting something about being hungry for breakfast. Gabe and Sam turned away from the scene of the fight at the same moment. They had made perhaps four steps back toward camp when they both heard from behind them, apparently from the battle scene, an odd short sound that stopped them in their tracks.

"Unh?" Gabe said. Sam shrugged. It did not sound like a groan, or any human sound, though at that distance they could not tell. They both looked back to the motionless, perfectly dead-looking Yankton circle. "Burk said sumpm about breakfast," Gabe said as they looked. "There's nobody alive in that pile an' I ain't goin' down there—not jes' yet anyhow. Let's go." He turned without waiting for a reply, and was off at a stone-rattling pace downhill, toward camp.

Sam did not wait or stand watching him, but almost as quickly turned in the opposite direction, and started toward the Yanktons without giving himself time to argue about what he was doing. The air toward the bottom of the hill was motionless, though still cool to the point of chill; there was no breeze down there. Sam glanced back to see how high the sun had got. Not high.

He did not know why he wanted to go look at the massacred Indians; he was as sure as Gabe had been that the sound was of nothing left there alive, and became surer as he walked steadily toward the silent heap of dead horses, men, squaws, and children out on the level stretch before him. Walking close to the edge of the Yankton circle; and then moving on around it, he kept his movements and his senses under control with some effort. There was a smell in the breezeless air, not yet the sharp odor of decay but the half-sweet stench of viscera and blood, like a smell Sam had known at hog-butcherings years before at his grandfather's farm. The red freshness had disappeared from the color of the blood and the surfaces of torn or broken flesh, under the steady slant of sunlight. He avoided looking closely at the tangles of bodies and gear, packs broken open and the commonplace objects that had been picked up and thrown once again on the heap by the departing Tetons.

Nor was he to learn what the sound had been which they had heard from the hilltop; it might have been some kind of animal or bird, or a dog of the Yanktons whining before it disappeared for good. It might have been just the kind of scraping or thumping or knocking about which the corpse of a recently dead animal might make when the legs stiffened or the gut swelled; something could have toppled in the crowded heap. He wondered only half seriously what the sound had been, and was glad enough to turn away from the whole shambles and walk straight south into odorless air, with only an uncomfortable shiver about his shoulder blades at the consciousness of so much death behind him. He was headed toward the course of the little stream on which their own camp was set, almost toward the spot where the Tetons had camped the night before.

He followed the steep slope of a briar-covered ridge that stood perhaps two hundred yards from the stream, taking a path that rabbits and deer had beaten hard through hundreds of seasons. Near the top of the ridge he heard a second sound, half a groan and half a call it seemed, and not far away. He turned suddenly toward it; it was as if he were expecting the sound, as if this unforeseen noise were the reason why he had turned back from the hilltop a while before and not gone with Gabe to camp and breakfast. He pushed the half leafless arms of a bush aside to move to the highest point on the ridge, and saw an open patch of ground, a patch marked, he could see at a glance, by the hoofs of a lot of horses. He looked again at the hoofmarks, and two or three tumbled bushes where the riders had passed before he saw the arrow lying there.

He felt as if his heart were turning over in his chest. It was a war arrow, with a loose-hung barbed point that had not pulled off but was turned a little sidewise from the line of the arrow itself. Why it had not pulled free as such arrowheads were designed to do was obvious at a glance; it was stained a single red-brown color from tip to feather, and sharply visible against the gray ground. The color was that of the drying blood of which he had already seen so much; the arrow had evidently passed clear through whatever creature it had struck. Sam had heard of arrows being driven right through buffalo bulls, shot at close range.

Trying to believe that one of the Tetons had shot a deer—or some kind of animal—there that morning, Sam moved onward almost against his will, pushing bushes aside and looking no farther ahead than he could help.

At the top of the rise, Bell came into his view all at once. She lay there half on her side, her legs bent slightly and her head resting on a tufted knob of earth, like any woman resting. Sam heard a long sigh or groan escape his own lips, as if he were himself an onlooker at the scene. Bell was not resting; he knew she could not rise easily, or rise at all again, but she opened her eyes and looked up at him impassively as if she might only be refusing because of some whim to sit up as she was expected to do. The arrow had apparently gone through her body just right of the center line of her chest. Her breathing was quiet and her voice came only in a whisper: "Water."

It was more than a hundred yards over rough ground to the stream, and he had no sense or recollection of how he got there; he realized only that he had no container for carrying water. He ran upstream a short way to the abandoned Teton camp, found a piece of deerhide and wondered if he could fold it in such a way that it would hold water, and then noticed a crude wooden porringer or bowl lying by the ashes of the fire. He marveled at his luck until he picked it up and saw it fall apart in his hand, held together only by a strand or two of the wood itself. Even so, he saw that it would hold water so long as he held the halves of the bowl together.

The next act of which he was aware was the difficult feat of holding the bowl to Bell's lips, lifting her head a little with one hand and holding the bowl together carefully with the other. After opening her eyes briefly as if it cost her some effort to raise the lids, she drank with her eyes closed, with the feeblest sort of greediness. She lay still then for a while as if unaware of his presence, and he set the bowl down with care, propped between two stones that might hold it together so firmly that all the water wouldn't leak away.

Bell seemed to lie there quietly enough, with a sumac bush and his own body shielding her face from the climbing sun. A branch of the red sumac extended out over her head, looking like a spray of some exotic flower set there for a color of death. She opened her eyes again at last, smoky dark as they always were, and looked at him calmly. There were smallest signs of expression about her nearly impassive countenance which Sam could read as unthinkingly as he might the changes in any white face. A week before, he could not have told that she was thinking anything out of the ordinary. He saw there now a look of concern, perhaps even love, that made him realize for a moment how shocked his own face must appear. He forced his lips into a smile for her, and touched her forehead with his palm in a brief caress. She did not smile; he had not expected that. She closed her eyes again.

He had no sense of passing time, and only later learned that much time had passed. The air was pleasant and warm, but he took off the shirt Bell had made for him and laid it about her legs and feet. If she felt it being tucked about her she made no sign. She opened her eyes once and asked for water, and keeping her eyes open and her gaze fixed on Sam she spoke for a little, very slowly, in English.

"Tetonwan," she said expressionlessly, of her own misfortune. "No mountain. No traps. I don't go with you now. Nothing." She paused so long that he thought she might not talk again. "The Yankton, all dead. I see the Tetonwan, too many, an' run to the Yankton. They kill me here. But they do not lif' my hair." She expressed something like pride in the odd frontier phrase, and Sam reached out and stroked her head lightly.

"No," he said.

"I hear the yells. Guns. Now no guns. All the Yankton are dead. The Tetonwan is gone to the buffalo country."

Sam nodded slowly.

She spoke an Indian name, then translated: "Deer-that-runs is dead, my brother. He dies in war. The black Injin is dead, The Feather. He asked me to go to the Canadas with him."

"Unh?" Sam had not known that the fugitive's plans had been so far acted upon.

"I do not go," Bell said. "I stayed with you to go to the mountains. You are a sojer an' a chief, an' kill the Wahpekute horse stealer." Another pause.

"Lucy," she said, and Sam for a moment did not understand the word at all. "Lucy medal." She lifted the hand nearest him for it. At first he did not think he had it with him, but remembered it then and fished it with some difficulty from the pocket of the light cloth shirt he still wore under his hunting shirt. By feel, he distinguished it from the Jefferson medal which also lay in the pocket. He laid the plain gold locket on Bell's palm, and at an infinitesimal gesture of her hand understood he was to open it and hold it up where she could see. He wondered, looking at her almost motionless eyes, how well she could see.

"Good squaw," she said. She looked at him as she had a few times in joking. "Good squaw?"

He joked too. "Well it beats hell out of me, Bell." He put the locket back in her outstretched hand, he hardly knew why. Her fingers closed over it.

"No matter," she said. She closed her eyes, and whether from the strain of speaking or increasing weakness, breathed more heavily. A thin bubble formed at the corner of her lips, colored with blood, and he brushed it away. She spoke once more, in whispers, three short sentences or phrases in the Yankton tongue. Her eyes remained closed.

She did not open them again or say anything more, and an indeterminate while later she died, with only a slight kind of tremor near the end. The Indian phrases had given her an air of remoteness unlike any Sam had ever sensed in her presence, and she died, for him, a purely Indian death, farther away and more unknown than she had ever seemed to be. But he knew exactly the instant when she died, and took a frayed square of blue cloth from his shirt pocket and laid it over her face. It fell in straight folds down the side of her face despite the creases that marked the cloth.

He stood up with difficulty, his knees cramped from having been bent so long a time. The red spray of sumac and the blue of the cloth seemed to shine too brilliantly before his eyes for a minute.

That sense, perhaps a moment of dizziness from standing too quickly, passed from his mind and he saw the hills he had known, and the same prairie. He felt suddenly calm again and obscurely bitter. He half turned to go, then turned back to retrieve his hunting shirt from where it lay about the dead girl's legs. He turned away from her and put it on over his head. Without looking back he set out for camp.

No one seemed in a hurry to question him once he had got to camp, and he had taken a swallow of the hot tea that had been awaiting him in a pan set in the coals, before Gabe spoke. "None of the Yanktons was alive, I guess, was they?"

It took him some moments to realize what the question was about. "No," he said. "All dead."

"Your squaw ain't been here," Joe Burk said from where he sat working over the breech of his rifle. Sam turned half around to look at him, but the trapper's eyes were on the gun.

"She's dead."

Burk looked up for a moment, and back to his work. Gabe, from the other side of the fire, half grunted half sighed his sympathy and said nothing for a few moments. When Sam only continued drinking his tea, however, he asked a question: "She wasn't with the Yanktons, was she?"

"No. She found the Tetons, and tried to get back to tell the Yanktons. They got her, over there on a ridge. They didn't get her scalp." He added the last remark because Bell had, and like her he felt some pride in it.

He rose and threw the dregs of his tea into the fire. "I'm tired," he said, and moved toward the tent. "I'm going to sleep for a little bit and then I've got to bury her." He felt for a moment almost indifferent, and lay down stupidly on the bed that he had built with such care and ingenuity.

He heard Burk say in an undertone to Gabe something about his probably not going west, now his little squaw was dead, and he called out irritably, "Hell yes, I'm going west in the morning." He knew that he wanted to lose himself somewhere in the wilderness. In the meantime he need a rest. He went off into a troubled sleep almost as soon as his head struck the blanket roll he used for a pillow.

VI

KATE and VIRGIL D. BOYLES

Virgil Dillon Boyles (1872-1965) and his sister Kate (1876-1959) collaborated in writing six novels between 1907 and 1926. Th first of these, *Langford of the Three Bars,* was a national best-seller, the second to come from South Dakota in a brief period of two years (the first being Will Lillibridge's *Ben Blair,* 1905).

Virgil was born in Illinois. Two years later the family moved to Dakota Territory where Kate was born in Olivet. Both were educated at Yankton College. Virgil went on to become a court reporter, a lawyer, and finally a judge. Kate married J. H. Bingham and settled in Chamberlain.

The Spirit Trail (1910) was their third novel.

THE SPIRIT TRAIL

Red Cloud, Chief of the Oglala Sioux, at his buffalo camp on Powder River, received the messengers from the Peace Commission courteously but did not hasten down to Fort Laramie in response to the urgent request. Instead, he sent word that he thought he should wait until the forts were abandoned and the road closed up before he signed the treaty.

The road in question was that highway which the Government had proposed to construct from the California trail near Fort Laramie, across by the way of the Powder River to the gold fields in Montana and Idaho; and the forts were those builded along its course to protect the work of construction from the attacks of Red Cloud and his Oglalas, who resented bitterly this invasion of the richest, in fact the only, buffalo range left to the Sioux Nation. The Government did not as yet altogether trust Red Cloud. It was late August before it finally determined to take the chief at his word and to withdraw all the troops from the forts. This resolve was put into execution, but still the great chief did not come down to meet the peace commissioners.

"It is so late now," he said. "I think I will put up my Winter's meat before I go down to sign."

So, all during that Fall, while both the Indian department and the Military waited in nerve-trying suspense and uneasiness, Red Cloud, taking his own good time, busied himself in drying buffalo meat, and curing hides for the fast vanishing fur trade.

"Will Red Cloud keep faith?" men asked themselves and each other many times during those long days of waiting.

"Faith? Faith in a redskin?" said a member of the Commission, an army officer who stood high in the Government's confidence, and who was distinguished in his day as a peerless Indian-fighter, though somewhat over-zealous perhaps. "Policy, if anything, or fear of the Great Father's vengeance, may bring him down to treat with us, but never good faith. I should not be at all surprised if he were plotting mischief right now."

"It is insolent, to say the least," grumbled a second member of the Commission, "to keep us waiting his pleasure with figurative fingers in our mouths, while he—goes hunting. It must be royal sport to keep the great Republic of the United States thus dangling —a right kingly conception of humor, and no mistake. For my part, I would with all my heart that I were stalking buffalo while my red friend danced to the never-ending time of my errant fancy. I should make him rue the day very bitterly that he taught me the game so well."

"Do not be afraid. Red Cloud will keep faith," said a new voice in the fort, calm yet full with the authority of confidence.

"How so? Do you come from the Powder? I thought you rode from the opposite direction."

"So I did," said the stranger, quietly. "I am not an emissary from Red Cloud. On the contrary, I have never seen this chief in my life. I have come directly from the Missouri River."

"On what, then, do you ground your so great faith?" asked someone, curiously.

"Because his is a righteous war," said the stranger, clearly, and he turned the steadfast lustre of his tired but brave gray eyes full upon his interlocutor.

"It is evident that you believe strongly in the Church Militant," said the grizzled old Indian-fighter, with a shrug of his shoulders and a glance at the plain gold cross gleaming in relief against the dark of the young man's waistcoat.

And the saddle-weary newcomer, remembering Ash Hollow and its stain, answered with a great sadness:

"Is it only thus that peace can come to this people—the peace of fear? Yes, I believe in fighting," he continued, the scintillation of a smile lighting up his rather grave features. "I am somewhat of a fighter myself. I fight a host of foes—the sun, moon, wind, thunder, lightning, the Aurora Borealis, Onkteri, Wakinyan, Takuxhanxkan, with all their satellites of serpents, lizards, frogs, owls, eagles, spirits of the dead, buzzards, ravens, foxes, wolves, and myriads of others, all under the evil tutelage of *wakan*-men. But more than all," and there was a ring in his voice that few who heard him ever forgot, "I believe that the heart of man is instinctively honest, and that it is treachery that begets treachery. Red Cloud is a man. Soon you shall know."

"And Red Cloud was not at Ash Hollow," said another voice in good English, and yet no white man had spoken. If it was the young priest's dusky companion who had thus given speech, he did not again transgress. His mouth was set in lines of strong-willed taciturnity. His sombre eyes above his high cheekbones gazed haughtily past the interested glances focused upon his dark face.

"Were you at Ash Hollow?" asked a bystander, pointedly.

There was no answer.

"Who are you?" asked another.

Still no answer.

"On my word, but you are a surly fellow," said the Indian-fighter, turning to saunter away.

The priest put his hand affectionately on the Indian's shoulder. A sudden quiet fell upon the bystanders. Without warning, the air seemed all at once charged with a strange expectancy.

"Just a minute, General," he said. "I want to present my friend, Running Bird. His father was Little Thunder, Chief of the Brule Sioux, who fought and died at—Ash Hollow."

It was a warm, bright, still day in October when the priest and his Indian friend, Running Bird, after many dusty days in the saddle, rode through the stockade gates of Fort Laramie. No one knew their errand, or cared, perhaps. The cross was following the sword into the Indian country—that was all. The Army was always in the van—the Church lagging behind. The Army was the real missionary after all. So those first soldiers preserved a patronizing, though kindly, tolerance toward the first missionaries; and at Washington, the Great Father tried to guide wisely the destinies of the one, while he looked forward hopefully to the utlimate triumph of both. The two men abode in the fort until the blue of October turned into the brown of November, and the wolves grew very bold indeed because their tawny skins were now the color of everything; until the thrifty hunter had his lodge stored full of meat for the Winter, though the reckless were still far afield; and on the ninth, Red Cloud, Chief of the Oglala Sioux, came down from his camp on the Powder and signed the treaty of peace.

*

It was July, and the snows melted from the mountains had swelled the great river until it slopped over its banks in the low places, backed itself up every ravine and gulch that drew to the high water level, and, when compressed within the narrow limits of high chalk-rock bluffs on either side, sprang forward and took the breach, rushing, roaring, swirling, leaping, in its race to get through and once more stretch itself, and the boom of whose frantic haste might be heard for a mile or more sounding upon the surface of the water or far inland through the light atmosphere. The heat of the noonday had spread filmy clouds between the earth and the sun with hints of rain in them, but so far they had brought only a fresher Summer breeze and sent it singing down the valley, where often, its right of way being disputed by some rocky promontory, it whipped the water for the insolence until the waves flew their white caps of unwilling submission, before it slipped whisperingly around the bend. Willow thickets, growing upon low bottom lands or upon islands where perhaps not long since a grain of sand had lodged on a submerged snag, and then another and another, until an island was formed, showed now but their wind-blown green tops like reeds in a marsh. On this side, now on that, as the changing river shifted its course, arose to sheer but varying heights the cut bluffs, some with white, staring, sphinx-like faces, others frowning darkly, but always fit monuments of a majestic solitude and of a history whose covers will never be opened, whose pictography never read. Up and down the river brooded the shadow of its centuries of silence and the mysterious charm of its remoteness, changed but infinitesimally since those never-to-be-forgotten days when Lewis and Clarke journeyed that way, giant pioneers who struck the first blow that sunk our frontier into the Western Ocean.

The sight and sound of a steamboat making its regal way through the tremendous current on that Summer day in the early seventies, surrounded as it was by these silent witnesses of an unwritten past, seemed to many of the passengers like an anachronism. The vessel was the *Far West* of the Coulson Packet Company, loaded at Yankton with Government supplies, and bound for the up-river forts and agencies. It was a strongly built stern-wheeler, its builders at Pittsburg bearing in mind always the idiosyncracies of the Missouri River, for traffic on whose waters it was especially designed; so that the push of the channel had but little effect in delaying the boat's usual rate of progress.

On the cool side of the upper deck sat the wife and daughter of the newly appointed agent of Big Bend Agency. At least the wife was sitting. The daughter walked the deck in her quick impatience.

"Are you tired already, Katharine?" asked the mother, a pale, slight, fair little woman, who was quite content to sit quietly in her chair while her tall daughter paced restlessly to and fro.

"Already, mother? When was I ever not tired of this—madcap and heartless demand of my father's?"

"I mean tired of this boat; and please don't call it heartless, dear. Your father only asked, and we—we came because it was our duty to come. It ought to be our pleasure. I am trying to make it mine. He is so very lonely."

"You mean that you came because he wanted you to, and I came because—well, perhaps I was ashamed to let my little mother show a braver spirit than mine; and perhaps I was too cowardly to be left alone; and still another perhaps," she said, crumpling her tall self once more into her chair and laughing affectionately, "I came to protect your beautiful soft hair, mother. I thought maybe when they went to take it,—those dreadful tomahawk men,—if I offered mine instead, they might accept the sacrifice because, you see, mine is yellower than yours though not half so pretty; but my hope lies in the fact that the savage mind, devoid of taste or judgment in art, would immediately grasp after the glitter and leave the gold."

"What nonsense!" said Mrs. Mendenhall, with a little laugh in which there was a minor note of tears and dread. "But I cannot help thinking, Katharine, that you had far better have remained at home, at least for the present. It will be very lonely for you."

"Home, mother?" said Katharine, and there was a peculiar, intent, almost tragic look in her beautiful eyes, tragic because of its hint of prophecy. "We are going home. We have left behind us everything that was sweet and pleasant and worth while, and we are going to a wilderness of loneliness and to dreary wastes of never ending crudeness and barbarism—but we are going home. We must never forget that."

"Not you, dear," said the older woman, quietly, tears springing to the faded blue eyes. "You will go back some day—very soon, perhaps; and I am an old woman, so what does it matter where I am so I be with my husband?"

"If I thought," said Katharine, with a quick change of mood, "really and truly thought that I should have to live the rest of my days among the Indians, I should jump from this deck down there into that yellow whirlpool right this minute. You needn't smile, mother. I mean it—almost. For it would come to that in the end. So why wait for the slow torture of approaching insanity? When my mind should be altogether lost, I should simply walk off one of those ghostly cliffs some dark night, and that would be the end. If I ever should lose my mind, those lonesome cliffs would haunt me to my undoing,—that I know,—so I should take the leap at once and spare myself the misery between. Now forgive me, little mother, for my brutal selfishness. I had to thrash it all out to you, hadn't I? It was the only way to regain my shreds and tatters of self-respect. I am happier now. I have talked out the demon of my unrest. I could bear even hours on a sand bar. I walk the deck no more."

She picked up a book that had fallen to the floor and opened it resolutely. Hers was a striking figure, sitting there in the shade of the eastern row of staterooms, a flower plucked from the very heart of civilization, being borne to the very heart of the Great Reservation, and so evidently against her choice if not against her will. The set face forced to its task of reading, and the drooping poise of the tall, beautifully rounded young body, both spoke eloquently of a life loved and shielded, humored and self-effaced for, until the queenly progress of it had altogether, without warning, come upon one of those quiet forces of nature that for all their quietness and all their unassumingness yet rule the world. The man had said, "Come," and the woman was coming. The man was Katharine Mendenhall's father, and the woman, the slight, pale little lady at her side. That was why she sat chafing on the upper deck of the *Far West,* bound for the upper river. The meeker woman, hearkening to the call of the man, had conquered. Katharine was twenty-four and her hair was yellow with gold as were the shining depths of that treasure locked and guarded within the storehouses of those darkly showing, splendid Indian hills, covered over with their wonderful forests of pines—so soon to set the passion of gain of a great country aflame, so that men would forget their honor, and chief magistrates their sacred trust, because of the lure there is in the shining gold. Her eyes were blue, a deep, dark blue, with a straightforward self-confident outlook. From the moment of coming aboard at Yankton she had so wrapped herself in the outer garments of reserve that no one had dared to speak to her as yet. Mrs. Mendenhall, on the contrary, at luncheon in the dining saloon, had made tentative advances toward fellowship with one or two persons who seemed, like her, to be coming into a far country.

"What noise is that?" asked Katharine, suddenly, laying down her book. "Is it thunder?"

"It is too continuous for thunder," replied the older woman, anxiously. "I have been hearing it for some time. Ask the Captain, Katharine, won't you? It gets on one's nerves."

"You must learn to do without such inconvenient things as nerves in this haunt of the savage, mother mine," said Katharine, laughingly, but she rose to obey the request. She had laid aside her silk travelling coat because of the cloudy heat of the afternoon, and she looked very neat and trim in her faultlessly made frock, as she made her way to the pilot-house with a calm assurance of her perfect right to do anything or to go anywhere she pleased in the world.

"That rumbling, Miss? That's rapids," responded the Captain, courteously. The pilot did not turn at the question. His bronzed face was intent; his eyes, trained to steadfastness by much looking forward, were fixed on the narrowing waters ahead.

"How can there be rapids in the Missouri?" demanded Katharine, unconvinced.

"I think the old river is cutting a new channel up there a ways— she's a horribly fickle creature. I reckon all that spread out water at the bend thrown over here and forcing itself through these narrow limits is causing the trouble."

"Is there any danger?" asked Katharine, with a little chill of apprehension.

"Not the least. The *Far West* will take that like a swallow on the wing. Nothing in this heathen river surprises her any more. Besides, she's built for it."

The roar of the rapids was unmistakable now to all, and in another moment the stanch steamer was almost staggering beneath the force of opposition it met to its further progress. The waves raced and roared and whirled. The thunder of their wild haste was deafening. But the boat rallied gallantly to the renewed pressure of steam and pursued her stately way. Katharine returned to her mother.

"We are losing time," she fretted, discontentedly.

"Are you in such great haste to meet your savage friends?" asked her mother, quietly.

"It's like—jumping into the river," said Katharine, whimsically. "I want to have it over with."

"Why, child, how still it is!" exclaimed Mrs. Mendenhall, strangely startled. "Is it because we are through the rapids?"

"Do you hear the engine?" asked Katharine, almost in a whisper. "Listen."

An eerie silence at first greeted their strained attention, but it was not long before the old familiar boom of the tumbling current came to them with a new distinctness. That was all. It seemed louder than before because of the cessation of other sound. It was the sudden stopping of the noise of the throbbing engine that had so modified the beat upon the ears that for the moment it seemed as if even the seething waters were quiet.

"We are standing still," cried Mrs. Mendenhall, in terror.

"Standing still?" said Katharine, with a forced composure. "Mother, we are floating down stream."

They did not drift long. Just below the rapids, the vessel staggered, strained a little, quivered through all her heavy timbers, and stood still. Instantly there was the wildest confusion throughout the steamer—but to the passengers' deck came the Captain, at once quelling the threatened panic with his clear, calm explanations.

"The engine broke down and we thought to let the boat drift below the rapids before we deemed it wise to anchor. There is not the least danger. No, we have not run on a snag—only a sand-bar. Nothing is wrong with the boat except the engine. No, we have not sprung a leak. It will be necessary to get a steam boat to tow us back to Yankton, and we shall be obliged to tie up two or three days for repairs. As it will be impossible to get a boat here until some time tomorrow, it would seem that we are doomed to spend the night on this sand-bar. It is extremely provoking." He paused to mop his heated face with his handkerchief.

"I am very anxious to go on," said Mrs. Mendenhall. "Do you think there will be any other boat going up the river right away?"

"I think not," the Captain replied. "The *Josephine* expects to leave Yankton in about a week, but by that time we will be two or three days on our journey. I am afraid there is no alternative but for you to wait until we get our engine repaired and are ready to make a new start." The Captain turned and walked away. It was not long, however, before the two ladies saw him returning, followed by two gentlemen.

"Let me present Mr. Hugh Hunt," he said, "Indian missionary, and Mr. Locke Raynor. Mr. Raynor has been appointed issue clerk at the Agency, I believe."

"Captain Maxwell informs me," said the man called Locke Raynor, in a voice that was slow and pleasing, "that you were anxious to reach the Agency with as little delay as possible. I am also very anxious to proceed. I take it that Mr. Hunt, too, does not greatly relish a stop-over. The Captain informs me that there are horses on board, and saddles, to be consigned to Major Mendenhall at the Agency, and he has suggested that we might take these animals and continue the trip overland. He also suggested that you might possibly like to accompany us. There are blankets and plenty of provisions. If you think you can put up with the hardships of such a journey, it will enable you to reach the Agency three or four days sooner than you will if you wait for the boat."

"If only Mr. Mendenhall had met us!" mourned the Major's lady.

"He was unavoidably detained?" asked Locke Raynor, politely.

"Yes. We found a telegram waiting for us at Yankton saying that the Indians were restless and that he dared not leave the Agency at present."

"I don't see why they had to go and get all worked up the very day my father was to meet us," fretted Katharine. "Why didn't they have their ridiculous old dances before we left home? Or if they were too contrary to do that, then they might at least have waited until we were safe in their wretched country. What is it all about, anyway?"

"Perhaps their medicine men need a little time for reflection behind steel bars, Miss Mendenhall. They have held communion with evil spirits so long that we need not fear that they will be too lonely in captivity. And I think their braves need the feel of good powder and lead. Some day, perhaps, we shall be sorry for our leniency."

The Priest had not yet spoken. He stood waiting, slight, pale-faced, quiet, with big gray eyes that were dark and burning with the lustre of the everlasting fires of his great soul—fires that burned so steadily that it seemed as if they must some time consume the spare frame.

"Then why don't they order out the soldiers?" demanded Katharine, impatiently.

"They have ordered them out often—very often. I do not think that this is the time for the soldiers, Miss Mendenhall," said the priest, quietly. His voice was low and musical with the cultured cadences in it that spoke of cities and home and the land of the rising sun. A tiny sob of homesickness came suddenly into Katharine's throat, but she smothered it quickly.

"You think there is no danger, then?" she asked.

"Of an outbreak? I hope not. I trust not."

"Won't you tell me what the trouble is?"

"It is only that General Custer has been sent to the Black Hills."

"And high time, too," said Captain Maxwell, decidedly.

"Perhaps," said the priest, with a strange smile. "But if he would go back to Fort Abraham Lincoln, Major Mendenhall might meet his wife and daughter."

"Does your mother ride, Miss Mendenhall?" asked Locke Raynor, observing an impatience on the part of the Captain to have the matter disposed of one way or another.

"Not of late. She used to be accounted a fine horsewoman."

"And you?"

"I can do—what I have to do," said Katharine, briefly.

"Then let me urge you to take to the horses," said Locke Raynor. "If there should be a general uprising—though that is surely a remote contingency—you might be indefinitely delayed; but once at the Agency, you will be safe, no matter what happens."

"It will be a very harsh journey," cautioned Hugh Hunt, gravely, "for gentlewomen. We have no tent, and the stage route is not an extraordinarily good one. The stage houses are very primitive. They are unaccustomed to rough-riding. It is very probable that we shall have rain."

Katharine turned to him quickly.

"Then you think there is danger if we choose the land journey?"

"From what source?"

"The Indians."

"The Indians? My Indians? No, I do not think there is any danger from that source."

"Please then, Captain Maxwell, put us ashore," said Katharine, decidedly. "I said I could stand hours on a sand bar, but I cannot. I should die. Anything is better than stagnation. I think we can make almost as good time riding as the steamer does, anyway, going up stream, and that will save my father a great deal of unnecessary suspense."

"As I explained to Mr. Raynor," said the Captain, "there are only two horses aboard for Major Mendenhall. They were doubtless intended especially for you ladies. But it is only a short distance to Springfield, where you can either secure more horses or wait for the stage. There will probably be others going as far as Springfield. So be it, then."

The men made short work of transferring their meagre effects to the skiff. Obliged as they would be to walk some little distance before finding horses for themselves, they saw the mistake of attempting to carry more than the strictest necessity demanded.

Safely ensconced in the stern with her mother, Katharine yet could not keep back a gasp of sheer dread as the small boat pulled away from the stranded steamer. The gloomy waste of choppy, racing waves between her and the distant shore were brought so close to her that in reaching to slap the sides of the frail craft, the water often splashed over, and once wet her arm to the elbow as she clung desperately to the side of the skiff.

"Do not be afraid," said Locke Raynor, with kindly assurance, as he plied one pair of oars with long, steady sweeps of unmistakable accustomedness. One of the steamer's crew bent to a second stand, so the little craft cut the current, pointing upstream, with a fair degree of directness.

But Katharine's involuntary gasp turned into a real cry of alarm as a sudden tremendous splash, followed almost instantaneously by another as great, sounded behind her.

"It is only your horses," said Locke, with a quiet smile. "They were pushed overboard so they would swim in the wake of our boat. Good boys! They have made a gallant recovery and are coming after us in fine shape—heads up—no slopping or kicking. There's grit for you."

It seemed as if this man must be always reassuring her, Katharine Mendenhall, who had never before been afraid of anything in all her proud young life. This man was a stranger. It was altogether within the bounds of possibility that he was one of those unfortunate beings who, having made serious mistakes in the places that knew them, wished to lose themselves in the wide and rough and unasking frontier. She had known of men dropping quietly out of their wonted niches, and people had said of such, vaguely: "They have gone West." Why was this unknown man observing her so closely as to be conscious of her least movement? She resented it, even while a quick faith in his power to guide them safely through the gloomy mazes of tossing water sprang into life and grew steadily.

"I thought maybe it was a—sea serpent," she said, trying to smile with a brave unconcern.

When the stragglers from the *Far West* arrived at Springfield, there were still some hours of daylight left. After consultation, the Agency party, consisting of Mrs. Mendenhall and Katharine, the Missionary and Locke Raynor, decided to push on as long as they could distinguish the trail and then to make their own camp for the night. Two extra horses were easily obtained, and the travellers soon left the little hill settlement and began their long overland journey to the Agency.

VII

STEWART EDWARD WHITE

White was born March 12, 1873, the son of millionaire T. Stewart White of Grand Rapids, Michigan. He learned to ride and hunt at an early age in California; while in high school back in Michigan he developed an interest in ornithology and became an expert on the birds of Michigan. After earning the M. A. degree at the University of Michigan in 1897, he joined the rush for gold, locating several claims in Rapid Canyon in South Dakota and working them for two years.

Following a law degree at Columbia University, 1903, he traveled with his wife to Africa and Asia. His more than fifty novels, written between 1901 and 1946, were largely based on outdoor adventures set in places he had visited during his travels. "Billy's Tenderfoot" takes place in the Black Hills in the 1870's and is taken from *Blazed Trail Stories,* published in 1904. White died in California in 1946.

BILLY'S TENDERFOOT

During one spring of the early seventies Billy Knapp ran a species of road-house and hotel at the crossing of the Deadwood and Big Horn trails through Custer Valley. Travellers changing from one to the other frequently stopped there over night. He sold accommodations for man and beast, the former comprising plenty of whiskey, the latter plenty of hay. That was the best anyone could say of it. The hotel was of logs, two-storied, with partitions of sheeting to insure a certain privacy of sight if not of sound; had three beds and a number of bunks; and boasted of a woman cook—one of the first in the Hills. Billy did not run it long. He was too restless. For the time being, however, he was interested and satisfied.

The personnel of the establishment consisted of Billy and the woman, already mentioned, and an ancient Pistol of the name of Charley. The latter wore many firearms, and had a good deal to say, but had never, as Billy expressed it, "made good." This in the West could not be for lack of opportunity. His functions were those of general factotum.

One evening Billy sat chair-tilted against the walls of the hotel waiting for the stage. By and by it drew in. Charley hobbled out, carrying buckets of water for the horses. The driver flung the reins from him with the lordly insolence of his privileged class, descended slowly, and swaggered to the bar-room for his drink. Billy followed to serve it.

"Luck," said the driver, and crooked his elbow.

"Anything new?" queried Billy.

"Nope."

"Held up?"

"Nope. Black Hawk's over in th' limestone."

That exhausted the situation. The two men puffed silently for a moment at their pipes. In an instant the driver turned to go.

"I got you a tenderfoot," he remarked then, casually; "I reckon he's outside."

"Guess I ambles forth and sees what fer a tenderfoot it is," replied Billy, hastening from behind the bar.

The tenderfoot was seated on a small trunk just outside the door. As he held his hat in his hand, Billy could see his dome-like bald head. Beneath the dome was a little pink-and-white face, and below that narrow, sloping shoulders, a flat chest, and bandy legs. He wore a light check suit, and a flannel shirt whose collar was much too large for him. Billy took this all in while passing. As the driver climbed to the seat, the hotel-keeper commented.

"Say Hen," said he, "would you stuff it or put it under a glass case?"

"I'd serve it, a lay Tooloose," replied the driver, briefly, and brought his long lash 8-shaped across the four startled backs of his horses.

Billy turned to the reinspection of his guest, and met a deprecating smile.

"Can I get a room here fer to-night?" he inquired in a high, piping voice.

"You kin," said Billy, shortly, and began to howl for Charley.

That patriarch appeared around the corner, as did likewise the cook, a black-eyed, red-cheeked creature, afterward counted by Billy as one of his eight matrimonial ventures.

"Snake this stranger's war-bag into th' shack," commanded Billy, "and, Nell, jest nat'rally rustle a few grub."

The stranger picked up a small hand-satchel and followed Charley into the building. When, a little later, he reappeared for

73

supper, he carried the hand-bag with him, and placed it under the bench which flanked the table. Afterward he deposited it near his hand while enjoying a pipe outside. Naturally, all this did not escape Billy.

"Stranger," said he, "yo' seems mighty wedded to that thar satchel."

"Yes, sir," piped the stranger. Billy snorted at the title. "I has some personal belongin's which is valuable to me." He opened the bag and produced a cheap portrait of a rather cheap-looking woman. "My mother that was," said he.

Billy snorted again and went inside. He hated sentiment of all kinds.

The two men sat opposite each other and ate supper, which was served by the red-cheeked girl. The stranger kept his eyes on his plate while she was in the room. He perched on the edge of the bench with his feet tucked under him and resting on the toes. When she approached, the muscles of his shoulders and upper arms grew rigid with embarrassment, causing strange awkward movements of the hands. He answered in monosyllables.

Billy ate expansively and earnestly. Toward the close of the meal Charley slipped into place beside him. Charley was out of humour, and found the meat cold.

"Damn yore soul, Nell," he cried, "this yere ain't fitten fer a *hog* to eat!"

The girl did not mind; nor did Billy. It was the country's mode of speech. The stranger dropped his knife.

"I don't wonder you don't like it, then," said he, with a funny little blaze of anger.

"Meanin' what?" shouted Charley, threateningly.

"You sure mustn't speak to a lady that way," replied the stranger, firmly, in his little piping voice.

Billy caught the point and exploded in a mighty guffaw.

"Bully fer you!" he cried, slapping his knee; "struck pyrites (he pronounced it pie-rights) fer shore that trip, Charley."

The girl, too, laughed, but quietly. She was just a little touched, though only this winter she had left Bismarck because the place would have no more of her.

In the face of Billy's approval, the patriarch fell silent.

About midnight the four inmates of the frontier hotel were awakened by a tremendous racket outside. The stranger arose, fully clothed, from his bunk, and peered through the narrow open window. A dozen horses were standing grouped in charge of a single mounted man, indistinguishable in the dark. Out of the open door a broad band of light streamed from the saloon, whence came the noise of voices and of boots tramping about.

"It is Black Hank," said Billy, at his elbow, "Black Hank and his outfit. He hitches to this yere snubbin'-post occasional."

Black Hank in the Hills would have translated to Jesse James farther south.

The stranger turned suddenly energetic.

"Don't you make no fight?" he asked.

"Fight?" said Billy, wondering. "Fight? Co'se not. Hank don't plunder *me* none. He jest ambles along an' helps himself, and leaves th' dust fer it every time. I jest lays low an' lets him operate. I never has no *dealin's* with him, understand. He jest nat'rally waltzes in an' plants his grub-hooks on what he needs. *I* don't know nothin' about it. *I'm* dead asleep."

He bestowed a shadowy wink on the stranger.

Below, the outlaws moved here and there.

"Billy!" shouted a commanding voice, "Billy Knapp!"

The hotel-keeper looked perplexed.

"Now, what's he tollin' *me* for?" he asked of the man by his side.

"Billy!" shouted the voice again, "come down here, you Siwash. I want to palaver with you!"

"All right, Hank," replied Billy.

He went to his "room," and buckled on a heavy belt; then —descended the steep stairs. The bar-room was lighted and filled with men. Some of them were drinking and eating; others were strapping provisions into portable form. Against the corner of the bar a tall figure of a man leaned smoking—a man lithe, active, and muscular, with a keen dark face, and black eyebrows which met over his nose. Billy walked silently to this man.

"What is it?" he asked, shortly. "This yere ain't in th' agreement."

"I know that," replied the stranger.

"Then leave yore dust and vamoose."

"My dust is there," replied Black Hank, placing his hand on a buckskin bag at his side, "and you're paid, Billy Knapp. I want to ask you a question. Standing Rock has sent fifty thousand dollars in greenbacks to Spotted Tail. The messenger went through here to-day. Have you seen him?"

"Nary messenger," replied Billy, in relief. "Stage goes empty."

Charley had crept down the stairs and into the room.

"What in hell are yo' doin' yere, yo' ranikaboo ijit?" inquired Billy, truculently.

"That thar stage ain't what you calls *empty*," observed Charley, unmoved.

A light broke on Billy's mind. He remarked the valise which the stranger had so carefully guarded; and though his common-

75

sense told him that an inoffensive non-combatant such as his guest would hardly be chosen as express messenger, still the bare possibility remained.

"Yo're right," he agreed, carelessly, "thar is one tenderfoot, who knows as much of ridin' express as a pig does of a ruffled shirt."

"I notes he's almighty particular about that carpet-bag of his'n," insisted Charley.

The man against the counter had lost nothing of the scene. Billy's denial, his hesitation, his half-truth all looked suspicious to him. With one swift, round sweep of the arm he had Billy covered. Billy's hands shot over his head without the necessity of command.

The men ceased their occupations and gathered about. Scenes of this sort were too common to elicit comment or arouse excitement. They knew perfectly well the *laissez-faire* relations which obtained between the two Westerners.

"Now," said Black Hank, angrily, in a low tone, "I want to know why in hell you tried that monkey game!"

Billy, wary and unafraid, replied that he had tried no game, that he had forgotten the tenderfoot for the moment, and that he did not believe the latter would prove to be the sought-for express messenger.

One of the men, at a signal from his leader, relieved Billy's heavy belt of considerable weight. Then the latter was permitted to sit on a crackerbox. Two more mounted the stairs. In a moment they returned to report that the upper story contained no human beings, strange or otherwise, except the girl, but that there remained a small trunk. Under further orders, they dragged the trunk down into the bar-room. It was broken open and found to contain nothing but clothes—of the plainsman's cut, material, and state of wear; a neatly folded Mexican saddle showing use, and a raw-hide quirt.

"Hell of a tenderfoot!" said Black Hank, contemptuously.

The outlaws had already scattered outside to look for the trail. In this they were unsuccessful, reporting, indeed, that not the faintest sign indicated escape in any direction.

Billy knew his man. The tightening of Black Hank's close-knit brows meant but one thing. One does not gain chieftainship of any kind in the West without propping his ascendency with acts of ruthless decision. Billy leaped from his cracker-box with the suddenness of the puma, seized Black Hank firmly about the waist, whirled him into a sort of shield, and began an earnest struggle for the instant possession of the outlaw's drawn revolver. It was a gallant attempt, but an unsuccessful one. In a moment Billy was pinioned to the floor, and Black Hank was rubbing his abraded fore-arm. After that the only question was whether it should be rope or bullet.

Now, when Billy had gone downstairs, the stranger had wasted no further time at the window. He had in his possession fifty thousand dollars in greenbacks which he was to deliver as soon as possible to the Spotted Tail agency in Wyoming. The necessary change of stage lines had forced him to stay over night at Billy Knapp's hotel.

The messenger seized his bag and softly ran along through the canvas-partitioned room wherein Billy slept, to a narrow window which he had already noticed gave out almost directly into the pine woods. The window was of oiled paper, and its catch baffled him. He knew it should slide back; but it refused to slide. He did not dare break the paper because of the crackling noise. A voice at his shoulder startled him.

"I'll show you," whispered the red-cheeked girl.

She was wrapped loosely in a blanket, her hair falling about her shoulders, and her bare feet showed beneath her coverings. The little man suffered at once an agony of embarrassment in which the thought of his errand was lost. It was recalled to him by the girl.

"There you are," she whispered, showing him the open window.

"Thank you," he stammered, painfully, "I assure you—I wish——"

The girl laughed under her breath.

"That's all right," she said, heartily, "I owe you that for calling old whiskers off his bronc," and she kissed him.

The messenger, trembling with self-consciousness, climbed hastily through the window; ran the broad loop of the satchel up his arm; and, instead of dropping to the ground, as the girl had expected, swung himself lightly into the branches of a rather large scrub-oak that grew near. She listened to the rustle of the leaves for a moment as he neared the trunk, and then, unable longer to restrain her curiosity in regard to the doings below, turned to the stairway.

As she did so, two men mounted. They examined the three rooms of the upper story hastily but carefully, paying scant attention to her, and departed swearing. In a few moments they returned for the stranger's trunk. Nell followed them down the stairs as far as the doorway. There she heard and saw things, and fled in bitter dismay to the back of the house when Billy Knapp was overpowered.

At the window she knelt, clasping her hands and sinking her head between her arms. Women in the West, at least women like Nell, do not weep. But she came near it. Suddenly she raised her head. A voice next to her ear had addressed her.

She looked here and there and around, but could discover nothing.

"Here, outside," came the low, guarded voice, "in the tree."

Then she saw that the little stranger had not stirred from his first alighting-place.

"Beg yore pardon, ma'am, fer startling you or fer addressing you at all, which I shouldn't, but——"

"Oh, never mind that," said the girl, impatiently, shaking back her hair. So deprecating and timid were the tones, that almost without an effort of the imagination she could picture the little man's blushes and his half-sidling method of delivery. At this supreme moment his littleness and lack of self-assertion jarred on her mood. "What're you doin' there? Thought you'd vamoosed."

"It was safer here," explained the stranger, "I left no trail."

She nodded comprehension of the common-sense of this.

"But, ma'am, I took the liberty of speakin' to you because you seems to be in trouble. Of course, I ain't got no right to *ask,* an' if you don't care to tell me——"

"They're goin' to kill Billy," broke in Nell, with a sob.

"What for?"

"I don't jest rightly make out. They's after someone, and they thinks Billy's cacheing him. I reckon it's you. Billy ain't cacheing nothin', but they thinks he is."

"It's me they's after, all right. Now, you know where I am, why don't you tell them and save Billy?"

The girl started, but her keen Western mind saw the difficulty at once.

"They thinks Billy pertects you jest th' same."

"Do you love him?" asked the stranger.

"God knows I'm purty tough," confessed Nell, sobbing, "but I jest do that!" and she dropped her head again.

The invisible stranger in the gloom fell silent, considering.

"I'm a pretty rank proposition, myself," said he at last, as if to himself, "and I've got a job on hand which same I oughta put through without givin' attention to anything else. As a usual thing folks don't care fer me, and I don't care much fer folks. Women especial. They drives me plumb tired. I reckon I don't stack up very high in th' blue chips when it comes to cashin' in with the gentle sex, anyhow; but in general they gives me as much notice as they lavishes on a doodle-bug. I ain't kickin', you understand, nary bit; but onct in a dog's age I kind of hankers fer a decent look from one of 'em. I ain't never had no women-folks of my own, never. Sometimes I thinks it would be some scrumptious to know a little gal waitin' fer me somewhere. They ain't none. They never will be. I ain't built that way. You treated me white to-night. You're th' first woman that ever kissed me of her own accord."

The girl heard a faint scramble, then the soft *pat* of someone landing on his feet. Peering from the window she made out a faint, shadowy form stealing around the corner of the hotel. She put her hand to her heart and listened. Her understanding of the stranger's motives was vague at best, but she had caught his confession that her kiss had meant much to him, and even in her anxiety she felt an inclination to laugh. She had bestowed that caress as she would have kissed the cold end of a dog's nose.

The men below stairs had, after some discussion, decided on bullet. This was out of consideration for Billy's standing as a frontiersman. Besides, he had stolen no horses. In order not to delay matters, the execution was fixed for the present time and place. Billy stood with his back to the logs of his own hotel, his hands and feet bound, but his eyes uncovered. He had never lost his nerve. In the short respite which preparation demanded, he told his opponents what he thought of them.

"Proud?" he concluded a long soliloquy as if to the reflector of the lamp. "Proud?" he repeated, reflectively. "This yere Hank's jest that proud he's all swelled up like a poisoned pup. Ain't every-one kin corall a man sleepin' and git fifty thousand without turnin' a hair."

Black Hank distributed three men to do the business. There were no heroics. The execution of this man was necessary to him, not because he was particularly angry over the escape of the messenger—he expected to capture that individual in due time—but in order to preserve his authority over his men. He was in the act of moving back to give the shooters room, when he heard behind him the door open and shut.

He turned. Before the door stood a small consumptive-looking man in a light check suit. The tenderfoot carried two short-barrelled Colt's revolvers, one of which he presented directly at Black Hank.

" 'Nds up!" he commanded, sharply.

Hank was directly covered, so he obeyed. The new-comer's eye had a strangely restless quality. Of the other dozen inmates of the room, eleven were firmly convinced that the weapon and eye not directly levelled at their leader were personally concerned with themselves. The twelfth thought he saw his chance. To the bewildered onlookers there seemed to be a flash and a bang, instantaneous; then things were as before. One of the stranger's weapons still pointed at Black Hank's breast; the other at each of the rest. Only the twelfth man, he who had seen his chance, had collapsed forward to the floor. No one could assure himself positively that he had discerned the slightest motion on the part of the stranger.

"Now," said the latter, sharply, "one at a time, gentlemen. Drop yore gun," this last to Black Hank, "muzzle down. Drop it! Correct!"

One of the men in the back of the room stirred slightly on the ball of his foot.

"Steady, there!" warned the stranger. The man stiffened.

"Next gent," went on the little man, subtly indicating another. The latter obeyed without hesitation. "Next. Now you. Now you in th' corner."

One after another the pistols clattered to the floor. Not for an instant could a single inmate of the apartment, armed or unarmed, flatter himself that his slightest motion was unobserved. They were like tigers on the crouch, ready to spring the moment the man's guard lowered. It did not lower. The huddled figure on the floor reminded them of what might happen. They obeyed.

"Step back," commanded the stranger next. In a moment he had them standing in a row against the wall, rigid, upright, their hands over their heads. Then for the first time the stranger moved from his position by the door.

"Call her," he said to Billy, "th' girl."

Billy raised his voice. "Nell! Oh, Nell!"

In a moment she appeared in the doorway at the foot of the stairs, without hesitation or fear. When she perceived the state of affairs, she brightened almost mischievously.

"Would you jest as soon, ma'am, if it ain't troubling you too much, jest nat'rally sort of untie Billy?" requested the stranger.

She did so. The hotel-keeper stretched his arms.

"Now, pick up th' guns, please."

The two set about it.

"Where's that damn ol' reprobate?" inquired Billy, truculently, looking about for Charley.

The patriarch had quietly slipped away.

"You kin drop them hands," advised the stranger, lowering the muzzles of his weapons. The leader started to say something.

"You shut up!" said Billy, selecting his own weapons from the heap.

The stranger suddenly picked up one of the Colt's single-action revolvers which lay on the floor, and, holding the trigger back against the guard, exploded the six charges by hitting the hammer smartly with the palm of his hand. In the thrusting motion of this discharge he evidently had design, for the first six wine-glasses on Billy's bar were shivered. It was wonderful work, rattling fire, quicker than a self-cocker even. He selected another weapon. From a pile of tomato-cans he took one and tossed it into the air. Before it had fallen he had perforated it twice, and as it rolled along the floor he helped its progression by four more bullets which left streams of tomato-juice where they had hit. The room was full of smoke. The group watched, fascinated.

Then the men against the wall grew rigid. Out of the film of smoke long, vivid streams of fire flashed toward them, now right, now left, like the alternating steam of a locomotive's pistons. *Smash, smash! Smash, smash!* hit the bullets with regular thud. With the twelfth discharge the din ceased. Midway in the space between the heads of each pair of men against the wall was a round hole. No one was touched.

A silence fell. The smoke lightened and blew slowly through the open door. The horses, long since deserted by their guardians in favour of the excitement within, whinnied. The stranger dropped the smoking Colts, and quietly reproduced his own short-barrelled arms from his side-pockets, where he had thrust them. Billy broke the silence at last.

"That's *shootin'!*" he observed, with a sigh.

"Them fifty thousand is outside," clicked the stranger. "Do you want them?"

There was no reply.

"I aims to pull out on one of these yere hosses of yours," said he. "Billy he's all straight. He doesn't know nothin' about me."

He collected the six-shooters from the floor.

"I jest takes these with me for a spell," he continued. "You'll find them, if you look hard enough, along on th' trail—also yore broncs."

He backed toward the door.

"I'm layin' fer th' man that sticks his head out that door," he warned.

"Stranger," said Black Hank as he neared the door.

The little man paused.

"Might I ask yore name?"

"My name is Alfred," replied the latter.

Black Hank looked chagrined.

"I've hearn tell of you," he acknowledged.

The stranger's eye ran over the room, and encountered that of the girl. He shrank into himself and blushed.

"Good-night," he said, hastily, and disappeared. A moment later the beat of hoofs became audible as he led the bunch of horses away.

For a time there was silence. Then Billy, "By God, Hank, I means to stand in with you, but you let that kid alone, or I plugs you!"

"Kid, huh!" grunted Hank. "Alfred a kid! I've hearn tell of him."

"What've you heard?" inquired the girl.

"He's th' plumb best scout on th' southern trail," replied Black Hank.

The year following, Billy Knapp, Alfred, and another man named Jim Buckley took across to the Hills the only wagon-train that dared set out that summer.

VIII

MARIE L. McLAUGHLIN

Mrs. McLaughlin, wife of Major James McLaughlin (Indian agent at Standing Rock during the years when the Dakota were being settled on reservations), was born December 8, 1842, at Wabasha, Minnesota. Her grandmother, Ha-za-ho-ta-win, was a full-blood of the Medawakanton Band of the Sioux Tribe. In her book, *Myths and Legends of the Sioux,* she writes:

> "Having been born and reared in an Indian community, I at an early age acquired a thorough knowledge of the Sioux language, and having lived on Indian reservations for the past forty years [prior to 1913] in a position which brought me very near to the Indians, whose confidence I possessed, I have, therefore, had exceptional opportunities of learning the legends and folk-lore of the Sioux."

The following tales were taken from her book, also known as *Myths of the Sioux,* published in 1916.

THE BOUND CHILDREN

There once lived a widow with two children—the elder a daughter and the younger a son. The widow went in mourning for her husband a long time. She cut off her hair, let her dress lie untidy on her body and kept her face unpainted and unwashed.

There lived in the same village a great chief. He had one son just come old enough to marry. The chief had it known that he wished his son to take a wife, and all of the young women in the village were eager to marry the young man. However, he was pleased with none of them.

Now the widow thought. "I am tired of mourning for my husband and caring for my children. Perhaps if I lay aside by mourning and paint myself red, the chief's son may marry me."

83

So she slipped away from her two children, stole down to the river and made a bathing place thru the ice. When she had washed away all signs of mourning, she painted and decked herself and went to the chief's tepee. When his son saw her, he loved her, and a feast was made in honor of her wedding.

When the widow's daughter found herself forsaken, she wept bitterly. After a day or two she took her little brother in her arms and went to the tepee of an old woman who lived at one end of the village. The old woman's tumble down tepee was of bark and her dress and clothing was of old smoke-dried tent cover. But she was kind to the two waifs and took them in willingly.

The little girl was eager to find her mother. The old woman said to her: "I suspect your mother has painted her face red. Do not try to find her. If the chief's son marries her she will not want to be burdened with you."

The old woman was right. The girl went down to the river, and sure enough found a hole cut in the ice and about it lay the filth that the mother had washed from her body. The girl gathered up the filth and went on. By and by she came to a second hole in the ice. Here too was filth, but not so much as at the previous place. At the third hole the ice was clean.

The girl knew now that her mother had painted her face red. She went at once to the chief's tepee, raised the door flap and went in. There sat her mother with the chief's son at their wedding feast.

The girl walked up to her mother and hurled the filth in her mother's face.

"There," she cried, "you who forsake your helpless children and forget your husband, take that!"

And at once her mother became a hideous old woman.

The girl then went back to the lodge of the old woman, leaving the camp in an uproar. The chief soon sent some young warriors to seize the girl and her brother, and they were brought to his tent. He was furious with anger.

"Let the children be bound with lariats wrapped about their bodies and let them be left to starve. Our camp will move on," he said. The chief's son did not put away his wife, hoping she might be cured in some way and grow young again.

Everybody in camp now got ready to move; but the old woman came close to the girl and said:

"In my old tepee I have dug a hole and buried a pot with punk and steel and flint and packs of dried meat. They will tie you up like a corpse. But before we go I will come with a knife and pretend to stab you, but I will really cut the rope that binds you so that you can unwind it from your body as soon as the camp is out of sight and hearing."

And so, before the camp started, the old woman came to the place where the two children were bound. She had in her hand a knife bound to the end of a stick which she used as a lance. She stood over the children and cried aloud:

"You wicked girl, who have shamed your own mother, you deserve all the punishment that is given you. But after all I do not want to let you lie and starve. Far better kill you at once and have done with it!" and with her stick she stabbed many times, as if to kill, but she was really cutting the rope.

The camp moved on; but the children lay on the ground until noon the next day. Then they began to squirm about. Soon the girl was free, and she then set loose her little brother. They went at once to the old woman's hut where they found the flint and steel and the packs of dried meat.

The girl made her brother a bow and arrows and with these he killed birds and other small game.

The boy grew up a great hunter. They became rich. They built three great tepees, in one of which were stored rows upon rows of parfleche bags of dried meat.

One day as the brother went out to hunt, he met a handsome young stranger who greeted him and said to him:

"I know you are a good hunter, for I have been watching you; your sister, too, is industrious. Let me have her for a wife. Then you and I will be brothers and hunt together.

The girl's brother went home and told her what the young stranger had said.

"Brother, I do not care to marry," she answered. "I am now happy with you."

"But you will be yet happier married," he answered, "and the young stranger is of no mean family, as one can see by his dress and manners."

"Very well, I will do as you wish," she said. So the stranger came into the tepee and was the girl's husband.

One day as they were in their tent, a crow flew overhead, calling out loudly,

"Kaw, Kaw,

They who forsook the children have no meat."

The girl and her husband and brother looked up at one another.

"What can it mean?" they asked. "Let us send for Unktomi (the spider). He is a good judge and he will know."

"And I will get ready a good dinner for him, for Unktomi is always hungry," added the young wife.

When Unktomi came, his yellow mouth opened with delight

at the fine feast spread for him. After he had eaten he was told what the crow had said.

"The crow means," said Unktomi, "that the villagers and chief who bound and deserted you are in sad plight. They have hardly anything to eat and are starving."

When the girl heard this she made a bundle of choicest meat and called the crow.

"Take this to the starving villagers," she bade him.

He took the bundle in his beak, flew away to the starving village and dropped the bundle before the chief's tepee. The chief came out and the crow called loudly:

"Kaw, Kaw!

The children who were forsaken have much meat; those who forsook them have none."

"What can he mean," cried the astonished villagers.

"Let us send for Unktomi," said one, "he is a great judge; he will tell us."

They divided the bundle of meat among the starving people, saving the biggest piece for Unktomi.

When Unktomi had come and eaten, the villagers told him of the crow and asked what the bird's words meant.

"He means," said Unktomi, "that the two children whom you forsook have tepees full of dried meat enough for all the village."

The villagers were filled with astonishment at this news. To find whether or not it was true, the chief called seven young men and sent them out to see. They came to the three tepees and there met the girl's brother and husband just going out to hunt (which they did now only for sport).

The girl's brother invited the seven young men into the third or sacred lodge, and after they had smoked a pipe and knocked out the ashes on a buffalo bone the brother gave them meat to eat, which the seven devoured greedily. The next day he loaded all seven with packs of meat, saying:

"Take this meat to the villagers and lead them hither."

While they awaited the return of the young men with the villagers, the girl made two bundles of meat, one of the best and choicest pieces, and the other of liver, very dry and hard to eat. After a few days the camp arrived. The young woman's mother opened the door and ran in crying: "Oh, my dear daughter, how glad I am to see you." But the daughter received her coldly and gave her the bundle of dried liver to eat. But when the old woman who had saved the children's lives came in, the young girl received her gladly, called her grandmother, and gave her the package of choice meat with marrow.

Then the whole village camped and ate of the stores of meat

all the winter until spring came; and withal they were so many, there was such abundance of stores that there was still much left.

THE HERMIT, OR THE GIFT OF CORN

In a deep forest, far from the villages of his people, lived a hermit. His tent was made of buffalo skins, and his dress was made of deer skin. Far from the haunts of any human being this old hermit was content to spend his days.

All day long he would wander through the forest studying the different plants of nature and collecting precious roots, which he used as medicine. At long intervals some warrior would arrive at the tent of the old hermit and get medicine roots from him for the tribe, the old hermit's medicine being considered far superior to all others.

After a long day's ramble in the woods, the hermit came home late, and being very tired, at once lay down on his bed and was just dozing off to sleep, when he felt something rub against his foot. Awakening with a start, he noticed a dark object and an arm was extended to him, holding in its hand a flint pointed arrow.

The hermit thought, "This must be a spirit, as there is no human being around here but myself!" A voice then said: "Hermit, I have come to invite you to my home." "How (yes), I will come," said the old hermit. Wherewith he arose, wrapped his robe about him and followed.

Outside the door he stopped and looked around, but could see no signs of the dark object.

"Whoever you are, or whatever you be, wait for me, as I don't know where to go to find your house," said the hermit. Not an answer did he receive, nor could he hear any noises as though anyone was walking through the brush. Re-entering his tent he retired and was soon fast asleep. The next night the same thing occurred again, and the hermit followed the object out, only to be left as before.

He was very angry to think that anyone should be trying to make sport of him, and he determined to find out who this could be who was disturbing his night's rest.

The next evening he cut a hole in the tent large enough to stick an arrow through, and stood by the door watching. Soon the dark object came and stopped outside of the door, and said: "Grandfather, I came to———," but he never finished the sentence, for the old man let go his arrow, and he heard the arrow strike something which produced a sound as though he had shot into a sack of pebbles. He did not go out that night to see what his arrow had struck, but early next morning he went out and looked at the spot about where he thought the object had stood. There on the ground lay a little heap of corn, and from this little heap a small line of corn lay scattered along a path. This he followed far into the woods. When he came to a very small knoll the trail ended. At the end of the trail was a large circle, from which the grass had been scraped off clean.

"The corn trail stops at the edge of this circle," said the old man, "so this must be the home of whoever it was that invited me." He took his bone knife and hatchet and proceeded to dig down into the center of the circle. When he had got down to the length of his arm, he came to a sack of dried meat. Next he found a sack of Indian turnips, then a sack of dried cherries; then a sack of corn, and last of all another sack, empty except that there was about a cupful of corn in one corner of it, and that the sack had a hole in the other corner where his arrow had pierced it. From this hole in the sack the corn was scattered along the trail, which guided the old man to the cache.

From this the hermit taught the tribes how to keep their provisions when traveling and were overloaded. He explained to them how they should dig a pit and put their provisions into it and cover them with earth. By this method the Indians used to keep provisions all summer, and when fall came they would return to their cache, and on opening it would find everything as fresh as the day they were placed there.

The old hermit was also thanked as the discoverer of corn, which had never been known to the Indians until discovered by the old hermit.

THE MYSTERIOUS BUTTE

A young man was once hunting and came to a steep hill. The east side of the hill suddenly dropped off to a very steep bank. He stood on this bank, and at the base he noticed a small opening. On going down to examine it more closely, he found it was large enough to admit a horse or buffalo. On either side of the door were figures of different animals engraved into the wall.

He entered the opening and there, scattered about on the floor, lay many bracelets, pipes and many other things of ornament, as though they had been offerings to some great spirit. He passed through this first room and on entering the second it was so dark that he could not see his hands before his face, so becoming scared, he hurriedly left the place, and returning home told what he had seen.

Upon hearing this the chief selected four of his most daring warriors to go with this young man and investigate and ascertain whether the young man was telling the truth or not. The five proceeded to the butte, and at the entrance the young man refused to go inside, as the figures on either side of the entrance had been changed.

The four entered and seeing that all in the first chamber was as the young man had told, they went on to the next chamber and found it so dark that they could not see anything. They continued on, however, feeling their way along the walls. They finally found an entrance that was so narrow that they had to squeeze into it sideways. They felt their way around the walls and found another entrance, so low down that they had to crawl on their hands and knees to go through into the next chamber.

On entering the last chamber they found a very sweet odor coming from the opposite direction. Feeling around and crawling on their hands and knees, they discovered a hole in the floor leading downward. From this hole came up the sweet odor. They hurriedly held a council, and decided to go no further, but return to the camp and report what they had found. On getting to the first chamber one of the young men said: "I am going to take these bracelets to show that we are telling the truth." "No," said the other three, "this being the abode of some Great Spirit, you may have some accident befall you for taking what is not yours." "Ah! You fellows are like old women," said he, taking a fine bracelet and encircling his left wrist with it.

When they reached the village they reported what they had seen. The young man exhibited the bracelet to prove that it was the truth they had told.

Shortly after this, these four young men were out fixing up traps for wolves. They would raise one end of a heavy log and place a stick under, bracing up the log. A large piece of meat was placed about five feet away from the log and this space covered with poles and willows. At the place where the upright stick was put, a hole was left open, large enough to admit the body of a wolf. The wolf, scenting the meat and unable to get at it through the poles and willows, would crowd into the hole and working his body forward, in order to get the meat, would push down the brace and the log thus released would hold the wolf fast under its weight.

The young man with the bracelet was placing his bait under the log when he released the log by knocking down the brace, and the log caught his wrist on which he wore the bracelet. He could not release himself and called loud and long for assistance. His friends, hearing his call, came to his assistance, and on lifting the log found the young man's wrist broken. "Now," said they, "you have been punished for taking the wristlet out of the chamber of the mysterious butte."

Some time after this a young man went to the butte and saw engraved on the wall a woman holding in her hand a pole, with which she was holding up a large amount of beef which had been laid across another pole, which had broken in two from the weight of so much meat.

He returned to the camp and reported what he had seen. All around the figure he saw marks of buffalo hoofs, also marked upon the wall.

The next day an enormous herd of buffalo came near to the village, and a great many were killed. The women were busy cutting up and drying the meat. At one camp was more meat than at any other. The woman was hanging meat upon a long tent pole, when the pole broke in two and she was obliged to hold the meat up with another pole, just as the young man saw on the mysterious butte.

Ever after that the Indians paid weekly visits to this butte, and thereon would read the signs that were to govern their plans.

This butte was always considered the prophet of the tribe.

THE MAN AND THE OAK

There once lived a Sioux couple who had two children, a boy and a girl. Every fall this family would move away from the main camp and take up their winter quarters in a grove of timber some distance from the principal village. The reason they did this was that he was a great hunter and where a village was located for the winter the game was usually very scarce. Therefore, he always camped by himself in order to have an abundance of game adjacent to his camp.

All summer he had roamed around following the tribe to wherever their fancy might take them. During their travels this particular year there came to the village a strange girl who had no relatives there. No one seemed very anxious to take her into their family, so the great hunter's daughter, taking a fancy to the poor girl, took her to their home and kept her. She addressed her as sister, and the parents, on account of their daughter, addressed her as daughter.

This strange girl became desperately in love with the young man of the family, but being addressed as daughter by the parents, she could not openly show her feelings as the young man was considered her brother.

In the fall when the main village moved into a large belt of timber for their winter quarters, the hunter moved on to another place two days' travel from the main winter camp, where he would not be disturbed by any other hunters.

The young man had a tent by himself, and it was always kept nice and clean by his sister, who was very much attached to him. After a long day's hunt in the woods, he would go into his tent and lie down to rest, and when his supper was ready his sister would say, "My brother is so tired. I will carry his supper to him."

Her friend, whom she addressed as sister, would never go into the young man's tent. Along towards spring there came one night into the young man's tent a woman. She sat down by the door and kept her face covered so that it was hidden from view. She sat there a long time and finally arose and went away. The young man could not imagine who this could be. He knew that it was a long distance from the village and could not make out where the woman could have come from. The next night the woman came again and this time she came a little nearer to where the young man lay. She sat down and kept her face covered as before. Neither spoke a word. She sat there for a long time and then arose and departed. He was very much puzzled over the actions of this woman and decided to ascertain on her next visit who she was.

He kindled a small fire in his tent and had some ash wood laid on it so as to keep fire a long time, as ash burns very slowly and holds fire a long time.

The third night the woman came again and sat down still nearer his bed. She held her blanket open just a trifle, and he, catching up one of the embers, flashed it in her face; jumping up she ran hurriedly out of the tent. The next morning he noticed that his adopted sister kept her face hidden with her blanket. She chanced to drop her blanket while in the act of pouring out some soup, and when she did so he noticed a large burned spot on her cheek.

He felt so sorry for what he had done that he could eat no breakfast, but went outside and lay down under an oak tree. All day long he lay there gazing up into the tree, and when he was called for supper he refused, saying that he was not hungry, and for them not to bother him, as he would soon get up and go to bed. Far into the night he lay thus, and when he tried to arise he could not, as a small oak tree grew through the center of his body and held him fast to the ground.

In the morning when the family awoke they found the girl had disappeared, and on going outside the sister discovered her brother held fast to the earth by an oak tree which grew very rapidly. In vain were the best medicine men of the tribe sent for. Their medicine was of no avail. They said: "If the tree is cut down the young man will die."

The sister was wild with grief, and extending her hands to the sun, she cried: "Great Spirit, relieve my suffering brother. Any one who releases him I will marry, be he young, old, homely or deformed."

Several days after the young man had met with the mishap, there came to the tent a very tall man, who had a bright light encircling his body. "Where is the girl who promised to marry any one who would release her brother?" "I am the one," said the young man's sister. "I am the all-powerful lightning and thunder. I see all things and can kill at one stroke a whole tribe. When I make my voice heard the rocks shake loose and go rattling down the hillsides. The brave warriors cower shivering under some shelter at the sound of my voice. The girl whom you had adopted as your sister was a scorceress. She bewitched your brother because he would not let her make love to him. On my way here I met her traveling towards the west, and knowing what she had done, I struck her with one of my blazing swords, and she lies there now a heap of ashes. I will now release your brother."

So saying he placed his hand on the tree and instantly it crumbled to ashes. The young man arose, and thanked his deliverer.

Then they saw a great black cloud approaching, and the man said: "Make ready, we shall go home on that cloud." As the cloud approached near to the man who stood with his bride, it suddenly lowered and enveloped them and with a great roar and amidst flashes of lightning and loud peals of thunder the girl ascended and disappeared into the west with her Thunder and Lightning husband.

THE STORY OF THE PET CROW

Once upon a time there came to a large village a plague of crows. So thick were they that the poor women were sorely tried keeping them out of their tepees and driving them away from their lines of jerked buffalo meat. Indeed they got so numerous and were such a great nuisance that the Chief finally gave orders to his camp criers or heralds to go out among the different camps and announce the orders of their Chief, that war should be made upon the crows to extermination; that their nests were to be destroyed and all eggs broken. The war of extermination was to continue until not a crow remained, except the youngest found was to be brought to him alive.

For a week the war on the crows continued. Thousands of dead crows were brought in daily, and at the end of the week not a bird of that species could be seen in the neighborhood.

Those that escaped the deadly arrow of the warriors, flew away, never to return to those parts again.

At the end of the war made upon the crows, there was brought to the Chief's tepee the youngest found. Indeed, so young was the bird that it was only the great medicine of the Chief that kept him alive until he could hop about and find his own food. The Chief spent most of his time in his lodge teaching the young crow to understand and talk the language of the tribe. After the crow had mastered this, the Chief then taught him the languages of the neighboring tribes. When the crow had mastered these different languages the chief would send him on long journeys to ascertain the location of the camps of the different enemies.

When the crow would find a large Indian camp he would alight and hop about, pretending to be picking up scraps, but really keeping his ears open for anything he might hear. He would hang around all day, and at night when they would all gather in the large council tent (which always stood in the center of the village) to determine upon their next raid, and plan for a horse stealing trip, Mr. Crow was always nearby to hear all their plans discussed. He would then fly away to his master (the Chief) and tell him all that he had learned.

The Chief would then send a band of his warriors to lie in ambush for the raiding party, and, as the enemy would not suspect anything they would go blindly into the pitfall of death thus set for them. Thus the crow was the scout of this chief, whose reputation as a Wakan (Holy man) soon reached all of the different tribes. The Chief's warriors would intercept, ambush and annihilate every war party headed for his camp.

So, finally, learning that they could not make war on this chief's people unbeknown to them, they gave up making war on this particular band. When meat was running low in the camp this chief would send the crow out to look for buffalo. When he discovered a herd he would return and report to his master; then the chief would order out the hunters and they would return laden with meat. Thus the crow kept the camp all the time informed of everything that would be of benefit to them.

One day the crow disappeared, over which there was great grief among the tribe. A week had passed away, when Mr. Crow reappeared. There was great rejoicing upon his return, but the crow was downcast and would not speak, but sat with a drooping head perched at the top of the chief's tepee, and refused all food that was offered to him.

In vain did the chief try to get the crow to tell him the cause of his silence and seeming grief. The crow would not speak until the chief said: "Well, I will take a few of my warriors and go out and try to ascertain what has happened to cause you to act as you do."

Upon hearing this, the crow said: "Don't go. I dreaded to tell you what I know to be a fact, as I have heard it from some great medicine men. I was traveling over the mountains west of here, when I spied three old men sitting at the top of the highest peak. I very cautiously dropped down behind a rock and listened to their talk. I heard your name mentioned by one of them, then your brother's name was mentioned. Then the third, who was the oldest, said: 'In three days from today the lightning will kill those two brothers whom all the nations fear.'"

Upon hearing what the crow stated the tribe became grief stricken. On the morning of the third day the chief ordered a nice tepee placed upon the highest point, far enough away from the village, so that the peals of thunder would not alarm the babies of the camp.

A great feast was given, and after the feasting was over there came in six young maidens leading the war horses of the two brothers. The horses were painted and decorated as if for a charge on the enemy. One maiden walked ahead of the chief's horse bearing in her hands the bow and arrows of the great warrior. Next came two maidens, one on either side of the prancing war steed, each holding a rein. Behind the chief's horse came the fourth maiden. Like the first, she bore in her hands the bow and arrows of the chief's brother. Then the fifth and sixth maidens each holding a rein, walked on either side of the prancing horse of the chief's brother. They advanced and circled the large gathering and finally stopped directly in front of the two brothers, who immediately arose and taking their bows and arrows vaulted lightly upon their war steeds, and singing their death song, galloped off amid a great cry of grief from the people who loved them most dearly.

Heading straight for the tepee that had been placed upon the highest point, adjacent to the village, they soon arrived at their destination and, dismounting from their horses, turned, waved their hands to their band, and disappeared within the tepee. Scarcely had they entered the lodge when the rumblings of distant thunder could be heard. Nearer, and nearer, came the sound, until at last the storm overspread the locality in all its fury. Flash upon flash of lightning burst forth from the heavens. Deafening peals of thunder followed each flash. Finally, one flash brighter than any of the others, one peal more deafening than those preceding it, and the storm had passed.

Sadly the warriors gathered together, mounted their horses and slowly rode to the tepee on the high point. Arriving there they looked inside the lodge and saw the two brothers lying cold and still in death, each holding the lariat of his favorite war horse. The horses also lay dead side by side in front of the tent. (From this came the custom of killing the favorite horse of a dead warrior at the burial of the owner).

As the Indians sadly left the hill to return home, they heard a noise at the top of the tepee, and looking up they saw the crow sitting on one of the splintered tepee poles. He was crying most pitifully, and as they rode off he flew up high in the air and his pitiful "caw" became fainter and fainter till at last they heard it no more. And from that day, the story goes, no crow ever goes near the village of that band of Indians.

IX

JOHN G. NEIHARDT

Acclaimed rather later in his life for *Black Elk Speaks,* first published in 1932 and rediscovered in 1961, Neihardt devoted many of his years to a long epic poem of the American West. Begun in 1912, the fifth and final volume of this epic was not published until 1941. *A Cycle of the West* includes (each part book-length) "The Song of Three Friends," "The Song of Hugh Glass," "The Song of Jed Smith," "The Song of the Indian Wars," and "The Song of the Messiah." Thus, the cycle is divided into two major parts—in subject matter—the mountain man and the Indian. Neihardt had the utmost respect and sympathy for both, and his treatment of the prominent men and events of the 19th-century American West is heroic and grand even while being realistic and authentic.

Neihardt was born in Illinois on January 8, 1881. In 1886 the family moved to a sod house in Kansas. At the age of sixteen, Neihardt graduated from college in Wayne, Nebraska. After teaching at a country school for a short time, he moved to Bancroft, later to become a shrine to his work. He assisted an Indian trader among the Omahas, edited a weekly newspaper, and then lived frequently among the Sioux Indians as he wrote fiction and poetry. He did other things, and he won many awards and honors, but he concentrated mostly on writing and on learning about his Indian friends. He died on November 3, 1973.

"The Song of the Messiah," first published in 1935, is concerned with the dark days of the Sioux, the coming of the Ghost Dance religion (started by a Paiute named Wo-vo-ka) in 1889, and the dashing of hope at Wounded Knee on December 29, 1890. Two sections of the poem are reprinted here.

THE SONG OF THE MESSIAH

The Earth was dying slowly, being old.
A grandam, crouched against an inner cold
Above the scraped-up ashes of the dear,
She babbled still the story of the year
By hopeless moons; but all her bloom was snow.
Mere stresses in a monody of woe,

Her winters stung the moment, and her springs
were only garrulous rememberings
Of joy that made them sadder than the fall.
And mournful was the summer, most of all,
With fruitfulness remembered—bounteous sap
For happy giving, toddlers in her lap
And nuzzlers at her breast, and more to be,
And lovers eager still, so dear was she,
So needed and so beautiful to woo!

Ten years had grown the sorrow of the Sioux,
Blood-sown of one ingloriously slain,
Whose dusty heart no sorcery of rain
Would sprout with pity, flowering for his own;
Nor could the blizzard's unresolving moan
Remind him of his people unconsoled.
Old as the earth, the hearts of men were old
That year of 'eighty-seven in the spring.

O once it was a very holy thing,
Some late March night, to waken to the moan
Of little waters, when the South, outblown,
Had left the soft dark clear of other sound;
When you could feel things waking underground
And all the world turned spirit, and you heard
Still thunders of the everlasting Word
Straining the hush.—Alas, to lie awake
Remembering, when time is like the ache
Of silence wedded, barren, to a wraith!

True to an empty ritual of faith,
The geese came chanting as they used to do
When there was wonder yet; when, blue on blue,
The world was wider than a day in June,
And twice the northbound bison lost the moon
Trailing the summer up the Sioux domain.
What myriads now would hear the whooping crane
And join the green migration?

                                  Vision, sound,
Song from the green and color from the ground,
Scent in the wind and shimmer on the wing,
A cruel beauty, haunting everything,
Disguised the empty promise. In the sloughs
The plum bush, crediting the robin's news,

Made honey of it, and the bumblebee
Hummed with the old divine credulity
The music of the universal hoax.
Among the public cottonwoods and oaks
The shrill jays coupled and the catbird screamed,
Delirious with the dream the old Earth dreamed
Of ancient nuptials, ecstasies that were.
For once again the warm Rain over her
Folded the lover's blanket; nights were whist
To hear her low moan running in the mist,
Her secret whispers in the holy dark.
And every morning the deluded lark
Sang hallelujah to a widowed world.

May sickened into June. The short-grass curled.
Of evenings thunder mumbled 'round the sky;
But clouds were phantoms and the dawns were dry,
And it were better nothing had been born.
Sick-hearted in the squalor of the corn,
Old hunters brooded, dreaming back again
The days when earth still bore the meat of men—
Bull-thunders in a sky-wide storm of cows!—
Till bow-grips tightened on the hated plows
And spear-hands knuckled for an empty thrust.
The corn-stalks drooping in the bitter dust,
Despairing mothers widowed in the silk,
With swaddled babies dead for want of milk,
Moaned to the wind the universal dearth.

There was no longer magic in the earth;
No mystery was vital in the air;
No spirit in the silence anywhere
Made doubly sure a wonder that was sure.
To live was now no more than to endure
The purposeless indignity of breath,
Sick for the brave companion that was Death,
Now grown a coward preying on the weak.
However might the hungry-hearted seek
Upon a starry hill, however high,
A knowing Presence, everywhere the sky
Was like a tepee where the man lies stark
And women wail and babble in the dark
Of what the dawn can never bring to light.

The big Cheyenne lay dying, and the White;
And all the little creeks forgot their goals.
Crows feasted by the dusty water-holes.
Gaunt grew the Niobrara, ribbed with sand.
A wasting fever fed upon the Grand
And with the famishing Moreau it crawled.
All day and every day the hotwind bawled.
The still nights panted in a fever-swoon.
Dead leaves were falling in the harvest moon
And it was autumn long before the frost.
Back came the wild geese wailing for the lost—
Not there, not there! Back came the mourning crane.
A sunset darkened with a loveless rain;
The Northwest wakened and a blind dawn howled.

The winter deepened. Evil spirits prowled
And whimpered in the jungles of the cold,
Wolves of the ancient darkness that were old
Before the Morning took the Land to wife
And all the souls came loving into life
Save these alone, the haters of the warm.
Men heard them screaming by upon the storm;
And when the sharp nights glittered and were still
And any sound was big enough to fill
The world with clamor, they were gnawing fear.

The strangely wounded bodies of the dear
Grew alien. Scarce the father knew the child
So stricken, and the mother, so defiled,
By her own fire became a dreaded thing.
Wide roamed the evil spirits, ravening,
Till every village fed the Faceless Guest
With little hungers that forgot the breast
And aged wants too long denied to care.

In vain against the formless wolves of air
The holy men wrought magic. Songs that ran
Beyond the hoarded memories of man,
With might beyond the grip of words, they sang;
But still the hidden claw and secret fang
Were mightier, and would not go away.
Grotesqueries of terror shaped in clay
To simulate the foe, and named with names
Of dreadful sound, were given to the flames;

But it was hope that perished. Empty air
Was peopled for the haunted fever-stare;
And when some final horror loosed the jaw,
What shape could image what the dying saw
That none might ever see and live to tell?

By night when sleep made thin the hollow shell
Between what is forever and what seems,
Came voices, awful in a hush of dreams,
Upon the old; and in that dreams are wise
When hearing is but silence and the eyes
Are dark with sun and moon, and weird news spread.
"There is no hope for us," the old men said,
"For we have sold our Mother to the lust
Of strangers, and her breast is bitter dust,
Her thousand laps are empty! She was kind
Before the white men's seeing made us blind
And greedy for the shadows they pursue.
The fed-on-shadows shall be shadows too;
Their trails shall end in darkness. We have sinned;
And all our story is a midnight wind
That moans a little longer and is still.
There was a time when every gazing hill
Was holy with the wonder that it saw,
And every valley was a place of awe,
And what the grass knew never could be told.
It was the living Spirit that we sold—
And what can help us?"

                Still the evil grew.
It fell upon the cattle, gaunt and few,
That pawed the crusted winter to the bone.
The weirdly wounded flesh of them was blown
To putrid bubbles. Diabolic fire
Burned out the vain last animal desire
In caving paunches, and their muzzles bled.
They staggered, staring. And the wolves were fed.

So Hunger throve. And many of the lean,
Who, having eyes for seeing, had not seen,
And, having ears for hearing, had not heard,
Fed hope a little with the wrathful word
And clamored 'round the agencies. "Our lands,"
They said, "we sold to you for empty hands

And empty bellies and a white man's lie!
Where is the food we bought? Our children die!
The clothing? For our people shiver. Look!
The money for the ponies that you took
Ten snows ago? The Great White Father's friends
Have stolen half the little that he sends.
The starving of our babies makes them fat.
We want to tell the Great White Father that.
We cannot live on promises and lies."

But there were weighty matters for the wise
In Washington, and bellies that were round;
And gold made music yonder, and the sound
Of mourning was a whisper.

                So the young,
In whom wild blood was like a torrent flung
Upon a rock, grew sullen, brooding war.
What was it that the Sioux were waiting for?
To die like cattle starving in a pen?
Was it not better men should run as men
To meet the worst?

           And wrinkled warriors sighed,
Remembering the way their brothers died
Of old to make the living rich in tales.
"Go up the hills," they said, "and search the vales,
And count our battle-ponies by their breaths—
Ten thousand smokes! The grass they eat is death's,
And spirits hear the whisper of their feet.
Dream back for fighting men their bison meat;
Unlive these many winters of our sin
That makes us weak: then let the war begin,
And we will follow mighty men and tall.
Where are they?"

         And the young men thought of Gall,
The wild man-reaper of the Little Horn,
Grown tame at last, a sweater in the corn,
A talker for the white man and his way.
They thought of Red Cloud, doddering and gray,
And of the troubled twilight of his eyes,
Turned groundward now; of Spotted Tail, the wise,
Become a story seven winters old;
And, better to be sung than to be told,

The glory that was Crazy Horse. Alas!
Somewhere the heart and hand of him were grass
Upon a lonely hill!

                           The winter died.
Once more, as though a wish too long denied,
Became creative in a fond belief,
The old Earth cast her ragged weeds of grief,
And listened for the well-belovèd's words,
Until her hushes filled with singing birds
And many-rivered music. Only men
Were paupers in the faith to dream again,
Rebuilding heaven with the stuff of woe.

But when the northern slopes forgot the snow
And song betrayed the secret of the nest
Too dear to keep, begotten of the West
A timid rumor wandered—vaguely heard,
As troubled sleepers hear the early bird
And lose it in the unbelieving night.
'Twas all of wrong grown weaker than the right,
Of fatness for the lowly and the lean,
And whirlwinds of the spirit sweeping clean
The prairie for the coming of the dead.
And many strove to say what someone said
That someone said, who had it from the Crows,
To whom Cheyennes or else Arapahoes
Had brought it from the Snakes. And one by one
Strange tongues had brought it from the setting sun
Across the starving lands where men endure
To live upon the locust and are poor
And rabbit-hearted. And a valley lay
Among the mountains where the end of day
Clings long, because those mountains are the last
Before the prairie that is never grassed
Rolls on forever in dissolving hills.
And in that valley where the last light spills
From peaks of vision, so the rumor ran,
There lived a man—or was he but a man?—
Who once had died, and verily had trod
The Spirit Land, and from the lips of God
He knew how all this marvel was to be.

'Twas very far away.

                    A naked tree
Awakened by the fingers of the Spring,
But lacking the believing sap to sing,
Has nothing but the winter moan to give.

The vague tale made it harder still to live
Where men must dream the right and bear the wrong.
And so another summer, like a song,
Sad with an unforgettable refrain—
Green promises forgotten by the Rain—
Droned to the dying cadence of the leaves.
And winter came.

                    But as the wood believes
At last the evangelic winds of March,
When eagerly the bare apostate larch
Avows the faith of cedars in the sun,
And cottonwoods confess the Living One,
And scrub-oaks, feeling tall against the blue,
Grow priestly with the vision; so the Sioux
Thought better of the iterated tale.
For every westwind knew about the vale
Beneath the shining summits far away;
And southwinds hearkened what they had to say,
And northwinds listened, ceasing to deride.
The man had died, and yet he had not died,
And he had talked with God, and all the dead
Were coming with the whirlwind at their head,
And there would be new earth and heaven!
                                        So
It happened, when the grass began to grow
That spring of 'eighty-nine, the dream took root
In hearts long fallow. And the fateful fruit
Greened in the corn-denying summer heat;
And dry moons mellowed it and made it sweet
Before the plum took color, or the smoke
That was the gray-green rabbit-berry broke
Along the gullies into ruddy sparks.
It seemed no secret to the meadow larks.
In clamorous and agitated flights
The crows proclaimed it. In the stifling nights,
When latent wonder made the four winds still,
The breathless watching of a starry hill
Revealed some comprehension not for speech.
And wheresoever men might gather, each

Would have some new astonishment to share.
But when the smell of frost was in the air
Of mornings, though the noons were summer yet,
The oft-shared wonder only served to whet
The hunger for a wonder real as cold
And empty bellies.

                  So the wise and old
Held council. "Let us see him with our eyes
And hear him with our ears—this man who dies
And talks to God—that we may know the way;
For all our words are shadows, and the day
Is yonder, if the day be anywhere.
And who would go?"

                Good Thunder, Kicking Bear,
Short Bull, Flat Iron would, and Yellow Breast.
So once again the man-compelling West,
Sad mother of dissolving worlds, lured on.
And when the awed adventurers were gone,
Behind them fell the curtain of the snow.

And now the moon was like an elkhorn bow
Drawn to the shaft-head, wanting but a mark;
And now a shield against the doubting dark;
And now it withered, and was lost again:
And as the moon, the phasic hope of men
Measured the winter, slow with many a lack.
For less and less the jaded news came back
From regions nearer to the setting sun—
Re-echoings of wonders said and done—
That faith might flourish briefly in the green:
And sorrow filled the silences between
With troubled voices. What if, far away,
As sunset proves but ordinary day,
The dream-pursuers only sped their dreams?

But when along the cataleptic streams
Spasmodic shudders ran; and in the lee
Of browning slopes the furred anemone,
Already awed by what might happen next,
Stood waiting; and the silences were vexed,
Between crank winds, with moaning in the sloughs—
Though still the grasses slumbered—came the news
Of those five seekers homing. Like a fire
Before a banked-up southwind of desire

Unleashed at last, it swept the tawny land.
The smoke of it was all along the Grand
When first the valley of Moreau took light
From where it bloomed in tumult on the White,
Seeding the fallows of the Big Cheyenne.
The living Christ had come to earth again!
And those who saw Him face to face, and heard,
Were bringing back the wonder of the Word
Whereby the earth and heavens would be new!

And suddenly the prairie took the hue
Of faith again. The rivers understood;
And every budding, gaunt-limbed cottonwood
Experienced the Cleansing of the Blood.
The tall clouds bent above the lowly mud.
A holy passion whitened into flame
Among the plum-brush.

                    Then the seekers came
With awe upon their faces.

                    *

                    Every day
No Water's Camp was growing near the mouth
Of White Clay Creek, lean-flowing in the drouth.
What matter if the doomed, unfriendly sky,
The loveless grudging Earth, so soon to die,
Ignored the supplication of the lean?
Rains of the spirit, wonders in the green,
Bloom of the heart and thunders of the Truth,
Waking the deathless meadow lark of youth,
Were yonder. So the village grew. And most
Who came there felt the leading of the ghost;
But if the clever in their own regard,
Amused contenders that the hills were hard
And could not flow, came mockingly to see,
They saw indeed.

                    They saw the Holy Tree,
A sapling cottonwood with branches lopped,
Set in the center of a ring, and topped
With withered leaves. Around it and around,
Weaving a maze of dust and mournful sound,
The women and children and the men
Joined hands and shuffled, ever and again

Rounding a weird monotony of song,
Winged with the wail of immemorial wrong,
And burdened with the ancient hope at prayer.
And now and then one turned a knowing stare
Upon the empty dazzle of the skies,
Muttering names, and then, as one who dies.
Slumped to the dust and shivered and was still.
And more and more were seized upon, until
The ring was small of those who could not see;
And weeping there beneath the withered tree,
They sang and prayed.

                  But when the sleepers woke
To stagger from the dust, the words they spoke,
As in a dream, were beautiful and strange.
And many a scoffer felt a still swift change
Come over things late darkened with the light
Of common day; as in a moony night
The rapt sleepwalker lives and is aware,
Past telling, in the landscape everywhere
About him till no alien thing can be,
And every blade of grass and weed and tree,
Seed-loving soil and unbegetting stone,
Glow with the patient secret they have known
These troubled whiles, and even men shall know.
One moment, shrewdly smiling at a show,
The clever ones could see a common pole,
The antic grandmas, little children, droll
With grownup airs, the clowning men who wept,
And dust. But suddenly, as though they slept
And dreamed till then, to wake at last and see,
Swift saps of meaning quickened to a tree
The rootless bole, the earth-forgotten thing
With starveling leafage; and the birds would sing
Forever in that shielding holiness.
A joy that only weeping can express
This side of dying, swept them like a rain
Illumining with lightning that is pain
The life-begetting darkness that is sorrow.

So there would be more dancers on the morrow
To swell the camp.

                The Moon When Ponies Shed
Had aged and died; and, risen from the dead,

The Moon of Fatness, only in the name,
Haunted the desert heavens and became
A mockery of plenty at the full,
Remembering the thunders of the bull,
The lowing of the countless fatted cows,
Where now it saw the ghostly myriads browse
Along a thousand valleys, still and sere.
But mightily the spirit of the year,
At flood, poured out upon the needy ones
The Light that has the dazzle of the sun's
For shadow, till the very blind could see.

And then it was beneath the withered tree
Young Black Elk stood and sent a voice and wept;
And little had he danced until he slept
The sleep of vision; for a power lay
Upon him from a child, and men could say
Strange things about his seeing that were true,
And of the dying made to live anew
By virtue of the power. When he fell
The sun was high. When he awoke to tell
The silent crowd that pressed about the place
Of what he saw, with awe upon its face
The full moon rose and faltered, listening.

It was, he said, like riding in a swing,
Afraid of falling; for the swing rose high;
And faster, deeper into empty sky
It mounted, till the clutching hands let go,
And, like an arrow leaping from a bow,
He clove the empty spaces, swift and prone.
Alone he seemed, and terribly alone,
For there was nothing anywhere to heed
The helpless, headlong terror of the speed,
Until a single eagle feather blew
Before him in that emptiness and grew
Into a spotted eagle, leading on
With screaming cries.

                          The terror now was gone.
He seemed to float; but looking far below,
He saw strange lands and rivers come and go
In silence yonder. Far ahead appeared
A mighty mountain. Once again he feared,

For it was clothed in smoke and fanged with flame
And voiced with many thunders. On it came
And passed beneath. Then stretching everywhere
Below him, vivid in the glowing air,
A young earth blossomed with eternal spring;
And in the midst thereof a sacred ring
Of peoples throve in brotherly content;
And he could see the good Red Road that went
Across it, south to north; the hard Black Road
From east to west, where bearers of the load
Of earthly troubles wander blind and lost.
But in the center where the two roads crossed,
The roads men call the evil and the good,
The place was holy with the Tree that stood
Earth-rooted yonder. Nourished by the four
Great Powers that are one, he saw it soar
And be the blooming life of all that lives,
The Holy Spirit that the good grass gives
To animals, and animals to men,
And they give back unto the grass again;
But nothing dies.

     On every drying rack,
The meat was plenty. Hunters coming back
Sang on the hills, the laden ponies too.

Now he descended where the great Tree grew
And there a man was standing in the shade;
A man all perfect, and the light He made
Was like a rainbow 'round Him, spreading wide
Until the living things on every side,
Above Him and below, took fire and burned
One holy flame.

     "Then suddenly He turned
Full face upon me and I tried to see,"
Young Black Elk said, "what people His might be;
But there was cloud, and in the cloud appeared
So many stranger faces that I feared,
Until His face came smiling like a dawn.
And then between two blinks the man was gone;
But 'round the Tree there, standing in a ring,
Twelve women and twelve men began to sing:
'Behold! the people's future shall be such!'
I saw their garments and I wondered much

What these might mean, for they were strangely wrought.
And even as I thought, they heard my thought
And sang reply: 'The people clad as we
Shall fear no evil thing; for they shall see
As you have seen it. Hundreds shall be flame.'

Then I was blinded with a glow that came
Upon them, and they vanished in bright air
And wordless singing.

          Standing lonely there,
I thought about my father who is dead
And longed to find him. But a great Voice said,
'Go back and tell; for there is yet more wrong
And sorrow!'

             Then a swift wind came along
And lifted me; and once again I knew
The fearful empty speed. Face down I flew
And saw a rushing river full of foam,
And crowds of people trying to get home
Across it; but they could not; and I wept
To hear their wailing. Still the great wind kept
Beneath me. And you see that I am here."

Young Black Elk ceased; and, thinking of the dear
Good days of plenty now became a tale,
A woman, old and withered, raised a wail
Of bitter mourning: "It was even so
The way the young man saw it. Long ago
I can remember it was just the same,
The time before the bad Wasichus came,
That greedy people! All good things are dead,
And now I want to die." Her sorrow spread
Among the women like a song of pain,
As when the ponies, heavy with the slain,
Return from battle and the widows crowd
About them, and the mothers.

          When the shroud
Of moony silence fell upon their woe,
Young Black Elk spoke again: "What shall be so
Forever, I have seen. I did not sleep;
I only woke and saw it. Do not weep;

For it is only being blind that hurts.
Tomorrow you shall make these holy shirts
For us to wear the way I saw them worn.
Clothed in the Holy Spirit, none shall mourn
Or come to harm along the fearful road."

So on the morrow happy women sewed
In all the tepees, singing as they made
Of odds and ends and empty sacks of trade,
The rags and tatters of their earthly need,
Unearthly raiment, richly wrought indeed
For all the love they stitched in every hem.
And good old men of power painted them
With sacred meaning: blue upon the breast,
A moon of promise leading to the west,
The end of days; and, blue upon the back,
A morning star to glimmer on the black
And fearful road; the neck and fringes red,
The hue of life. An eagle feather sped
On either arm the homing of the soul.
And mighty with the meaning of the whole,
The work was finished.

               Death became afraid
Before the dancing people so arrayed
In vision of the deathless. Hundreds burned
With holiness.

              But when the cherries turned
From red to black, while Summer slowly died
And in her waiting hushes prophesied
The locust, and the lark forgot his song,
There fell the shadow of the coming wrong
And yet more sorrow that were left to bear.

The Agent came to see; and he was there
With all his world about him. It was sure
And solid, being builded to endure
With granite guess and rumor of the eyes,
Convincingly cemented with surmise
Against all winds of fancy and of fraud.
The height of it was high; the breadth was broad;
The length was long; and, whether bought or sold,
The worths thereof were weighable in gold,

His one concession to the mysteries.
As common as the growing of its trees,
And natural as having wakened there
Quite obviously living and aware,
His world was known.

              So clearly they were mad,
These dancing heathen, ludicrously clad
For superstitious doings in a day
Of Christian light and progress! Who could say
What devilment they hatched against the whites,
What lonely roofs would flare across the nights
To mark a path of murder!

                  It must cease.

Surrounded by the Indian police,
Who sat their mounts importantly, half proud
And half abashed to wear before the crowd
Of relatives the master's coat of blue,
He spoke: "This thing is foolish that you do,
And you must stop it!" Still as though a trance
Had fallen on the interrupted dance,
The people listened while a half-breed hurled
The feeble thunder of a dying world
Among them: "It is bad and you must stop!
Go home and work! This will not raise a crop
To feed you!"

           Yet awhile the silence held,
The tension snapping with a voice that yelled
Some word of fury; and a hubbub broke.

As when across the dust and battle-smoke
The warrior hails the warrior—"Hokahey!
Have courage, brother! Let us die today!"—
The young men clamored, running for their guns.
And swarming back about the hated ones,
They faltered, waiting for the first to kill.
Then momently again the place went still,
But for the clicking locks. And someone cried:
"Your people tortured Jesus till He died!
You killed our bison and you stole our land!
Go back or we will kill you where you stand!

This dance is our religion! Go and bring
Your soldiers, if you will. Not anything
Can hurt us now. And if they want to die,
Go bring them to us!"

                              Followed by the cry,
As by a stinging whip, the Agent went.

That night one mourned: "It was not what you meant!"
Alone upon a hill he prayed and wept;
"Not so you taught me when my body slept.
Great Spirit, give them eyes, for they are lost!"

X

HAMLIN GARLAND

Although Garland wrote more than fifty books, his major work is concerned with what he called the "Middle Border," a wide strip of land comprising parts of Wisconsin, Iowa, and South Dakota. He was born in Wisconsin in 1860 but moved while he was a boy to Iowa. Shortly before Dakota Territory was divided into two states, Garland's family was homesteading there on the prairie. In 1884 Garland went to Boston where he studied and taught for a few years. In 1887 he visited Wisconsin, Iowa, and Dakota and apparently decided at this time to become a writer and to take this Middle Border area as his subject matter and place in an effort to portray the region realistically. In spite of the fact that he settled in Chicago in 1893 and then in New York in 1916, he continued to write of the prairie and of the Mississippi Valley. Often the tone of his novels and stories was one of moral indignation against the conditions and weather and climate that made farming and other Middle West activities difficult and often kept people from doing more than surviving.

Some of his bleakest comments have been made about eastern South Dakota, but "Among the Corn-Rows" offers some relief from Garland's frequent grimness.

Some of his best-known books are *Main-Travelled Roads,* 1890 (from which this story is taken), *Rose of Dutcher's Cooly,* 1895, *A Son of the Middle Border,* 1917, *A Daughter of the Middle Border,* 1921, and *Trail-makers of the Middle Border,* 1926. A prolific writer, and considered important as a chronicler of the Middle West in the first third of the 20th century, Garland died in Hollywood in 1940.

AMONG THE CORN-ROWS

"But the road sometimes passes a rich meadow, where the songs of larks and bob-o'-links and blackbirds are tangled.

Rob held up his hands, from which the dough depended in ragged strings.

"Biscuits," he said, with an elaborate working of his jaws, intended to convey the idea that they were going to be specially delicious.

Seagraves laughed, but did not enter the shanty door. "How do you like baching it?"

113

"Oh, don't mention it!" entreated Rob, mauling the dough again. "Come in an' sit down. What in thunder y' standin' out there for?"

"Oh, I'd rather be where I can see the prairie. Great weather!"

"*Im*-mense!"

"How goes breaking?"

"Tip-top! A *leetle* dry now; but the bulls pull the plough through two acres a day. How's things in Boomtown?"

"Oh, same old grind."

"Judge still lyin'?"

"Still at it."

"Major Mullens still swearin' to it?"

"You hit it like a mallet. Railroad schemes are thicker 'n prairie-chickens. You've got grit, Rob. I don't have anything but crackers and sardines over to my shanty, and here you are making soda-biscuit."

"I have t' do it. Couldn't break if I didn't. You editors c'n take things easy, lay around on the prairie, and watch the plovers and medderlarks; but we *settlers* have got to work."

Leaving Rob to sputter over his cooking, Seagraves took his slow way off down toward the oxen grazing in a little hollow. The scene was characteristically, wonderfully beautiful. It was about five o'clock in a day in late June, and the level plain was green and yellow, and infinite in reach as a sea; the lowering sun was casting over its distant swells a faint impalpable mist, through which the breaking teams on the neighboring claims ploughed noiselessly, as figures in a dream. The whistle of gophers, the faint, wailing, fluttering cry of the falling plover, the whir of the swift-winged prairie-pigeon, or the quack of a lonely duck, came through the shimmering air. The lark's infrequent whistle, piercingly sweet, broke from the longer grass in the swales near by. No other climate, sky, plain, could produce the same unnamable weird charm. No tree to wave, no grass to rustle, scarcely a sound of domestic life; only the faint melancholy soughing of the wind in the short grass, and the voices of the wild things of the prairie.

Seagraves, an impressionable young man (junior editor of the Boomtown *Spike*), threw himself down on the sod, pulled his hat-rim down over his eyes, and looked away over the plain. It was the second year of Boomtown's existence, and Seagraves had not yet grown restless under its monotony. Around him the gophers played saucily. Teams were moving here and there across the sod, with a peculiar noiseless, effortless motion, that made them seem as calm, lazy, and insubstantial as the mist through which they made their way; even the sound of passing wagons was a sort of low, well-fed, self-satisfied chuckle.

Seagraves, "holding down a claim" near Rob, had come to see his neighboring "bach" because feeling the need of company; but now that he was near enough to hear him prancing about getting supper, he was content to lie alone on a slope of the green sod.

The silence of the prairie at night was well-nigh terrible. Many a night, as Seagraves lay in his bunk against the side of his cabin, he would strain his ear to hear the slightest sound, and be listening thus sometimes for minutes before the squeak of a mouse or the step of a passing fox came as a relief to the aching sense. In the daytime, however, and especially on a morning, the prairie was another thing. The pigeons, the larks, the cranes, the multitudinous voices of the ground-birds and snipes and insects, made the air pulsate with sound—a chorus that died away into an infinite murmur of music.

"Hello, Seagraves!" yelled Rob from the door. "The biscuits are 'most done."

Seagraves did not speak, only nodded his head, and slowly rose. The faint clouds in the west were getting a superb flame-color above and a misty purple below, and the sun had shot them with lances of yellow light. As the air grew denser with moisture, the sounds of neighboring life began to reach the air. Children screamed and laughed, and afar off a woman was singing a lullaby. The rattle of wagons and the voices of men speaking to their teams multiplied. Ducks in a neighboring lowland were quacking sociably. The whole scene took hold upon Seagraves with irresistible power.

"It is American," he exclaimed. "No other land or time can match this mellow air, this wealth of color, much less the strange social conditions of life on this sunlit Dakota prairie."

Rob, though visibly affected by the scene also, couldn't let his biscuit spoil, or go without proper attention.

"Say, ain't y' comin' t' grub?" he asked, impatiently.

"In a minute," replied his friend, taking a last wistful look at the scene. "I want one more look at the landscape."

"Landscape be blessed! If you'd been breakin' all day—Come, take that stool an' draw up."

"No; I'll take the candle-box."

"Not much. I know what manners are, if I am a bulldriver."

Seagraves took the three-legged and rather precarious-looking stool and drew up to the table, which was a flat broad box nailed up against the side of the wall, with two strips of board nailed at the outer corners for legs.

"How's that f'r a lay-out?" Rob inquired proudly.

"Well, you *have* spread yourself! Biscuit and canned peaches and sardines and cheese. Why, this is—is—prodigal."

"It ain't nothin' else."

Rob was from one of the finest counties of Wisconsin, over toward Milwaukee. He was of German parentage, a middle-sized, cheery, wide-awake, good-looking young fellow—a typical claim-holder. He was always confident, jovial, and full of plans for the future. He had dug his own well, built his own shanty, washed and mended his own clothing. He could do anything, and do it well. He had a fine field of wheat, and was finishing the plough-ing of his entire quarter-section.

"This is what I call settin' under a feller's own vine an' fig tree"—after Seagraves' compliments—"an' I like it. I'm my own boss. No man can say 'come here' 'n' 'go there' to me. I get up when I'm a min' to, an' go t' bed when I'm a min' to."

"Some drawbacks, I s'pose?"

"Yes. Mice, f'r instance, give me a devilish lot o' trouble. They get into my flour-barrel, eat up my cheese, an' fall into my well. But it ain't no use t' swear."

> " 'The rats and the mice made such a strife
> He had to go to London to buy him a wife.' "

quoted Seagraves. "Don't blush. I've probed your secret thought."

"Well, to tell the honest truth," said Rob, a little sheepishly, leaning across the table, "I ain't satisfied with my style o' cookin'. It's good, but a little too plain, y' know. I'd like a change. It ain't much fun to break all day, and then go to work an' cook y'r own supper."

"No, I should say not."

"This fall I'm going back to Wisconsin. Girls are thick as huckleberries back there, and I'm goin' t' bring one back, now you hear me."

"Good! That's the plan," laughed Seagraves, amused at a cer-tain timid and apprehensive look in his companion's eye. "Just think what a woman would do to put this shanty in shape; and think how nice it would be to take her arm and saunter out after supper, and look at the farm, and plan, and lay out gardens and paths, and tend the chickens!"

Rob's manly and self-reliant nature had the settler's typical buoyancy and hopefulness, as well as a certain power of analysis, which enabled him now to say: "The fact is, we fellers holdin' claims out here ain't fools clear to the *rine*. We know a *couple* o' things. Now I didn't leave Waupac County f'r fun. Did y' ever see Waupac? Well, it's one o' the handsomest counties the sun ever shone on, full o' lakes and rivers and groves of timber. I miss 'em all out here, and I miss the boys an' girls; but they wa'n't no chance there f'r a feller. Land that was good was so

116

blamed high you couldn't touch it with a ten-foot pole from a balloon. Rent was high, if you wanted t' rent, an' so a feller like me had t' get out, an' now I'm out here, I'm goin' t' make the most of it. Another thing," he went on, after a pause—"we fellers workin' out back there got more 'n' more like *hands,* an' less like human beings. Y' know, Waupac is a kind of a summer resort, and the people that use' t' come in summers looked down on us cusses in the fields an' shops. I couldn't stand it. By God!" he said, with a sudden impulse of rage quite unusual, "I'd rather live on an iceberg and claw crabs f'r a livin' than have some feller passin' me on the road an' callin' me 'fellah!' "

Seagraves knew what he meant, but listened in astonishment at this outburst.

"I consider myself a sight better 'n' any man who lives on somebody else's hard work. I've never had a cent I didn't earn with them hands." He held them up, and broke into a grin. "Beauties, ain't they? But they never wore gloves that some other poor cuss earned."

Seagraves thought them grand hands, worthy to grasp the hand of any man or woman living.

"Well, so I come West, just like a thousand other fellers, to get a start where the cussed European aristocracy hadn't got a holt on the people. I like it here—course I'd like the lakes an' meadows of Waupac better—but I'm my own boss, as I say, and I'm goin' to *stay* my own boss if I haf to live on crackers an' wheat coffee to do it; that's the kind of a hair-pin I am."

In the pause which followed, Seagraves, plunged deep into thought by Rob's words, leaned his head on his hand. This working farmer had voiced the modern idea. It was an absolute overturn of all the ideas of nobility and special privilege born of the feudal past. Rob had spoken upon impulse, but that impulse appeared to Seagraves to be right.

"I'd like to use your idea for an editorial, Rob," he said.

"*My* ideas!" exclaimed the astounded host, pausing in the act of filling his pipe. "My ideas! Why, I didn't know I had any."

"Well, you've given me some, anyhow."

Seagraves felt that it was a wild, grand upstirring of the modern democrat against the aristocrat, against the idea of caste and the privilege of living on the labor of others. This atom of humanity (how infinitesimal this drop in the ocean of humanity!) was feeling the nameless longing of expanding personality, and had already pierced the conventions of society, and declared as *nil* the laws of the land—laws that were survivals of hate and prejudice. He had exposed also the native spring of the emigrant

117

by uttering the feeling that it is better to be an equal among peasants than a servant before nobles.

"So I have good reasons f'r liking the country," Rob resumed, in a quiet way. "The soil is rich, the climate good so far, an' if I have a couple o' decent crops you'll see a neat upright goin' up here, with a porch and a bay-winder."

"And you'll still be living here alone, frying leathery slap-jacks an' chopping 'taters and bacon."

"I think I see myself," drawled Rob, "goin' around all summer wearin' the same shirt without washin', an' wipin' on the same towel four straight weeks, an' wearin' holes in my socks, an' eatin' musty gingersnaps, mouldy bacon, an' canned Boston beans f'r the rest o' my enduring days! Oh, yes; I guess *not!* Well, see y' later. Must go water my bulls."

As he went off down the slope, Seagraves smiled to hear him sing:

"I wish that some kind-hearted girl
Would pity on me take,
And extricate me from the mess I'm in.
The angel—how I'd bless her,
If this her home she'd make,
In my little old sod shanty on the plain."

The boys nearly fell off their chairs in the Western House dining room, a few days later, at seeing Rob come into supper with a collar and neck-tie as the finishing touch of a remarkable outfit.

"Hit him, somebody!"

"It's a clean collar!"

"He's started f'r Congress!"

"He's going to get married," put in Seagraves, in a tone that brought conviction.

"What!" screamed Jack Adams, O'Neill, and Wilson, in one breath. "That man?"

"That man," replied Seagraves, amazed at Rob, who coolly took his seat, squared his elbows, pressed his collar down at the back, and called for the bacon and eggs.

The crowd stared at him in a dead silence.

"Where's he going to do it?" asked Jack Adams. "Where's he going to find a girl?"

"Ask him," said Seagraves.

"I ain't tellin'," put in Rob, with his mouth full of potato.

"You're afraid of our competition."

"That's right; *our* competition, Jack; not *your* competition. Come, now, Rob, tell us where you found her."

"I ain't found her."

"What! And yet you're goin' away t' get married!"

118

"I'm goin' to' bring a wife back with me ten days fr'm date."

"I see his scheme," put in Jim Rivers. "He's goin' back East somewhere, an' he's goin' to propose to every girl he meets."

"Hold on!" interrupted Rob, holding up his fork. "Ain't quite right. Every *good lookin'* girl I meet."

"Well, I'll be blanked!" exclaimed Jack, impatiently; "that simply lets me out. Any man with such a cheek ought to——"

"Succeed," interrupted Seagraves.

"That's what I say," bawled Hank Whiting, the proprietor of the house. "You fellers ain't got any enterprise to yeh. Why don't you go to work an' help settle the country like men? Cause y' ain't got no sand. Girls are thicker 'n huckleberries back East. I say it's a dum shame!"

"Easy, Henry," said the elegant bank-clerk, Wilson, looking gravely about through his spectacles. "I commend the courage and the resolution of Mr. Rodemaker. I pray the lady may not

'Mislike him for his complexion,
The shadowed livery of the burning sun'. "

"Shakespeare," said Adams at a venture.

"Brother in adversity, when do you embark? Another Jason on an untried sea."

"Hay!" said Rob, winking at Seagraves. "Oh, I go tonight—night train."

"And return?"

"Ten days from date."

"I'll wager a wedding supper he brings a blonde," said Wilson, in his clean-cut, languid speech.

"Oh, come, now, Wilson; that's too thin! We all know that rule about dark marryin' light."

"I'll wager she'll be tall," continued Wilson. "I'll wager *you,* friend Rodemaker, she'll be blonde and tall."

The rest roared at Rob's astonishment and confusion. The absurdity of it grew, and they went into spasms of laughter. But Wilson remained impassive, not the twitching of a muscle betraying that he saw anything to laugh at in the proposition.

Mrs. Whiting and the kitchen-girls came in, wondering at the merriment. Rob began to get uneasy.

"What is it? What is it?" said Mrs. Whiting, a jolly little matron.

Rivers put the case. "Rob's on his way back to Wisconsin t' get married, and Wilson has offered to bet *him* that his wife will be a blonde and tall, and Rob dassent bet!" And they roared again.

"Why, the idea! the man's crazy!" said Mrs. Whiting.

The crowd looked at each other. This was hint enough; they sobered, nodding at each other.

"Aha; I see; I understand."

"It's the heat."

"And the Boston beans."

"Let up on him, Wilson. Don't badger a poor irresponsible fellow. I *thought* something was wrong when I saw the collar."

"Oh, keep it up!" said Rob, a little nettled by their evident intention to "have fun" with him.

"Soothe him—*soo-o-o-othe* him!" said Wilson. "Don't be harsh."

Rob rose from the table. "Go to thunder! You fellows make me tired."

"The fit is on him again!"

He rose disgustedly and went out. They followed him in single file. The rest of the town "caught on." Frank Graham heaved an apple at him, and joined the procession. Rob went into the store to buy some tobacco. They followed, and perched like crows on the counters till he went out; then they followed him, as before. They watched him check his trunk; they witnessed the purchase of the ticket. The town had turned out by this time.

"Waupac!" announced the one nearest the victim.

"Waupac!" said the next man, and the word was passed along the street up town.

"Make a note of it," said Wilson; "Waupac—a county where a man's proposal for marriage is honored upon presentation. Sight drafts."

Rivers struck up a song, while Rob stood around, patiently bearing the jokes of the crowd:

> "We're lookin' rather seedy now,
> While holdin' down our claims,
> And our vittles are not always of the best,
> And the mice play slyly round us
> As we lay down to sleep
> In our little old tarred shanties on the claim.

> "Yet we rather like the novelty
> Of livin' in this way,
> Though the bill of fare is often rather tame;
> And we're happy as a clam
> On the land of Uncle Sam
> In our little old tarred shanty on the claim."

The train drew up at length, to the immense relief of Rob, whose stoical resignation was beginning to weaken.

"Don't y' wish y' had sand?" he yelled to the crowd, as he plunged into the car, thinking he was rid of them.

But no; their last stroke was to follow him into the car, nodding, pointing to their heads, and whispering, managing in the half-minute the train stood at the platform to set every person in the car staring at the "crazy man." Rob groaned, and pulled his hat down over his eyes—an action which confirmed his tormentors' words and made several ladies click their tongues in sympathy—"Tlck! tlck! poor fellow!"

"All *abo-o-o-a-rd!*" said the conductor, grinning his appreciation at the crowd, and the train was off.

"Oh, won't we make him groan when he gets back!" said Barney, the young lawyer who sang the shouting tenor.

"We'll meet him with the timbrel and the harp. Anybody want to wager? I've got two to one on a short brunette," said Wilson.

II

"Follow it far enough and it may pass the bend in the river where the water laughs eternally over its shallows."

A corn-field in July is a hot place. The soil is hot and dry; the wind comes across the lazily murmuring leaves laden with a warm sickening smell drawn from the rapidly growing, broad-flung banners of the corn. The sun, nearly vertical, drops a flood of dazzling light upon the field over which the cool shadows run, only to make the heat seem the more intense.

Julia Peterson, faint with hunger, was toiling back and forth between the corn-rows, holding the handles of the double-shovel corn-plough, while her little brother Otto rode the steaming horse. Her heart was full of bitterness, her face flushed with heat, and her muscles aching with fatigue. The heat grew terrible. The corn came to her shoulders, and not a breath seemed to reach her, while the sun, nearing the noon mark, lay pitilessly upon her shoulders, protected only by a calico dress. The dust rose under her feet, and as she was wet with perspiration it soiled her till with a woman's instinctive cleanliness, she shuddered. Her head throbbed dangerously. What matter to her that the kingbird pitched jovially from the maples to catch a wandering blue-bottle fly, that the robin was feeding its young, that the bobolink was singing? All these things, if she saw them, only threw her bondage to labor into greater relief.

Across the field, in another patch of corn, she could see her father—a big, gruff-voiced, wide-bearded Norwegian—at work also with a plough. The corn must be ploughed, and so she toiled on, the tears dropping from the shadow of the ugly sun-bonnet she wore. Her shoes, coarse and square-toed, chafed her feet; her hands, large and strong, were browned, or, more properly, *burnt,* on the backs by the sun. The horse's harness *"creak*-cracked" as he swung steadily and patiently forward, the moisture pouring from his sides, his nostrils distended.

The field ran down to a road, and on the other side of the road ran a river—a broad, clear, shallow expanse at that point, and the eyes of the boy gazed longingly at the pond and the cool shadow each time that he turned at the fence.

"Say, Jule, I'm goin' in! Come, can't I? Come—say!" he pleaded, as they stopped at the fence to let the horse breathe.

"I've let you go wade twice."

"But that don't do any good. My legs is all smarty, 'cause ol' Jack sweats so." The boy turned around on the horse's back and slid to his rump. "I can't stand it!" he burst out, sliding off and darting under the fence. "Father can't see."

The girl put her elbows on the fence and watched her little brother as he sped away to the pool, throwing off his clothes as he ran, whooping with uncontrollable delight. Soon she could hear him splashing about in the water a short distance up the stream, and caught glimpses of his little shiny body and happy face. How cool that water looked! And the shadows there by the big basswood! How that water would cool her blistered feet! An impulse seized her, and she squeezed between the rails of the fence, and stood in the road looking up and down to see that the way was clear. It was not a main-travelled road; no one was likely to come; why not?

She hurriedly took off her shoes and stockings—how delicious the cool, soft velvet of the grass!—and sitting down on the bank under the great basswood, whose roots formed an abrupt bank, she slid her poor blistered, chafed feet into the water, her bare head leaned against the huge tree-trunk.

And now, as she rested, the beauty of the scene came to her. Over her the wind moved the leaves. A jay screamed far off, as if answering the cries of the boy. A kingfisher crossed and re-crossed the stream with dipping sweep of his wings. The river sang with its lips to the pebbles. The vast clouds went by majestically, far above the tree-tops, and the snap and buzzing and ringing whir of July insects made a ceaseless, slumberous undertone of song solvent of all else. The tired girl forgot her work. She began to dream. This would not last always. Some one would come to release her from such drudgery. This was her constant, tenderest, and most secret dream. *He* would be a Yankee, not a Norwegian; the Yankees didn't ask their wives to work in the field. He would have a home. Perhaps he'd live in town—perhaps a merchant! And then she thought of the drug clerk in Rock River who had looked at her—A voice broke in on her dream, a fresh, manly voice.

"Well, by jinks! if it ain't Julia! Just the one I wanted to see!"

The girl turned, saw a pleasant-faced young fellow in a derby hat and a fifteen-dollar suit of diagonals.

"Bob Rodemaker! How come——"

She remembered her situation, and flushed, looked down at the water and remained perfectly still.

"Ain't ye goin' to shake hands? Y' don't seem very glad t' see me."

She began to grow angry. "If you had any eyes, you'd see."

Rob looked over the edge of the bank, whistled, turned away. "Oh, I see! Excuse *me!* Don't blame yeh a bit, though. Good weather f'r corn," he went on, looking up at the trees. "Corn seems to be pretty well forward," he continued, in a louder voice, as he walked away, still gazing into the air. "Crops is looking first-class in Boomtown. Hello! This Otto? H'yare, y' little scamp! Get on to that horse agin. Quick, 'r I'll take y'r skin off an' hang it on the fence. What y' been doin'?"

"Ben in swimmin'. Jimminy, ain't it fun! When 'dy' get back?" said the boy, grinning.

"Never you mind!" replied Rob, leaping the fence by laying his left hand on the top rail. "Get on to that horse." He tossed the boy up on the horse, hung his coat on the fence. "I s'pose the ol' man makes her plough same as usual?"

"Yup," said Otto.

"Dod ding a man that'll do that! I don't mind if it's necessary, but it ain't necessary in his case." He continued to mutter in this way as he went across to the other side of the field. As they turned to come back, Rob went up and looked at the horse's mouth. "Gettin' purty near of age. Say, who's sparkin' Julia now —anybody?"

"Nobody 'cept some ol' Norwegians. She won't have them. Por wants her to, but she won't."

"Good f'r her. Nobody comes t' see her Sunday nights, eh?"

"Nope; only 'Tias Anderson an' 'Ole Hoover; but she goes off an' leaves 'em."

"Chk!" said Rob, starting old Jack across the field.

It was almost noon, and Jack moved reluctantly. He knew the time of day as well as the boy. He made this round after distinct protest.

In the meantime Julia, putting on her shoes and stockings, went to the fence and watched the man's shining white shirt as he moved across the corn-field. There had never been any special tenderness between them, but she had always liked him. They had been at school together. She wondered why he had come back at this time of the year, and wondered how long he would stay. How long had he stood looking at her? She flushed again at the thought of it. But he wasn't to blame; it was a public road. She might have known better.

She stood under a little popple-tree, whose leaves shook musically at every zephyr, and her eyes through half-shut lids roved over the sea of deep-green, glossy leaves, dappled here and there by cloud shadows, stirred here and there like water by the wind, and out of it all a longing to be free from such toil rose like a breath, filling her throat and quickening the motion of her heart. Must this go on forever, this life of heat and dust and labor? What did it all mean?

The girl laid her chin on her strong red wrists, and looked up into the blue spaces between the vast clouds—aërial mountains dissolving in a shoreless azure sea. How cool and sweet and restful they looked! If she might only lie out on the billowy, snow-white, sunlit edge! The voices of the driver and the ploughman recalled her, and she fixed her eyes again upon the slowly nodding head of the patient horse, on the boy turned half about on his saddle, talking to the white-sleeved man, whose derby hat bobbed up and down quite curiously, like the horse's head. Would she ask him to dinner? What would her people say?

"Phew! it's hot!" was the greeting the young fellow gave as he came up. He smiled in a frank, boyish way, as he hung his hat on the top of a stake and looked up at her. "D' y' know, I kind o' enjoy gettin' at it again? Fact. It ain't no work for a girl, though," he added.

"When 'd you get back?" she asked, the flush not yet out of her face. Rob was looking at her thick, fine hair and full Scandinavian face, rich as a rose in color, and did not reply for a few seconds. She stood with her hideous sun-bonnet pushed back on her shoulders. A kingbird was chattering overhead.

"Oh, a few days ago."

"How long y' goin' t' stay?"

"Oh, I d' know. A week, mebbe."

A far-off halloo came pulsing across the shimmering air. The boy screamed "Dinner!" and waved his hat with an answering whoop, then flopped off the horse like a turtle off a stone into water. He had the horse unhooked in an instant, and had flung his toes over the horse's back, in act to climb on, when Rob said:

"H'yare, young feller! wait a minute. Tired?" he asked the girl, with a tone that was more than kindly, it was almost tender.

"Yes," she replied, in a low voice. "My shoes hurt me."

"Well, here y' go," he replied, taking his stand by the horse, and holding out his hand like a step. She colored and smiled a little as she lifted her foot into his huge, hard, sunburned hand.

"Oop-a-daisy!" he called. She gave a spring, and sat on the horse like one at home there.

Rob had a deliciously unconscious, abstracted, businesslike air. He really left her nothing to do but enjoy his company, while he went ahead and did precisely as he pleased.

"We don't raise much corn out there, an' so I kind o' like to see it once more."

"I wish I didn't have to see another hill of corn as long as I live!" replied the girl, bitterly.

"Don't know as I blame yeh a bit. But, all the same, I'm glad you was working in it to-day," he thought to himself, as he walked beside her horse toward the house.

"Will you stop to dinner?" she inquired bluntly, almost surlily. It was evident there were reasons why she didn't mean to press him to do so.

"You bet I will," he replied; "that is, if you want I should."

"You know how we live," she replied evasively. "If you can stand it, why—" She broke off abruptly.

Yes, he remembered how they lived in that big, square, dirty, white frame house. It had been three or four years since he had been in it, but the smell of the cabbage and onions, the penetrating, peculiar mixture of odors, assailed his memory as something unforgettable.

"I guess I'll stop," he said, as she hesitated. She said no more, but tried to act as if she were not in any way responsible for what came afterward.

"I guess I c'n stand f'r one meal what you stand all the while," he added.

As she left them at the well and went to the house he saw her limp painfully, and the memory of her face so close to his lips as he helped her down from the horse gave him pleasure at the same time that he was touched by its tired and gloomy look. Mrs. Peterson came to the door of the kitchen, looking just the same as ever. Broad-faced, unwieldy, flabby, apparently wearing the same dress he remembered to have seen her in years before,—a dirty drab-colored thing,—she looked as shapeless as a sack of wool. Her English was limited to, "How de do, Rob?"

He washed at the pump, while the girl, in an attempt to be hospitable, held the clean towel for him.

"You're purty well used up, eh?" he said to her.

"Yes; it's awful hot out there."

"Can't you lay off this afternoon? It ain't right."

"No. *He* won't listen to that."

"Well, let me take your place."

"No; there ain't any use o' that."

Peterson, a brawny, wide-bearded Norwegian, came up at this moment, and spoke to Rob in a sullen, gruff way.

"He ain't *very* glad to see me," said Rob, winking at Julia. "He ain't b'ilin' over with enthusiasm; but I c'n stand it, for your sake," he added, with amazing assurance; but the girl had turned away, and it was wasted.

At the table he ate heartily of the "bean swaagen," which filled a large wooden bowl in the centre of the table, and which was ladled into smaller wooden bowls at each plate. Julia had tried hard to convert her mother to Yankee ways, and had at last given it up in despair. Rob kept on safe subjects, mainly asking questions about the crops of Peterson, and when addressing the girl, inquired of the schoolmates. By skillful questioning, he kept the subject of marriage uppermost, and seemingly was getting an inventory of the girls not yet married or engaged.

It was embarrassing for the girl. She was all too well aware of the difference between her home and the home of her schoolmates and friends. She knew that it was not pleasant for her "Yankee" friends to come to visit her when they could not feel sure of a welcome from the tireless, silent, and grim-visaged old Norse, if, indeed, they could escape insult. Julia ate her food mechanically and it could hardly be said that she enjoyed the brisk talk of the young man, his eyes were upon her so constantly and his smile so obviously addressed to her. She rose as soon as possible and, going outside, took a seat on a chair under the trees in the yard. She was not a coarse or dull girl. In fact, she had developed so rapidly by contact with the young people of the neighborhood that she no longer found pleasure in her own home. She didn't believe in keeping up the old-fashioned Norwegian customs, and her life with her mother was not one to breed love or confidence. She was more like a hired hand. The love of the mother for her "Yulyie" was sincere though rough and inarticulate, and it was her jealousy of the young "Yankees" that widened the chasm between the girl and herself—an inevitable result.

Rob followed the girl out into the yard, and threw himself on the grass at her feet, perfectly unconscious of the fact that this attitude was exceedingly romantic and becoming to them both. He did it because he wanted to talk to her, and the grass was cool and easy; there wasn't any other chair, anyway.

"Do they keep up the ly-ceum and the sociables same as ever?"

"Yes. The others go a good 'eal, but I don't. We're gettin' such a stock round us, and father thinks he needs me s' much, I don't get out often. I'm gettin' sick of it."

"I sh'd think y' would," he replied, his eyes on her face.

"I c'd stand the churnin' and housework, but when it comes t' workin' outdoors in the dirt an' hot sun, gettin' all sunburned and chapped up, it's another thing. An' then it seems as if he gets stingier 'n' stingier every year. I ain't had a new dress in—I d'-know-how-long. He says it's all nonsense, an' mother's about as bad. *She* don't want a new dress, an' so she thinks I don't." The girl was feeling the influence of a sympathetic listener and was making up for the long silence. "I've tried t' go t' work, but they won't let me. They'd have t' pay a hand twenty dollars a month f'r the work I do, an' they like cheap help; but I'm not goin' t' stand it much longer, I can tell you that."

Rob thought she was very handsome as she sat there with her eyes fixed on the horizon, while these rebellious thoughts found utterance in her quivering, passionate voice.

"Yulie! Kom haar!" roared the old man from the well.

A frown of anger and pain came into her face. She looked at Rob. "That means more work."

"Say! let me go out in your place. Come, now; what's the use——"

"No; it wouldn't do no good. It ain't t'-day s' much; it's every day, and——"

Yu*lie!*" called Peterson again, with a string of impatient Norwegian.

"Well, all right, only I'd like to—"

"Well, good-by," she said, with a little touch of feeling. "When d' ye go back?"

"I don't know. I'll see y' again before I go. Good-by."

He stood watching her slow, painful pace till she reached the well, where Otto was standing with the horse. He stood watching them as they moved out into the road and turned down toward the field. He felt that she had sent him away; but still there was a look in her eyes which was not altogether——

He gave it up in despair at last. He was not good at analyses of this nature; he was used to plain, blunt expressions. There was a woman's subtlety here quite beyond his reach.

He sauntered slowly off up the road after his talk with Julia. His head was low on his breast; he was thinking as one who is about to take a decided and important step.

He stopped at length, and, turning, watched the girl moving along in the deeps of the corn. Hardly a leaf was stirring; the untempered sunlight fell in a burning flood upon the field; the grasshoppers rose, snapped, buzzed, and fell; the locust uttered its dry, heat-intensifying cry. The man lifted his head.

"It's a d—n shame!" he said, beginning rapidly to retrace his steps. He stood leaning on the fence, awaiting the girl's coming very much as she had waited his on the round he had made

127

before dinner. He grew impatient at the slow gait of the horse, and drummed on the rail while he whistled. Then he took off his hat and dusted it nervously. As the horse got a little nearer he wiped his face carefully, pushed his hat back on his head, and climbed over the fence, where he stood with elbows on the middle rail as the girl and boy and horse came to the end of the furrow.

"Hot, ain't it?" he said, as she looked up.

"Jimminy Peters, it's awful!" puffed the boy. The girl did not reply till she swung the plough about after the horse, and set it upright into the next row. Her powerful body had a superb swaying motion at the waist as she did this—a motion which affected Rob vaguely but massively.

"I thought you'd gone," she said gravely, pushing back her bonnet till he could see her face dewed with sweat, and pink as a rose. She had the high cheek-bones of her race, but she had also their exquisite fairness of color.

"Say, Otto," asked Rob, alluringly, "wan' to go swimmin'?"

"You bet," replied Otto.

"Well, I'll go a round if——"

The boy dropped off the horse, not waiting to hear any more. Rob grinned, but the girl dropped her eyes, then looked away.

"Got rid o' him mighty quick. Say, Julyie, I hate like thunder t' see you out here; it ain't right. I wish you'd—I wish——"

She could not look at him now, and her bosom rose and fell with a motion that was not due to fatigue. Her moist hair matted around her forehead gave her a boyish look.

Rob nervously tried again, tearing splinters from the fence. "Say, now, I'll tell yeh what I came back here for—t' git married; and if you're willin', I'll do it tonight. Come, now, whaddy y' say?"

"What've *I* got t' do 'bout it?" she finally asked, the color flooding her face, and a faint smile coming to her lips. "Go ahead. I ain't got anything——"

Rob put a splinter in his mouth and faced her. "Oh, looky here, now, Julyie! you know what I mean. I've got a good claim out near Boomtown—a *rattlin'* good claim; a shanty on it fourteen by sixteen—no tarred paper about it, and a suller to keep butter in, and a hundred acres o' wheat just about ready to turn now. I need a wife."

Here he straightened up, threw away the splinter, and took off his hat. He was a very pleasant figure as the girl stole a look at him. His black laughing eyes were especially earnest just now. His voice had a touch of pleading. The popple-tree over their heads murmured applause at his eloquence, then hushed to listen. A cloud dropped a silent shadow down upon them, and it sent a little thrill of fear through Rob, as if it were an omen of failure.

As the girl remained silent, looking away, he began, man-fashion, to desire her more and more as he feared to lose her. He put his hat on the post again and took out his jack-knife. Her calico dress draped her supple and powerful figure simply but naturally. The stoop in her shoulders, given by labor, disappeared as she partly leaned upon the fence. The curves of her muscular arms showed through her sleeve.

"It's all-fired lonesome f'r me out there on that claim, and it ain't no picnic f'r you here. Now, if you'll come out there with me, you needn't do anything but cook f'r me, and after harvest we can git a good layout o' furniture, an' I'll lath and plaster the house and put a little hell [ell] in the rear." He smiled, and so did she. He felt encouraged to say: "An' there we be, as snug as y' please. We're close t' Boomtown, an' we can go down there to church sociables an' things, and they're a jolly lot there."

The girl was still silent, but the man's simple enthusiasm came to her charged with passion and a sort of romance such as her hard life had known little of. There was something enticing about this trip to the West.

"What'll my folks say?" she said at last.

A virtual surrender, but Rob was not acute enough to see it. He pressed on eagerly:

"I don't care. Do you? They'll just keep y' ploughin' corn and milkin' cows till the day of judgment. Come, Julyie, I ain't got no time to fool away. I've got t' get back t' that grain. It's a whoopin' old crop, sure's y'r born, an' that means sompin purty scrumptious in furniture this fall. Come, now." He approached her and laid his hand on her shoulder very much as he would have touched Albert Seagraves or any other comrade. "Whady y' say?"

She neither started, nor shrunk nor looked at him. She simply moved a step away. "They'd never let me go," she replied bitterly. "I'm too cheap a hand. I do a man's work an' get no pay at all."

"You'll have half o' all I c'n make," he put in.

"How long c'n you wait?" she asked, looking down at her dress.

"Just two minutes," he said, pulling out his watch. "It ain't no use t' wait. The old man'll be jest as mad a week from now as he is to-day. Why not go now?"

"I'm of age in a few days," she mused, wavering, calculating.

"You c'n be of age to-night if you'll jest call on old Squire Hatfield with me."

"All right, Rob," the girl said, turning and holding out her hand.

"That's the talk!" he exclaimed, seizing it. "And now a kiss, to bind the bargain, as the fellah says."

"I guess we c'n get along without that."

"No, we can't. It won't seem like an engagement without it."

"It ain't goin' to seem much like one, anyway," she answered, with a sudden realization of how far from her dreams of courtship this reality was.

"Say, now Julyie, that ain't fair; it ain't treatin' me right. You don't seem to understand that I *like* you, but I do."

Rob was carried quite out of himself by the time, the place, and the girl. He had said a very moving thing.

The tears sprang involuntarily to the girl's eyes. "Do you mean it? If y' do, you may."

She was trembling with emotion for the first time. The sincerity of the man's voice had gone deep.

He put his arm around her almost timidly, and kissed her on the cheek, a great love for her springing up in his heart. "That settles it," he said. "Don't cry, Julyie. You'll never be sorry for it. Don't cry. It kind o' hurts me to see it."

He didn't understand her feelings. He was only aware that she was crying, and tried in a bungling way to soothe her. But now that she had given way, she sat down in the grass and wept bitterly.

"*Yulyie!*" yelled the old Norwegian, like a distant foghorn.

The girl sprang up; the habit of obedience was strong.

"No; you set right here, and I'll go round," he said. "*Otto!*"

The boy came scrambling out of the wood, half dressed. Rob tossed him upon the horse, snatched Julie's sun-bonnet, put his own hat on her head, and moved off down the corn-rows, leaving the girl smiling through her tears as he whistled and chirped to the horse. Farmer Peterson, seeing the familiar sun-bonnet above the corn-rows, went back to his work, with a sentence of Norwegian trailing after him like the tail of a kite—something about lazy girls who didn't earn the crust of their bread, etc.

Rob was wild with delight. "Git up there, Jack! Hay, you old corncrib! Say, Otto, can you keep your mouth shet if it puts money in your pocket?"

"Jest try me 'n' see," said the keen-eyed little scamp.

"Well, you keep quiet about my bein' here this afternoon, and I'll put a dollar on y'r tongue—hay?—what?—understand?"

"Show me y'r dollar," said the boy, turning about and showing his tongue.

"All right. Begin to practise now by not talkin' to me."

Rob went over the whole situation on his way back, and when he got in sight of the girl his plan was made. She stood waiting for him with a new look on her face. Her sullenness had given way to a peculiar eagerness and anxiety to believe in him. She was

130

already living that free life in a far-off, wonderful country. No more would her stern father and sullen mother force her to tasks which she hated. She'd be a member of a new firm. She'd work, of course, but it would be because she wanted to, and not because she was forced to. The independence and the love promised grew more and more attractive. She laughed back with a softer light in her eyes, when she saw the smiling face of Rob looking at her from her sun-bonnet.

"Now you mustn't do any more o' this," he said. "You go back to the house an' tell y'r mother you're too lame to plough any more to-day, and it's gettin' late, anyhow. To-night!" he whispered quickly. "Eleven! Here!"

The girl's heart leaped with fear. "I'm afraid."

"Not of *me*, are yeh?"

"No, I'm not afraid of you, Rob."

"I'm glad o' that. I—I want you—to *like* me, Julyie; won't you?"

"I'll try," she answered, with a smile.

"To-night, then," he said, as she moved away.

"To-night. Good-by."

"Good-by."

He stood and watched her till her tall figure was lost among the drooping corn-leaves. There was a singular choking feeling in his throat. The girl's voice and face had brought up so many memories of parties and picnics and excursions on far-off holidays, and at the same time such suggestions of the future. He already felt that it was going to be an unconscionably long time before eleven o'clock.

He saw her go to the house, and then he turned and walked slowly up the dusty road. Out of the Mayweed the grasshoppers sprang, buzzing and snapping their dull red wings. Butterflies, yellow and white, fluttered around moist places in the ditch, and slender, striped water-snakes glided across the stagnant pools at sound of footsteps.

But the mind of the man was far away on his claim, building a new house, with a woman's advice and presence.

It was a windless night. The katydids and an occasional cricket were the only sounds Rob could hear as he stood beside his team and strained his ear to listen. At long intervals a little breeze ran through the corn like a swift serpent, bringing to his nostrils the sappy smell of the growing corn. The horses stamped uneasily as the mosquitoes settled on their shining limbs. The sky was full of stars, but there was no moon.

"What if she don't come?" he thought. "Or *can't* come? I can't stand that. I'll go to the old man an' say, 'Looky here—' Sh!"

He listened again. There was a rustling in the corn. It was not like the fitful movement of the wind; it was steady, slower, and approaching. It ceased. He whistled the wailing, sweet cry of the prairie-chicken. Then a figure came out into the road—a woman—Julia!

He took her in his arms as she came panting up to him.

"Rob!"

"Julyie!"

A few words, the dull tread of swift horses, the rising of a silent train of dust, and then the wind wandered in the growing corn. The dust fell, a dog barked down the road, and the katydids sang to the liquid contralto of the river in its shallows.

XI

OSCAR MICHEAUX

Born into a farm family in Kentucky in the early 1880's, Oscar Micheaux was descended from a slave in Texas. He left home at the age of seventeen, and after a series of odd jobs here and there he became a Pullman porter and was able to travel into the West. He liked what he saw. When the Indian lands of the eastern part of the Rosebud Reservation were opened for sale in 1904, Micheaux was one of approximately 106,000 people who registered for a claim. He eventually settled in Gregory County.

The Conquest: The Story of a Negro Pioneer was published in 1913. It is an autobiographical novel, although Micheaux somewhat disguises it with place names that are usually identifiable in the Bonesteel-Gregory area. It is difficult to say exactly what Oscar Micheaux was: he was the grandson of a slave, he was a Pullman porter, he was a farmer, he was a writer of sorts, and later in life it was reported that, as a movie producer, he was living in New York, weighing over 300 pounds, and being driven to Chicago occasionally in a 16-cylinder car with a white chauffeur. Whatever else he was, Micheaux was a black pioneer in South Dakota who left a record of this part of his life. He died in 1951.

THE CONQUEST

It came a few days later in a restaurant in Council Bluffs, Iowa, when I heard the waiters, one white man and the other colored, saying, "I'm going to Oristown." "And where is Oristown?" I inquired, taking a stool and scrutinizing the bill of fare. "Oristown," the white man spoke up, drawing away at a pipe which gave him the appearance of being anything from a rover to a freight brakeman, "is about two hundred and fifty miles northwest of here in southern South Dakota, on the edge of the Little Crow Reservation, to be opened this summer." This is not the right name, but the name of an Indian chief living near where this is written.

Oristown is the present terminus of the C. & R. W. Ry. and he went on to tell me that the land in part was valuable, while some portions were no better than Western Nebraska. A part of the

Reservation was to be opened to settlement by lottery that summer and the registration was to take place in July. It was now April. "And the registration is to come off at Oristown?" I finished for him with a question. "Yes," he assented.

At Omaha the following day I chanced to meet two surveyors who had been sent out to the reservation from Washington, D. C. and who told me to write to the Department of the Interior for information regarding the opening, the lay of the land, quality of the soil, rainfall, etc. I did as they suggested and the pamphlets received stated that the land to be opened was a deep black loam, with clay subsoil, and the rainfall in this section averaged twenty-eight inches the last five years. I knew that Iowa had about thirty inches and most of the time was too wet, so concluded here at last was the place to go. This suited me better than any of the states or projects I had previously looked into, besides, I knew more about the mode of farming employed in that section of the country, it being somewhat similar to that in Southern Illinois.

On the morning of July fifth, at U. P. Transfer, Iowa, I took a train over the C. P. & St. L., which carried me to a certain town on the Missouri in South Dakota. I did not go to Oristown to register as I had intended but went to the town referred to, which had been designated as a registration point also. I was told by people who were "hitting" in the same direction and for the same purpose, that Oristown was crowded and lawless, with no place to sleep, and was overrun with tin-horn gamblers. It would be much better to go to the larger town on the Missouri, where better hotel accommodation and other conveniences could be had. So I bought a ticket to Johnstown, where I arrived late in the afternoon of the same day. There was a large crowd, which soon found its way to the main street, where numerous booths and offices were set up, with a notary in each to accept applications for the drawing. This consisted of taking oath that one was a citizen of the United States, twenty-one years of age or over. The head of a family, a widow, or any woman upon whom fell the support of a family, was also accepted. No person, however, owning over one hundred and sixty acres of land, or who had ever had a homestead before, could apply. The application was then enclosed in an envelope and directed to the Superintendent of the opening.

After all the applications had been taken, they were thoroughly mixed and shuffled together. Then a blindfolded child was directed to draw one from the pile, which became number one in the opening. The lucky person whose oath was contained in such envelope was given the choice of all the land thrown open for settlement. Then another envelope was drawn and that person was given the second choice, and so on until they were all drawn.

This system was an out and out lottery, but gave each and every applicant an equal chance to draw a claim, but guaranteed none. Years before, land openings were conducted in a different manner. The applicants were held back of a line until a signal was given and then a general rush was made for the locations and settlement rights on the land. This worked fairly well at first but there grew to be more applicants than land, and two or more persons often located on the same piece of land and this brought about expensive litigation and annoying disputes and sometimes even murder, over the settlement. This was finally abolished in favor of the lottery system, which was at least safer and more profitable to the railroads that were fortunate enough to have a line to one or more of the registration points.

At Johnstown, people from every part of the United States, of all ages and descriptions, gathered in crowded masses, the greater part of them being from Illinois, Iowa, Missouri, Minnesota, North Dakota, Kansas and Nebraska. When I started for the registration I was under the impression that only a few people would register, probably four or five thousand, and as there were twenty-four hundred homesteads I had no other thought than I would draw and later file on a quarter section. Imagine my consternation when at the end of the first day the registration numbered ten thousand. A colored farmer in Kansas had asked me to keep him posted in regard to the opening. He also thought of coming up and registering when he had completed his harvest. When the throngs of people began pouring in from the three railroads into Johnstown (and there were two other points of registration besides) I saw my chances of drawing a claim dwindling from one to two, to one to ten, fifteen and twenty and maybe more. After three days in Johnstown I wrote my friend and told him I believed there would be fully thirty thousand people apply for the twenty-four hundred claims. The fifth day I wrote there would be fifty thousand. After a week I wrote there would be seventy-five thousand register, that it was useless to expect to draw and I was leaving for Kansas to visit my parents. When the registration was over I read in a Kansas City paper that one hundred and seven thousand persons had registered, making the chance of drawing one to forty-four.

Received a card soon after from the Superintendent of the opening, which read that my number was 6504, and as the number of claims was approximately twenty-four hundred, my number was too high to be reached before the land should all be taken. I think it was the same day I lost fifty-five dollars out of my pocket. This, combined with my disappointment in not drawing a piece of land, gave me a grouch and I lit out for the Louisiana Purchase Exposition at St. Louis with the intention of again getting into the P——n service for a time.

Ofttimes porters who had been discharged went to another city, changed their names, furnished a different set of references and got back to work for the same company. Now if they happened to be on a car that took them into the district from which they were discharged, and before the same officials, who of course recognized them, they were promptly reported and again discharged. I pondered over the situation and came to the conclusion that I would not attempt such deception, but avoid being sent back to the Chicago Western District. I was at a greater disadvantage than Johnson, Smith, Jackson, or a number of other common names, by having the odd French name that had always to be spelled slowly to a conductor, or any one else who had occasion to know me. Out of curiosity I had once looked in a Chicago Directory. Of some two million names there were just two others with the same name. But on the other hand it was much easier to avoid the Chicago Western District, or at least Mr. Miltzow's office and by keeping my own name, assume that I had never been discharged, than it was to go into a half dozen other districts with a new name and avoid being recognized. Arriving at this decision, I approached the St. Louis office, presented my references which had been furnished by other M—pls business men, and was accepted. After I had been sent out with a porter, who had been running three months, to show me how to run a car, I was immediately put to work. I learned in two trips, according to the report my tutor handed to the chief clerk, and by chance fell into one of the best runs to New York on one of the limited trains during the fair. There was not much knocking down on this run, but the tips, including the salary were good for three hundred dollars per month. I ran this from September first to October fourth and saved three hundred dollars. I had not given up getting a Dakota Homestead, for while I was there during the summer I learned if I did not draw a number I could buy a relinquishment.

This relates to the purchasing of a relinquishment:

An entryman has the right at any time to relinquish back to the United States all his right, title, and interest to and in the land covered by his filing. This land is then open to entry.

A claimholder who has filed on a quarter of land will have plenty of opportunity to relinquish his claim, for a cash consideration, so that another party may get a filing on it. This is called buying or selling a relinquishment. The amount of the consideration varies with quality of the land, and the eagerness of the buyer or seller, as the case may be.

Relinquishments are the largest stock in trade of all the real estate dealers, in a new country. Besides, everybody from the bank president down to the humble dish washer in the hotel, or the chore boy in the livery, the ministers not omitted, would, with guarded secrecy, confide in you of some choice relinquishment that could be had at a very low figure compared with what it was really worth.

When I left St. Louis on the night of October fourth I headed for Oristown to buy someone's relinquishment. I had two thousand, five hundred dollars. From Omaha the journey was made on the C. & R. W.'s one train a day that during these times was loaded from end to end, with everybody discussing the Little Crow and the buying of relinquishments. I was the only negro on the train and an object of many inquiries as to where I was going. Some of those whom I told that I was going to buy a relinquishment seemingly regarded it as a joke, judging from the meaning glances cast at those nearest them.

An incident occurred when I arrived at Oristown which is yet considered a good joke on a real estate man then located there, by the name of Keeler, who was also the United States Commissioner. He could not only sell me a relinquishment, but could also take my filing. I had a talk with Keeler, but as he did not encourage me in my plan to make a purchase I went to another firm, a young lawyer and a fellow by the name of Slater, who ran a livery barn, around the corner. Watkins, the lawyer, impressed me as having more ambition than practical business qualities. However, Slater took the matter up and agreed to take me over the reservation and show me some good claims. If I bought, the drive was gratis, if not four dollars per day, and I accepted his proposition.

After we had driven a few miles he told me Keeler had said to him that he was a fool to waste his time hauling a d— nigger around over the reservation; that I didn't have any money and was just "stalling." I flushed angrily, and said "Show me what I want and I will produce the money. What I want is something near the west end of the county. You say the relinquishments are cheaper there and the soil is richer. I don't want big hills or rocks nor anything I can't farm, but I want a nice level or gently rolling quarter section of prairie near some town to be, that has prospects of getting the railroad when it is extended west from Oristown." By this time we had covered the three miles between Oristown and the reservation line, and had entered the newly opened section which stretched for thirty miles to the west. As we drove on I became attracted by the long grass, now dead, which was of a

137

brownish hue and as I gazed over the miles of it lying like a mighty carpet I could seem to feel the magnitude of the development and industry that would some day replace this state of wildness. To the Northeast the Missouri River wound its way, into which empties the Whetstone Creek, the breaks of which resembled miniature mountains, falling abruptly, then rising to a point where the dark shale sides glistened in the sunlight. It was my longest drive in a buggy. We could go for three or four miles on a table-like plateau, then drop suddenly into small canyon-like ditches and rise abruptly to the other side. After driving about fifteen miles we came to the town, as they called it, but I would have said village of Hedrick—a collection of frame shacks with one or two houses, many roughly constructed sod buildings, the long brown grass hanging from between the sod, giving it a frizzled appearance. Here we listened to a few boosters and mountebanks whose rustic eloquence was no doubt intended to give the unwary the impression that they were on the site of the coming metropolis of the west. A county-seat battle was to be fought the next month and the few citizens of the sixty days declared they would wrest it from Fairview, the present county seat situated in the extreme east end of the county, if it cost them a million dollars, or one-half of all they were worth. They boasted of Hedrick's prospects, sweeping their arms around in eloquent gestures in alluding to the territory tributary to the town, as though half the universe were Hedrick territory.

Nine miles northwest, where the land was very sandy and full of pits, into which the buggy wheels dropped with a grinding sound, and where magnesia rock cropped out of the soil, was another budding town by the name of Kirk. The few prospective citizens of this burg were not so enthusiastic as those in Hedrick and when I asked one why they located the town in such a sandy country he opened up with a snort about some pinheaded engineer for the "guvment" who didn't know enough to jump straight up "a locating the town in such an all fired sandy place"; but he concluded with a compliment, that plenty of good water could be found at from fifteen to fifty feet.

This sandy land continued some three miles west and we often found springs along the streams. After ascending an unusually steep hill, we came upon a plateau where the grass, the soil, and the lay of the land, were entirely different from any we had as yet seen. I was struck by the beauty of the scenery and it seemed to charm and bring me out of the spirit of depression the sandy stretch brought upon me. Stretching for miles to the northwest and to the south, the land would rise in a gentle slope to a hog back, and as gently slope away to a draw, which drained to the south. Here the small streams emptied into a larger one, winding along like a snake's track, and thickly wooded with a growth of small hardwood timber. It was beautiful. From each side the land rose gently like huge wings, and spread away as far as the eye could reach. The driver brought me back to earth, after a mile of such fascinating observations, and pointing to the north, said: "There lays one of the claims." I was carried away by the first sight of it. The land appeared to slope from a point, or table, and to the north of that was a small draw, with water. We rode along the south side and on coming upon a slight raise, which he informed me was the highest part of the place, we found a square white stone set equally distant from four small holes, four or five feet apart. On one side of the stone was inscribed a row of letters which ran like this, SWC, SWQ, Sec. 29-97-72 W. 5th P. M., and on the other sides were some other letters similar to these. "What does all that mean?" I asked. He said the letters were initials describing the land and reading from the side next to the place we had come to see it, read: "The southwest corner of the southwest quarter of section twenty-nine, township ninety-seven, and range seventy-two, west of the fifth principal meridian."

When we got back to Oristown I concluded I wanted the place and dreamed of it at night. It had been drawn by a girl who lived with her parents across the Missouri. To see her, we had to drive to their home, and here a disagreement arose, which for a time threatened to·cause a split. I had been so enthusiastic over the place, that Slater figured on a handsome commission, but I had been making inquiries in Oristown, and found I could buy relinquishments much cheaper than I had anticipated. I had expected the price to be about one thousand, eight hundred dollars and came prepared to pay that much, but was advised to pay not over five hundred dollars for land as far west as the town of Megory, which was only four miles northwest of the place I was now dickering to buy. We had agreed to give the girl three hundred and seventy-five dollars, and I had partly agreed to give Slater two hundred dollars commission. However, I decided this was too much, and told him I would give him only seventy-five dollars. He was in for going right back to Oristown and calling the deal off, but when he figured up that two and a half day's driving would amount to only ten dollars, he offered to take one hundred dollars. But I was obstinate and held out for seventy-five dollars, finally giving him eighty dollars, and in due time became the proud owner of a Little Crow homestead.

All this time I had been writing to Jessie. I had written first while I was in Eaton, and she had answered in the same demure manner in which she had received me at our first meeting, and had continued answering the letters I had written from all parts of the continent, in much the same way. For a time I had quit writing, for I felt that she was really too young and not taking me seriously enough, but after a month, my sister wrote me, asking why I did not write to Jessie; that she asked about me every day. This inspired me with a new interest and I began writing again.

I wrote her in glowing terms all about my advent in Dakota, and as she was of a reserved disposition, I always asked her opinion as to whether she thought it a sensible move. I wanted to hear her say something more than: "I was at a cantata last evening and had a nice time," and so on. Furthermore, I was skeptical. I knew that a great many colored people considered farming a deprivation of all things essential to a good time. In fact, to have a good time, was the first thing to be considered, and everything else was secondary. Jessie, however, was not of this kind. She wrote me a letter that surprised me, stating, among other things, that she was seventeen and in her senior high school. That she thought I was grand and noble, as well as practical, and was sorry she couldn't find words to tell me all she felt, but that which satisfied me suited her also. I was delighted with her answer and wrote a cheerful letter in return, saying I would come to see her, Christmas.

* * * * *

After the presidential election of that year I went to South America with a special party, consisting mostly of New York capitalists and millionaires. We traveled through the southwest, crossing the Rio Grand at Eagle Pass, and on south by the way of Toreon, Zacatecas, Aguas Calientes, Guadalajara, Puebla, Tehauntepec and to the southwest coast, sailing from Salina Cruz down the Pacific to Valparaiso, Chile, going inland to Santiago, thence over the Trans-Andean railway across the Andes and onward to the western plateau of Argentina.

Arriving at the new city of Mendoza, we visited the ruins of the ancient city of the same name. Here, in the early part of the fifteenth century, on a Sunday morning, when a large part of the people were at church, an earthquake shook the city. When it passed, it left bitter ruin in its wake, the only part that stood intact being one wall of the church. Of a population of thirteen thousand, only sixteen hundred persons escaped alive. The city was rebuilt later, and at the time we were there it was a beautiful place of about twenty-five thousand population. At this place a report of bubonic plague, in Brazil, reached us. The party became frightened and beat it in post haste back to Valparaiso, setting sail immediately for Salina Cruz, and spent the time that was scheduled for

a tour of Argentina, in snoopin' around the land of the Monte-
zumas. This is the American center of Catholic Churches; the
home of many gaudy Spanish women and begging peons; where
the people, the laws, and the customs, are two hundred years
behind those of the United States. Still, I thought Mexico very
beautiful, as well as of historical interest.

One day we journeyed far into the highlands, where lay the
ancient Mexican city of Cuernavaca, the one time summer home
of America's only Emperor, Maximilian. From there we went to
Puebla, where we saw the old Cathedral which was begun in 1518,
and which at that time was said to be the second largest in the
world. We saw San Louis Potosi, and Monterey, and returned by
the way of Loredo, Texas. I became well enough acquainted with
the liberal millionaires and so useful in serving their families that
I made five hundred and seventy-five dollars on the trip, besides
bringing back so many gifts and curiosities of all kinds that I had
enough to divide up with a good many of my friends.

Flushed with prosperity and success in my undertakings since
leaving Southern Illinois less than three years before, I went to
M—boro to see my sister and to see whether Miss Rooks had
grown any. I was received as a personage of much importance
among the colored people of the town, who were about the same
kind that lived in M—pls; not very progressive, excepting with
their tongues when it came to curiosity and gossip. I arrived in
the evening too late to call on Miss Rooks and having become
quite anxious to see her again, the night dragged slowly away,
and I thought the conventional afternoon would never come again.
Her father, who was an important figure among the colored people, was a mail carrier and brought the mail to the house that
morning where I stopped. He looked me over searchingly, and I
tried to appear unaffected by his scrutinizing glances.

By and by two o'clock finally arrived, and with my sister I
went to make my first call in three years. I had grown quite tall
and rugged, and I was anxious to see how she looked. We were
received by her mother who said: "Jessie saw you coming and
will be out shortly." After a while she entered and how she had
changed. She, too, had grown much taller and was a little stooped
in the shoulders. She was neatly dressed and wore her hair done
up in a small knot, in keeping with the style of that time. She
came straight to me, extended her hand and seemed delighted
to see me after the years of separation.

After awhile her mother and my sister accommodatingly found
an excuse to go up town, and a few minutes later with her on the
settee beside me, I was telling of my big plans and the air castles
I was building on the great plains of the west. Finally, drawing

her hand into mine and finding that she offered no resistance, I put my arm around her waist, drew her close and declared I loved her. Then I caught myself and dared not go farther with so serious a subject when I recalled the wild, rough, and lonely place out on the plains that I had selected as a home, and finally asked that we defer anything further until the claim on the Little Crow should develop into something more like an Illinois home.

"O, we don't know what will happen before that time," she spoke for the first time, with a blush as I squeezed her hand.

"But nothing can happen," I defended, nonplused, "can there?"

"Well, no," she answered hesitatingly, leaning away.

"Then we will, won't we?" I urged.

"Well, yes," she answered, looking down and appearing a trifle doubtful. I admired her the more. Love is something I had longed for more than anything else, but my ambition to overcome the vagaries of my race by accomplishing something worthy of note, hadn't given me much time to seek love.

I went to my old occupation of the road for awhile and spent most of the winter on a run to Florida, where the tipping was as good as it had been on the run from St. Louis to New York. However, about a month before I quit I was assigned to a run to Boston. By this time I had seen nearly all the important cities in the United States and of them all none interested me so much as Boston.

What always appeared odd to me, however, was the fact that the passenger yards were right at the door of the fashionable Back Bay district of Huntington Avenue, near the Hotel Nottingham, not three blocks from where the intersection of Huntington Avenue and Boylton Street form an acute angle in which stands the Public Library, and in the opposite angle stands Trinity Church, so thickly purpled with aristocracy and the memory big with the tradition of Philip Brooks, the last of that group of mighty American pulpit orators, of whom I had read so much. A little farther on stands the Massachusetts Institute of Technology.

The mornings I spent wandering around the city, visiting Faneuil Hall, the old State House, Boston commons, Bunker Hill, and a thousand other reminders of the early heroism, rugged courage, and far seeing greatness of Boston's early citizens. Afternoons generally found me on Tremont or Washington Street attending a matinee or hearing music. There once I heard Caruso, Melba, and two or three other grand opera stars in the popular Rigeletto Quartette, and another time I witnessed "Siberia" and the gorgeous and blood-curdling reproduction of the Kishneff Massacre, with two hundred people on the stage. On my last trip to Boston I saw Chauncy Olcott in "Terrence the Coach Boy," a romance of old

Ireland with the scene laid in Valley Bay, which seemed to correspond to the Back Bay a few blocks away.

Dear old Boston, when will I see you again, was my thought as the train pulled out through the most fashionable part of America, so stately and so grand. Even now I recall the last trip with a sigh. If the Little Crow, with Oristown as its gateway, was a land of hope; through Massachusetts; Worcester, with the Polytechnic Institute arising in the back ground; Springfield, and Smith School for girls, Pittsfield, Brookfield, and on to Albany on the Hudson, is a memory never to be forgotten, which evolved in my mind many long years afterward, in my shack on the homestead.

* * * * *

I left St. Louis about April first with about three thousand dollars in the bank and started again for Oristown, this time to stay. I had just paid Jessie a visit and I felt a little lonely. With the grim reality of the situation facing me, I now began to steel my nerves for a lot of new experience which soon came thick and fast.

Slater met the train at Oristown, and as soon as he spied me he informed me that I was a lucky man. That a town had been started adjoining my land and was being promoted by his brother and the sons of a former Iowa Governor, and gave every promise of making a good town, also, if I cared to sell, he had a buyer who was willing to pay me a neat advance over what I had paid. However, I had no idea of parting with the land, but I was delighted over the news, and the next morning found me among Dad Durpee's through stage coach passengers, for Calias, the new town joining my homestead, via Hedrick and Kirk. As we passed through Hedrick I noticed that several frame shacks had been put up and some better buildings were under way. The ground had been frozen for five months, so sod-house building had been temporarily abandoned.

It was a long ride, but I was beside myself with enthusiasm. Calias finally loomed up, conspicuously perched on a hill, and could be seen long before the stage arrived, and was the scene of much activity. It had been reported that a colored man had a claim adjoining the town on the north, so when I stepped from the stage before the postoffice, the many knowing glances informed me that I was being looked for. A fellow who had a claim near and whom I met in Oristown, introduced me to the Postmaster whose name was Billinger, an individual with dry complexion and thin, light hair. Then to the president of the Townsite Company, second of three sons of the Iowa Governor.

My long experience with all classes of humanity had made me somewhat of a student of human nature, and I could see at a glance that here was a person of unusual agressiveness and a great capacity for doing things. As he looked at me his eyes seemed to bore clear through, and as he asked a few questions his searching look would make a person tell the truth whether he would or no. This was Ernest Nicholson, and in the following years he had much to do with the development of the Little Crow.

* * * * *

That evening at the hotel he asked me whether I wished to double my money by selling my relinquishment. "No," I answered, "but I tell you what I do want to do," I replied firmly. "I am not here to sell; I am here to make good or die trying; I am here to grow up with this country and prosper with the growth, if possible. I have a little coin back in old "Chi." (my money was still in the Chicago bank) "and when these people begin to commute and want to sell, I am ready to buy another place." I admired the fellow. He reminded me of "the richest man in the world" in "The Lion and the Mouse," Otis Skinner as Colonel Phillippi Bridau, an officer on the staff of Napoleon's Army in "The Honor of the Family," and other characters in plays that I greatly admired, where great courage, strength of character, and firm decision were displayed. He seemed to have a commanding way that one found himself feeling honored and willing to obey.

But getting back to the homestead. I looked over my claim and found it just as I had left it the fall before, excepting that a prairie fire during the winter had burned the grass. The next morning I returned to Oristown and announced my intentions of buying a team. The same day I drew a draft for five hundred dollars with which to start.

Now if there is anywhere an inexperienced man is sure to go wrong in starting up on a homestead, it is in buying horses. Most prospective homesteaders make the same mistake I did in buying horses, unless they are experienced. The inefficient man reasons thus: "Well, I will start off economically by buying a cheap team" —and he usually gets what he thought he wanted, "a cheap team."

If I had gone into the country and bought a team of young mares for say three hundred dollars, which would have been a very high price at that time, I would have them yet, and the increase would have kept me fairly well supplied with young horses, instead of scouting around town looking for something cheaper, in the "skate" line, as I did. I looked at so many teams around Oristown that all of them began to look alike. I am sure I must have looked at five hundred different horses, more in an effort to appear as a conservative buyer than to buy the best team. Finally I ran onto an "Oklahoma" grafter by the name of Nunemaker.

He was a deceiving and unscrupulous rascal, but nevertheless possessed a pleasing personality, which stood him in good in his schemes of deception, and we became quite chummy. He professed to know all about horses—no doubt he did, but he didn't put his knowledge at my disposal in the way I thought he should, being a friend, as he claimed. He finally persuaded me to buy a team of big plugs, one of which was so awkward he looked as though he would fall down if he tried to trot. The other was a powerful four-year-old gelding, that would have never been for sale around Oristown if it hadn't been that he had two feet badly wire cut. One was so very large that it must have been quite burdensome for the horse to pick it up, swing it forward and put it down, as I look back and see him now in my mind.

When I was paying the man for them I wondered why Nunemaker led him into the private office of the bank, but I was not left long in doubt. When I crossed the street one of the men who had tried to sell me a team jumped me with: "Well, they got you, did they?" his voice mingled with sarcasm and a sneer.

"Got who?" I returned questionly.

"Does a man have to knock you down to take a hint?" he went on in a tone of disappointment and anger. "Don't you know that man Nunemaker is the biggest grafter in Oristown? I would have sold you that team of mine for twenty-five dollars less'n I offered 'em, if the gol-darn grafter hadn't of come to me'n said, 'give me twenty-five dollars and I will see that the coon buys the team.' I would have knocked him down with a club if I'd had one, the low life bum." He finished with a snort and off he went.

"Stung, by cracky," was all I could say, and feeling rather blue I went to the barn where the team was, stroked them and hoped for the best.

I then bought lumber to build a small house and barn, an old wagon for twenty dollars, one wheel of which the blacksmith had forgotten to grease, worked hard all day getting loaded, and wearied, sick and discouraged, I started at five o'clock P.M. to drive the thirty miles to Calias. When I was out two miles the big old horse was wobbling along like a broken-legged cow, hobbling, stumbling, and making such a burdensome job of walking, that I felt like doing something desperate. When I looked back the wheel that had not been greased was smoking like a hot box on the Twentieth Century Limited.

The sun was nearly down and a cold east wind was whooping it up at about sixty miles an hour, chilling me to the marrow. The fact that I was a stranger in a strange land, inhabited wholly by people not my own race, did not tend to cheer my gloomy spirits. I decided it might be all right in July but never in April. I pulled my wagon to the side of the road, got down and unhitched and jumped on the young horse, and such a commotion as he did make. I am quite sure he would have bucked me off, had it not for his big foot being so heavy, he couldn't raise it quick enough to leap. Evidently he had never been ridden. When I got back to Oristown and put the team in the barn and warmed up, I resolved to do one thing and do it that night. I would sell the old horse, and I did, for twenty-two-fifty. I considered myself lucky, too. I had paid one hundred and ninety dollars for the team and harness the day before.

I sat down and wrote Jessie a long letter, telling her of my troubles and that I was awfully, awfully, lonesome. There was only one other colored person in the town, a barber who was married to a white woman, and I didn't like him.

The next day I hired a horse, started early and arrived at Calias in good time. At Hedrick I hired a sod mason, who was also a carpenter, at three dollars a day and we soon put up a frame barn large enough for three horses; a sod house sixteen by fourteen with a hip roof made of two by fours for rafters, and plain boards with tar paper and sod with the grass turned downward and laid side by side, the cracks being filled with sand. The house had two small windows and one door, that was a little short on account of my getting tired carrying sod. I ordered the "contractor" to put the roof on as soon as I felt it was high enough to be comfortable inside.

The fifth day I moved in. There was no floor, but the thick, short buffalo grass made a neat carpet. In one corner I put the bed, while in another I set the table, the one next the door I placed the stove, a little two-hole burner gasoline, and in the other corner I made a bin for the horses grain.

* * * * *

It must have been about the twentieth of April when I finished building. I started to "batch" and prepared to break out my claim. Having only one horse, it became necessary to buy another team. I decided to buy mules this time. I remembered that back on our farm in southern Illinois, mules were thought to be capable of doing more work than horses and eat less grain. So when some boys living west of me came one Sunday afternoon, and said they could sell me a team of mules, I agreed to go and see them the next day. I thought I was getting wise. As proof of such wisdom I determined to view the mules in the field. I followed them around the field a few times and although they were not fine looking, they seemed to work very well. Another great advantage was, they were cheap, only one hundred and thirty-five dollars for the team and a fourteen-inch-rod breaking plow. This looked to me like a bargain. I wrote him a check and took the mules home with me. Jack and Jenny were their names, and I hadn't owned Jack two days before I began to hate him. He was lazy, and when he went down hill, instead of holding his head up and stepping his front feet out, he would lower the beam and perform a sort of crowhop. It was too exasperating for words and I used to strike him viciously for it, but that didn't seem to help matters any.

I shall not soon forget my first effort to break prairie. There are different kinds of plows made for breaking the sod. Some kind that are good for one kind of soil cannot be used in another. In the gummy soils of the Dakotas, a long slant cut is the best. In fact, about the only kind that can be used successfully, while in the more sandy lands found in parts of Kansas and Nebraska, a kind is used which is called the square cut. The share being almost at right angles with the beam instead of slanting back from point to heel. Now in sandy soils this pulls much easier for the grit scours off any roots, grass, or whatever else would hang over the share. To attempt to use this kind in wet, sticky land, such as was on my claim, would find the soil adhering to the plow share, causing it to drag, gather roots and grass, until it is impossible to keep the plow in the ground. When it is dry, this kind of plow can be used with success in the gummy land; but it was not dry when I invaded my homestead soil with my big horse, Jenny and Jack, that first day of May, but very wet indeed.

To make matters worse, Doc, the big horse, believed in "speeding." Jenny was fair but Jack, on the landside, was affected with "hook-worm hustle," and believed in taking his time. I tried to help him along with a yell that grew louder as I hopped, skipped, and jumped across the prairie, and that plow began hitting and missing, mostly missing. It would gouge into the soil up to the beam, and the big horse would get down and make a mighty pull, while old Jack would swing back like the heavy end of a ball bat when a player draws to strike, and out would come the plow with a skip, skip, skip; the big horse nearly trotting and dragging the two little mules, that looked like two goats beside an elephant. Well, I sat down and gave up to a fit of the blues; for it looked bad, mighty bad for me.

I had left St. Louis with two hundred dollars in cash, and had drawn a draft for five hundred dollars more on the Chicago bank, where my money was on deposit, and what did I have for it? One big horse, tall as a giraffe; two little mules, one of which was a torment to me; a sod house; an old wagon. As I faced the situation there seemed nothing to do but to fight it out, and I turned wearily to another attempt, this time with more success. Before I had started breaking I had invited criticism. Now I was getting it on all sides. I was the only colored homesteader on the reservation, and as an agriculturist it began to look mighty bad for the colored race on the Little Crow.

Finally, with the assistance of dry weather, I got the plow so I could go two or three rods without stopping, throw it out of the ground and clear the share of roots and grass. Sometimes I managed to go farther, but never over forty rods, the entire summer.

I took another course in horse trading or mule trading, which almost came to be my undoing. I determined to get rid of Jack. I decided that I would not be aggravated with his laziness and crow-hopping any longer than it took me to find a trade. So on Sunday, about two weeks after I bought the team, a horse trader pulled into Calias, drew his prairie schooner to a level spot, hobbled his horses—mostly old plugs of diverse descriptions, and made preparation to stay awhile. He had only one animal, according to my horse-sense (?), that was any good, and that was a mule that he kept blanketed. His camp was so situated that I could watch the mule, from my east window, and the more I looked at the mule, the better he looked to me. It was Wednesday noon the following week and old Jack had become almost unbearable. My continuing to watch a good mule do nothing, while I continued to fret my life away trying to be patient with a lazy brute, only added to my restlessness and eagerness to trade. At noon I entered the barn and told old Jack I would get rid of him. I would swap him to that horse trader for his good mule as soon as I watered him. He was looking pretty thin and I thought it would be to my advantage to fill him up.

During the three days the trader camped near my house he never approached me with an offer to sell or trade, and it was with many misgivings that I called out in a loud, breezy voice and David Harum manner; "Hello, Governor, how will you trade mules?" "How'll I trade mules? did you say how'll I trade mules? Huh, do you suppose I want your old mule? drawing up one side of his face and twisting his big red nose until he resembled a German clown."

"O, my mule's fair," I defended weakly.

"Nothing but an old dead mule," he spit out grabbing old Jack's tail and giving him a yank that all but pulled him over. "Look at him, look at him," he rattled away like an auctioneer.

"Go on, Mr. Colored Man, you can't work me that way." He continued stepping around old Jack, making pretentions to hit him on the head. Jack may have been slow in the field, but he was swift in dodging, and he didn't look where he dodged either. I was standing at his side holding the reins, when the fellow made one of his wild motions, and Jack nearly knocked my head off as he dodged. "Naw sir, if I considered a trade, that is if I considered a trade at all, I would have to have a lot of boot" he said with an important air.

"How much?" I asked nervously.

"Well, sir," he spoke with slow decision; I would have to have twenty-five dollars."

"What!" I exclaimed, at which he seemed to weaken; but he didn't understand that my exclamation was of surprise that he only wanted twenty-five dollars, when I had expected to give him seventy-five dollars. I grasped the situation, however, and leaning forward, said hardly above a whisper, my heart was so near my throat: "I will give you twenty," as I pulled out my roll and held a twenty before his eyes, which he took as though afraid I would jerk it away; muttering something about it not being enough, and that he had ought to have had twenty-five. However, he got old Jack and the twenty, gathered his plugs and left town immediately. I felt rather proud of my new possession, but before I got through the field that afternoon I became suspicious. Although I looked my new mule over and over often during the afternoon while plowing, I could find nothing wrong. Still I had a chilly premonition, fostered, no doubt, by past experience, that something would show up soon, and in a few days it did show up. I learned afterward the trader had come thirty-five miles to trade me that mule.

The mule I had traded was only lazy, while the one I had received in the trade was not only lazy, but "ornery" and full of tricks that she took a fiendish delight in exercising on me. One of her favorites was to watch me out of her left eye, shirking the while, and crowding the furrow at the same time, which would pull the plow out of the ground. I tried to coax and cajole her into doing a decent's mule's work, but it availed me nothing. I bore up under the aggravation with patience and fortitude, then determined to subdue the mule or become subdued myself. I would lunge forward with my whip, and away she would rush out from under it, brush the other horse and mule out of their places and throw things into general confusion. Then as soon as I was straightened out, she would be back at her old tricks, and I am almost positive that she used to wink at me impudently from her vantage point. Added to this, the coloring matter with which the trader doped her head, faded, and she turned grey headed in two weeks, leaving me with a mule of uncertain and doubtful age, instead of one seven going on eight as the trader represented her to be.

I soon had the enviable reputation of being a horse trader. Whenever anybody with horses to trade came to town, they were advised to go over to the sod house north of town and see the colored man. He was fond of trading horses, yes, he fairly doted on it. Nevertheless with all my poor "horsejudgment" I continued to turn the sod over day after day and completed ten or twelve acres each week.

XII

IKE BLASINGAME

Born in Texas in 1884, Ike Blasingame was in the ranching business all of his working life. He grew up on a ranch. When his father died in 1898, Ike went to work for the noted Texas cattle companies, the XIT, the LX, and the Matador. It was with the Matador Land and Cattle Company that he came north to the Cheyenne River Indian Reservation in 1904. As part of his job on this large leased range, he "repped" with the surrounding outfits—the Sword and Dagger, the L7, and Turkey Tracks. The company sent him to Canada for three years, and after the South Dakota lease was closed out he started his own ranch on the Little Moreau River, married Clara Condon in Timber Lake, and raised three children. In 1934, during the drouth, he moved to Wyoming and later to California where he managed ranches until 1960. He died in 1962.

"Storm and Stampede" is a chapter from his book, *Dakota Cowboy*, published in 1958. The action in this episode takes place in 1905.

STORM AND STAMPEDE

All spring the weather had been mild. Plentiful rain and sunshine brought grass up by leaps and bounds, so the Matador began working through their pastures early. Since I was to ride the broncs again, I took them and others of the rough string out to the wagon, for I was to help with this work.

We started clearing the Strip of stock that had wandered in there during winter. April drifted into May and animals had shed their winter hair. All of the other big outfits were moving herds or working their ranges, too. The H O had started from their ranch out near the Black Hills, to their reservation lease with a herd of over twelve hundred cattle. The H O men rode big horses, carrying a lot of Belgian blood, the only outfit to have these big horses. They were pretty tough to ride. With this drive, they were also bringing several hundred mares. One band was headed by a big eastern stud, the others by range studs. The Sword & Dagger, an outfit just to the south, straightening out their livestock also, were out with their wagon. There was nothing to indicate that anything other than summer was near at hand. Certainly, the cloudy, warm morning of May 5, 1905, was pleasant enough. But rain began falling before noon, the summery breeze became icy, and the rain changed rapidly to snow, blanketing everything—the makings of a blizzard growing by the hour!

Our Matador wagon was on the Trail near Tony Akers Corners. Con, sniffing the north wind like a longhorn steer, felt from this storm's approach that we could expect a bad time. So he ordered the wagons to move and camp down on the Moreau, in the timber between Pete Le Beau's and Landreaux' place, where there was plenty of wood for the cookstove. The tents kept us dry while the snow pelted us continually for two days and nights. It fell in huge flakes that at times so filled the air that objects ten feet away were not visible.

We turned the horses loose in the timber, except a few that we kept close to the tents, and they fared all right. While it got pretty cold, there was little wind in the timber and the horses stood bunched together a good deal of the time. Snow piled up on their backs like a blanket, but we didn't lose any horses at all. The ones we kept up were blanketed and saddled, which helped to keep them warm.

But other outfits, caught on higher ground where wind could hit them, lost many horses, especially those that had been stabled all winter in log barns and were slick as seals. The H O's held their big herd in the whipping gale for a while, but had to let them go. They drifted into the rough country along the Cheyenne. The band of mares with the big stud from an eastern farm all died, but some of the others, with native studs that kept them moving about, got through all right.

Art Bivins, a Sword & Dagger man, told me later how he had wrapped his pet cow horse, Papoose, in his best quilt to save him. Long years afterward, when Papoose was in his twenties, he became my children's cherished companion.

After this terrible storm, the sun came out again, the weather warmed up and the snow melted, revealing the frightful livestock tragedy. Range cattle and horses had died like flies in a heavy frost—some of them still standing up against a fence or a tree. Dead animals lay everywhere. One Indian owner, Herbert, who branded his horses with the figures 24 connected, lost twenty-four of them in one pile. It was the same all over—livestock died due to chilling from the sudden, extreme change in weather so late in spring. The May 1905 snowstorm remains historically the worst killer of range animals, and doubtless was the worst spring storm ever known on the reservation.

For a while, the weather held nice, and we went back to work.

Then, with June, came the heaviest rains I can remember. Lightning and thunder were frightful. Once, during a week's downpour, the soppy ground was totally unable to absorb any more water and we had to dip deep holes to drain water away from the cook's tent. We were camped on Bear Neckless Creek, northeast of where La Plant is now. Virgin Creek, to the west, was flooded out of banks. We couldn't work, nor even move camp to higher ground, because of the deep, sticky gumbo mud. The wagons simply couldn't be pulled through the heavy underfoot for the gumbo would roll up on the wheels until they became so wide and packed they couldn't turn. Had we undertaken a move, we would have mired down completely, and so would the teams. Fifteen years later, where the saddle horses bogged nearly to their knees when penned and circling the rope corral was plainly marked by a different, darker green type of grass which came up where the gumbo top soil was stomped and churned under by their hoofs. This, to me, was a strange thing, suggesting that perhaps several feet down under the present soil of that region might be a far different sort of plant life which was somehow covered over in the long ago.

While we were forced to stay there, I saw my first Indian killed by lightning. Gray Bear lived on Virgin Creek, west of the crossing. One morning, while waiting for drier weather, we were sunning beds, pulling mud balls from horses' tails, braiding them, and tying them up out of reach of more mud. We saw a team of Indian ponies hitched to a squaw wagon inching through the gumbo, coming our way. It was the Gray Bear squaw with four or five youngsters, and in the back of the rig lay a large, tarp-covered form. She drove up to the roundup tent and stopped. Con stepped out to her rig and Mrs. Gray Bear told him that lightning had killed her husband when he went to the pasture to catch a horse. She and the kids had loaded him into the light wagon and waited for Virgin Creek to go down so she could cross over. Now she was taking him to the Agency, twenty-five miles distant, through all that mud, to bury him.

It was noon, and Con invited her to eat with us, which she did. We all helped the kids get plates and heap them with grub. The woman had been married to Charley Ducharm before Gray Bear and her hitched up. Charley was with our wagon then. Some of the kids were his and went right over to him. He helped them fill their plates but didn't speak to the squaw, and she took no notice of him.

Some of us took a quick look at Gray Bear under the tarp. He had been dead several days and was a rough-looking sight.

After the team had rested, Mrs. Gray Bear started out again. Con offered to send an escort with her and the corpse, but she refused. She said she would get there all right by herself, and she did.

Lightning was an ever-present danger to a cowboy. Working livestock in natural lightning country, we had many close calls. Among ourselves, we had a theory that hot, sweaty cattle or horses "drawed" electricity; that they were a likely target when the fire-devils in the clouds got to splitting the sky apart. Most any old cowboy can tell of the way a horse's mane and tail almost sparks just before a storm. The hairs stand out separately as if a little hurricane is blowing in from underneath. On nights when a black storm hovers overhead, soft phosphorus lights glow on the tips of a horse's ears, like little candles, moving as he twitches and turns them while watching everything out in the dark. On many bad nights, I've seen these same little balls of light on the tips of the cattle's horns, and the glow is considerable when many cattle are bunched. Such are cowboy's memories of the stormy nights, night-guarding a herd, and to claim that a man is without fear of lightning just isn't true.

Those were the nights that a herd was hard to hold, for they were fearful, too, and would run with the storm. Weather has stampeded many a herd, and not always from lightning and hail, either. Snow and a fierce gale with it has turned many a herd and sent them drifting in a lope with the wind. But lightning has the strongest grip on creatures of the outdoors, man or beast. A stampede has led many a cowboy to a near miss with death while riding to stop a running herd. But not all to the bad was lightning those times. By its dazzling flashes, a man could see mortal danger ahead, affording a split-second's time for his mount to leap aside or over it; or to stop in his tracks, to save his and his rider's life.

Lightning is full of strange tricks. It runs a crazy pattern that is as unpredictable as the streak it cuts across a dark cloud. I've seen it strike one horse, yet not harm the one beside him. I saw it kill a man and burn everything off of him except his shirt collar, tie, and boots—even his socks were burned.

Contrary to the old legend that lightning never strikes twice in the same place, I know that it will not only strike in the same spot more than once, but I've watched a bolt hit Coffee Buttes, saw it keep on bouncing, striking with fire flying as it went from ridge to ridge a half-dozen times before it grounded. And more than once on the same night.

Coffee Buttes is a series of high ridges that were in the Matador pasture near the Missouri. They were noted for fiendish lightning, and we rarely had a herd to hold there but what a hellish mean storm got set to give us the works. The worst lightning I ever saw in my life was near these buttes the night the herd was hit.

We had been working the beef pasture nearest the Missouri, gathering all of the two- and three-year-old winter-drifted stock out of that end to take them to the back pasture where everything not going to market that fall belonged.

We had worked the range to Coffee Buttes and had a herd of a thousand. That afternoon, away off to the northwest, we could see a storm brewing. Oscar Buford and I rode out to relieve the others on day herd. The storm by then looked cyclone-black, edged in ruffled hailstone-and-wind green. It was right over us by then, as I circled around the cattle and watched it. We couldn't bed the steers in the face of such weather coming up. They simply wouldn't lie down, but we had to try to hold them if at all possible.

The wagon was camped just over a little knoll not far from us.

I had gone around the herd and met the other guard a couple of times, and I was singing a little, if you could call such sounds singing. I had just pushed a few edgy steers closer to the others and rode on around the outside of others, when a bolt of chain lightning split the sky wide open! One blinding prong shot straight down and hit the herd where I had just passed only a few moments before. One hundred steers went to the ground, and the tail end of the strike flattened me and my night horse, Dick. Twenty steers lay in a heap that never moved again. The others stumbled to their feet, stunned and wobbly. I cannot recall having any feeling at all. I just didn't know what had happened. I was dazed and scrambling around on the ground the first I remember. Dick was doing the same, trying to stay near me, nickering pitifully.

Oscar saw everything that happened from the other side of the herd. He didn't wait for anything or even look back. Scared as ever a man could be, he swung his horse around and rode like hell to tell Con and the men that "Ike and half of the herd are dead!" Everyone in camp rode out to us and saw me trying to get on my horse, both of us still staggering from the shock, while the lightning doubled its violence. The herd was moving, too, gathering speed for a stampede. When the bolt had hit, the steers had bunched and milled for a time before the leaders led off. But the men from the wagon got there just in time to hold them, and Con had the whole herd moved a half-mile away from the dead steers, out onto a flat place for the night. He sent me to the wagon and to bed. Extra men stayed to help guard and the black tempest swept on over us with very little rain. After a night's sleep, I was all right again, but ever after, my best night horse, Dick, was spoiled. He went completely frantic in an electric storm, and could never again be used for night-guarding.

There couldn't help being many wild stampedes where thousands of half-tame cattle were handled on a semi-frontier where virgin soil had never known the plow; where the rocks, the streams, the butte landmarks with their tall Indian water signs on the highest point seemed to have existed always; where the wild life and the forage, down through the centuries, were changed only by the hand of Mother Nature. Her forces—sun, wind, rain, snow, blizzard, hail, drouth—all these had changed the land but little. Not yet had the destructive hand of white man torn asunder the ages-old region, in his quest to make it over into something he believed was better. And only time would tell the havoc he wrought.

Although there were stampedes of frightened cattle, they were not always the bloody, hair-raising affairs some "tellers" would have you believe, but wild enough to stir up plenty of excitement, and they were always dangerous.

Once, at Short White Man Dam, six miles out on the Strip from Evarts, we had a mixup that was a dandy. A half-dozen outfits, the L7's, H O, Turkey Track, the Sword & Dagger, Matador, the H A T's, and possibly other outfits, were all in to the rails receiving the spring shipment of thin stuff from the south. All of these cattle had to be taken to their ranges and turned loose, no matter where they were. The wagons were camped about a half-mile apart. Some of the shipments were short—that is, not all of the stock arrived at the same time, so it caused some outfits to delay until everything arrived. All of the outfits were anxious to leave just as soon as they could. These were the times when Evarts swarmed with cowboys, and many a hilarious night that wild little cow town knew. Every outfit had from eight to twelve men, and with time to spare they made things lively. Some of it was cheerful hell-raising; some of it wasn't, but actually the happier side predominated.

One day, the L7's received all their cattle and were ready to leave at daybreak. But for some reason that night, their herd broke away and overran half of the surrounding herds, some of them ready to start out, too, the next morning. The Sword & Dagger let their two thousand head go, under pressure. Some outfits held part of their stock out of the stampede, but more than six thousand were well scrambled in the night's run.

Next morning, the L7's sent out word that their men would round up everything, which they did, but of course, the other outfits sent men to help, too. When the cattle were thrown into a big roundup, ten or twelve men went to cutting cattle according to the brands they were representing. The big roundup was separated into quarters, and each one moved back far enough so that the men had room to work and to hold the cut from each quarter. I helped with the separating. We cut cattle to the center, cut them to the sides—just wherever the different brands belonged, while reps took them away as fast as they could. Twenty-five cowboys held the big roundup together as the brand men rode among the stock, separating them. Other cowboys held the different cuts from mixing again with the main roundup, no matter who they might belong to, and as night came on the guards were doubled. Eventually, all brands and herds were back again where they belonged.

This job was just over when an amusing incident touched off another stampede that was as wild as any, but didn't involve so many herds. It happened in daylight, which helped some, but it showed how little it takes to set off a stampede.

A man on a pinto horse came riding down a trail near one of these ringy, or edgy, and well-spooked herds still being detained, waiting for late trains. A big black dog trotted close to the horse's heels, minding his own business, excepting for an occasional side trip to sniff for a rabbit, and maybe to yelp a little. A young fellow, not much more than a kid, who was helping hold the herd saw them coming, feared that the pair might cause trouble when the cattle spotted them, since they were still cranky enough to run at a sudden puff of wind. So he rode around to the wagon to tell the boss what he saw in the distance. "Man coming over yonder," he said. "Got a dog a-follerin' his horse," he added helpfully.

The wagon boss was grouchy enough at best, and without considering what the kid said, he growled, "Mind your own business, kid!" The kid turned away and rode back to his place at the herd. Shortly thereafter, the steers saw the approaching pair. A bunch of them jumped, rattling their hocks; others caught the cue and inside of minutes the whole herd, heads up, tails curled over their backs, and horns cracking against others, stampeded completely out of control. They ran for two hours before they could be turned into a "mill"—or run in a circle and stopped.

But the granddad of all stampedes I ever took part in was on Bear Neckless Creek, with a Matador herd. There is usually some reason for cattle stampeding, but a lot of the time, no one knows but the cattle themselves why they take off. "Some instinct" men will tell you, but I don't know. Sometimes a man on guard causes it by doing a careless thing—lighting a cigarette, or getting down off his horse. At times, a hard cough will do the trick. It could be something in the wind, or a night horse nickering for a reason known only to himself. There are times when a herd will "break" in broad daylight, but it happens mostly at night. Cattle are slow animals, but they are fast enough when scared. A herd of a thousand can get to their feet as quickly as one can, hoofs rattling, running before they are half up—a mystery how they get the "flash" to go at the same instant. Herds have been known to "jump" but not run—that is, to get on their feet from the ground where they had been resting an instant before. There would be a heavy roll of sound and every steer would be standing, alerted and on his feet, ready to run, and if they did take off, every head would swing in the same direction at the same moment.

Most of us old cowmen have seen some lively stampedes in our time and we like to recall them, remembering that the cattle we handled back in those unforgettable days weren't slow to put up a fight if molested a little—yet we handled thousands of them with little trouble. A man had to know the nature of these wild critters.

The stampede on Bear Neckless, when the Matador herd split wide open, happened while we were taking cattle to the back pasture. Besides the Matador men, there were at least a dozen reps from other outfits, as well as Indian owners looking for their strays, so our horse *remuda* numbered at least 175 head. Each rep had from eight to ten head, and, of course, the Matador men had theirs.

In spite of muddy, rain weather, we were getting along pretty well with the roundup of that part of the range, and had a herd of about two thousand head when we reached Bear Neckless. The wagon camped for the night on a little knoll above the creek. As night came on, away off in the north, a whole skyful of bumpy clouds began to show up and move toward us. Each man with the wagon always kept a night horse. If he was gentle, he was staked out with a rope, but if he was bad about getting loose, he was tied to the bedwagon wheel. Most of them were saddled and ready for their owners to go on night guard when their turn came, or so they would have horses if anything happened in the night.

Among the reps was a young Indian named His Horse Is Fast. He lived on the Moreau, and that night he kept up a sort of a cream-colored horse. He had saddled him, and with the oncoming storm in mind, he had covered his saddle with his big yellow slicker, tying it down so it wouldn't come off. Somehow, during the night the horse got loose and wandered along the creek, probably grazing and looking for other horses. We were holding the steer herd just north of the wagon, and north of them the night hawk guarded the saddle horses. The loose horse had worked around north of the *remuda,* when just about midnight a helluva rainstorm hit us and the lightning flashed almost continuously. The stock in both herds were restless, all on their feet, heads

158

pointing south and backs humped to the storm coming in on them.

When lightning began tearing the sky apart in dead earnest right above us, with deafening thunder crashing right on its heels, the gelding belonging to His Horse Is Fast made a run for the other horses. In the zig-zag lightning, the night hawk saw him coming, and just as he reached the *remuda*, a terrific bolt of chain lightning and crashing thunder streaked over the entire Up-Above, plainly revealing the big white thing charging down on them, white "wings" (the sleeves of the slicker) flailing and flapping all about him as he tore in among them. The rising wind struck, too, just then, and he chose that instant to nicker just as loud as he could! Who knows what he told the others? Perhaps he screamed that the devil himself was riding his tail. Anyway, in a short split-second, the *remuda* whirled away in a wild run. They swept through the steers, who were ready for action, too, and they broke away also, and the whole works ran over and around camp, breaking loose nearly every night horse—and they ran, too.

A night guard is broken up into four shifts of two hours each, between eight p.m. and four a.m., and that night I was to go on the two o'clock guard. I wasn't asleep, but had rolled out my bed on the south side of the wagon. Not far from me was old Dick. He would stand staked with just a little pin shoved into the ground. We used little iron pins shaped like a corkscrew, with a handle on top. They were easily twisted into the ground. A swivel around the top allowed the rope to turn about it without tangling up.

By the lightning, I could see he was still there, and after the uproar had mostly passed by, I got on him and followed the stampede. We ran steers and horses the rest of the night, and daylight found us—Dick and me—about ten miles away, on Stove Creek. I had lost track of the steers, but had kept up with about seventy-five head of saddle horses. A dozen of them were saddled or dragging a rope around their necks. One was Con's old white night horse, Walker, and he had Con's saddle on his back.

Dick was nearly played out by the night's run. I turned him loose to travel with the bunch after I caught Walker, and started the others back toward camp. Men who had a saddle and horse were out looking for me, but most everyone was afoot until I got there with the horses. That was one stampede we never got together again. Some of the scared horses headed south and ran over the Turkey Track fence that night. Most of the reps were completely afoot, for their horses had headed for home as soon as it got daylight and they got their bearings. His Horse Is Fast had neither horses nor saddle. He lost all of them in the night's run. No one was hurt, but we sure had a stampede to remember.

And we had to begin all over getting the same region rounded up again.

About ten days later, we had a good-sized herd at Coffee Butte, and once more hit the same old bad night. I often wondered why Con continued to camp there when we so seldom escaped trouble. It certainly was a mean place to be when an electric storm moved in, but this time a rather comical incident occurred there.

As night came on, we had no sooner bedded the herd than a threatening storm began building up just as the first guard was going on. All of us were jumpy and wishing we were anywhere but there—especially me. But the worst scared one of all of us was a long-legged, big-mouthed fellow named Rufe. He came from Georgia, and "Suh, he was a much a-feared of the damnable lightning, Suh!"

Con was a quiet man, but he didn't like to be told his business. All of us hoped he would turn the herd loose in the face of what was about to hit us, but we kept our mouths shut and let him decide the matter. We knew that to start bellyaching was a good way to get to stand night guard on those cattle. But Rufe wouldn't shut up. He kept advising Con against "holding the herd," until we wanted to plant a fist in his mouth, for some of us who knew Con well could see faint signs that he might turn loose.

As Con rode by, we heard Rufe yell: "Con, you suttinly don't intind tryin' to hold this here herd an' that helluva storm 'bout to pounce on us?" Con didn't answer, and all the more we wanted to choke the mouthy Rufe.

After Con rode around a while longer and everything got blacker by the minute, he said, "Just drift the herd up to the head of Stove Creek breaks," which wasn't far. "Turn them loose and everybody go to bed tonight. If the storm stampedes them they will hit the Turkey Track fence and we'll round up in the morning." That sure sounded good to all of us. The storm beat over us, but we were snug in our bedrolls and didn't give a damn. We could soon gather the herd again, come daylight.

Right after that, Frank Mitchell came out to the wagon and talked to Con. He had word that Matador steers were in Turkey Track range, so a rep had to go and work with them. Next morning, Con told me to take my horses and go to the "Tracks," the short-cut name we gave to the Turkey Tracks. Since I had several broncs extra, I was to give them to the cowboys I thought could ride them, leaving me with a regular ten-horse string. So I cut my horses from the *remuda,* packed my bed on Dick, saddled up, and started the rest of my mounts toward the Turkey Track range to the south.

XIII

OLE E. RÖLVAAG

Rölvaag was born on April 22, 1876, on the Island of Donna Helgeland, Norway, in a small fishing town. At fourteen he was told by his father that he was incapable of learning and was taken out of school and put to work on the fishing boats. But the little town had a good library and Ole read American and British novels and decided that he did not want to be a sailor all his life. He borrowed money from an American uncle farming near Elk Point and came to the United States in 1896. He began by working on his uncle's farm, but after he had saved some money he enrolled in school at Canton and then moved on to St. Olaf College in Minnesota. After he graduated, at the age of twenty-eight, he borrowed money again and returned to Norway for a year of graduate study. In 1906 he returned, to become a professor of Norwegian at St. Olaf. In 1908 he married and also became a naturalized citizen. He remained at St. Olaf College until his death in 1931.

Giants in the Earth, his first and best-known novel, was, like the other four, written in Norwegian (published 1927) and then translated into English. There is some argument as to whether these novels (or some of them) are more Norwegian than they are American. However that argument is resolved, the fact remains that *Giants in the Earth* is a classic novel of people coming from another land and trying to make a new life on the prairie. The selection here is taken from the beginning of the novel as the Norwegian immigrants first come onto the prairie.

TOWARD THE SUNSET

I

Bright, clear sky over a plain so wide that the rim of the heavens cut down on it around the entire horizon . . . Bright, clear sky, to-day, to-morrow, and for all time to come.

. . . And sun! And still more sun! It set the heavens afire every morning; it grew with the day to quivering golden light— then softened into all the shades of red and purple as evening fell. . . . Pure colour everywhere. A gust of wind, sweeping across the plain, threw into life waves of yellow and blue and green. Now and then a dead black wave would race over the scene . . . a cloud's gliding shadow . . . now and then. . . .

It was late afternoon. A small caravan was pushing its way through the tall grass. The track that it left behind was like the wake of a boat—except that instead of widening out astern it closed in again.

"Tish-ah!" said the grass. . . . "Tish-ah, tish-ah!" . . . Never had it said anything else—never would it say anything else. It bent resiliently under the trampling feet; it did not break, but it complained aloud every time—for nothing like this had ever happened to it before. . . . "Tish-ah, tish-ah!" it cried, and rose up in surprise to look at this rough, hard thing that had crushed it to the ground so rudely, and then moved on.

A stocky, broad-shouldered man walked at the head of the caravan. He seemed shorter than he really was, because of the tall grass around him and the broad-brimmed hat of coarse straw which he wore. A few steps behind him followed a boy of about nine years of age. The boy's blond hair was clearly marked against his brown, sunburnt neck; but the man's hair and neck were of exactly the same shade of brown. From the looks of these two, and still more from their gait, it was easy to guess that here walked father and son.

Behind them a team of oxen jogged along; the oxen were drawing a vehicle which once upon a time might have been a wagon, but which now, on account of its many and grave infirmities, ought long since to have been consigned to the scrap heap—exactly the place, in point of fact, where the man had picked it up. Over the wagon box long willow saplings had been bent, in the form of arches in a church chancel!—six of them in all. On these arches, and tied down to the body on each side, were spread first of all two handwoven blankets, that might well have adorned the walls of some manor house in the olden times; on top of the blankets were thrown two sheepskin robes, with the wool side down, which were used for bed-coverings at night. The rear of the wagon was stowed full of numberless articles, all the way up to the top. A large immigrant chest at the bottom of the pile, very long and high, devoured a big share of the space; around and above it were piled household utensils, tools, implements, and all their clothing.

Hitched to this wagon and trailing behind was another vehicle, homemade and very curious-looking, so solidly and quaintly constructed that it might easily have won a place in any museum. Indeed, it appeared strong enough to stand all the jolting from the Atlantic to the Pacific. . . . It, too, was a wagon, after a fashion; at least, it had been intended for such. The wheels were made from pieces of plank fitting roughly together; the box, considerably wider than that of the first wagon, was also loaded full of provisions and household gear, covered over with canvas and lashed down securely. Both wagons creaked and groaned loudly every time they bounced over a tussock or hove out of a hollow. . . . "Squeak, squeak!" said the one. . . . "Squeak, squeak!" answered the other. . . . The strident sound broke the silence of centuries.

A short distance behind the wagons followed a brindle cow. The caravan moved so slowly that she occasionally had time to stop and snatch a few mouthfuls, though there was never a chance for many at a time. But what little she got in this way she sorely needed. She had been jogging along all day, swinging and switching her tail, the rudder of the caravan. Soon it would be night, and then her part of the work would come—to furnish milk for the evening porridge, for all the company up ahead.

Across the front end of the box of the first wagon lay a rough piece of plank. On the right side of this plank sat a woman with a white kerchief over her head, driving the oxen. Against her thigh rested the blond head of a little girl, who was stretched out on the plank and sleeping sweetly. Now and then the hand of the mother moved across the child's face to chase away the mosquitoes, which had begun to gather as the sun lowered. On the left side of the plank, beyond the girl, sat a boy about seven years old—a well-grown lad, his skin deeply tanned, a certain clever, watchful gleam in his eyes. With hands folded over one knee, he looked straight ahead.

This was the caravan of Per Hansa, who with his family and all his earthly possessions was moving west from Fillmore County, Minnesota, to Dakota Territory. There he intended to take up land and build himself a home; he was going to do something remarkable out there, which should become known far and wide. No lack of opportunity in that country, he had been told! . . . Per Hansa himself strode ahead and laid out the course; the boy Ole, or *Olamand*, followed closely after, and explored it. Beret, the wife, drove the oxen and took care of little Anna Marie, pet-named *And-Ongen* (which means "The Duckling"), who was usually bubbling over with happiness. Hans Kristian, whose everyday name was *Store-Hans* (meaning "Big Hans," to distinguish him from his godfather, who was also named Hans, but who, of course, was three times his size), sat there on the wagon, and saw to it that everyone attended to business. . . . The cow Rosie trailed behind, swinging and switching her tail, following the caravan farther and farther yet into the endless vista of the plain.

"Tish-ah, tish-ah!" cried the grass. . . . "Tish-ah, tish-ah!" . . .

The caravan seemed a miserably frail and Lilliputian thing as it crept over the boundless prairie toward the sky line. Of road or trail there lay not a trace ahead; as soon as the grass had straightened up again behind, no one could have told the direction from which it had come or whither it was bound. The whole train—Per Hansa with his wife and children, the oxen, the wagons, the cow, and all—might just as well have dropped down out of the sky. Nor was it at all impossible to imagine that they were trying to get back there again; their course was always the same— straight toward the west, straight toward the sky line. . . .

Poverty-stricken, unspeakably forlorn, the caravan creaked along, advancing at a snail's pace, deeper and deeper into a bluish-green infinity—on and on, and always farther on. . . . It steered for Sunset Land! . . .

For more than three weeks now, and well into the fourth, this caravan had been crawling across the plain. . . . Early in the journey it had passed through Blue Earth; it had left Chain Lakes behind; and one fine day it had crept into Jackson, on the Des Moines River. But that seemed ages ago. . . . From Jackson, after a short lay-up, it had pushed on westward—always westward—to Worthington, then to Rock River. . . . A little west of Rock River, Per Hansa had lost the trail completely. Since then he had not been able to find it again; at this moment he literally did not know where he was, nor how to get to the place he had to reach. But Split Rock Creek must lie out there somewhere in the sun; if he could only find that landmark, he could pick his way still farther without much trouble. . . . Strange that he hadn't reached Split Rock Creek before this time! According to his directions, he should have been there two or three days ago; but he hadn't seen anything that even looked like the place. . . . Oh, my God! If something didn't turn up soon! . . . My God! . . .

The wagons creaked and groaned. Per Hansa's eyes wandered over the plain. His bearded face swung constantly from side to side as he examined every inch of ground from the northeast to the southwest. At times he gave his whole attention to that part of the plain lying between him and the western sky line; with head bent forward and eyes fixed and searching, he would sniff the air, like an animal trying to find the scent. Every now and then he glanced at an old silver watch which he carried in his left hand; but his gaze would quickly wander off again, to take up its fruitless search of the empty horizon.

It was now nearing six o'clock. Since three in the afternoon he had been certain of his course; at that time he had taken his bearings by means of his watch and the sun. . . . Out here one had to get one's cross-bearings from the very day itself—then trust to luck. . . .

For a long while the little company had been silent. Per Hansa turned halfway around, and without slackening his pace spoke to the boy walking behind.

"Go back and drive for a while now, Ola.* . . . You must talk to mother, too, so that it won't be so lonesome for her. And be sure to keep as sharp a lookout as you can."

"I'm not tired yet!" said the boy, loath to leave the van.

"Go back, anyway! Maybe you're not, but I can feel it beginning to tell on me. We'll have to start cooking the porridge pretty soon. . . . You go back, and hold her on the sun for a while longer."

"Do you think we'll catch up with them to-night, Dad?" The boy was still undecided.

"Good Lord, no! They've got too long a start on us. . . . Look sharp, now! If you happen to see anything suspicious, sing out!" . . . Per Hansa glanced again at his watch, turned forward, and strode steadily onward.

Ole said no more; he stepped out of the track and stood there waiting till the train came up. Then Store-Hans jumped down nimbly, while the other climbed up and took his seat.

"Have you seen anything?" the mother asked in an anxious voice.

"Why, no . . . not yet," answered the boy, evasively.

"I wonder if we shall ever see them again," she said, as if speaking to herself, and looked down at the ground. "This seems to be taking us to the end of the world . . . beyond the end of the world!"

Store-Hans, who was still walking beside the wagon, heard what she said and looked up at her. The buoyancy of childhood shone in his brown face. . . . Too bad that mother should be so scared! . . .

"Yes, Mother, but when we're both steering for the sun, we'll both land in the same place, won't we? . . . The sun is a sure guide, you know!"

These were the very words which he had heard his father use the night before; now he repeated them. To Store-Hans the truth of them seemed as clear as the sun itself; in the first place, because dad had said it, and then because it sounded so reasonable.

He hurried up alongside his father and laid his hand in his— he always felt safer thus.

The two walked on side by side. Now and then the boy stole

* In most dialects of Norway the name Ole becomes Ola when spoken.

a glance at the face beside him, which was as stern and fixed as the prairie on which they were walking. He was anxious to talk, but couldn't find anything to say that sounded grown-up enough; and so he kept quiet. At last, however, the silence grew too heavy for him to bear. He tried to say indifferently, just like his father:

"When I'm a man and have horses, I'm going to make a road over these plains, and . . . and put up some posts for people to follow. Don't you think that'll be a good idea?"

A slight chuckle came from the bearded face set toward the sun.

"Sure thing, Store-Hans—you'll manage that all right. . . . I might find time to help you an hour or two, now and then."

The boy knew by his father's voice that he was in a talkative mood. This made him so glad, that he forgot himself and did something that his mother always objected to; he began to whistle, and tried to take just as long strides as his father. But he could only make the grass say: "Swish-sh, swish-sh!"

On and on they went, farther out toward Sunset Land—farther into the deep glow of the evening.

The mother had taken little Anna up in her lap and was now leaning backward as much as she could; it gave such relief to her tired muscles. The caresses of the child and her lively chatter made her forget for a moment care and anxiety, and that vague sense of the unknown which bore in on them so strongly from all directions. . . . Ole sat there and drove like a full-grown man; by some means or other he managed to get more speed out of the oxen than the mother had done—she noticed this herself. His eyes were searching the prairie far and near.

Out on the sky line the huge plain now began to swell and rise, almost as if an abscess were forming under the skin of the earth. Although this elevation lay somewhat out of his course, Per Hansa swung over and held straight toward the highest part of it.

The afternoon breeze lulled, and finally dropped off altogether. The sun, whose golden lustre had faded imperceptibly into a reddish hue, shone now with a dull light, yet strong and clear; in a short while, deeper tones of violet began to creep across the red. The great ball grew enormous; it retreated farther and farther into the empty reaches of the western sky; then it sank suddenly. . . . The spell of evening quickly crowded in and laid hold of them all; the oxen wagged their ears; Rosie lifted her voice in a long moo, which died out slowly in the great stillness. At the moment when the sun closed his eye, the vastness of the plain seemed to rise up on every hand—and suddenly the landscape had grown desolate; something bleak and cold had come into the silence, filling it with terror. . . . Behind them, along the way they had come, the plain lay dark green and lifeless, under the gathering shadow of the dim, purple sky.

Ole sat motionless at his mother's side. The falling of evening had made such a deep impression on him that his throat felt dry; he wanted to express some of the emotions that overwhelmed him, but only choked when he tried.

"Did you ever see anything so beautiful!" he whispered at last, and gave a heavy sign. . . . Low down in the northwest, above the little hill, a few fleecy clouds hovered, betokening fair weather; now they were fringed with shining gold, which glowed with a mellow light. As if they had no weight, they floated lightly there. . . .

The mother drew herself forward to an upright position. She still held the child in her lap. Per Hansa and Store-Hans were walking in the dusk far up ahead. For the last two days Per had kept well in advance of the caravan all the time; she thought she knew the reason why.

"Per," she called out, wearily, "aren't we going to stop soon?"

"Pretty soon." . . . He did not slacken his pace.

She shifted the child over into the other arm and began to weep silently. Ole saw it, but pretended not to notice, though he had to swallow big lumps that were forcing themselves up in his throat; he kept his eyes resolutely fixed on the scene ahead.

"Dad," he shouted after a while, "I see a wood over there to the westward!"

"You do, do you? A great fellow you are! Store-Hans and I have seen that for a long time now."

"Whereabouts is it?" whispered Store-Hans, eagerly.

"It begins down there on the slope to the left, and then goes around on the other side," said his father. "Anyway, it doesn't seem to be much of a wood."

"D'you think they are there?"

"Not on your life! But we're keeping the right course, anyhow."

"Have the others been this way?"

"Of course they have—somewhere near, at any rate. There's supposed to be a creek around here, by the name of Split Rock Creek, or whatever they call it in English."

"Are there any people here, do you think?"

"People? Good Lord, no! There isn't a soul around these parts."

The sombre blue haze was now closing rapidly in on the caravan. One sensed the night near at hand; it breathed a chill as it came.

At last Per Hansa halted. "Well, I suppose we can't drive any farther to-day. We and the animals would both drop pretty soon." With these words he faced the oxen, held his arms straight out

167

like the horizontal beam of a cross, shouted a long-drawn "Whoa!"
—and then the creaking stopped for that day.

III

The preparations for the night were soon made; each had his
own task and was now well used to it. Store-Hans brought the
wood; it lay strapped under the hind wagon and consisted of small
logs and dry branches from the last thicket they had passed.

Ole got the fireplace ready. From the last wagon he brought
out two iron rods, cleft in one end; these he drove into the ground
and then went back to the wagon for a third rod, which he laid
across the other two. It was also his duty to see that there was
water enough in the keg, no matter where they happened to stop;
for the rest of it, he was on hand to help his mother.

The father tended to the cattle. First he lifted the yoke off
the oxen and turned them loose; then he milked Rosie and let her
go also. After that he made up a bed for the whole family under
the wagon.

While the mother waited for the pot to boil she set the table.
She spread a home-woven blanket on the ground, laid a spoon
for each one on it, placed a couple of bowls for the milk, and
fetched the dishes for the porridge. Meanwhile she had to keep
an eye on And-Ongen, who was toddling about in the grass near
by. The child stumbled, laughed, lay there a moment chattering
to herself, then got up, only to trip on her skirt and tumble headlong again. Her prattling laughter rang on the evening air. Now
and then the voice of the mother would mingle with it, warning
the child not to stray too far.

Store-Hans was the first to get through with his task; he stood
around awhile, but, finding nothing more to do, he strolled off
westward. He was itching to know how far it was to the hill out
there; it would be great fun to see what things looked like on the
other side! . . . Now he started off in that direction. Perhaps he
might come across the others? They surely must be somewhere.
Just think, if he could only find them! He would yell and rush
in on them like an Indian—and then they would be scared out
of their senses! . . . He had gone quite far before he paused to
look back. When he did so the sight sent a shiver over him; the
wagons had shrunk to two small specks, away off on the floor of
a huge, dusky room. . . . I'd better hurry at once, he thought;
mother will surely have the porridge ready by this time! His legs
had already adopted the idea of their own accord. But thoughts
of his mother and the porridge didn't quite bring him all the feeling of safety he needed; he hunted through his mind for a few

strains of a hymn, and sang them over and over in a high-pitched, breaking voice, until he had no more breath left to sing with. . . . He didn't feel entirely safe until the wagons had begun to assume their natural size once more.

The mother called to them that supper was ready. On the blanket stood two dishes of porridge—a large dish for the father and the two boys, a smaller one for the mother and And-Ongen. The evening milk was divided between two bowls, and set before them; Rosie, poor thing, was not giving much these days! The father said that he didn't care for milk this evening, either; it had a tangy taste, he thought; and he drank water with his porridge. But when Ole also began to complain of the tangy taste and asked for water, the father grew stern and ordered him to go ahead and get that drop of milk down as quick as he could! There was nothing else on the table but milk and porridge.

Suddenly Ole and Store-Hans flared up in a quarrel; one blamed the other for eating too close to the edge, where the porridge was coolest. The father paused in his meal, listening to them a moment, then chuckled to himself. Taking his spoon and cutting three lines through the crust of the porridge, he quickly settled the matter between them.

"There you are! Here, Store Hans, is your land; now take it and be satisfied. Ola, who is the biggest, gets another forty. . . . Shut up your mouths, now, and eat!" Per Hansa himself got the smallest share that evening.

Aside from this outbreak it was quiet at the table. A spell of silence lay upon them and they were not able to throw it off. . . . As soon as the father had eaten he licked his spoon carefully, wiped it off on his shirt sleeve, and threw it on the blanket. The boys did likewise as they finished; but And-Ongen wanted to tuck her spoon in her dress and keep it there till morning.

They sat around in the same silence after they were done. Then she who was the smallest of them repeated in a tiny voice:

"Thanks to Thee, Our Lord and Maker. . . .

"Now I want to go to sleep in your lap!" she said, after the Amen. She climbed up into her mother's lap and threw her arms around her neck.

"Oh, how quickly it grows dark out here!" the mother murmured.

Per Hansa gave a care-free shrug of his shoulders. "Well," he said, dryly, "the sooner the day's over, the sooner the next day comes!"

But now something seemed to be brewing back there over the prairie whence they had come. Up from the horizon swelled a supernatural light—a glow of pale yellow and transparent green, mingled with strange touches of red and gold. It spread upward as they watched; the colors deepened; the glow grew stronger, like the witching light of a fen fire.

All sat silently gazing. It was And-Ongen, hanging around her mother's neck, who first found her voice.

"Oh, look! . . . She is coming up again!"

In solemn grandeur the moon swung up above the plain. She had been with them many nights now; but each time she seemed as wonderful a sight as ever. To-night a hush fell on their spirits as they watched her rise—just as the scene had hushed them the evening before, far away to the eastward somewhere on the plain. The silvery beams grew stronger; the first pale fen fire began to shimmer and spread; slowly the light mellowed into a mist of green and yellow and blue. And-Ongen exclaimed that the moon was much bigger to-night; but it had seemed bigger the night before also. Store-Hans again solemnly told her the reason for it— that the moon had to grow, just as she did! This seemed to her quite logical; she turned to her mother and asked whether the moon had milk and porridge every evening, too.

Per Hansa had been sitting on the tongue of the wagon, smoking his pipe. Now he got up, knocked out the ashes carefully, put his pipe in his pocket, and wound up his watch. These duties done, he gave the order to turn in for the night.

A little while later they all lay under the quilts, gazing off into the opalescent glow. When the mother thought that the children had gone to sleep she asked, soberly:

"Do you suppose we'll ever find the others again?"

"Oh yes—I'm sure of it . . . if they haven't sunk through the ground!"

This was all Per Hansa said. He yawned once or twice, long and heavily, as if he were very sleepy, and turned away from her.

. . . And after that she said no more, either.

IV

Truth to tell, Per Hansa was not a bit sleepy. For a long while he lay wide awake, staring into the night. Although the evening had grown cool, sweat started out on his body from time to time, as thoughts which he could not banish persisted in his mind.

He had good reason to sweat, at all the things he was forced to lie there and remember. Nor was it only to-night that these heavy thoughts came to trouble him; it had been just the same all through the day, and last night, too, and the night before. And now, the moment he had lain down, they had seized upon him with renewed strength; he recalled keenly all the scruples and misgivings that had obsessed his wife before they had started out on this long journey—both those which had been spoken and those which had been left unsaid. The latter had been the worst; they had seemed to grow deeper and more tragic as he had kept prying into them in his clumsy way. . . . But she wasn't a bit stupid, that wife of his! As a matter of fact, she had more sense than most people. Indeed she had!

. . . No, it wasn't a pleasant situation for Per Hansa, by any means. He had not seen a happy moment, day or night, since the mishap had struck them on the second afternoon this side of Jackson. There the first wagon had got stuck in a mud hole; in pulling it out they had wrecked it so hopelessly that he had been forced to put back to Jackson for repairs. Under the circumstances, it had seemed to him utterly senseless to hold up all the rest of the company four days. He simply wouldn't listen to their waiting for him; for they had houses to build and fields to break, if they were to get anything into the ground this season. They must go on without him; he'd come along all right, in his own good time. . . . So they had given him full instructions about the course he was to follow and the halting places where he was to stop for the night; it had all seemed so simple to him at the time. Then they had started on together—Tönseten, who knew the way, and Hans Olsa, and the two Solum boys. They all had horses and strong new wagons. They travelled fast, those fellows! . . .

If he only had paid some attention to Hans Olsa, who for a long while had insisted on waiting for him. But he had overruled all their objections; it was entirely his own doing that Hans Olsa and the others had gone on, leaving him behind.

But he soon had learned that it wasn't so easy. Hadn't he lost his way altogether the other day, in the midst of a fog and drizzling rain? Until late in the afternoon that day he hadn't had the faintest idea what direction he was taking. It had been after this experience that he had formed the habit of keeping so far ahead of the caravan. He simply couldn't endure listening to her constant questions—questions which he found himself unable to answer. . . .

The only thing he felt sure of was that he wasn't on the right track; otherwise he would have come across the traces of their camps. It was getting to be a matter of life and death to him to find the trail—and find it soon. . . . A devil of a jaunt it would be to the Pacific Ocean—the wagon would never hold out *that* long! . . . Oh yes, he realized it all too well—a matter of life and death. There weren't many supplies left in the wagon. He had depended on his old comrade and Lofot-man, Hans Olsa, for everything.

Per Hansa heaved a deep sigh; it came out before he could stop it. . . . Huh!—it was an easy matter enough for Hans Olsa! He had ample means, and could start out on a big scale from the beginning; he had a wife in whose heart there wasn't a speck of fear! . . . The Lord only knew where they were now—whether they were east or west of him! And they had Tönseten, too, and his wife Kjersti, both of them used to America. Why, they could talk the language and everything. . . .

And then there were the Solum boys, who had actually been born in this country. . . . Indeed, east or west, it made no difference to them where they lay that night.

But here was he, the newcomer, who owned nothing and knew nothing, groping about with his dear ones in the endless wilderness! . . . Beret had taken such a dislike to this journey, too— although in many ways she was the more sensible of the two. . . . Well, he certainly had fixed up a nice mess for himself, and no mistake!

He wondered why he had ever left Fillmore County; as he lay there thinking it over, he couldn't understand what had prompted him to do such a thing. He could easily have found a job there and stayed until his wife got up from childbed; then he could have moved west next spring. This had been what she had wanted, though she had never said it in so many words.

The quilt had grown oppressively heavy; he threw it aside. . . . How long it took her to get to sleep to-night! Why wouldn't she try to get as much rest as possible? Surely she knew that it would be another day to-morrow? . . .

. . . Just so that confounded wagon didn't go to pieces again! . . .

V

The night wore on. The children slept quietly and peacefully. The mother also seemed to have found rest at last. Per Hansa thought that she was sound asleep; he began to move slowly away from her. He threw his hand over on the quilt between them as if making a motion in his sleep. . . . No, she didn't stir; he lay quiet for a while, then moved again. In so doing his hand happened to fall on that of Store-Hans; it was so chubby and round, that hand, so healthy and warm, and quite firm for the hand of only a child. Per Hansa lay still for a long time, holding the boy's hand with a desperate earnestness. . . . Slowly the troublesome thoughts seemed to lighten and lift; his courage ebbed back again; surely everything would come out all right in the end!

Little by little he slipped the quilt off, crept out of bed as quietly as a mouse, got into his trousers, and pulled on his shoes.

Outside, the misty sheen of the moonlight shimmered so brightly that it blinded him. Near at hand, the prairie was bathed in a flood of tarnished green; farther off the faint blue tones began to appear, merging gradually into the purple dimness that shrouded all the horizon.

Per Hansa looked for the North Star, found it, turned about until he had it over his right shoulder; then he glanced at his watch, took a few steps, hesitated, and looked back as if taking a bearing of the wagons and the star. The next moment he faced about resolutely, and hurried off westward.

It felt good to be moving again; he almost broke into a trot. There were the oxen, busily grazing; they needed to get their fill all right, poor devils! . . . Rosie lay closer to the wagons; his eyes had passed over her at first, a dark spot in the vague, deceptive light. The cow must have noticed the shadow gliding along so swiftly; she gave a long moo. . . . This enraged Per Hansa; he broke into a run and got out of her sight as quickly as he could, for fear she would moo again. . . . If she only hadn't waked Beret!

He set his course toward the point where he thought the crest of the ridge must lie. Now and then he stopped and looked around, to find out if he could still see the wagons. When he had lost them at last, and they were wholly swallowed up in the night, he gave an involuntary gasp—but clenched his teeth and went on.

The ridge lay farther off than he had thought. He had walked for a solid hour before he finally reached what he felt to be the highest point; he reckoned that he must be at least four miles from camp. . . . There he fell to examining the ground carefully; but first of all he looked at his watch again, and then at the North Star and the moon, trying to fix the bearings of the camp in his mind.

On the other side of the ridge the lay of the land seemed to be different; the slope was a little steeper; a thick underbrush covered it; through the tall bushes the moonlight shimmered strangely. . . . Per Hansa felt no fear, but every sense within him was alert. First he searched the northerly slope of the hill, beyond the edge of the thicket, stooping over as he went, his eyes scanning every foot of the ground. When he had found no trace of what he was looking for, he came back to the same starting point and searched an equal distance in the opposite direction; but he discovered nothing on this tack, either.

Now he began to walk along the edge of the thicket, in and out, crisscrossing the line in every direction; he pushed his way into each little grassless opening, and kicked over the earth there, before he went on. Sweat was running off him in streams. A quarter of an hour went by; he was still searching frantically. . . . All at once, right at the edge of the woods, he struck a piece of level ground with a larger clearing on it; in the middle of this clearing lay a wide, round patch in the grass. Per Hansa threw himself down on his knees, like a miser who has found a costly treasure; he bent over and sniffed the ground. His blood throbbed; his hands shook as he dug. . . . Yes, he was right—here there had been a fire! It couldn't have been many days ago, either; the smell of the ashes was still fresh. . . . His eyes had grown so moist and dim that he had to wipe them. . . . But he wasn't crying—no, not yet! . . .

He began to crawl around on all fours, farther and farther down the slope. Suddenly he stopped, sat up on his haunches, and held something in his hand that he was examining closely. . . .

"I'll be damned if it isn't fresh horse dung!" . . . His voice rang with a great joy. He tried the stuff between his fingers—crumbled it, sniffed at it . . . there was no doubting the fact any longer.

Now he got up, walking erectly with a confident step, like a man who has just made a lucky strike, and began to search along the whole slope. . . . He might as well go ahead and find the ford to-night; then he wouldn't be delayed by hunting for it in the morning. The underbrush thickened as he made his way down the slope. . . . Here, then, was Split Rock Creek; and here they had camped, as Tönseten had said they would! . . .

Once he had reached the edge of the creek, it did not take him long to find the ford that the others had used; the ruts still stood there plainly, as fresh and deep as if they had been made that very day. For a while he paused at the edge of the water, and looked about him. . . . Had they chosen the best crossing, after all? The bank of the creek on the other side formed a bend; the brink looked pretty steep. At last he waded out into the water, with his shoes still on. . . . Oh, well, the grade wasn't so steep that the oxen couldn't easily make it; there would be a bad jolt here at the edge, but after that they would have an even slope up the bank. . . . Stepping out on the opposite shore, he stood as if rooted to the ground.

. . . "What in the devil . . . !"

Per Hansa bent over and picked up the object that lay before him; he held it out in the moonlight, turned it over and over in his hands, smelled of it . . . then took a bite.

. . . "By God! if it isn't one of Hans Olsa's dried mutton legs!"

He straightened himself up and gazed with deep thankfulness into the quivering bluish-green haze that glowed all around him.

. . . "Yes, that's the way it goes, when people have more than they can take care of!" . . . He stuck the mutton leg under his arm; whistling a love ballad of Nordland, which seemed to have come into his mind unconsciously, he crossed the creek again.

On the way back he took his own time. Nothing mattered now; the night was fair and mild; his aching weariness was gone; he felt refreshed and strengthened. His wife and children were sleeping safe and sound; of food they still had supplies for a couple of weeks; and now he had found the trail again and could be certain of it all the way to Sioux Falls. . . . That wretched wagon was the only difficulty; it would have to hang together for a few days more! . . .

When he drew near enough to the wagons to make them out clearly in the moonlight, he slackened his pace, and a shiver passed over him.

Wasn't some one sitting there on the wagon tongue? Surely that was a human form?

In growing apprehension he hurried on.

"Good Heavens, Beret! What are you doing out here in the middle of the night?" His voice was full of alarm, yet softened by his great concern for her.

"It felt so awful to lie there alone, after you had gone. . . . I could hardly breathe . . . so I got up."

The words came with difficulty; he realized that her voice was hoarse with weeping; he had to pull himself sharply together in order to keep his own tears back.

"Were you awake, Beret? . . . You shouldn't lie awake that way in the night!" he said, reproachfully.

"How can I sleep? . . . You lie there tossing back and forth, and say nothing! . . . You might have told me. I know very well what's the matter!"

Suddenly she could stand it no longer. She ran over to him, flung her arms around his neck, and leaned close against him. The dam of her pent-up tears broke in a flood of emotion; she wept long and bitterly.

"Now calm yourself, dear. . . . You *must* calm yourself, Beret-girl!" . . . He had put his arm lovingly around her, but found it hard to speak. . . . "Don't you see that I've got one of Hans Olsa's dried mutton legs under my arm?" . . .

. . . That night Per Hansa was good to his wife.

XIV

WILL OTIS LILLIBRIDGE

Dr. Lillibridge was a native South Dakotan, born in Union County on December 18, 1877. He graduated from the College of Dentistry at the State University of Iowa in 1898 and set up a practice in Sioux Falls. In 1904 he married Edith Mary Keller. A year later his first novel was published; *Ben Blair,* with some similarities to Owen Wister's *The Virginian,* became a national best seller. Six more books were published between 1907 and 1911—the last two posthumously—a remarkable feat for a professional man who had to do his writing at night after a busy day.

Lillibridge paid the toll. He died of tuberculosis in 1909. Two years after his death a book of stories called *A Breath of Prairie* was published, and it is from this collection that the following long story (actually a novella) was taken.

ARCADIA IN AVERNUS

"For they have sown the wind, and they shall reap the whirlwind."

CHAPTER I — PRELUDE

Silence, the silence of double doors and of padded walls was upon the private room of the down-town office. Across the littered, ink-stained desk a man and a woman faced each other. Threads of gray lightened the hair of each. Faint lines, delicate as pencillings, marked the forehead of the woman and radiated from the angles of her eyes. A deep fissure unequally separated the brows of the man, and on his shaven face another furrow added firmness to the mouth. Their eyes met squarely, without a motion from faces imperturbable in middle age and knowledge of life.

The man broke silence slowly.

176

"You mean," he hesitated, "what that would seem to mean?"

"Why not?" A shade of resentment was in the answering voice.

"But you're a woman"—

"Well—"

"And married—"

The note of resentment became positive. "What difference does that make?"

"It ought to." The man spoke almost mechanically. "You took oath before man and higher than man—"

The woman interrupted him shortly.

"Another took oath with me and broke it." She leaned gracefully forward in the big chair until their eyes met. "I'm no longer bound."

"But I—"

"I love you!" she interjected.

The man's eyebrows lifted.

"Love?" he inflected.

"Yes, love. What is love but good friendship—and sex?"

The man was silent.

A strong white hand slid under the woman's chin and her elbow met the desk.

"I meant what you thought," she completed slowly.

"But I cannot—"

"Why?"

"It destroys all my ideas of things. Your promise to another—"

"I say he's broken his promise to me."

"But your being a woman—"

"Why do you expect more of me because I'm a woman? Haven't I feelings, rights, as well as you who are a man?" She waited until he looked up. "I ask you again, won't you come?"

The man arose and walked slowly back and forth across the narrow room. At length he stopped by her chair.

"I cannot."

In swift motion his companion stood up facing him.

"Don't you wish to?" she challenged.

The hand of the man dropped in outward motion of deprecation.

"The question is useless. I'm human."

"Why shouldn't we do what pleases us, then?" The voice was insistent. "What is life for if not for pleasure?"

"Would it be pleasure, though? Wouldn't the future hold for us more of pain than of pleasure?"

"No never." The words came with a slowness that meant finality. "Why need to-morrow or a year from now be different from to-day unless we make it so?"

177

"But it would change unconsciously. We'd think and hate ourselves."

"For what reason? Isn't it Nature that attracts us to each other and can Nature be wrong?"

"We can't always depend upon Nature," commented the man absently.

"That's an artificial argument, and you know it." A reprimand was in her voice. "If you can't depend upon Nature to tell you what is right, what other authority can you consult?"

"But Nature has been perverted," he evaded.

"Isn't it possible your judgment instead is at fault?"

"It can't be at fault, here." The voice was neutral as before. "Something tells us both it would be wrong—to do—as we want to do."

Once more they sat down facing each other, the desk between them as at first.

"Artificial convention, I tell you again." In motion graceful as nature the woman extended her hand, palm upward, on the polished desk top. "How could we be other than right? What do we mean by right, anyway? Is there any judge higher than our individual selves, and don't they tell us pleasure is the chief aim of life and as such must be right?"

The muscles at the angle of the man's jaw tightened involuntarily.

"But pleasure is not the chief end of life."

"What is, then?"

"Development—evolution."

"Evolution to what?" she insisted.

"That we cannot answer as yet. Future generations must and will give answer."

"It's for this then that you deny yourself?" A shade almost of contempt was in the questioning voice.

The taunt brought no change of expression to the man's face. "Yes."

The woman walked over to a bookcase, and, drawing out a volume, turned the pages absently. Without reading a word, she came back and looked the man squarely in the face.

"Will denying yourself help the world to evolve?"

"I think so."

"How?"

"My determination makes me a positive force. It is my Karma for good, that makes my child stronger to do things."

"But you have no child,"—swiftly.

Their eyes met again without faltering.

"I shall have—sometime."

178

Silence fell upon them.

"Where were you a century ago?" digressed the woman.

"I wasn't born."

"Where will your child be a hundred years from now?"

"Dead likewise, probably; but the force for good, the Karma of the life, will be passed on and remain in the world."

Unconsciously they both rose to their feet.

"Was man always on the earth?" she asked.

The question was answered almost before spoken.

"No."

"Will he always be here?"

"Science says 'no.'"

The woman came a step forward until they almost touched.

"What then becomes of your life of denial?" she challenged.

"You make it hard for me," said the man, simply.

"But am I not right?" She came toward him passionately. "I come near you, and you start." She laid her hand on his. "I touch you, and your eyes grow warm. Both our hearts beat more quickly. Look at the sunshine! It's brighter when we're so close together. What of life? It's soon gone—and then? What of convention that says 'no'? It's but a farce that gives the same thing we ask— at the price of a few words of mummery. Our strongest instincts of nature call for each other. Why shouldn't we obey them when we wish?" She hesitated, and her voice became tender. "We would be very happy together. Won't you come?"

The man broke away almost roughly.

"Don't you know," he demanded, "it's madness for us to be talking like this? We'll be taking it seriously, and then—"

The woman made a swift gesture of protest.

"Don't. Let's be honest—with each other, at least. I'm tired of pretending to be other than I am. Why did you say 'being true to my husband'? You know it's mockery. Is it being true to live with a man I hate because man's law demands it, rather than true to you whom Nature's law sanctions? Don't speak to me of society's right and wrong! I despise it. There is no other tribunal than Nature, and Nature says 'Come.'"

The man sat down slowly and dropped his head wearily into his hands.

"I say again, I cannot. I respect you too much. We're intoxicated now being together. In an hour, after we're separate—"

She broke in on him passionately.

"Do you think a woman says what I have said on the spur of the moment? Do you think I merely happened to see you to-day, merely happened to say what I've said? You know better. This has been coming for months. I fought it hard at first; with convention, with your idea of right and wrong. Now I laugh at them both. Life is life, and short, and beyond is darkness. Think what atoms we are; and we struggle so hard. Our life that seems to us so short—and so long! A thousand, perhaps ten thousand such, end to end, and we have the life of a world. And what is that? A cycle! A thing self-created, self-destructive: then of human life—nothingness. Oh, it's humorous! Our life, a ten thousandth part of that nothingness; and so full of tiny—great struggles and worries!" She was silent a moment, her throat trembling, a multitude of expressions shifting swiftly on her face.

"Do you believe in God?" she questioned suddenly.

"I hardly know. There must be—"

"Don't you suppose, then, He's laughing at us now?" She hesitated again and then went on, almost unconsciously. "I had a dream a few nights ago." The voice was low and very soft. "It seemed I was alone in a desert place, and partial darkness was about me. I was conscious only of listening and wondering, for out of the shadow came sounds of human suffering. I waited with my heart beating strangely. Gradually the voices grew louder, until I caught the meaning of occasional words and distinctly saw coming toward me the figure of a man and a woman bearing a great burden, a load so great that both together bent beneath the weight and sweat stood thick upon their brows. The edges of the burden were very sharp so that the hands of the man and the woman bled from the wounds and their shoulders were torn grievously where the load had shifted: those of the woman more than the man, for she bore more of the weight. I marvelled at the sight.

"Suddenly an intense brightness fell about me and I saw, near and afar, other figures each bearing similar burdens. The light passed away, and I drew near the man and questioned him.

" 'What rough load is that you carry?' I asked.

" 'The burden of conventionality,' answered the man, wearily and with a note of surprise in his voice.

" 'Why do you bear it needlessly?' I remonstrated.

" 'We dare not drop it,' said the woman, hopelessly, 'lest that light, which is the searchlight of public opinion, return, showing us different from the others.'

"Even as she spoke the illumination again fell upon us, and by its brightness I saw a drop of blood gather slowly from the wounds on the woman's hand and fall into the dust at her feet."

A silence fell upon the inmates of the tiny muffled office.

"But the burden isn't useless," said the man, gently. "The condemnation of society is an hourly reality. From the patronage of others we live. The sun burns us, but we submit, for in return it gives life."

The woman arose with an abrupt movement, and looked down at him coldly.

"Are you a man, and use those arguments?" An expression akin to contempt formed about her mouth. "Are you afraid of a united voice the individuals of which you despise?"

The first hint of restrained passion was in the answering voice.

"You taunt me in safety, for you know I love you." He looked up at her unhesitatingly. "Man's law is artificial, that I know; but it's made for conditions which are artificial, and for such it's right. Were we as in the beginning, Nature's law, which beside the law of man is no law, would be right; but we're of the world as it is now. Things are as they are, and we must conform or pay the price." He hesitated. His face settled back into a mask. "And that price of non-conformity is too high," he completed steadily.

The eyes of the woman blazed and her hands tightened convulsively.

"Oh, you're frozen—fossilized, man! I called you man! You're not a man at all, but a nineteenth century machine! You're run like a motor, from a power house; by the force of conventional thought, over wires of red tape. Fie on you! I thought to meet a human being, not a lifeless thing." She looked at him steadily, her chin in the air, a world of scorn in her face. "Go on sweating beneath the useless load! Go on building your structure of artificiality that ends centuries from now in nothingness! Here's happiness to you in your empty life of self-effacement, with your machine prompted acts, years considered!" Without looking at him, one hand made scornful motion of dismissal. "Good-bye, ghost of man; I wash my hands of you."

"Wait, Eleanor!" The man sprang to his feet, the mask lifting from his face, and there stood revealed a multitude of emotions, unseen of the world, that flashed from the depths of his brown eyes and quivered in the angles of his mouth. He came quickly over and took her hand between his own.

"I'm proud of you,"—a world of tenderness was in his voice— "unspeakably proud—for I love you. I've done my best to keep us apart, yet all the time I believed with you. Nature is higher than man, and no power on earth can prove it otherwise." He looked into the softest of brown eyes, and his voice trembled. "Beside you the world is nothing. Its approval or its condemnation are things to be laughed at. With you I challenge conventionality—society—everything." He bent over her hand almost reverently and touched it softly with his lips.

"Farewell—until I come," he said.

A man and a woman emerged from the dilapidated day-car
as it drew up before the tiny, sanded station which marked the
terminus of the railway. The man was tall, clean-shaven, quick
of step and of glance. The woman was likewise tall, well-gloved,
and, strange phenomenon at a country station, carried no parcels.

Though easily the centre of attention, the couple were far from
being alone. On the contrary, the car and platform fairly swarmed
with humanity. Men mostly composed the throng that alighted—
big, weather-stained fellows in rough jeans and denims. In the
background, as spectators moved or lounged a sprinkling of others:
thinner, lighter, enveloped in felt, woollen and buckskin, a fringe
of heavy hair peeping out at their backs beneath the broad hat-
brims. A few women were intermingled. Coarsely gowned, sun-
browned, they stood; themselves like suns, but each the centre
of a system of bleach-haired minor satellites. It was into this
heterogeneous mass that the tall man elbowed his way, a neat
grip in either hand; the woman following closely in his wake,
her skirts carefully lifted.

Clear of the out-flowing stream the man put down the satchels,
and looked over the heads of the motley crowd into the still more
motley street beyond. Two short rows of one-story buildings, distinctive by the brightness of new lumber on their sheltered side,
bordered a narrow street, half clogged by the teams of visiting
farmers. Not the faintest clue to a hostelry was visible, and the
eyes of the man wandered back, interrupting by the way another
pair of eyes frankly inquisitive.

The curious one was short; by comparison his face was still
shorter, and round. From his chin a tiny tuft of whiskers protruded, like the handle of a gourd. Never was countenance more
unmistakably labelled good-humored, Americanized German.

The eyes of the tall man stopped.

"Is there a hotel in this"—he groped for a classification—
"this city?" he asked.

A rattling sound, startlingly akin to the agitated contents of
over-ripe vegetables, came from somewhere in the internal mechanism of the small man. Inferentially, the inquiry was amusing
to the questioned, likewise the immediately surrounding listeners
who became suddenly silent, gazing at the stranger with the wonder
of young calves.

At length the innate spirit of courtesy in the German triumphed
over his amusement.

"Hans Becher up by the postoffice takes folks in." The inward
commotion showed indications of resumption. "I never heard,

though, that he called his place a hotel!"

"Thank you," and the circle of silence widened.

The man and the woman walked up the street. Beneath their feet the cottonwood sidewalk, despite its newness, was warped in agony under sun and storm. Big puddles of water from a recent rain stood in the hollows of the roadway, side by side with tufts of native grasses fighting bravely for life against the intruder— Man. A fresh, indescribable odor was in their nostrils; an odor which puzzled them then, but which later they learned to recognize and never forgot—the pungent scent of buffalo grass. A stillness, deeper than of Sabbath, unbelievable to urban ears, wrapped all things, and united with an absence of broken sky line, to produce an all-pervading sense of loneliness.

Hans Becher did not belie his name. He was very German. Likewise the little woman who courtesied at his side. Ditto the choice assortment of inquisitive tow-heads, who stared wide-eyed from various corners. He shook hands at the door with each of his guests,—which action also was unmistakably German.

"You would in my house—put up, you call it?" he inquired in labored English, while the little woman polished two speckless chairs with her apron, and with instinctive photographic art placed them stiffly side by side for the visitors.

"Yes, we'd like to stay with you for a time," corroborated the tall man.

The little German ran his fingers uncertainly through his hair for a moment; then his round face beamed.

"We should then become to each other known. Is it not so?" Without pausing for an answer, he put out a big hand to each in turn. "I am Hans Becher, and this—with elaborate indications— "this my wife is—Minna."

Minna courtsied dutifully, lower than before. The little Bechers were not classified, but their connection was apparent. They calmly sucked their thumbs.

The lords of creation obviously held the rostrum. It was the tall man who responded.

"My name is Maurice, Ichabod Maurice." He looked at the woman, his companion, from the corner of his eye. "Allow me, Camilla, to present Mr. Becher." Then turning to his hosts, "Camilla Maurice: Mr. and Mrs. Becher."

The tall lady shook hands with each.

"Pleased to meet you," she said, and smiled a moment into their eyes. Thus Camilla Maurice made friends.

There were a few low-spoken words in German and Minna vanished.

"She will dinner make ready," Hans explained.

The visitors sat down in their chairs, with Hans opposite studying them narrowly; singly and together.

"The town is very new," suggested Ichabod.

"One year ago it was not." The German's short legs crossed each other nervously and their owner seized the opportunity to make further inspection. "It is very new," he repeated absently.

Camilla Maurice stood up.

"Might we wash, Mr. Becher?" she asked.

The ultimate predicament was all at once staring the little man in the face.

"To be sure. . . . I might have known. . . . You will a room—desire." . . . He ran his fingers through his hair, and inspiration came. "Mr. Maurice," he motioned, "might I a moment with you—speak?"

"Certainly, Mr. Becher."

The German saw light, and fairly beamed as he sought the safe seclution of the doorway.

"She is your sister or cousin—*nein?*" he asked

There was the faintest suggestion of a smile in the corners of Ichabod's mouth.

"No, she is neither my sister nor my cousin, Mr. Becher."

Hans heaved a sigh of relief: it had been a close corner.

"She is your wife. One must know," and he mopped his brow.

"Certainly—one must know," very soberly.

Alone together in the little unfinished room under the rafters, the woman sat down on the corner of the bed, physical discomfort forgotten in feminine curiosity.

"Those names—where did you get them?" she queried.

"They came to me—at the moment," smiled the man.

"But the cold-blooded horror of them! . . . Ichabod!"

"The glory has departed."

His companion started, and the smile left the man's face.

"And Camilla?"—slowly.

"Attendant at a sacrifice."

Of a sudden the room became very still.

Ichabod, exploring, discovered a tiny wash basin and a bucket of water.

"You wished to wash, Camilla?"

The woman did not move.

"They were very kind"—she looked through the window with the tiny panes: "have we any right to—lie to them?"

"We have not lied."

"Tacitly."

"No. I'm Ichabod Maurice and you're Camilla Maurice. We have not lied."

"But—"

"The past is dead, dead!"

The woman's face dropped into her hands. Woman ever weeps instinctively for the dead.

"You are sorry that it is—so?" There was no bitterness in the man's voice, but he did not look at her, and Camilla misunderstood.

"Sorry!" She came close, and a soft warm face pressed tightly against his face. "Sorry!" Her arms were around him. "Sorry!" again repeated. "No! No! No! No, without end! I'm not sorry. I'm Camilla Maurice, the happiest woman in the world!"

Later they utilized the tin basin and the mirror with a crack across its centre. Dinner was waiting when they went below.

To a casual observer, Hans had been very idle while they were gone. He sat absently on the doorstep, watching the grass that grew almost visibly in the warm spring sun. Occasionally he tapped his forehead with his finger tips. It helped him to think, and just now he sadly needed assistance.

"Who were these people, anyway?" he wondered. Not farmers, certainly. Farmers did not have hands that dented when you pressed them, and farmers' wives did not lift their skirts daintily from behind. Hans had been very observant as his visitors came up the muddy street. No, that was not the way of farmers' wives: they took hold at the sides with both hands, and splashed right through on their heels.

Hans pulled the yellow tuft on his chin. What could they be, then? Not summer boarders. It was only early spring; and, besides, although the little German was an optimist, even he could not imagine any one selecting a Dakota prairie for an outing. Yet . . . No, they could not be summer boarders.

But what then? In his intensity Hans actually forgot the grass and, unfailing producer of inspiration, ran his fingers frantically through his mane.

"Ah—at last—of course!" The round face beamed and a hard hand smote a harder knee, joyously. That he had not remembered at once! It was the new banker, to be sure. He would tell Minna, quite as a matter of fact, for there could be no mistake. Hank Junge, the machine agent, and Eli Stevens, the proprietor of the corner store, had said only yesterday there was to be a bank. Looking up the street the little man spied a familiar figure, and sprang to his feet as though released by a spring, his hand already in the air. There was Hank Judge, now, and he didn't know—

"Dinner, Hans," announced Minna at his elbow.

Holding the child of his brain hard in both hands lest it should escape prematurely, the little German went inside to preside over a repast, the distinctively German incense of which ascended most appetizingly.

Hans, junior, in a childish treble, spoke an honest little German blessing, beginning *"Mein Vater von Himmel,"* and emphasized by the raps of Hans senior's knuckles on certain other small heads to keep their owners quiet.

"Fresh lettuce and radishes!" commented Camilla, joyously.

"Raised in our own garden *hinein,"* bobbed Minna, in ecstasy.

"And sauerkraut—" began Ichabod.

"From cabbages so large," completed Hans, spreading his arms to designate an imaginary vegetable of heroic proportions.

"They must have grown very fast to be so large in May," commented Camilla.

Hans and Minna exchanged glances—pitying, superior glances —such as we gave behind the backs of the infirm, or the very old; and the subject of vegetables dropped.

"A great country for a bank, this," commented Mr. Becher, with infinite *finesse* and between intermittent puffs at a hot potato.

"Is that so?"

Hans nodded violent confirmation, then words, English words, being valuable to him, he came quickly to the test.

"You will build for the bank yourself, is it not so?"

It was not the German and Minna who exchanged glances this time.

"No, I shall not build for the bank myself, Mr. Becher."

"You will rent, perhaps?" Hans's faith was beautiful.

"No, I shall not rent."

The German's face fell. To have wasted all that thought; for after all it was not the banker!

Minna, senior, stared in surprise, and her attention being diverted, Minna the younger seized the opportunity to inundate herself with a cup of hot coffee.

The spell was broken.

"I'm going to take a homestead," explained Ichabod.

Hans's fork paused in mid-air and his mouth forgot to close. At the point where the German struck, the earth was very hard.

"So?" he interrogated, weakly.

At this juncture the difference between the two Minnas, which had been transferred from the table to the kitchen, was resumed; and although Ichabod ate the remaining kraut to the last shred, and Camilla talked to Hans of the *Vaterland* in his native German, each knew the occasion was a failure. An ideal had been raised, the ideal of a Napoleon of finance, a banker; and that ideal materializing, lo there stood forth a farmer! *Ach Gott von Himmel!*

After dinner Hans stood in the doorway and pointed out the land-office. Ichabod thanked him, and under the impulse of habit felt in his pocket for a cigar. None was there, and all at once he remembered Ichabod Maurice did not smoke. Strange he should have such an abominable inclination to do so just then; but nevertheless the fact remained. Ichabod Maurice never had smoked.

He started up the street.

A small man, with very high boots and a very long moustache, sat tipped back in the sun in front of the land-office. He was telling a story; a good one, judging from the attention of the row of listeners. He grasped the chair tightly with his left hand while his right, holding a cob pipe, gesticulated actively. The story halted abruptly as Ichabod came up.

"Howdy!" greeted the little man.

Maurice nodded.

"Don't let me interrupt you," he temporized.

"Not at all," courtesied the teller of stories, as he led the way inside. "I've told that one until I'm tired of it, anyway." He tapped the ashes from his pipe-bowl, meditatively. "A fellow has to kill the time some way, though, you know."

"Yes, I know," acquiesced Ichabod.

The agent took a chair behind the battered pine desk, and pointed to another opposite.

"Any way I can help you?" he suggested.

"Yes," answered Maurice. "I'm thinking of taking a homestead."

The agent looked his visitor up and down and back again; then, being native born, his surprise broke forth in idiom.

"Well, I'm jiggered!" he avowed.

It was Ichabod's turn to make observation.

"I believe you; you look it," he corroborated at length.

Again the little man stared; and in the silence following, a hungry-looking bird-dog thrust his thin muzzle in at the door, and sniffed.

"Get out," shouted the owner at the intruder, adding in extenuation: "I'm busy." He certainly was "jiggered."

Ichabod came to the rescue.

"I called to learn how one goes at it to take a claim," he explained. "The *modus operandi* isn't exactly clear in my mind."

The agent braced up in his chair.

"I suppose you'll say it's none of my business," he commented, "but as a speculation you'd do a lot better to buy up the claims of poor cusses who have to relinquish, than to settle yourself."

"I'm not speculating. I expect to build a house, and live here."

"As a friend, then, let me tell you you'll never stand it." A stubby thumb made motion up the narrow street. "You see this town. I won't say what it is—you realize for yourself; but bad as it is, it's advanced civilization alongside of the country. You'll have to go ten miles out to get any land that's not taken." He stopped and lit his pipe. "Do you know what it means to live alone ten miles out on the prairie?"

"I've never lived in the country."

"I'll tell you, then, what it means." He put down his pipe and looked out at the open door. His face changed; became softer, milder, younger. His voice, when he spoke, added to the impression of reminiscence, bearing an almost forgotten tone of years ago.

"The prairie!" he apostrophized. "It means the loneliest place on God's earth. It means that living there, in life you bury yourself, your hopes, your ambitions. It means you work ever to forget the past—and fail. It means self, always; morning, noon, night; until the very solitude becomes an incubus. It means that in time you die, or, from being a man, become as the cattle." The speaker turned for the first time to the tall man before him, his big blue eyes wide open and round, his voice an entreaty.

"Don't move into it, man. It's death and worse than death to such as you! You're too old to begin. One must be born to the life; must never have known another. Don't do it, I say."

Ichabod Maurice, listening, read in that appeal, beneath the words, the wild, unsatisfied tale of a disappointed human life.

"You are dissatisfied, lonesome— There was a time years ago perhaps—"

"I don't know." The glow had passed and the face was old again, and heavy. "I remember nothing. I'm dead, dead." He drew a rough map from his pocket and spread it out before him.

"If you'll move close, please, I'll show you the open lands."

For an hour he explained homesteads, pre-emptions and tree claims, and the method of filing and proving up. At parting, Ichabod held out his hand.

"I thank you for your advice," he said.

The man behind the desk puffed stolidly.

"But don't intend to follow it," he completed.

Instinctively, metaphor sprang to the lips of Ichabod Maurice.

"A small speck of circumstance, which is near, obliterates much that is in the distance." He turned toward the door. "I shall not be alone."

The little agent smoked on in silence for some minutes, gazing motionless at the doorway through which Ichabod had passed

188

out. Again the lean bird-dog thrust in an apologetic head, dutifully awaiting recognition. At length the man shook his pipe clean, and leaned back in soliloquy.

"Man, woman, human nature; habit, solitude, the prairie." He spoke each word slowly, and with a shake of his head. "He's mad, mad; but I pity him"—a pause—"for I know."

The dog whined an interruption from the doorway, and the man looked up.

"Come in, boy," he said, in recognition.

Chapter III — The Wonder of Prairie

Ichabod and Camilla selected their claim together. A fair day's drive it was from the little town; a half-mile from the nearest neighbor, a Norwegian, without two-score English words in his vocabulary. Level it was, as the surface of a lake or the plane of a railroad bed.

Together, too, they chose the spot for their home. Camilla sobbed over the word; but she was soon dry-eyed and smiling again. Afterwards, side by side, they did much journeying to and from the nearest sawmill—each trip through a day and a night—thirty odd miles away. The mill was a small, primitive affair, almost lost in the straggling box-elders and soft maples that bordered the muddy Missouri, producing, amid noisy protestations, the most despisable of all lumber on the face of the globe—twisting, creeping, crawling cottonwood.

Having the material on the spot, Ichabod built the house himself, after a plan never before seen of man; joint product of his and Camilla's brains. It took a month to complete; and in the meantime, each night they threw their tired bodies on the brown earth, indifferent to the thin canvas, which alone was spread between them and the stars.

Too utterly weary for immediate sleep, they listened to the sounds of animal life—wholly unfamiliar to ears urban trained—as they stood out distinct by contrast with a silence otherwise absolute as the grave.

. . . The sharp bark of the coyote, near or far away; soft as an echo, the gently cadenced tremolo of the prairie owl. To these, the mere opening numbers of the nightly concerts, the two exotics would listen wonderingly; then, of a sudden, typical, indescribable, lonely as death, there would boom the cry which, as often as it was repeated, recalled to Ichabod's mind the words of the little man in the land-office, "loneliest sound on earth"—the sound which, once heard, remains forever vivid—the night call of the prairie rooster. Even now, new and fascinating as it all was, at the last wailing cry the two occupants of the tent would reach out in the darkness until their hands met. Not till then would they sleep.

In May, they finished and moved their few belongings into the odd little two-room house. True to instinct, Ichabod had built a fireplace, though looking in any direction until the earth met the sky, not a tree was visible; and Camilla had added a cozy reading corner, which soon developed into a sleeping corner,—out-of-door occupations in sun and wind being insurmountable obstacles to mental effort.

But what matter! One straggling little folio, the local newspaper, made its way into the corner each week—and that was all. They had cut themselves off from the world, deliberately, irrevocably. It was but natural that they should sleep. All dead things sleep!

Month after month slipped by, and the first ripple of local excitement and curiosity born of their advent subsided. Ichabod knew nothing of farming, but to learn was simple. It needed only that he watch what his neighbors were doing, and proceed to do likewise. He learned soon to hold a breaking-plough in the tough prairie sod, and to swear mightily when it balked at an unusually tough root. As well, he came to know the oily feel of flax as he scattered it by hand over the brown breaking. Later he learned the smell of buckwheat blossoms, and the delicate green coloring of sod corn, greener by contrast with its dark background.

Nor was Camilla idle. The dresses she had brought with her, dainty creations of foreign make, soon gave way to domestic productions of gingham and print. In these, the long brown hands neatly gloved, she struggled with a tiny garden, becoming in ratio as passed the weeks, warmer, browner, and healthier.

"Are you happy?" asked Ichabod, one day, observing her thus amid the fruits of her hands.

Camilla hesitated. Catching her hand, Ichabod lifted her chin so that their eyes met.

"Tell me, are you happy?" he repeated.

Another pause, though her eyes did not falter.

"Happier than I ever thought to be." She touched his sleeve tenderly. "But not completely so, for—" she was not looking at him now,— "for I love you, and—and—I'm a woman."

They said no more; and though Ichabod went back to his team, it was not to work. For many minutes he stood motionless, a new problem of right and wrong throbbing in his brain.

Fall came slowly, bringing the drowsy, hazy days of so-called Indian Summer. It was the season of threshing, and all day long to the drowse of the air was added, near and afar, all-prevading through the stillness, the sleepy hum of the separator. Typical voice of the prairie was that busy drone, penetrating to the ears as the ubiquitous odor of the buffalo grass to the nostril, again bearing resemblance in that, once heard, memory would reproduce the sound until recollection was no more.

Winter followed, and they, who had thought the earth quiet before, found it still now indeed. Even the voice of the prairie-chicken was hushed; only the sharp knife-like cutting of spread wings told of a flock's passage at night. The level country, mottled white with occasional drifts, and brown from spots blown bare by the wind, stretched out seemingly interminable, until the line of earth and sky met.

Idle perforce, the two exotics would stand for hours in the sunshine of their open doorway, shading their eyes from the glare and looking out, out into the distance that was as yet only a name—and that the borrowed name of an Indian tribe.

"What a country!" Camilla would say, struck each time anew with a never-ending wonder.

"Yes, what a country," Ichabod would echo, unconscious that he had repeated the same words in the same way a score of times before.

In January, a blizzard settled upon them, and for two days and nights they took turns keeping the big kitchen stove red hot. The West knows no such storms, now. Man has not only changed the face of the earth, but, in so doing, has annihilated that terror of the past,—the Dakota blizzard.

In those days, though, it was very real, as Ichabod learned. He had prepared for winter, by hauling a huge pile of cordwood and stacking it, as a protection to windward, the full length of the little cabin, thinking the spot always accessible; but he had builded in ignorance.

The snow first commenced falling in the afternoon. By the next morning the tiny house was buried to the window sashes. Looking out, there could be seen but an indistinct slanting white wall, scarcely ten feet away: a screen through which the sunlight filtered dimly, like the solemn haze of a church. The earth was not silent, now. The falling of the sleet and snow was as the striking of fine shot, and the sound of the wind a steady unceasing moan, resembling the sigh of a big dynamo at a distance.

Slowly, inch by inch, during the day the snow crept up the window panes until, before the coming of darkness without, it fell within. Banked though they were on three sides, on the fourth side, unprotected, the cold penetrated bitterly,—a cold no living thing could withstand without shelter. Then it was that Ichabod and Camilla feared to sleep, and that the long vigil began.

By the next morning there was no light from the windows. The snow had drifted level with the eaves. Icabod stood in the narrow window frame, and, lowering the glass from the top, beat a hole upward with a pole to admit air. Through the tunnel thus formed there filtered the dull gray light of day: and at its end, obstructing, there stood revealed a slanting drab wall,—a condensed milky way.

The storm was yet on, and he closed the window. To get outside for fuel that day was impossible, so with an axe Icabod chopped a hole through the wall into the big pile and on wood thus secured sawed steadily in the tiny kitchen, while the kerosene lamp at his side sputtered, and the fire crackled in a silence, like that surrounding a hunted animal in its den.

Many usual events had occurred in the lives of the wandering Ichabod and Camilla, which had been forgotten; but the memory of that day, the overwhelming, incontestible knowledge of the impotency of wee, restless, inconsequent man, they were never to forget.

"Tiny, tiny, mortal!" laughed the storm. "To think you would combat Nature, would defy her, the power of which I am but one of many, many manifestations!" And it laughed again. The two prisoners, listening, their ears to the tunnel, heard the sound, and felt to the full its biting mockery.

Next day the siege was raised, and the sun smiled as only the sun can smile upon miles and miles of dazzling snow crystals. Ichabod climbed out—by way of the window route— and worked for hours with a shovel before he had a channel from the tiny, submerged shanty to the light of day beyond. Then together he and Camilla stood side by side in the doorway, as they had done so many times before, looking about them at the boundless prairie, drifted in waves of snow like the sea: the wonder of it all, ever new, creeping over them.

"What a country!" voiced Camilla.

"What a country, indeed," echoed Ichabod.

"Lonely and mysterious as Death."

"Yes, as Death or—Life."

Chapter IV — A Revelation

Time, unchanging automaton, moved on until late spring. Paradox of nature, the warm brown tints of chilly days gave place under the heat of slanting suns to the cool green of summer. All at once, sudden as though autochthonal, there appeared meadowlarks and blackbirds: dead weeds or man-erected posts serving in lieu of trees as vantage points from which to sing. Ground squirrels whistled cheerily from newly broken fields and roadways. Coveys of quail, tame as barn-yard fowls, played about the beaten paths, and ran pattering in the dust ahead of each passing team. Again, from its winter's rest, lonely, uncertain as to distance, came the low, booming call of the prairie rooster. Nature had awakened, and the joy of awakening was upon the land.

Of a morning in May the faded, dust-covered day-coach drew in at the tiny prairie village. A little man alighted. He stood a moment on the platform, his hands deep in his pockets, a big black cigar between his teeth, and looked out over the town. The coloring of the short straggling street was more weather-stained than a year ago, yet still very new, and the newcomer smiled as he looked; a big broad smile that played about his lips, turning up the corners of his brown moustache, showing a flash of white teeth, and lighting a pair of big blue eyes which lay, like a woman's, beneath heavy lashes. In youth, that smile would have been a grin; but it was no grin now. The man was far from youth, and about the mouth and eyes were deep lines, which told of one who knew of the world.

Slowly the smile disappeared, and as it faded the little man puffed harder at the cigar. Evidently something he particularly wished to explain would not become clear to his mind.

"Of all places," he soliloquized, "to have chosen—this!"

He started up the street, over the irregular warping sidewalk.

"Hotel, sir-r?" The formula was American, the trilling r's distinctly German.

The traveller turned at the sound, to make acquaintance with Hans Becher; for it was Hans Becher, very much metamorphosed from the retiring German of a year ago. He made the train regularly now.

The small man nodded and held out his grip; together they walked up the street. In front of the hotel they stopped, and the stranger pulled out his watch.

"Is there a livery here?" he asked.

"Yes; at the street end—the side to the left hand."

"Thanks. I'll be back with you this evening."

Hans Becher stared, open-mouthed, as the man moved off.

"You will not to dinner return?"

The little man stopped, and smiled without apparent reason.

"No. Keep the grip. I expect to lunch," again he smiled without provocation, "elsewhere. By the way," he added, as an afterthought, "can you tell me where Mr. Maurice—Ichabod Maurice —lives?"

The German nodded violent confirmation of a direction indicated by his free hand.

"Straight out, eight miles. Little house with *"paint"*—strong emphasis on the last—*"white* paint."

"Thanks."

Hans saw the escape of an opportunity.

"They are friends of yours, perhaps?"—he grasped at it.

The little man did not turn, but the smile that seemed almost a habit, sprang to his face.

"Yes, they're—friends of mine," he corroborated.

Hans, personification of knowledge, stood bobbing on the door-step, until the trail of smoke vanished from sight, then brought the satchel inside and set it down hard.

"Her brother has come," he announced to the wide-eyed Minna.

"Wessen Bruder?" Minna was obviously excited, as attested by the lapse from English.

"Are we not now Americans naturalized?" rebuked Hans, icily. Suddenly he thawed. "Whose brother! The brother of Camilla Maurice, to be sure."

Minna scrutinized the bag, curiously.

"Did he so—inform you?" she questioned unadvisedly.

"It was not necessary. I have eyes."

Offended masculine dignity clumped noisily toward the door; instinctive feminine diplomacy sprang to the rescue.

"You are so wise, Hans!"

And Peace, sweet Peace, returned to the household of Becher.

Meanwhile the little man had secured a buggy, and was jogging out into the country. He drove very leisurely, looking about him curiously. Of a sudden he threw down his cigar, and sniffed at the air.

"Buffalo grass, I'll wager! I've heard of it," and in the instinctive action of every newcomer he sniffed again.

Camilla Maurice sat in front of her tiny house, the late morning sun warm about her; one hand supported a book, slanted carefully to avoid the light, the other held the crank of a barrel-churn. As she read, she turned steadily, the monotonous *chug! chug!* of the tumbling cream drowning all other sounds.

Suddenly the shadow of a horse passed her and a rough livery buggy stopped at her side. She looked up. Instinctively her hand dropped the crank, and her face turned white; then equally involuntarily she returned to her work, the the *chug! chug!* continued.

"Does Ichabod Maurice," drawling emphasis on the name, "live here?" asked a voice.

"He does." Camilla's chin was trembling; her answer halted abruptly.

The man looked down at her, genuine amusement depicted upon his face.

"Won't you please stop your work for a moment, Camilla?"

With the name, one hand made swift movement of deprecation. "Pardon if I mistake, but I take it you're Camilla Maurice?"

"Yes, I'm Camilla Maurice."

"Quite so! You see, Ichabod and I were old chums together in college—all that sort of thing; consequently I've always wanted to meet—"

The woman stood up. Her face still was very white, but her chin did not tremble now.

"Let's stop this farce," she insisted. "What is it you wish?"

The man in the buggy again made a motion of deprecation.

"I was just about to say, that happening to be in town, and incidentally hearing the name, I wondered if it were possible . . . But, pardon, I haven't introduced myself. Allow me—" and he bowed elaborately. "Arnold, Asa Arnold. . . . You've heard Ichabod mention my name, perhaps?"

The woman held up her hand.

"Again I ask, what do you wish?"

"Since you insist, first of all I'd like to speak a moment with Ichabod." His face changed suddenly. "For Heaven's sake, Eleanor, if he must alter his name, why did he choose such a barbaric substitute as Ichabod?"

"Were he here"—evenly—"he'd doubtless explain that himself."

"He's not here, then?" No banter in the voice now.

"Never fear"—quickly—"he'll return."

A moment they looked into each other's eyes; challengingly, as they had looked unnumbered times before.

"As you suggest, Eleanor," said the man, slowly, "this farce has gone far enough. Where may I tie this horse? I wish to speak with you."

Camilla pointed to a post, and silently went toward the house. Soon the man followed her, stopping a moment to take a final puff at his cigar before throwing it away.

Within the tiny kitchen they sat opposite, a narrow band of warm spring sunshine creeping in at the open door separating them. The woman looked out over the broad prairie, her color a trifle higher than usual, the lids of her eyes a shade nearer together—that was all. The man crossed his legs and waited, looking so small that he seemed almost boyish. In the silence, the drone of feeding poultry came from the back-yard, and the sleepy breathing of the big collie on the steps sounded plainly through the room.

A minute passed. Neither spoke. Then, with a shade of annoyance, the man shifted in his chair.

"I thought, perhaps, you'd have something you wished to say. If not, however—" He paused meaningly.

"You said a moment ago, you wished to speak to *me.*"

"As usual, you make everything as difficult as possible." The shade of annoyance became positive. "Such being the case, we may as well come to the point. How soon do you contemplate bringing this—this incident to a close?"

"The answer to that question concerns me alone."

An ordinary man would have laughed; but Asa Arnold was not an ordinary man—not at this time.

"As your husband, I can't agree with you."

Camilla Maurice took up his words, quickly.

"You mistake. You're the husband of Eleanor Owen. I'm not she."

The man went on calmly, as though there had been no interruption.

"I don't want to be hard on you, Eleanor. I don't think I have been hard on you. A year has passed, and I've known you were here from the first day. But this sort of thing can't go on indefinitely; there's a limit, even to good nature. I ask you again, when are you coming back?"

The woman looked at her companion, for the first time steadily. Even she, who knew him so well, felt a shade of wonder at the man who could adjust all the affairs of his life in the same voice with which he ordered his dinner. Before, she had always thought this attitude of his pure affectation. Now she knew better, knew it mirrored the man himself. He had done this thing. Knowing her whereabouts all the time, he had allotted her the past year, as an employer would grant a holiday to an assistant. Now he asked her to return to the old life, as calmly as one returns in the fall to the city home after an outing! Only one man in the world could have done that thing, and that man was before her— her husband by law—Asa Arnold!

The wonder of it all crept into her voice.

"I'm not coming back, can't you understand? I'm never coming back," she repeated.

The man arose and stood in the doorway.

"Don't say that," he said very quietly. "Not yet. I won't begin, now, after all these years to make protestations of love. The thing called Love we've discussed too often already, and without result. Anyway, that's not the point. We never pretended to be lovers, even when we were married. We were simply useful, very useful to each other."

Camilla started to interrupt him, but, preventing, he held up his hand.

"We talked over a certain possibility—one now a reality—before we were married." He caught the look upon her face. "I don't say it was ideal. It simply *was*," he digressed slowly in answer, then hurried on: "That was only five years ago, Eleanor, and we were far from young." He looked at her, searchingly. "You've not forgotten the contract we drew up, that stood above the marriage obligation, above everything, supreme law for you and me?" Instinctively his hand went to an inner pocket, where the rustle of a paper answered his touch. "Remember; it's not a favor I ask of you, but the fulfilment of your own word. Think a moment before you say you'll never return."

Camilla Maurice found an answer very difficult. Had he been angry, or abusive, it would have been easy; but as it was—

"You overlook the fact of change. A lifetime isn't required for that."

"I overlook nothing." The man went back to his chair. "You remember, as well as I, that we considered the problem of change—and laughed at it. I repeat, we're no longer in swaddling clothes."

"Be that as it may, I tell you the whole world looks different to me now." The speaker struggled bravely, but the ghastliness of such a discussion wore on her nerves, and her face twitched. "No power on earth could make me keep that contract since I've changed."

The suggestion of a smile played about the man's mouth.

"You've succeeded, perhaps, in finding that for which we searched so long in vain, an æsthetic, non-corporeal love?"

"I refuse to answer a question which was intended as an insult." The words out of her mouth, the woman regretted them.

"Though quick yourself to take offence, you seem at no great pains to avoid giving affront to another." The man voiced the reprimand without the twitch of an eyelid, and finished with another question: "Have you any reason for doing as you've done, other than the one you gave?"

"Reason! Reason!" Camilla Maurice stared again. "Isn't it reason enough that I love him, and don't love you? Isn't it sufficient reason to one who has lived until middle life in darkness that a ray of light is in sight? Of all people in the world, you're the one who should understand the reason best!"

"Would any of those arguments be sufficient to break another contract?"

"No, but one I didn't mention would. Even when I lived with

you, I was of no more importance than a half-dozen other women."

"You didn't protest at time of the agreement. You knew then my belief and," Arnold paused meaningly, "your own."

A memory of the past came to the woman; the dark, lonely past, which, even yet, after so many years, came to her like a nightmare; the time when she was a stranger in a strange town, without joy of past or hope of future; most lonely being on God's earth, a woman with an ambition—and without friends.

"I was mad—I see it now—lonely mad. I met you. Our work was alike, and we were very useful to each other." One white hand made motion of repugnance at the thought. "I was mad, I say."

"Is that your excuse for ignoring a solemn obligation?" Arnold looked her through. "Is that your excuse for leaving me for another, without a word of explanation, or even the conventional form of a divorce?"

It was just that explanation—this—I wished to avoid. It's hard for us both, and useless."

"Useless!" The man quickly picked up the word. "Useless! I don't like the suggestion of that word. It hints of death, and old age, and hateful things. It has no place with the living."

He drew a paper from his pocket, slowly, and spread it on his knee.

"Pardon me for again recalling past history, Eleanor; but to use a word that is dead! . . . You must have forgotten—" The writing, a dainty, feminine hand, was turned toward her, tauntingly, compellingly.

The man waited for some response; but Camilla Maurice was silent. That bit of paper, the shadow of a seemingly impossible past, made her, for the time, question her identity, almost doubt it.

Five years ago, almost to the day, high up in a city building, in a dainty little room, half office, half *atelier,* a man and a woman had copied an agreement, each for the other, and had sworn an oath ever to remain true to that solemn bond. . . . She had brought nothing to him, but herself; not even affection. He, on the other hand, had saved her from a life of drudgery by elevating her to a position where, free of the necessity of struggling for a bare existence, she might hope to consummate the fruition of at least a part of her dreams. On her part . . . .

"Witnesseth: The said Eleanor Owen is at liberty to follow her own inclinations as she may see fit; she is to remain free of any and all responsibilities and restrictions such as customarily attach to the supervision of a household, excepting as she may elect

to exercise her wifely prerogatives; being absolutely free to pursue whatsoever occupation or devices she may desire or choose, the same as if she were yet a spinster.....

"In Consideration of Which: The said Eleanor Owen agrees never so to comport herself that by word or conduct will she bring ridicule. . . . dishonor upon the name. . . ."

Recollection of it all came to her with a rush; but the words ran together and swam in a maddening blur—the roar from the street below, dull with distance; the hum of the big building, with its faint concussions of closing doors; the air from the open window, not like the sweet prairie air of to-day, but heavy, smoky, typical breath of the town, yet pregnant with the indescribable throb of spring, impossible to efface or to disguise! The compelling intimacy and irrevocability of that memory overwhelmed her, now; a dark, evil flood that blotted out the sunshine of the present.

The paper rustled, as the man smoothed it flat with his hand.

"Shall I read?" he asked.

The woman's face stood clear—cruelly clear—in the sunlight; about her mouth and eyes there was an expression which, from repetition, we have learned to associate with the circle surrounding a new-made grave: an expression hopelessly desperate, desperately hopeless.

Of a sudden her chin trembled and her face dropped into her hands.

"Read, if you wish"; and the smooth brown head, with its thread of gray, trembled uncontrollably.

"Eleanor!" with a sudden vibration of tenderness in his voice. "Eleanor," he repeated.

But the woman made no response.

The man had taken a step forward; now he sat down again, looking through the open doorway at the stretch of green prairie, with the road, a narrow ribbon of brown, dividing it fair in the middle. In the distance a farmer's wagon was rumbling toward town, a trail of fine dust, like smoke, suspended in the air behind. It rattled past, and the big collie on the step woke to give furious chase in its wake, then returned slowly, a little conscious under the stranger's eye, to sleep as before. Asa Arnold sat through it all, still as one devitalized; an expression on his face no man had ever seen before; one hopeless, lonely, akin to that of the woman.

"Read, if you wish," repeated Camilla, bitterly.

For a long minute her companion made no motion.

"It's unnecessary," he intoned at last. "You know as well as

I that neither of us will ever forget one word it contains." He hesitated and his voice grew gentle. "Eleanor, you know I didn't come here to insult you, or to hurt you needlessly;—but I'm human. You seem to forget this. You brand me less than a man, and then ask of me the unselfishness of a God!"

Camilla's white face lifted from her hands.

"I ask nothing except that you leave me alone."

For the first time the little man showed his teeth.

"At last you mention the point I came here to arrange. Were you alone, rest assured I shouldn't trouble you."

"You mean—"

"I mean just this. I wouldn't be human if I did what you ask—if I condoned what you've done and are still doing." He was fairly started now, and words came crowding each other; reproachful, tempestuous.

"Didn't you ever stop to think of the past—think what you've done, Eleanor?" He paused without giving her an opportunity to answer. "Let me tell you, then. You've broken every manner of faith between man and woman. If you believe in God, you've broken faith with Him as well. Don't think for a moment I ever had respect for marriage as a divine institution, but I did have respect for you, and at your wish we conformed. You're my wife now, by your own choosing. Don't interrupt me, please. I repeat, God has no more to do with ceremonial marriage now than he had at the time of the Old Testament and polygamy. It's a man-made bond, but an obligation nevertheless, and as such, at the foundation of all good faith between man and woman. It's this good faith you've broken." A look of bitterness flashed over his face.

"Still, I could excuse this and release you at the asking, remaining your friend, your best friend as before; but to be thrown aside without even a 'by your leave,' and that for another man—" He hesitated and finished slowly:

"You know me well enough, Eleanor, to realize that I'm in earnest when I say that while I live the man has yet to be born who can take something of mine away from me."

Camilla gestured passionately.

"In other words: while growling hard at the dog who approached your bone, you have no hesitation in stealing from another!" The accumulated bitterness of years of repression spoke in the taunt.

Across the little man's face there fell an impenetrable mask, like the armor which dropped about an ancient ship of war before the shock of battle.

"I'm not on trial. I've not changed my name—" he nodded

significantly toward the view beyond the open door,— "and sought seclusion."

Again the bitterness of memory prompted Camilla to speak the harshest words of her life.

"No, you hadn't the decency. It was more pleasure to thrust your shame daily in my face."

Arnold's color paled above the dark beard line; but the woman took no heed.

"Why did you wait a year," continued the bitter voice, "to end in—this? If it must have been—why not before?"

"I repeat, I'm not on trial. If you've anything to say, I'll listen."

Something new in the man's face caught Camilla's attention, softened the tone of her voice.

"I've only this to say. You've asked for an explanation and a promise; but I can give you neither. If there ever comes a time when I feel they're due you, and I'm able to comply, I'll give them both gladly." The absent look of the past returned to her eyes. "Even if I wished, I couldn't give you an explanation now. I can't make myself understand the contradiction. Somehow, knowing you so long, your beliefs crept insistently into my loneliness. It seems hideous now, but I was honest then. I believed them, too. I don't blame you; I only pity you. You were the embodiment of protest against the established, of the non-responsibility of the individual, of skepticism in everything. Your eternal 'why' covered my horizon. Every familiar thing came to bear a question I couldn't answer. My whole life seemed one eternal doubt. One thing I'd never known, and I questioned it most of all; the one thing I know now to be the truth,—the greatest truth in the world." For an instant the present crowded the past from Camilla's mind, but only for an instant. "Whatever I was at the time, you'd made me—with your deathless 'why.' When I signed the obligation of that day, I believed it was of my own free will; but I know now it was you who wrote it for both of us—you, with your perpetual interrogation. I don't accuse you of doing this deliberately, maliciously. We were both deceived; but none the less the fact remains." A shadow, almost of horror, passed over her face.

"Time passed, and though you didn't know, I was in Hell. Reason told me I was right. Instinct, something, called me a drag. I tried to compromise, and we were married. Then, for the first time, came realization. We were the best of friends,—but only friends."

"You wonder how I knew. I didn't tell you then. I couldn't. I could only feel, and that not clearly. The shadow of your 'why' was still dark upon me. What I vaguely felt then, though, I know

now; as I recognize light or cold or pain." Her voice assumed the tone of one who speaks of mysteries; slow, vibrant. "In every woman's mind the maternal instinct should be uppermost; before everything, before God,—unashamed, inevitable. It's unmistakably the distinction of a good woman from a bad. The choosing of the father of her child is a woman's unfailing test of love."

The face of the man before her dropped into his hands, but she did not notice.

"Gropingly I felt this, and the knowledge came almost as an inspiration. It gave a clue to—"

"Stop!" The man's eyes blazed, as he leaped from his chair. "Stop!"

He took a step forward, his hand before him, his face twitching uncontrollably. The collie on the step awoke, and seeing his mistress threatened, growled ominously.

"Stop, I tell you!" Arnold choked for words. This the man of "why," whom nothing before could shake!

Camilla paled as her companion arose, and the dog, bristling, came inside the room.

"Get out!" blazed the man, with a threatening step, and the collie fled.

The interruption loosed words which came tumbling forth in a torrent, as Arnold returned to face her.

"You think I'm human, and yet tell me that to my face?" His voice was terrible. "You women brand men cruel! No man on earth would speak as you have spoken to a woman he'd lived with for four years!" The sentences crowded over each other, like water over a fall—his eyes flashing like a spray.

"I told you before, I'm not on trial; that it was not my place to defend. I don't do so now; but since you've spoken, I'll answer your question. You ask why I didn't come a year ago, hinting that I wanted to be more cruel. God! the blindness and injustice of you women! Because we men don't show—Bah! . . . I was paying my own price. We weren't living by the marriage vow; it was but a farce. Our own contract was the vital thing, and it had said—But I won't repeat. God, it was bitter! But I thought you'd come back. I loved you still." He paused for words, breathing hard.

"You say, I'll never know what love is. Blind! I've always loved you until this moment, when you killed my love. You say I was untrue. It's false. I swear it before—you, as you were once, —when you were my god. Had you trusted me, as I trusted you, there'd have been no thought of unfaithfulness in your mind."

The woman sank back in the chair, her face covered, her whole body trembling; but Asa Arnold went on like the storm.

"Yes, I was ever true to you. From the first moment we met, and against my own beliefs. You didn't see. You expected me to protest it daily: to repeat the tale as a child repeats its lesson for a comfit. Blind, I say, blind! You'll charge that I never told you that I loved you. You wouldn't have believed me, even had I done so. Besides, I didn't realize that you doubted, until the time when you were learning—" he walked jerkily across the room and took up his hat,— "learning the thing you threw in my face." He started to leave, but stopped in the doorway, without looking back. "You tell me you've suffered. For the first time in my life I say to another human being: I hope so." He turned, unsteadily, down the steps.

"Wait," pleaded the woman. "Wait!"

The man did not stop, or turn.

Camilla Maurice sank back in the chair, weak as one sick unto death, her mind a throbbing, whirling chaos,—as of a patient under an anæsthetic. Something she knew she ought to do, intended doing, and could not. She groped desperately, but overwhelming, insistent, there had developed in her a sudden, preventing tumult—in paradox, a confusion in rhythm—like the beating of a great hammer on an anvil, only incredibly more swift than blows from human hands. Over and over again she repeated to herself the one word: "wait," "wait," "wait," but mechanically now, without thought as to the reason. Then, all at once, soft, all-enfolding, kindly Nature wrapped her in darkness.

She awoke with the big collie licking her hand, and a numbness of cramped limbs that was positive pain. A long-necked pullet was standing in the doorway, with her mouth open; others stood wondering, beyond. The sun had moved until it no longer shone in at the tiny south windows, and the shadow of the house had begun to lengthen.

Camilla stood up in the doorway; uncertain, dazed. A great lump was on her forehead, which she stroked absently, without surprise at its presence. She looked about the yard, and, her breath coming more quickly, at the prairie. A broad green plain, parted by the road squarely in the centre, smiled at her in the sunlight. That was all. She stepped outside and shaded her eyes with her hand. Not a wagon nor a human being was in sight.

Again the weakness and the blackness came stealing over her; she sank down on the doorstep.

"O God, what have I done!" she wailed.

The hens returned to their search for bugs; but the big collie stayed by her side, whimpering and fondling her hand.

The keen joy of life was warmly flooding Ichabod Maurice this spring day. Not life for the sake of an ambition or a duty, but delight in the mere animal pleasure of existence. He had risen early, and, a neighbor with him, they had driven forth: stars all about, perpendicular, horizontal, save in the reddening east, upon their long day's drive to the sawmill. The two teams plodded along steadily, their footfall muffled in the soft prairie loam; the earth elsewhere soundless, with a silence which even yet was a marvel to the city man.

The majesty of it held him silent until day dawned, and with the coming of the sun there woke in unison the chorus of joyous animal life. Then Ichabod, his long legs dangling over the dashboard, lifted up a voice untrained as the note of a loon, and sang lustily, until his companion on the wagon ahead,—boy-faced, man-bodied,—grinned perilously.

The long-visaged man was near happiness that morning,—unbelievably near. By nature unsocial, by habit, city inbred, artificially taciturn, there came with the primitive happiness of the moment the concomitant primitive desire for companionship. He smiled self-tolerantly when, obeying an instinct, he wound the lines around the seat, and went ahead to the man, who grinned companionably as he made room beside him.

"God's country, this." Ichabod's hand made an all-including gesture, as he seated himself comfortably, his hat low over his eyes.

"Yes, sir," and the grin was repeated.

The tall man reflected. Sunburned, roughly dressed, unshaven as he, Maurice, was, this boy-man never failed the word of respect. Ichabod examined him curiously out of his shaded lids. Big brown hands; body strong as a bull; powerful shoulders; neck turned like a model; a soft chin under a soft, light beard; gentle blue eyes—all in all, a face so open that its very legibility seemed a mark. It reddened now, under the scrutiny.

"Pardon," said Ichabod. "I was thinking how happy you are."

"Yes, sir." And the face reddened again.

Ichabod smiled.

"When is it to be, Ole?"

The big body wriggled in blissful embarrassment.

"As soon as the house is built,"—confusedly.

"You're building very fast, eh?"

The Swede grinned confirmation. Words were of value to Ole.

"I see the question was superfluous," and Ichabod likewise

smiled in genial comradery. A moment later, however, the smile vanished.

"You're very content as it is Ole," he digressed, equivocally; "but—supposing—Minna were already the wife of a friend?"

The Swede stared in breathless astonishment.

"She isn't, though," he gasped at length in startled protest.

"But supposing—"

"It would be so. I couldn't help it."

"You'd do nothing?" rank anarchy in the suggestion.

"What would there be to do?"

Ichabod temporized.

"Supposing again, she loved you, and didn't love her husband?"

Ole scratched his head, seeing very devious passages beyond.

"That would be different," and he crossed his legs.

Ichabod smiled. The world over, human nature is fashioned from one mould.

"Supposing, once more, it's a year from now,—five years from now. You've married Minna, but you're not happy. She's grown to hate you,—to love another man?"

Ole's faith was beautiful.

"It's not to be thought of. It's impossible!"

"But supposing," urged Ichabod.

The boy-man was silent for a very long minute; then his face darkened, and the soft jaw grew hard.

"I don't know—" he said slowly,— "I don't know, but I think I kill that man."

Ichabod did not smile this time.

"We're all much alike, Ole. I think you would."

They drove on; far past the town, now; the sun high in the sky; dew sparkling like prisms innumerable; the prairie colorings soft as a rug—its varied greens of groundwork blending with the narrow line of fresh breaking rolling at their feet.

"You were born in this country?" asked Ichabod suddenly.

"In Iowa. It's much like this—only rougher."

"You'll live here, always?"

The Swede shook his head and the boy's face grew older.

"No; some day, we're going to the city—Minna and I. We've planned."

Ichabod was thoughtful a minute.

"I'm a friend of yours, Ole."

"A very good friend," repeated the mystified Swede.

"Then, listen, and don't forget." The voice was vibrant, low, but the boy heard it clearly above the noise of the wagon. "Don't do it, Ole; in God's name, don't do it! Stay here, you'll be happy." He looked the open-mouthed listener deep in the eyes. "If you ever say a prayer, let it be the old one, even though it be an insult to a just God:—'Lead us not into temptation.' Avoid, as you would avoid death, the love of money, the fever of unrest, the desire to become greater than your fellows, the thirst to know and to taste all things, which is the spirit of the city. Live close to Nature, where all is equal and all is good; where sleep comes in the time of sleep, and work when it is day. Do that labor which comes to you at the moment, leaving to-morrow to Nature." He crossed his long legs, and pressed his hat down over his eyes. "Accept life as Nature gives it, day by day. Don't question, and you'll find it good." He repeated himself slowly. "That's the secret. Don't doubt, or question anything."

In the Swede's throat there was a rattling, which presaged speech, but it died away.

"Do you love children, Ole?" asked Ichabod, suddenly.

The boy face flushed. Ole was very young.

"I—" he lagged.

"Of course you do. Every living human being does. It's the one good instinct, which even the lust of gain doesn't down. It's the tie that binds,—the badge of brotherhood which makes the world one." He gently laid his hand on the broad shoulder beside him.

"Don't be ashamed to say you love children, boy, though the rest of the world laugh,—for they're laughing at a lie. They'll tell you the parental instinct is dying out with the advance of civilization; that the time will come when man will educate himself to his own extinction. It's false, I tell you, absolutely false." Ichabod had forgotten himself, and he rushed on, far above the head of the gaping Swede.

"There's one instinct in the world, the instinct of parenthood, which advances eternal, stronger, infinitely, as man's mind grows stronger. So unvarying the rule that it's almost an index of civilization itself, advancing from a crude instinct of the body-base and animal—until it reaches the realm of the mind: the highest, the holiest of man's desires: yet stronger immeasurably, as with the educated, things of the mind are stronger than things of the body. Those who deny this are fools, or imposters,—I know not which. To do so is to strike at the very foundation of human nature,—but impotently,—for in fundamentals, human nature is good." Unconsciously, a smile flashed over the long face.

"Talk about depopulating the earth! All the wars of primitive man were inadequate. The vices of civilization have likewise failed. Even man's mightiest weapon, legislation, couldn't stay the tide for a moment, if it would. While man is man, and woman is woman, that long, above government, religion,—life and death itself,—will reign supreme the eternal instinct of parenthood."

Ichabod caught himself in his own period and stopped, a little ashamed of his earnestness. He sat up in the seat preparatory to returning to his own wagon, then dropped his hand once more on the boy's shoulder.

"I'm old enough to be your father, boy, and have done, in all things, the reverse of what I advised you. Therefore, I know I was wrong. We may sneer and speak of poetry when the words proceed from another, my boy; but, as inevitable as death, there comes to every man the knowledge that he stands accursed of Nature, who hasn't heard the voice of his own child call 'father!' "

He clambered down, leaving the speechless Ole sprawling on the wagon-seat. Back in his own wagon, he smiled broadly to himself.

"Strange, how easily the apple falls when it's ripe," he soliloquized.

They drove on clear to the mill without another word; without even a grin from the broad-faced Ole, who sat in ponderous thought in the wagon ahead. To a nature such as his the infrequency of a new idea gives it the force of a cataclysm; during its presence, obliterating everything else.

It was nearly noon when they reached the narrow fringe of trees and underbrush—deciduous and wind-tortured all—which bordered the big, muddy, low-lying Missouri; and soon they could hear the throb of the engine at the mill, and the swish of the saw through the green lumber; a sound that heard near by, inevitably carries the suggestion of scalpel and living flesh. Nothing but green timber was sawed thereabout in those days. The country was settling rapidly, lumber was imperative, and available timber very, very limited.

Returning, the heavy loads grumbled slowly along, so slowly that it was nearly evening, and their shadows preceded them by rods when they reached the little prairie town. They stopped to water their teams; and Ole, true to the instincts of his plebeian ancestry, went in search of a glass of beer. He returned, quickly, his face very red.

"A fellow in there is talking about—about Mrs. Maurice," he blurted.

"In the saloon, Ole?"

The Swede repeated the story, watching the tall man from the corner of his eye.

A man, very drunk, was standing by the bar, and telling how, in coming to town, he had seen a buggy drive away from the Maurice home very fast. He had thought it was the doctor's buggy and had stopped in to see if any one was sick.

The fellow had grinned here and drank some more, before finishing the story; the surrounding audience winking at each other meanwhile, and drinking in company.

Then he went on to tell how Camilla Maurice had sat just inside the doorway, her face in her hands, sobbing,—so hard she hadn't noticed him; and—and—it wasn't the doctor who had been there at all!

Ichabod had been holding a pail of water so that a horse might drink. At the end he motioned Ole very quietly, to take his place.

"Finish watering them, and—wait for me, please."

It was far from what the Swede had expected; but he accepted the task, obediently.

The only saloon of the town stood almost exactly opposite Hans Becher's place, flush with the street. A long, low building, communicating with the outer world by one door—*sans* glass—its single window in front and at the rear lit it but imperfectly at midday, and now at early evening made faces almost indistinguishable, and cast kindly shadow over the fly specks and smoke stains of a low roof. A narrow pine bar, redolent of tribute absorbed from innumerable passing "schooners," stretched the entire length of the room at one side; and back of it, in shirt sleeves and stained apron, presided the typical bar-keeper of the frontier. All this Ichabod saw as he stepped inside; then, himself in shadow, he studied the group before him.

Railroad and cattle men, mostly, made up the gathering, with a scant sprinkling of farmers and others unclassified. A big, ill-dressed fellow was repeating the tale of scandal for the benefit of a newcomer; the narrative moving jerkily over hiccoughs, like hurdles.

"—I drew up to th' house quick, an' went up th' path quiet like,"—he tapped thunderously on the bar with a heavy glass for silence—"quiet—sh-h—like; an' when I come t' th' door, ther' 'twas open, an'—as I hope—hope t' die, . . . drink on me, b'ys, allery'—set 'm up, Barney ol' b'y, m' treat, . . . hope t' die, ther' she sat, like this—" He looked around mistily for a chair, but none was convenient, and he slid flat to the floor in their midst, his face in his hands, blubbering dismally in imitation. . . . "Sat (hic) like this; rockin' an' moanin' n' callin' his name: Asa—Asa—Asa—(hic) Arnold—'shure's I'm a sinner she—"

He did not finish. Very suddenly the surrounding group had scattered, and he peered up through maudlin tears to learn the cause. One man alone stood above him. The room had grown still as a church.

The drunken one blinked his watery eyes and showed his yellow teeth in a convivial grin.

"G'devnin', pard. . . . Serve th'—th' gem'n, Barney; m' treat."
Again the teeth obtruded. "Was jes'—"

"Get up!"

He of the story winked harder than before.

"Bless m'—" He paused for an expletive, hiccoughed, and forgetting what had caused the halt, stumbled on:—"Didn' rec'gniz' y' b'-fore. Shake, ol' boy. S—sh-orry for y'." Tears rose copiously. "Tough—when feller's wife—"

Interrupting suddenly a muffled sound like the distant exhaust of a big engine—the meeting of a heavy boot with an obstacle on the floor. "Get up!"

A very mountain of human brawn resolved itself upward; a hand on its hips; a curse on its lips.

"You damned lantern-faced—" No hiccough now, but a pause from pure physical impotence, pending a doubtful struggle against a half-dozen men.

"Order, gentlemen!" demanded the bar-keeper, adding emphasis by hammering a heavy bottle on the bar.

"Let him go," commanded Ichabod very quietly; but they all heard through the confusion. "Let him go."

The country was by no means the wild West of the story-papers, but it was primitive, and no man thought, then, of preventing the obviously inevitable.

Ichabod held up his hand, suggestively, imperatively, and the crowd fell back, silent,—leaving him facing the big man.

"You'll apologize!" The thin jaw showed clear, through the shade of brown stubble on Ichabod's face.

For answer, the big man leaning on the bar exhibited his discolored teeth and breathed hard.

"How shall it be?" asked Ichabod.

A grimy hand twitched toward a grimier hip.

"You've seen the likes of this—"

Ichabod turned toward the spectators.

"Will any man lend me—"

"Here—"

"Here—"

"And give us a little light."

"Outside," suggested the saloon-keeper.

"We're not advertising patent medicine," blazed Ichabod, and the lamps were lit immediately.

Once more the long-visaged man appealed to the group lined up now against the bar.

"Gentlemen—I never carried a revolver a half-hour in my life. Is it any more than fair that I name the details?"

"Name 'm quick," acquiesced his big opponent before the others could speak.

"Thanks, Mr. Duggin," with equal swiftness. "These, then, are the conditions." For three seconds, that seemed a minute, Ichabod looked steadily between his adversary's bushy eyebrows. "The conditions," he repeated, "are, that starting from opposite ends of the room, we don't fire until our toes touch in the middle line."

"Good!" commended a voice; but it was not big Duggin who spoke.

"I'll see that it's done, too,"—added a listening cattleman, grasping Ichabod by the hand.

"And I."

The building had been designed as a bowling-alley and was built the entire length of the lot. With an alacrity born of experience, the long space opposite the bar was cleared, and the belligerents stationed one at either end, their faces toward the wall. Midway between them a heavy line had been drawn with chalk, and beside it stood a half-dozen grim men, their hands resting suggestively on their hips. The room was again very quiet, and from out-of-doors penetrated the shrill sound of a schoolboy whistling "Annie Laurie" with original variations. So exotic seemed the entire scene in its prairie setting, that it might have been transferred bodily from the stage of a distant theatre and set down here,—by mistake.

"Now," directed a voice. "You understand, men. You're to face and walk to the line. When your feet touch—fire; and," warningly—"remember, not before. Ready, gentlemen. Turn."

Ichabod faced about, the cocked revolver in his hand, the name Asa Arnold singing in his ears. A terrible cold-white anger was in his heart against the man opposite, who had publicly caused the resurrection of this hated, buried thing. For a moment it blotted out all other sensations; then, rushing, crowding came other thoughts,—vision from boyhood down. In the space of seconds, faded scenes of the dead past took on sudden color and as suddenly vanished. Faces, he had forgotten for years, flashed instantaneously into view. Voices long hushed in oblivion, re-embodied, spoke in accents as familiar as his own. Inwardly he was seething with the myriad shifting pictures of a drowning man. Outwardly he walked those half-score steps to the line, unflinchingly; came to certain death,—and waited: personification of all that is cool and deliberate—of the sudden abundant nerve in emergencies which comes only to the highly evolved.

Duggin, the big man, turned likewise at the word and came part way swiftly; then stopped, his face very pale. Another step he took, with another pause, and with great drops of perspiration gathering on his face, and on the backs of his hands. Yet another start, and he came very near; so near that he gazed into the blue of Ichabod's eyes. They seemed to him now devil's eyes, and he halted, looking at them, fingering the weapon in his hand, his courage oozing at every pore.

Out of those eyes and that long, thin face stared death; not hot, sudden death, but nihility, cool, deliberate, that waited for one! The big beads on his forehead gathered in drops and ran down his cheeks. He tried to move on, but his legs only trembled beneath him. The hopeless, unreasoning terror of the frightened animal, the raw recruit, the superstitious negro, was upon him. The last fragment of self-respect, of bravado even, was in tatters. No object on earth, no fear of hereafter, could have made him face death in that way, with those eyes looking into his.

The weapon shook from Duggin's hand to the floor,—with a sound like the first clatter of gravel on a coffin lid; and in abasement absolute he dropped his head; his hands nerveless, his jaw trembling.

"I beg your pardon—and your wife's," he faltered.

"It was all a lie? You were drunk?" Ichabod crossed the line, standing over him.

A rustle and a great snort of contempt went around the room; but Duggin still felt those terrible eyes upon him.

"I was very drunk. It was all a lie."

Without another word Ichabod turned away, and almost immediately the other men followed, the door closing behind them. Only the bar-keeper stood impassive, watching.

That instant the red heat of the liquor returned to the big man's brain and he picked up the revolver. Muttering, he staggered over to the bar.

"D—n him—the hide-faced—" he cursed. "Gimme a drink, Barney. Whiskey, straight."

"Not a drop."

"What?"

"Never another drop in my place so long as I live."

"Barney, damn you!"

"Get out! You coward!"

"But, Barney—"

"Not another word. Go."

Again Duggin was sober as he stumbled out into the evening.

Ichabod moved slowly up the street, months aged in those last few minutes. Reaction was inevitable, and with it the future instead of the present, stared him in the face. He had crowded

the lie down the man's throat, but well he knew it had been useless. The story was true, and it would spread; no power of his
could prevent. He could not deceive himself, even. That name!
Again the white anger born of memory, flooded him. Curses on
the name and on the man who had spoken it! Why must the
fellow have turned coward at the last moment? Had they but
touched feet over the line—

Suddenly Ichabod stopped, his hands pressed to his head. Camilla, home—alone! And he had forgotten! He hurried back to
the waiting Swede, an anathema that was not directed at another,
hot on his lips.

"All ready, Ole," he announced, clambering to the seat.

The boy handed up the lines lingeringly.

"Here sir." Then uncontrollable, long-repressed curiosity broke
the bounds of deference. "You—heard him, sir?"

"Yes."

Ole edged toward his own wagon.

"It wasn't so?"

"Duggin swore it was a lie."

"He—"

"He swore it was false, I say."

They drove out into the prairie and the night; the stars looking down, smiling, as in the morning which was so long ago, the
man had smiled,—looking upward.

"Tiny, tiny mortal," they twinkled, each to the other. "So
small and hot, and rebellious. Tiny, tiny, mortal!"

But the man covered his face with his hands, shutting them out.

Chapter VI — By a Candle's Flame

Asa Arnold sat in the small upstairs room at the hotel of Hans
Becher. It was the same room that Ichabod and Camilla had
occupied when they first arrived; but he did not know that. Even
had he known, however, it would have made slight difference;
nothing could have kept them more constantly in his mind than
they were at this time. He had not slept any the night before; a
fact which would have spoken loudly to one who knew him well;
and this morning he was very tired. He lounged low in the oak
chair, his feet on the bed, the usual big cigar in his mouth.

This morning, the perspective of the little man was anything
but normal. Worse than that, he could not reduce it to the normal,
try as he might.

His meeting with Camilla yesterday had produced a deep and
abiding shock; for either of them to have been so moved signified

the stirring of dangerous forces. They—and especially himself—who had always accepted life, even crises, so calmly; who had heretofore laughed at all display of emotion—for them to have acted as they had, for them to have spoken to each other the things they had spoken, the things they could not forget, that he never could forgive—it was unbelievable! It upset all the established order of things!

His anger of yesterday against Camilla had died out. She was not to blame; she was a woman, and women were all alike. He had thought differently before; that she was an exception; but now he knew better. One and all they were mere puppets of emotion, and fickle.

In a measure, though, as he had excused Camilla he had incriminated Ichabod. Ichabod was the guilty one, and a man. Ichabod had filched from him his possession of most value; and without even the form of a by-your-leave. The incident of last evening at the saloon (for he had heard of it in the hour, as had every one in the little town) had but served to make more implacable his resentment. By the satire of circumstances it had come about that he again, Asa Arnold, had been the cause of another's defending the honor of his own wife,—for she was his wife yet,—and that other, the defender, was Ichabod Maurice!

The little man's face did not change at the thought. He only smoked harder, until the room was blue; but though he did not put the feeling in words even to himself, he knew in the depths of his own mind that the price of that last day was death. Whether it was his own death, or the death of Ichabod, he did not know; he did not care; but that one of them must die was inevitable. Horrible as was the thought, it had no terror for him, now. He wondered that it did not have; but, on the contrary, it seemed to him very ordinary, even logical—as one orders a dinner when he is hungry.

He lit another cigar, calmly. It was this very imperturbability of the little man which made him terrible. Like a great movement of Nature, it was awful from its very resistlessness; its imperviability to appeal. Steadily, as he had lit the cigar, he smoked until the air became bluer than before. In a ghastly way, he was trying to decide whose death it should be,—as one decides a winter's flitting, whether to Florida or California; only now the question was: should it be suicide, or,—as in the saloon yesterday,—leave the decision to Chance? For the time the personal equation was eliminated; the man weighed the evidence as impartially as though he were deciding the fate of another.

He sat long and very still; until even in the daylight the red cigar-end grew redder in the haze. Without being conscious of

213

the fact, he was probably doing the most unselfish thinking of his life. What the result of that thought would have been no man will ever know, for of a sudden, interrupting, Hans Becher's round face appeared in the doorway.

"Ichabod Maurice to see you," coughed the German, obscured in the cloud of smoke which passed out like steam through the opening.

It cannot be said that Asa Arnold's face grew impassive; it was that already. Certain it was, though, that behind the mask there occurred, at that moment, a revolution. Born of it, the old mocking smile sprang to his lips.

"The devil fights for his own," he soliloquized. "I really believe I,"—again the smile,—"I was about to make a sacrifice."

"Sir?"

"Thank you, Hans."

The German's jaw dropped in inexpressible surprise.

"Sir?" he repeated.

"You made a decision for me, then. Thank you."

"I do not understand."

"Tell Mr. Maurice I shall be pleased to see him."

The round face disappeared from the door.

"*Donnerwetter!*" commented the little landlord in the safe seclusion of the stairway. Later, in relating the incident to Minna, he tapped his forehead, suggestively.

Ichabod climbed the stair alone. "To your old room," Hans had said; and Ichabod knew the place well. He knocked on the panel, a voice answered: "Come," and he opened the door. Arnold had thrown away his cigar and opened the window. The room was clearing rapidly.

Ichabod stepped inside and closed the door carefully behind him. A few seconds he stood holding it, then swung it open quickly and glanced down the hallway. Answering, there was a sudden, scuttling sound, not unlike the escape of frightened rats, as Hans Becher precipitately disappeared. The tall man came back and for the second time slowly closed the door.

Asa Arnold had neither moved nor spoken since that first word,—"come"; and the self-invited visitor read the inaction correctly. No man, with the knowledge Ichabod possessed, could have misunderstood the challenge in that impassive face. No man, a year ago, would have accepted that challenge more quickly. Now —But God only knew whether or no he would forget,—now.

For a minute, which to an onlooker would have seemed interminable, the two men faced each other. Up from the street came the ring of a heavy hammer on a sweet-voiced anvil, as Jim Donovan, the blacksmith, sharpened anew the breaking ploughs which were battling the prairie sod for bread. In the street below, a group of farmers were swapping yarns, an occasional chorus of guffaws interrupting to punctuate the narrative. The combatants heard it all, as one hears the drone of the cicada on a sleepy summer day; at the moment, as a mere colorless background which later, Time, the greater adjuster, utilizes to harmonize the whole memory.

Ichabod had been standing; now he sat down upon the bed, his long legs stretched out before him.

"It would be useless for us to temporize," he initiated. "I've intruded my presence in order to ask you a question." The long fingers locked slowly over his knees. "What is your object here?"

The innate spirit of mockery sprang to the little man's face.

"You're mistaken," he smiled; "so far mistaken, that instead of your visit being an intrusion, I expected you"—an amending memory came to him—"although I wasn't looking for you quite so soon, perhaps." He paused for an instant, and the smile left his lips.

"As to the statement of object. I think"—slowly—"a disinterested observer would have put the question you ask into my mouth." He stared his tall visitor up and down critically, menacingly. Of a sudden, irresistibly, a very convulsion shot over his face. "God, man, you're brazen!" he commented cumulatively.

Ichabod had gambled with this man in the past, and had seen him lose half he possessed without the twitch of an eyelid. A force which now could cause that sudden change of expression—no man on earth knew, better than Ichabod, its intensity. Perhaps a shade of the same feeling crept into his own answering voice.

"We'll quarrel later, if you wish,"—swiftly. "Neither of us can afford to do so now. I ask you again, what are your intentions?"

"And I repeat, the question is by right mine. It's not I who've changed my name and—and in other things emulated the hero of the yellowback."

Ichabod's face turned a shade paler, though his answer was calm.

"We've known each other too well for either to attempt explanation or condemnation. You wish me to testify first." The long fingers unclasped from over his knee. "You know the story of the past year: it's the key to the future."

A smile, sardonic, distinctive, lifted the tips of Arnold's big moustaches.

"Your faith in your watchful Gods is certainly beautiful."

Ichabod nursed a callous spot on one palm.

"I understand,"—very slowly. "At least, you'll answer my question now, perhaps," he suggested.

"With pleasure. You intimate the future will be but a repetition of the past. It'll be my endeavor to give that statement the lie."

"You insist on quarrelling?"

"I insist on but one thing,"—swiftly. "That you never again come into my sight, or into the sight of my wife."

One of Ichabod's long hands extended in gesture.

"And I insist you shall never again use the name of Camilla Maurice as your wife."

The old mocking smile sprang to Asa Arnold's face.

"Unconsciously, you're amusing," he derided. "The old story of the mouse who forbids the cat. . . . You forget, man, she is my wife."

Ichabod stood up, seemingly longer and gaunter than ever before.

"Good God, Arnold," he flashed, "haven't you the faintest element of pride, or of consistency in your make-up? Is it necessary for a woman to tell you more than once that she hates you? By your own statement your marriage, even at first, was merely of convenience; but even if this weren't so, every principle of the belief you hold releases her. Before God, or man, you haven't the slightest claim, and you know it."

"And you—"

"I love her."

Asa Arnold did not stir, but the pupils of his eyes grew wider, until the whole eye seemed black.

"You fool!" he accented slowly. "You brazen egoist! Did it never occur to you that others than yourself could love?"

Score for the little man. Ichabod had been pinked first.

"You dare tell me to my face you loved her?"

"I do."

"You lie!" blazed Ichabod. "Every word and action of your life gives you the lie!"

Not five minutes had passed since he came in and already he had forgotten!

Asa Arnold likewise was upon his feet and they two faced each other,—a bed length between; in their minds the past and future a blank, the present with its primitive animal hate blazing in their eyes.

"You know what it means to tell me that." Arnold's voice was a full note higher than usual. "You'll apologize?"

"Never. It's true. You lied, and you know you lied."

The surrounding world turned dark to the little man, and the dry-goods box with the tin dipper on its top, danced before his eyes. For the first time in his memory he felt himself losing self-control, and by main force of will he turned away to the window. For the instant all the savage of his nature was on the surface, and he could fairly feel his fingers gripping at the tall man's throat.

A moment he stood in the narrow south window, full in the smiling irony of Nature's sunshine; but only a moment. Then the mocking smile that had become an instinctive part of his nature spread over his face.

"I see but one way to settle this difficulty," he intimated.

A taunt sprang to Ichabod's tongue, but was as quickly repressed.

"There is but one, unless—" with meaning pause.

"I repeat, there is but one."

Ichabod's long face held like wood.

"Consider yourself, then, the challenged party."

They were both very calm, now; the immediate exciting cause in the mind of neither. It seemed as if they had been expecting this time for years, had been preparing for it.

"Perhaps, as yesterday, in the saloon?" The points of the big moustaches twitched ironically. "I promise you there'll be no procrastination as—at certain cases recorded."

The mockery, malice inspired, was cleverly turned, and Ichabod's big chin protruded ominously, as he came over and fairly towered above the small man.

"Most assuredly it'll not be as yesterday. If we're going to reverse civilization, we may as well roll it away back. We'll settle it alone, and here."

Asa Arnold smiled up into the blue eyes.

"You'd prefer to make the adjustment with your hands, too, perhaps? There'd be less risk, considering—" He stopped at the look on the face above his. No man vis-á-vis with Ichabod Maurice ever made accusation of cowardice. Instead, instinctive sarcasm leaped to his lips.

"Not being of the West, I don't ordinarily carry an arsenal with me, in anticipation of such incidents as these. If you're prepared, however,—" and he paused again.

Ichabod turned away; a terrible weariness and disgust of it all— of life, himself, the little man,—in his face. A tragedy would not be so bad, but this lingering comedy of death— One thing alone was in his mind: to have it over, and quickly.

"I didn't expect—this, either. We'll find another way."

He glanced about the room. A bed, the improvised commode, a chair, a small table with a book upon it, and a tallow candle— an idea came to him, and his search terminated.

"I may—suggest—" he hesitated.

217

"Go on."

Ichabod took up the candle, and, with his pocket-knife, cut it down until it was a mere stub in the socket, then lit a match and held the flame to the wick, until the tallow sputtered into burning.

"You can estimate when that light will go out?" he intimated impassively.

Asa Arnold watched the tall man, steadily, as the latter returned the candle to the table and drew out his watch.

"I think so," *sotto voce.*

Ichabod returned to his seat on the bed.

"You are not afraid, perhaps, to go into the dark alone?"

"No."

"By your own hand?"

"No," again, very slowly. Arnold understood now.

"You swear?" Ichabod flashed a glance with the question.

"I swear."

"And I."

A moment they both studied the sputtering candle.

"It'll be within fifteen minutes," randomed Ichabod.

Arnold drew out his watch slowly.

"It'll be longer."

That was all. Each had made his choice; a trivial matter of one second in the candle's life would decide which of these two men would die by his own hand.

For a minute there was no sound. They could not even hear their breathing. Then Arnold cleared his throat.

"You didn't say when the loser must pay his debt," he suggested.

Ichabod's voice in answer was a trifle husky.

"It won't be necessary." A vision of the future flashed, sinister, inevitable. "The man who loses won't care to face the necessity long."

Five minutes more passed. Down the street the blacksmith was hammering steadily. Beneath the window the group of farmers had separated; their departing footsteps tapping into distance and silence.

Minna went to the street door, calling loudly for Hans, Jr., who had strayed,—and both men started at the sound. The quick catch of their breathing was now plainly audible.

Arnold shifted in his chair.

"You swear—" his voice rang unnaturally sharp, and he paused to moisten his throat,—"you swear before God you'll abide by this?"

"I swear before God," repeated Ichabod slowly.

A second, and the little man followed in echo.

"And I—I swear, I, too, will abide."

Neither man remembered that one of this twain, who gave the oath before the Deity, was an agnostic, the other an atheist!

A lonely south wind was rising, and above the tinkle of the blacksmith's hammer there sounded the tap of the light shade as it flapped in the wind against the window-pane. Low, drowsy, moaning,—typical breath of prairie,—it droned through the loosely built house, with sound louder, but not unlike the perpetual roar of a great sea-shell.

Ten minutes passed, and the men sat very still. Both their faces were white, and in the angle of the jaw of each the muscles were locked hard. Ichabod was leaning near the candle. It sputtered and a tiny globule of hot tallow struck his face. He winced and wiped the drop off quickly. Observing, Arnold smiled and opened his lips as if to make comment; then closed them suddenly, and the smile passed.

Two minutes more the watches ticked off; very, very slowly. Neither of the men had thought, beforehand, of this time of waiting. Big drops of sweat were forming on both their faces, and in the ears of each the blood sang madly. A haze, as from the dropping of a shade, seemed to have formed and hung over the room, and in unison sounds from without acquired a certain faintness, like that born of distance. Through it all the two men sat motionless, watching the candle and the time, as the fascinated bird watches its charmer; as the subject watches the hypnotist,— as if the passive exercise were the one imperative thing in the world.

"Thirteen minutes."

Unconsciously, Arnold was counting aloud. The flame was very low, now, and he started to move his chair closer, then sank back, a smile, almost ghastly, upon his lips. The blaze had reached the level of the socket, and was growing smaller and smaller. Two minutes yet to burn! He had lost.

He tried to turn his eyes away, but they seemed fastened to the spot, and he powerless. It was as though death, from staring him in the face, had suddenly gripped him hard. The panorama of his past life flashed through his mind. The thoughts of the drowning man, of the miner who hears the rumble of crumbling earth, of the prisoner helpless and hopeless who feels the first touch of flame,—common thought of all these were his; and in a space of time which, though seeming to him endless, was in reality but seconds.

Then came the duller reaction and the events of the last few minutes repeated themselves, impersonally, spectacularly,—as though they were the actions of another man; one for whom he felt very sorry. He even went into the future and saw this same man lying down with a tiny bottle in his hand, preparing for the sleep from which there would be no awakening,—the sleep which, in anticipation, seemed so pleasant.

Concomitant with this thought the visionary shaded into the real, and there came the determination to act at once, this very afternoon, as soon as Ichabod had gone. He even felt a little relief at the decision. After all, it was so much simpler than if he had won, for then—then—He laughed gratingly at the thought. Cursed if he would have known what to have done, then!

The sound roused him and he looked at his watch. A minute had passed, fourteen from the first and the flame still sputtered. Was it possible after all—after he had decided—that he was not to lose, that the decision was unnecessary? There was not in his mind the slightest feeling of personal elation at the prospect, but rather a sense of injury that such a scurvy trick should be foisted off upon him. It was like going to a funeral and being confronted, suddenly, with the grinning head of the supposed dead projecting through the coffin lid. It was unseemly!

Only a minute more: a half now—yes, he would win. For the first time he felt that his forehead was wet, and he mopped his face with his handkerchief jerkily; then sank back in the chair, instinctively shooting forward his cuffs in motion habitual.

"Fifteen seconds." There could be no question now of the result; and the outside world, banished for the once, returned. The blacksmith was hammering again, the strokes two seconds apart, and the fancy seized the little man to finish counting by the ring of the anvil.

"Twelve, ten, eight," he counted slowly. "Six" was forming on the tip of the tongue when of a sudden the tiny flame veered far over toward the holder, sputtered and went out. For the first time in those interminable minutes, Arnold looked at his companion. Ichabod's face was within a foot of the table, and in line with the direction the flame had veered. Swift as thought the small man was on his feet, white anger in his face.

"You blew that candle!" he challenged.

Ichabod's head dropped into his hands. An awful horror of himself fell crushingly upon him; an abhorrence of the selfishness that could have forgotten—what he forgot; and for so long,— almost irrevocably long. Mingled with this feeling was a sudden thanksgiving for the boon of which he was unworthy; the memory at the eleventh hour, in time to do as he had done before his word was passed. Arnold strode across the room, his breath coming fast, his eyes flashing fire. He shook the tall man by the shoulder roughly.

"You blew that flame, I say!"

Ichabod looked up at the furious, dark face almost in surprise.

"Yes, I blew it," he corroborated absently.

"It would have burned longer."

"Perhaps—I don't know."

Arnold moved back a step and the old smile, mocking, maddening, spread over his face; tilting, perpendicular, the tips of the big moustaches.

"After all—" very slowly— "after all, then, you're a coward."

The tall man stood up; six-feet-two, long, bony, immovable: Ichabod himself again.

"You know that's a lie."

"You'll meet me again,—another way, then?"

"No, never!"

"I repeat, you're a cursed coward."

"I'd be a coward if I did meet you," quickly.

Something in Ichabod's voice caught the little man's ear and held him silent, as, for a long half-minute, the last time in their lives, the two men looked into each other's eyes.

"You'll perhaps explain." Arnold's voice was cold as death. "You have a reason?"

Ichabod walked slowly over to the window and leaned against the frame. Standing there, the spring sunshine fell full upon his face, drawing clear the furrows at the angles of his eyes and the gray threads of his hair. He paused a moment, looking out over the broad prairie shimmering indistinctly in the heat, and the calm of it all took hold of him, shone in his face.

"I've a reason," very measuredly, "but it's not that I fear death, or you." He took up his hat and smoothed it absently. "In future I shall neither seek, nor avoid you. Do what you wish—and God judge us both." Without a glance at the other man, he turned toward the door.

Arnold moved a step, as if to prevent him going.

"I repeat, it's my right to know why you refuse." His feet shifted uneasily upon the floor. "Is it because of another—Eleanor?"

Ichabod paused.

"Yes," very slowly. "It's because of Eleanor—*and* another."

The tall man's hand was upon the knob, but this time there was no interruption. An instant he hesitated; then absently, slowly, the door opened and closed. A moment later indistinct, descending steps sounded on the stairway.

Alone, Asa Arnold stood immovable, looking blindly at the closed door, listening until the tapping feet had passed into silence. Then, in a motion indescribable, of pain and of abandon, he sank back into the single chair.

His dearest enemy would have pitied the little man at that moment!

Chapter VII—The Price of the Leap

In the chronology of the little town, day followed day, as monotonously as ticks the tall clock on the wall. Only in multiple they merged into the seasons which glided so smoothly, one into the other, that the change was unnoticed, until it had taken place.

Thus three months passed by, and man's work for the year was nearly done. The face of the prairie had become one of many colors; eternal badge of civilization as opposed to Nature, who paints each season with its own hue. Beside the roadways great, rank sunflowers turned their glaring yellow faces to the light. In every direction stretched broad fields of flax; unequally ripening, their color scheme ranging from sky blue of blossoms to warm browns of maturity. Blotches of sod corn added here and there a dash of green to the picture. Surrounding all, a setting for all, the unbroken virgin prairie, mottled green and brown, stretched, smiling, harmonious, beneficent; a land of promise and of plenty for generations yet unborn.

All through the long, hot summer Asa Arnold had stayed in town, smoking a big pipe in front of the hotel of Hans Becher. Indolent, abnormally indolent, a stranger seeing him thus would have commented; but, save Hans the confiding, none other of the many interested observers were deceived. No man merely indolent sleeps neither by night nor by day; and it seemed the little man never slept. No man merely indolent sits wide-eyed hour after hour, gazing blankly at the earth beneath his feet—and uttering never a word. Brooding, not dreaming, was Asa Arnold; brooding over the eternal problem of right and wrong. And, as passed the slow weeks, he moved back—back on the trail of civilization, back until Passion and not Reason was the god enthroned; back until one thought alone was with him morning, noon, and night,—and that thought preponderant, overmasting, deadly hate.

Observant Curtis, the doctor, shrugged his shoulders.

"The old, old trail," he satirized.

It was to Bud Evans, the little agent, that he made the observation.

"Which has no ending," completed the latter.

The doctor shrugged afresh.

"That has one inevitable termination," he refuted.

"Which is—"

"Madness—sheer madness."

The agent was silent a moment.

"And the end of that?" he suggested.

Curtis pursed his lips.

"Tragedy, or a strait-jacket. The former, in this instance."

Evans was silent longer than before.

"Do you really mean that?" he queried at last, significantly.

"I've warned Maurice,"—sententiously. "I can do no more."

"And he?" quickly.

"Thanked me."

"That was all?"

"That was all."

The two friends looked at each other, steadily; yet, though they said no more, each knew the thought of the other, each knew that in future no move of Asa Arnold's would pass unnoticed, unchallenged.

Again, weeks, a month, passed without incident. It was well along in the fall and of an early evening that a vague rumor of the unusual passed swiftly, by word of mouth, throughout the tiny town. Only a rumor it was, but sufficient to set every man within hearing in motion.

On this night Hans Becher had eaten his supper and returned to the hotel office, as was his wont, for an evening smoke, when, without apparent reason, Bud Evans and Jim Donovan, the blacksmith, came quietly in and sat down.

"Evening," they nodded, and looked about them.

A minute later Dr. Curtis and Hank Judge, the machine man, dropped unostentatiously into chairs. They likewise muttered "Evening," and made observation from under their hat-brims. Others followed rapidly, until the room was full and dark figures waited outside. At last Curtis spoke.

"Your boarder, Asa Arnold, where is he, Hans?"

The unsuspecting German blew a cloud of smoke.

"He a while ago went out." Then, as an afterthought: "He will return soon."

Silence once more for a time, and a steadily thickening haze of smoke in the room.

"Did he have supper, Hans?" queried Bud Evans, impatiently.

Again the German's face expressed surprise.

"No, it is waiting for him. He went to shoot a rabbit he saw."

The men were on their feet.

"He took a gun, Hans?"

"A rifle, to be sure." The mild brown eyes glanced up reproachfully. "A man does not go hunting without— . . . What is this!" he completed in consternation, as, finding himself suddenly alone, he hurried outside and stood confusedly scratching his bushy poll, in the block of light surrounding the open doorway.

The yard was deserted. As one snuffs a candle, the men had vanished. Hans' pipe had gone out and he went inside for a match. Though the stars fell, the German must needs smoke. Only a minute he was gone, but during that time a group of horse-men had gathered in the street. Others were coming across lots, and still others emerging from the darkness of alleys. Some were mounted; some led by the rein, wiry little bronchos. Watching, it almost seemed to the German that they sprang from the ground.

"Are you all ready?" called a voice, Bud Evans' voice.

"Here—"

"Here—"

"All ready?"

"Yes—"

"We're off, then."

There was a sudden, confused trampling, as of cattle in stam-pede; a musical creaking of heavy saddles; a knife-like swish of many quirts through the air; a chorus of dull, chesty groans as the rowels of long spurs bit the flanks of the mustangs, and they were gone—down the narrow street, out upon the prairie, their hoof beats pattering *diminuendo* into silence; a cloud of dust, grayish in the starlight, marking the way they had taken.

Jim Donovan, the blacksmith, came running excitedly up from a side street. He stopped in front of the hotel, breathlessly. Hold-ing his sides, he followed with his eyes the trail of dust leading out into the night.

"Have they gone?" he panted. "I can't find another horse in town."

"Where is it to?" sputtered the German.

"Have they gone, I say?"

Hans gasped.

"Yes, to be sure."

"They'll never make it." The blacksmith mopped his brow with conviction. "He has an hour's start."

Hans grasped the big man by the coat.

"Who is too late?" he emphasized. "Where are they going?"

Jim Donovan turned about, great pity for such density in his eyes.

"Is it possible you don't understand? It's to Ichabod Maurice's they're going, to tell him of Arnold." The speaker mopped his face anew. "It's useless though. They're too late," he completed.

"But Arnold is not there," protested the German. "He went for

224

a rabbit, out on the breaking. He so told me."

"He lied to you. He's mad. I tell you they're too late," repeated the smith, obstinately.

Hans clung tenaciously to the collar.

"Some one knew and told them?" He pointed in the direction the dust indicated.

"Yes, Bud Evans; but they wouldn't believe him at first, and" bitterly—"and waited." Donovan shook himself free, and started down the walk. "I'm going to bed," he announced conclusively.

Meanwhile the cloud of dust was moving out over the prairie like the wind. The pace was terrific, and the tough little ponies were soon puffing steadily. Small game, roused from its sleep by the roadside, sprang winging into the night. Once a coyote, surprised, ran a distance confusedly ahead in the roadway; then, an indistinct black ball, it vanished amongst the tall grass.

Well out on the prairie, Bud Evans, the leader, raised in his stirrups and looked ahead. There was no light beyond where the little cottage should be. The rowels of his spur dug anew at the flank of his pony as he turned a voice like a fog-horn back over his shoulder.

"The place is dark, boys," he called. Hurry."

Answering, a muttering sound, not unlike an approaching storm, passed along the line, and in accompaniment the quirts cut the air anew.

Silent as the grave was the little farmstead when, forty odd minutes from the time of starting, they steamed up at the high fence bounding the yard. One of Ichabod's farm horses whinnied a lone greeting from the barn as they hastily dismounted and swarmed within the inclosure.

"We're too late," prophesied a voice.

"I'm glad my name's not Arnold, if we are," responded another, threateningly.

Hurrying up the path in advance, the little land-agent stumbled over a soft, dark object, and a curse fell from his lips as he recognized the dead body of the big collie.

"Yes, we're too late," he echoed.

The door of the house swung ajar, creaking upon its hinges; and, as penetrates the advance wave of a flood, the men swarmed through the doorway inside, until the narrow room was blocked. Simultaneously, like torches, lighted matches appeared aloft in their hands, and the tiny whitewashed room flashed into light. As simultaneously there sprang from the mouth of each man an oath, and another, and another. Waiting outside, not a listener but knew the meaning of that sound; and big, hairy faces crowded tightly to the one small window.

For a moment not a man in the line stirred. Death was to them no stranger; but death such as this—

In more than one hand the match burned down until it left a mark like charcoal, and without calling attention. One and all they stood spellbound, their eyes on the floor, their lips unconsciously uttering the speech universal of anger and of horror, the instinctive language of anathema.

On the floor, sprawling, as falls a lifeless body, lay the long Ichabod. On his forehead, almost geometrically near the centre, was a tiny, black spot, around it a lighter red blotch; his face otherwise very white; his hair, on the side toward which he leaned, a little matted; that was all.

Prostrate across him, in an attitude of utter abandon, reposed the body of a woman, soft, graceful, motionless now as that of the man: the body of Camilla Maurice. One hand had held his head and was stained dark. On her lips was another stain, but lighter. The meaning of that last mark came as a flash to the spectators, and the room grew still as the figures on the floor.

Suddenly in the silence the men caught their breath, with the quick guttural note that announces the unexpected. That there was no remaining life they had taken for granted—and Camilla's lips had moved! They stared as at sight of a ghost; all except Curtis, the physician.

"A lamp, men," he demanded, pressing his ear to Camilla's chest.

"Help me here, Evans," he continued without turning. "I think she's fainted is all," and together they carried their burden into the tiny sleeping-room, closing the door behind.

That instant Ole, the Swede, thrust a curious head in at the outer doorway. He had noticed the light and the gathering, and came to ascertain their meaning. Wondering, his big eyes passed around the waiting group and from them to the floor. With that look self-consciousness left him; he crowded to the front, bending over the tall man and speaking his name.

"Mr. Maurice," he called. "Mr. Maurice."

He snatched off his own coat, rolling it under Ichabod's head, and with his handkerchief touched the dark spot on the forehead. It was clotted already and hardening, and realization came to the boy Swede. He stood up, facing the men, the big veins in his throat throbbing.

"Who did this?" he thundered, crouching for a spring like a great dog. "Who did this, I say?"

It was the call to action. In the sudden horror of the tragedy the big fellows had momentarily forgotten their own grim epilogue. Now, at the words, they turned toward the door. But the Swede was in advance, blocking the passage.

"Tell me first who did this thing," he challenged, threateningly.

A hand was laid gently upon his shoulder.

"Asa Arnold, my boy," answered a quiet voice, which continued, in response to a sudden thought, "You live near here; have you seen him to-night?"

The Swede dropped the bar.

"The little man who stays with Hans Becher?"

The questioner nodded.

"Yes, a half-hour ago." The boy-man understood now. "He stopped at my house, and—"

"Which direction did he go?"

Ole stepped outside, his arm stretched over the prairie, white now in the moonlight.

"That way," he indicated. "East."

As there had been quiescence before, now there was action. No charge of cavalry was ever more swift than their sudden departure.

"East, toward Schooner's ranch," was called and repeated as they made their way back to the road; and, following, the wiry little bronchos groaned in unison as the back cinch to each one of the heavy saddles, was, with one accord, drawn tight. Then, widening out upon the reflected whiteness of prairie, there spread a great black crescent. A moment later came silence, broken only by the quivering call of a lone coyote.

Ole watched them out of sight, then turned back to the door; the mood of the heroic passed, once more the timid, retiring Swede. But now he was not alone. Bud Evans was quietly working over the body on the floor, laying it out decently as the quick ever lay out the dead.

"Evans," called the doctor from the bedroom. As the agent responded, Ole heard the smothered cry of a woman in pain.

The big boy hesitated, then sat down on the doorstep. There was nothing now for him to do, and suddenly he felt very tired. His head dropped listlessly into his hands; like a great dog, he waited, watching.

Minutes passed. On the table the oil lamp sputtered and burned lower. Out in the stable the horse repeated its former challenging whinny. Once again through the partition the listener caught the choking wail of pain, and the muffled sound of the doctor's voice in answer.

At last Bud Evans came to the door, his face very white. "Water," he requested, and Ole ran to the well and back. Then, impassive, he sat down again to wait.

Time passed, so long a time it seemed to the watcher that the riders must soon be returning. Finally Evans emerged from the side room, walking absently, his face gray in the lamplight.

The Swede stood up.

"Camilla Maurice, is she hurt?" he asked.

The little agent busied himself making a fire.

"She's dead," he answered slowly.

"Dead, you say?"

"Yes, dead,"—very quietly.

The fire blazed up and lit the room, shining unpityingly upon the face of the man on the floor.

Evans noticed, and drawing off his own coat spread it over the face and hands, covering them from sight; then, uncertain, he returned and sat down, mechanically holding his palms to the blaze.

A moment later Dr. Curtis appeared at the tiny bedroom entrance; and, emerging as the little man had done before him, he closed the door softly behind. In his arms he carried a blanket, carefully rolled. From the depths of its folds, as he slowly crossed the room toward the stove, there escaped a sudden cry, muffled, unmistakable.

The doctor sank down wearily in a chair. Ole, the boy-faced, without a question brought in fresh wood, laying it down on the floor very, very softly.

"Will he—live?" asked Bud Evans, suddenly, with an uncertain glance at the obscuring blanket; and hearing the query, the Swede paused in his work to listen.

The big doctor hesitated, and cleared his throat.

"I think so; though—God forgive me—I hope not." And he cleared his throat again.

XV

KENNETT HARRIS

An Englishman, born in 1865, Kennett Harris came to South Dakota in the late 1880's with his brother. His first job was weeding onions, but in the following years he homesteaded, started a newspaper, and worked as clerk for Fall River County. During the Spanish-American War he spent some time in Cuba. Many of the stories he wrote for the *Saturday Evening Post* and other national magazines were set in the Black Hills area, although he eventually settled in Pasadena, California. He died in 1930.

Harris seems to have published only one book, *Meet Mr. Stegg,* 1920, which is a collection of those stories which were set in the Black Hills around the turn of the century and which qualify as frontier humor, perhaps even as tall tales. Harris introduces a narrator, the fictional character known as Mr. Stegg, who tells the stories. The introduction to the book and one of the tales are reprinted here.

INTRODUCTORY

Ladies and gentlemen, meet Mr. Stegg.

To do this, many of you will have to travel into a far country; all the way up between 43° 20′ and 44° 45′ north latitude into the Territory of Dakota, and to get into the Territory you will, all of you, have to go back into the past a little. But the Black Hills country is well worth while visiting and living in. I who tell you this am not to be suspected of ulterior motives, having, at the present time, no real estate interests there—only friends, and Mr. Stegg is one of them. I hope that you will think Mr. Stegg worth while when you have made his acquaintance.

Sam Stegg, the old bullwhacker turned granger.

Here, perhaps, it may be well to explain that a bullwhacker and a cowpuncher are two different things. A bullwhacker is a gentleman who hauls freight on wagons drawn by oxen from remote centers of commerce, such as was Sidney, Nebraska, to outposts of civilization like, say Custer, Rapid City and Deadwood, as they were in an earlier day; so, you see, he is professionally more akin to the muleskinner. To be a good bullwhacker, one must be an excellent pedestrian, a fluent and vociferous speaker of the language customarily addressed to oxen, tough as a hickory knot, inured to hardship and extremes of weather, resourceful in emergency, an expert in the manifold uses of baling wire, possessed of a digestive apparatus not inferior to the ordinary feed-grinder and less susceptible to the action of corrosive liquids, patient as Job, yet a man of action and indomitable courage.

Mr. Stegg has all these qualifications, as he has demonstrated during many years back and forth on the old Sidney trail, and he has other qualities. That he is the soul of hospitality is not so very remarkable in a country where hospitality is the invariable rule, but when to the abundant and not badly cooked ranch fare that he sets before his guests he adds the diversion of his inexhaustible yarns, he achieves a distinction in entertainment. It is not to be supposed that he originated the sadly portentous phrase "that reminds me," but there is no doubt that his reminder is set on a hair trigger. A breath will set it off, but once started, its mechanism has to run down of itself. Men who live much in the great solitudes often seem to lose the faculty of speech in a great measure and become taciturn and laconic when the opportunity of social intercourse presents itself; but not so Mr. Stegg. He is always glad of a chance to talk and makes the most of it. He is a complete chronicle of the Hills bound in brown leather; he knows everybody; he was on familiar terms with such sinister celebrities as Wild Bill, Fly-specked Billy and Lame Johnny and was among those present at their something-of-the-suddenest departure from this life. On the other hand, he is on equally familiar terms with judges, senators, bankers and others of the respectable and mighty or mighty respectable, who know better than to put on any airs with him, even if they had the inclination. He knew most of them when.

The stock tender at the Box Elder stage station is favored with more of Mr. Stegg's society than any one else. The two are congenial and, moreover, near neighbors, as proximity is reckoned in the Hills. But whether at the Station or at the store in Blue-blanket, all but necessary business is suspended when the old man arrives and the crowd gather around him, confident that they will hear something worth repeating. Sometimes he is asked for documents substantiating what he relates, but even that little pleasantry is not often indulged in.

Mr. Stegg is a listener, as well as a talker; eager and greedy for gossip, he has heard much and forgotten nothing. Regarding certain things, he can be as close-mouthed as a sprung trap, and this known fact, as well as his sympathetic and genial nature, has made him the recipient of many confidences, especially from the young of both sexes, concerning whom his interest is unflagging and his curiosity insatiable. He religiously attends all the dances within a radius of sixty miles, and the withered, bald-headed, gray-bearded old reprobate can dance as well as any of the boys and better than most of them, not confining himself to squares, by any means. And, believe it or not, the girls like to dance with him. He has an ingratiating twinkle in his sharp old eye, a fatherly and benign manner and he knows how to say the things that girls like to hear even from old men. A ladies' man, if you please! You may remember that I put the ladies first in my introduction.

It is rather strange, considering all this, that there is not, and, as far as is known, never has been a Mrs. Stegg. I like to fancy that in his youth there was some romance with an unhappy ending, that, nevertheless, left no trace of bitterness in his good heart. At all events I have concluded that of the many roads that he has traveled, actually or vicariously, the one of which he has the most vivid memories and whose scenes and incidents dwell most pleasantly in his mind is that universal path that never did, and never will run smooth.

TOBERMORY

Jimmy Good-Voice-Flute had been pestering the trader for gratuitous cigarettes for at least half an hour after he had got all that was coming to him for his beaver pelts, and when he surreptitiously slipped a dollar-and-fifty-cent skinning knife under his blanket and tried to look innocent the trader's patience gave out completely. The old bullwhacker watched the ensuing action with grave interest, and even left his seat on a nail keg by the stove to view the continuation of the proceedings 'outside' the store. He viewed them from the inside, however, through a clear patch that he rubbed on the frost-covered window, first closing the door to keep out the zero cold.

It was an interesting spectacle. It takes an active and speedy white person to keep within kicking distance of a running Oglala Indian in the prime of life and good condition. To actually kick him three times and make up the ground lost on each occasion, which the trader did, constitutes a record performance. The course ran over ground covered with a light snow, around the hay corral and to the steep bank overhanging the creek, Jimmy demonstrating the aptness of the first two-thirds of his family name as they went. The trader stopped at the creek bank; the Indian went on, down and through.

When the breathless advance agent of commerce returned the old bullwhacker complimented him on his form, but deprecated his violence.

"I was something of a foot racer myself when I was some younger," he said, "but I don't believe I'd have allowed you much of a handicap. Nevertheless, Ike, a man hadn't ought to let his heels outrun his head like you done. I reckon it's no more than natural and human for to feel a mite peevish once in a spell. We can't all be like Old Man Tobermory, but we can smother our honest feelings, sort of—or we ought to could—when it ain't to our interest to show 'em."

"Who's Tobermory?" inquired the trader, picking up the skinning knife and returning it to stock.

"When Young-Man-Afraid-of-the-Soap has got you knotted up in rawhide and wired to a sapling you'll be sorry for this," pursued the old bullwhacker, shaking his head with much seriousness. "When the squaws are singing happy little songs as they stick lighted pine splinters into your shrinking form you'll be a-cursing of the day when you humbled the haughty spirit of the noble red man."

"Who's Tobermory?" repeated the trader.

"When the Badface band exhumes the tomahawk and the shrill warwhoops is a-ringing through the forest aisles you'll regret that you hadn't extended the right hand of fellowship to him instead of the sole of your number nine," the old bullwhacker went on. "An Injun has got his feelings, the same as you and me, and you injured that one in a tender and sensitive spot, Ike."

"I aimed to," replied the trader. "Who—"

"You've just about forfeited his friendship," sighed the old bullwhacker. "He won't be easy now until he's got red hair hanging in his tepee. Is this here shack insured?"

"You never stopped to listen when folks got to talking about me," remarked the trader. "I come into the Mandan Territory before I growed hair of any color at all, and I was eating baled hay without spitting out the wire before I was three years old. All I wear boots for is the looks of the thing. Who was Tobermory? I was asking you."

"That's what I'm trying to tell you," said the old bullwhacker. "Well, he was a man that wouldn't never have treated nobody the way you done a while ago. He was mild and gentle in his ways, Old Man Tobermory was. Moses wasn't nothing to him for meekness, and he claimed that Job, seemed like to him, was a lee-eetle mite disposed to kick on slight provocation. Not that he wanted to criticize Mr. Job or be finding fault with him, but— well, it seemed like Satan might have made out a tolerable case against him if he had wanted to bad enough. 'Still,' says Tobermory, 'I got to own that I never had no boils myself on me.' Then he strokes his old gray whiskers all the way down from his chin to the buttons on his pants. 'I reckon mabbe it's because I've always et a heap of corn bread and sorghum molasses with the rest of my victuals; what do you reckon? How does a fellow go about it to get boils, anyway? I'd like to try 'em.' You see he sort of prided himself on being patient.

"Well, he come into the territory from Missouri or Iowa or somewheres—him and his old woman and the two boys—and they settled on the Belle Fourche, near where the Gooseneck Ranch was. If you'll believe me he broke forty-odd acres of sod with a yoke of balky steers and never said a word out of the way. What's more, he kept good friends with the man who sold him them steers and told him they'd pull the tongue of a wagon— friends with him for years after. Lent him money, by Godfrey!"

"Did you ever pay him back?" inquired the trader.

"Do you want to hear about this?" demanded the old bullwhacker. "All right then! One day he went out to the pasture where he'd had ten head of three-year-old colts and found the fence wire cut and the colts gone.

" 'Too bad!' he says. 'Too bad! Well, the Lord gave, and the Lord taketh away. I ain't got no kick coming.'

"His biggest boy, Arch, who was with him, was nosing round the tracks where the wire was cut. 'The Lord didn't take 'em away,' says Arch. 'It was a couple of sons-of-guns riding half-shod ponies. See if it wasn't! And they headed straight for no place they could ride round that was anyways populous, the way their trail runs. I reckon we might tag along after them, just out of curiosity, paw. You fog along and I'll go to the house and get you a gun and overtake you.'

" 'What do I want with a gun?' asks Tobermory. 'This ain't the Fourth of July for to make a joyful noise, and we ain't out after meat. I'm sorry to see you getting notions like that into your head, sonny. If them Sabeans need them colts worse than what I do they're welcome to them; but I don't know that it wouldn't be just as well to explain to them that I'm a poor man and leave it to their better feelings whether it wouldn't be the right thing for them to let us take 'em back—if we catch up with them.'

" 'All right, pappy,' says Arch. 'If you'd sooner talk 'em to death than kill 'em outright I'm agreeable. I guess they deserve it—the naughty, bad, wicked things! I don't blame you for feeling sort of vindictive.'

" 'Why, Archie!' says Tobermory. 'Why, boy, I ain't feeling a particle vindictive. I can't figure how in time you should think such a thing as that of me. No, I ain't mad at 'em. All I said was that I'd tell 'em how things was with me. They hadn't ought to mind that. Do you recken they'd mind—if I just told 'em? You know we really do need them colts, Archie. 'Course we could get along without 'em, but—'

"Arch had got too far ahead to hear good, so he stopped talking and followed along the trail, which was tolerable plain so that the boy was making right good time. It was all Tobermory could do to keep him in sight. The balance of the morning they rode about south and an hour after noon they come into sight of Bear Butte and pretty soon Arch pulled up at the top of a rise.

" 'Look over there,' he says, pointing with his finger, and there about a mile away they made out a bunch of horses and some men milling round under some cottonwoods.

" 'There's more than ten head there, and there's more than two men,' says Tobermory; and then he seen that Arch had got a little Spencer carbine under his leg and was pulling it out. 'I'd like for you to put that back, Archie,' he says. 'Remember, them that takes the sword shall perish by the sword, and the same applies to guns. I didn't see you had that when we started or I'd have asked you to leave it at home.'

" 'We might as well go back then,' says Arch, reining round. 'I feel bashful when I meet a bunch of perfect strangers and ain't properly attired and fixed up like other men; and I bet that every last one of them fellows is wearing the very latest styles in artillery and has got 'em on straight. Let's go home, pappy.'

" 'All right, son,' says Tobermory. 'Tell ma to set out a bite for me on the table and not to wait up.' Saying which he trots along toward the cottonwoods. Arch made a move to pull out the carbine again, but he was a good boy and 'most always done what his daddy told him, so he just cussed a streak and then put out after the old gentleman; and they both arrived together, just at the same time that Black Jack Frushin kicked his last at the looped end of rope that was slung over a limb of one of the trees.

"The party consisted of Alonzo Dolby and his merry little band of stranglers, who had accidently happened on Frushin and a partner of his, name of Gus Minnick, who was driving four other horses besides the Tobermory ten, all with brands that wasn't vented, and no good excuse. They had give the boys a fair— well, a fair-to-middling trial, and had got as far as one up and one to play when the Tobermorys come up and sort of diverted attention.

"Dolby knew Old Man Tobermory and gave him glad welcome. 'If we had known you was coming we'd have sure delayed the performance,' he says; 'but you can have a seat for the second act, which is just a-going to begin.'

" 'Do you mean to tell me that you've hung that poor boy just because he had a few cayuses that didn't properly belong to him?' says Tobermory in horror-struck tones.

"Dolby said he sort of reckoned that they had, kind of, and asked him what was his own opinion about it, judging from the looks of the late Mr. Frushin.

"Old Man Tobermory wagged his head mighty sorrowful. 'And do you mean to say that you're figuring on hanging that one too?' he asks, pointing with his finger to Gus Minnick, who was all wound round and waiting.

" 'You might say we got definite intentions bordering on decisions thataway,' Dolby told him. 'You see, Tobe,' he says, 'we've got to do something to show that we ain't approving this here promiscuous stock-rustling and general helling round. We don't want the idea to get out that we don't take a warm and practical interest in good morals. We aim to be an uplifting and elevating force in the community, and we will now proceed to uplift and elevate Brother Minnick.'

" 'Hold on, 'Lonzo!' says Tobermory. 'I just want to say a word or two before you do anything rash. You ain't agoing to improve no man's morals by treating him as if he was a family wash. Once you've hung him you've spoiled all his chances for future usefulness. He ain't going to distinguish himself in no walk of life you can mention, from that out, the way I look at it. And what's more, it ain't kind or considerate, noways. You wouldn't like it yourself. No, sir! None of you gentlemen wouldn't. I don't claim it's the right thing to go round gathering up folks' horses without asking or saying something about it; but I don't believe Mr. Minnick here has had the advantages that some of us has had, and I believe he's sorry right now that he done so. And I think if you asked him he'd promise that he wouldn't do it no more—wouldn't you, Mr. Minnick? You think it over and you'll see that you've done wrong. You don't aim to do wrong, do you?'

"Minnick looked up at Dolby. 'Do I have to take this as well?' he asks. 'Ain't this against the constitution providing against cruel and unusual punishments? It's all right, I suppose, if you say so. You've got me tied.'

" 'I told you so, pappy,' whispers Arch, nudging the old man.

" 'You hush, son!' says Tobermory. 'I reckon he thinks I'm making sport of him, which sure would be a cruelty and which I wouldn't do and ain't. 'Lonzo, you turn this boy loose and I'll take him back to the ranch with me where he won't be led astray by bad company and will have good books and moral influences and steady work and wages and regular square meals. I've got a heap of faith in this boy. If I was a betting man I'd be willing to bet I can reform him, even if appearances is against him now.'

" 'We'd like to oblige you, Tobe,' says Dolby, 'but you're a heap too hopeful. All said and done, Mr. Minnick is a horse thief.'

" 'All said and done, they're mostly my horses,' says Tobermory. 'If I'm willing to overlook it I guess you gentlemen ought to be. Now I'd just like to say a few words to prove that I'm right about this.'

" 'For the love of heaven let him take the dirty son-of-a-gun!' says one of the party. 'A few words is good with me, and he's sure said 'em aplenty. I like to see a good lively hanging as well as the next fellow, but I ain't agoing to hold out for it if Mr. Tobermory is agoing to object at any more length.'

"That got another man started. Seemed like Minnick had shot off the tip of his ear and the soreness had worked all through his system. He expressed himself according, and then Gus chirped up and told him that his ears was too long anyway. 'You certainly couldn't expect me to shoot you in the brain,' says Gus.

" 'Now don't you boys get to fussing and quarreling,' says Tobermory. 'It ain't seemly. Gus, you poor, misguided fellow, are you willing to come home with me and behave yourself?'

" 'Suits me,' says Gus.

" 'There you are!' says Old Man Tobermory, as pleased as pie. 'He says he'll behave himself, and what more could you ask?'

"So, after a little more, back and forth, they untied Gus, and him and the old man and Arch and the colts started back. Gus acted kind of quiet and thoughtful for a spell. They had gone four or five miles before he spoke. Then he says to Old Man Tobermory: 'You was mentioning wages a while back. How much do you reckon you want to pay me, Mister Man?'

"Arch heard him. 'Why, you slit-eyed, crooked-nosed, small-souled, bandy-legged blister!' says he. 'I've a notion to drag you out of that saddle and jam you a yard and a half into the ground. Wages!'

"Gus slid his hand down to his hip before he took time to think that it was waste motion. Then he remembered that 'Lonzo Dolby had forgot to return him the personal property that he was reaching for, and spurred off to one side to avoid the rush that Arch started to make. Old Man Tobermory edged in between them pretty lively and told Arch to behave.

" 'I'm perfectly ashamed of you, son,' he said. 'I don't know what on earth Mr. Minnick is agoing to think of such manners—talking about a gentleman's features and limbs, what he ain't noways to blame for, right to his face! Why, you act as if you'd never had no raising. You excuse him, Mr. Minnick; he doesn't mean no harm; he's just young and thoughtless. You and him is agoing to be the best kind of friends or I miss my guess.'

" 'You miss it about a statutory mile if he ever makes them kind of cracks again,' says Gus. 'Such language applied to me 'most always occasions a coolness in the applicationer sort of approximating the temperature of a wedge. If I hadn't a high respect for you I'd be miffed about it as it is.'

" 'You apologize, Archie,' says Tobermory. 'You apologize, like a good boy.'

" 'Sure,' says Arch, with a sweet, dutiful smile. 'I done wrong, pa. Mr. Minnick, I hope you'll overlook it. I wouldn't sleep more than twelve hours at a stretch if I thought I'd really hurt your tender feelings and got you to disliking me. I apologize. Sure! I'd apologize to a polecat—any polecat—to please pa.'

" 'Now that's handsome,' says Tobermory, with his crinkled-up, benevolent grin. 'That's more like my boy Archie. Now about them wages: I'm willing to pay what's fair—thirty-five a month; and if we do well and don't have no losses I'll raise it at the end of the season.'

" 'Well, that ain't much,' says Gus; 'but I've took a fancy to you, and then you done me a favor a little while ago, so if your old woman ain't no more than an average bad cook I'll help you out.'

" 'I feel sure that ma'll do her level best to please you, since you're so kind and obliging,' says Arch. 'Any time the grub is cold you just tell me and I'll make it hot for you. I'll make it so damned hot for you——'

" 'Archie,' " says the old man.

" 'Yes, I see that me and Archie is agoing to be the best kind of friends,' says Gus, and his eyes was slittier than ever when he said it.

"Now I take the same view of human nature as Tobermory," observed the old bullwhacker. "I claim there's some good in most folks if we could only find it. The trouble is that we don't look hard enough. Ain't that right? Tobermory figured that Gus had just mislaid his redeeming qualities, but they was in him somewheres, hid away under a mess of orneriness where nobody'd ever guess they could have been put. Him being about two-thirds granger, he looked on Gus as a barren forty and proceeded to water him with words of wisdom and fertilize him with forgiveness and warm his soil with sunny smiles, all the time a-scattering seeds of kindness and going down on all fours to see of some of them wasn't beginning to sprout. You try that on some of your Injun brothers some time, Ike, and see if it don't pay. I read once about a kind-hearted old settler who found a poor starving redskin out in the snow and took him into his humble cabin and fed him up a lot and warmed him and turned him loose with a grubstake, and years after——"

"Years ago, you was speaking of Tobermory," hinted the trader.

"Well, Gus didn't seem to sprout worth a cent," the old bullwhacker resumed. "About that time I lived neighbors to the Tobermorys—not more than twelve miles away—and Arch Tobermory used to happen along once in a while and unload his mind concerning Gus and the old man. I used to like to listen to Arch. He had a natural gift for language that he had to keep under a bushel, as you might say, while he was round home, account of the old man. You don't often run across sons like Archie. He was different to the most. He couldn't help feeling that Gus was this, that and the other, and he thought that his old daddy was doomed to a heap of disappointment in his plans for reform; but he walked wide of Gus for the most part and only let himself out when he was alone, according to what he said, except once or twice, and when Tobermory wasn't round. I reckon that was the truth. As for Tobermory himself:

" 'Bless his dear old whiskers!' says Arch to me. 'He's dead certain that he's going to make that libel on a decent hyena over into a model for the young. He thinks he can sweeten the mess of meanness until it's fit to fill scent sachets and put in bureau drawers. You can't tell pa that a rattlesnake with a sore tummy ain't no fit playmate for the children; he won't believe you. He smokes his darned old pipe and tells me to be patient like he is. If you ask me, I'm a surprise to myself, considering how the color of Gus' hair annoys me; but all I can do is stay round and see that the gentleman doesn't burn the house up some fine night. You wait, though! Yes, he mighty nigh crisped us already. Give me half a chance and I'll sure reach out and wipe that smut off the nose of Creation!'

" 'I believe you are sort of prejudiced against him,' I says. 'There's no telling but your daddy may soften him yet, hard as he is.'

" 'I'd like to soak him good and see what that would do,' says Arch, sort of studying. 'The only other way I know to soften that asafetida pill is to pound him into a pulp.'

"I said I should have thought that he would forget himself some odd time and eradicate the son-of-a-gun.

" 'Pa always watches out for that,' says Arch. 'I might slip past the old gent,' he says, 'but it would be like killing a good neighbor's worthless pet dog because he showed his teeth at you. Pa would never get over it.'

" 'Didn't you never tell Gus about how he reminds you of all them members of the animal kingdom?' I asks him.

" 'I've mentioned it to him in private; but then I'm keeping the guns locked up, and he knows that if I once laid hands on him I'd pull him apart and take chances on being able to put him together again,' says Arch. 'He's tried to assassinate me by accident a couple of times and I have to watch him close, but otherwise our relations is cordial. I keep thinking that he'll run to the end of the picket rope and throw himself, but it begins to look doubtful. The other day he got mad with the best cow we've got because she switched her tail in his face, so he ups with the milk stool and busts her head wide open. Pa did tell him that wasn't no way to act, but he told him more in sorrow than in anger, and Gus overlooked the seeming harshness of the remark when he seen how pa regretted it.'

" 'It certainly was hasty of Gus,' says I. 'I think I'd have remonstrated a few myself. Did he kill the cow?'

" 'Her hide is on the fence and her meat is salted down for the winter,' says Arch. 'Then, the day before yesterday—I guess you seen the smoke—he set the grass afire down the valley where we was agoing to cut hay next week. There ain't no kind of work Gus hates worse than haying, and there ain't none that he likes any better. All is, we'll have to buy hay this fall or let the stock rustle through the winter. If I had catched him there would have been some eradicating done right there, but it was pa happened along while he was touching her off in the third place. Pa spoiled his coat and singed off a considerable whisker trying to put the fire out, but the wind got the start of him.'

" 'I suppose pa made allowances for him,' says I.

" 'The low-flung liar said that he done it for a joke on the grasshoppers,' says Arch. 'He claimed that he never thought about the hay once. Of course pa had to own up that anybody was liable to forget once in a while, but he did hope that Gus would try to be more thoughtful.'

"You'd have thought, being as uncharitable as tinkling cymbals, that Gus would have took a chance and a few horses and lit out, after a general massacre of the Tobermory family; but 'Lonzo Dolby had passed word about him to all the ranches and the stock-association men, and as the Kansas rustlers was somewhat active about that time 'Lonzo had his scouts pretty well organized, particularly in the dark of the moon; so, altogether, the chance was a slim one. Arch figured it out that way at first, but later on he come round to my opinion that Gus was softening. For a while, I don't deny, the old man's proteege acted up real aggravating; trying to teach little Sammy Tobermory to swear and chew tobacco premature, as you might say, before them accomplishments was proper and befitting. That looked like pure devilment; but it may have been ignorance. And taking Mis' Tobermory's gold watch and the brooch that had her grandfather's hair into it and trading them to a whisky peddler and then getting himself intoxicated and cutting down the three-year-old apple orchard that was just getting ready to bear—that was another thing.

" 'And all pa does is fill up a bucket with rich orient pearls and tote them out to his trough,' says Arch. 'Ma's talking of packing up and going back East to her folks with little Sammy,' he says. 'Pa tells her that if she feels that way and won't be persuaded he can't stop her, but it's his duty to be patient with Gus and what would the boy do if there wasn't nobody to give him a helping hand. "It's a cinch that he'd help himself," says ma. You see Gus undertook to grease the wagon the other day, and he wiped the thimbles off with ma's best petticoat that was hanging to sun, because it saved him walking all the way to the barn for a piece of old gunny sack.'

"But, as I say, things begun to change. 'The constant drip of water wears away the hardest stone,' as the fellow says, and, along come fall, Gus begun to act more like the common run of humanity. Aside from feeding bread and strychnine to some of the chickens—which may have been out of scientific interest—and a few things like that, he didn't do nothing out of reason, and he begun to quit insulting the old man and trying to kill Arch. Arch owned up that he had turned his back more than once without anything happening—as long as a minute at a time. He told me that Gus had toted in a pail of water for Mis' Tobermory without even being asked and shucked half a wagonload of squaw corn the same day. Pa sent him to town instead of Arch and he come back you might say sober, and with all the mail.

" 'That's right good news,' I says. 'If your daddy doesn't take all the cussedness out of him he'll go to the United States Senate yet.'

" 'It begins to look thataway,' says Arch, sort of looking down his nose and fetching a deep sigh.

" 'Ain't you glad?' I asks him. 'You don't act like it,' I says.

" 'Sure I'm glad!' says he, but he didn't look like it.

" 'Certainly, I'm tickled 'most to pieces,' he busts out again after a little. 'Why wouldn't I be pleased to see a fellow creature a-turning from the paths of gall and bitterness and walking in the straight and narrow way that leadeth unto a good team and wagon and a cow not to speak of summer's wages all winter. That's what pa is figuring on giving him to start him on a ranch, and I wouldn't be surprised if he raised the bid before spring. Yes, sir, Gus allows he'll settle down on a claim somewheres near us so's he can get over often to see pa and get the benefit of his advice. You bet I'm plumb joyful about it.'

"Well, there it was; and I ain't got the slightest doubt but if nothing hadn't happened to the contrary Gus would have settled down and him and Arch would have been like brothers, same as the old man had said they would be. I kept on thinking thataway for about a week after Arch went away, quirting his horse for shying at the gatepost—'which wasn't like my boy Archie,' as Old Man Tobermory used to say. I made allowances, because I knew that all along the youngster had figured that sometime he'd get to crawl Mr. Minnick's hump for reasons that his daddy couldn't kick at, and here was Mr. Minnick blasting that sweet hope with a short fuse and a double shot of virtuousness.

"Well, I reckon it was about two weeks after that when Arch come back again. It was one of these here bright clear mornings 'when all Nature seems to smile,' as the fellow says. Like in the month of May when the lambs did skip and play and the birds was a-singing to a charm—only some colder, and it wasn't the birds a-singing. I'd just stepped to the door to throw out my dishwater when I heard a song that wasn't never rendered by nothing that wore feathers. It come clear and strong on the morning breeze, with happy yelps on the high notes like a timber wolf a-serenading the amber moon:

> " 'With my hippy, hippy, hippy,
>   And my hippy, hippy, hi;
> With my hippy, hippy, hippy,
>   Ya-hoo-oo ee-ee—ha-ay——'

"And here comes Arch Tobermory, loping along over the trail, beating time with his hat on his horse's neck. He stopped singing when he seen me and pulled his horse in to a walk, and when he got up to where I was his face was as long as a fiddle.

" 'How, colah!' I says. 'If you ain't emptied the bottle I don't mind if I do join you, early as it is.'

" 'I forget once in a while,' says Arch, sort of sheepish, as he followed me in. 'No, I ain't got none and ain't had none,' he says. 'Ho hum! I just forget.'

" 'With my hip ——'

" 'Doggone it! Somebody ought to kick me good. It's a world of sorrow, Uncle Billy. We're here to-day and gone to-morrow— like the flowers that bloom in the spring and is cut down, as pappy says.

" 'With my hippy ——'

" 'Oh, shucks! Have you got the makings, Uncle Billy? Poor pappy! Poor pappy!'
" 'What's the matter with him?' I asks. I was kind of worried at the curious way Arch was acting. He ain't sick, is he?' I asks.
" 'Why, it ain't him; it's Gus,' says Arch. 'Poor Gus! If you've got a stock of this smoking I'll take a sack home to pappy. That's what I come for. Yes,' he says, lighting his cigarette and dragging on it kind of ravenous, 'poor Gus has left us, poor Gus has.'
I asked him how that come.
" 'Well, the old gent sent him to town again,' says Arch. 'He was to have been back the next morning, but he claimed he met a friend. If that was so I don't blame him for staying three days to enjoy the novelty, but it seems to me hard to believe. But he come back. Pa had been real uneasy for them three days, but he wouldn't let me ride over and borrow from you. "I've got faith in that boy," he kept saying. "He'll be back any minute now. You can't tell me that he ain't got a single spark of gratitude in him, after all I've done for him. He wouldn't cause me anguish and suffering all this time if something hadn't happened to him. But I look for him any minute. He's good at heart, Gus is."
" 'Well, finally Gus did come. I don't blame pa the least in the world, mind. If that ax hadn't been right handy——I don't know. It takes a heap to get pa started, but he's sure hard to stop when he really moves—and sudden. Mighty spry for a man of his age. I was proud of him! Ho hum! Yes, we laid Gus where the waving willows grow.'
"I stared at him. I says: 'You don't mean to say that your pa—Samuel J. Tobermory——'
"Arch nodded. 'Yes,' says he, 'with the ax.'

" 'With my hippy, hippy——'

" 'Oh, sugar! Yes, pa said that he'd stood a good deal from Gus and had been forbearing and long-suffering and lenient all that could be expected, but when the thankless whelp come back without the smoking tobacco he thought it was just a lee-eetle too much. Well, I've got to be going or pa'll get anxious about me.'

He jumps up and jams my good tobacco down in his pocket and busts through the door in a hurry.

" 'Poor Gus!' he says as he throws his leg over the saddle. Then he went off on the keen run, into the golden glory of the morn, a-splashing the dancing, rippling water of the ford into bright-hued rainbows of peaceful promise, as it were, whilst a-floating back behind him on the breeze, like I mentioned it had floated on ahead of him, come once more the exulting strain:

> " 'With my hippy, hippy, hippy,
> And my hippy, hippy, hi;
> *With my hippy, hippy, hippy,*
> Ya-hoo-oo ee-ee—ha-ay——' "

XVI

EDITH EUDORA KOHL

Edith Eudora Ammons was born in Illinois in 1884 and came to South Dakota with her sister, Ida Mary, in 1908. Apparently an early example of the "liberated woman," Edith homesteaded near McClure with only her sister to help in the difficult work. The farm did not provide a living for them, and so Edith began a newspaper while her sister taught school. Later, Edith established the Ammons Post Office and a store, but when the buildings were destroyed by fire in 1909 she left South Dakota, first going to Wyoming where she married Aaron Wesly Kohl, and then settling in Denver. After Mr. Kohl died, Edith turned her attention to writing. During the rest of her life she remembered South Dakota and was a benefactress of the Presho area. She died in Denver in 1959.

Mrs. Kohl's novel, *Land of the Burnt Thigh,* 1938, takes place during the agricultural settlement of South Dakota and is written with the kind of authority and sensitivity that makes the story seem autobiographical, although the author disclaims that possibility in her introductory remarks. "A Shack on the Prairie" is the first chapter of her novel.

A SHACK ON THE PRAIRIE

At sunset we came up out of the draw to the crest of the ridge. Perched on the high seat of the old spring wagon, we looked into a desolate land which reached to the horizon on every side. Prairie which had lain untouched since the Creation save for buffalo and roving bands of Indians, its brown grass scorched and crackling from the sun. No trees to break the endless monotony or to provide a moment's respite from the sun.

The driver, sitting stooped over on the front seat, half asleep, straightened up and looked around, sizing up the vacant prairie.

"Well," he announced, "I reckon this might be it."

But this couldn't be it. There was nothing but space, and sun-baked plains, and the sun blazing down on our heads. My sister pulled out the filing papers, looking for the description the United States Land Office had given her: Section 18, Range 77W—about thirty miles from Pierre, South Dakota.

"Three miles from the buffalo waller," our driver said, mumbling to himself, ignoring the official location and looking back as though measuring the distance with his eye. "Yeah, right in here—somewhere."

"But," faltered Ida Mary, "there was to be a house—"

"Thar she is!" he announced, pointing his long whip in the direction of the setting sun. "See that shack over yonder?"

Whipping up the tired team with a flick of the rawhide, he angled off across the trackless prairie. One panic-stricken look at the black, tar-papered shack, standing alone in that barren expanse, and the last spark of our dwindling enthusiasm for homesteading was snuffed out. The house, which had seemed such an extraordinary stroke of luck when we had heard of it, looked like a large but none too substantial packing-box tossed haphazardly on the prairie which crept in at its very door.

The driver stopped the team in front of the shack, threw the lines to the ground, stretched his long, lank frame over the wheel and began to unload the baggage. He pushed open the unbolted door with the grass grown up to the very sill, and set the boxes and trunk inside. Grass. Dry, yellow grass crackling under his feet.

"Here, why don't you get out?" he said sharply. "It's sundown and a long trip back to town."

Automatically we obeyed. As Ida Mary paid him the $20 fee, he stood there for a moment sizing us up. Homesteaders were all in his day's work. They came. Some stayed to prove up the land. Some didn't. We wouldn't.

"Don't 'pear to me like you gals are big enough to homestead." He took his own filled water jug from the wagon and set it down at the door, thus expressing his compassion. Then, as unconcerned as a taxi driver leaving his passengers at a city door, he drove away, leaving us alone.

Ida Mary and I fought down the impulse to run after him, implore him to take us back with him, not to leave us alone with the prairie and the night, with nothing but the packing-box for shelter. I think we were too overwhelmed by the magnitude of our disaster even to ask for help.

We stared after him until the sudden evening chill which comes with the dusk of the frontier roused us to action.

Hesitantly we stepped over the low sill of the little shack, feeling like intruders. Ida Mary, who had been so proud of finding a claim with a house already built, stared at it without a word, her round, young face shadowed by the brim of her straw hat drawn and tired.

It was a typical homestead shack, about 10 x 12 feet, containing only one room, and built of rough, foot-wide boards, with a small cellar window on either side of the room. Like the walls, the door was of wide boards. The whole house was covered on the outside with tar paper. It had obviously been put together with small concern for the fine points of carpentry and none whatever for appearance. It looked as though the first wind would pick it up and send it flying through the air.

It was as unprepossessing within as it was outside. In one corner a homemade bunk was fastened to the wall, with ropes crisscrossed and run through holes in the 2 x 4 inch pieces of lumber which formed the bed, to take the place of springs. In another corner a rusty, two-hole oil stove stood on a drygoods box; above it another box with a shelf in it for a cupboard. Two rickety, homemade chairs completed the furnishings.

We tried to tell ourselves that we were lucky; shacks were not provided for homesteaders, they had to build their own—but Ida Mary had succeeded in finding one not only ready built but furnished as well. We did not deceive ourselves or each other. We were frightened and homesick. Whatever we had pictured in our imaginations, it bore no resemblance to the tar-paper shack without creature comforts; nor had we counted on the desolation of prairie on which we were marooned.

Before darkness should shut us in, we hurriedly scrambled through our provisions for a can of kerosene. Down in the trunk was a small lamp. We got it out and filled it. And then we faced each other, speechless, each knowing the other's fear—afraid to voice it. Matches! They had not been on our list. I fumbled hastily through the old box cupboard with its few dust-covered odds and ends. Back in a corner was an old tobacco can. Something rattled lightly as I picked it up—matches!

We were too weary to light a fire. On a trunk which we used as a table, we spread a cold lunch, tried to swallow a few bites and gave it up. The empty space and the black night had swallowed us up.

"We might as well go to bed," said Ida Mary dully.

"We'll start back home in the morning," I declared, "as soon as it is daylight."

Oddly enough, we had never questioned the impulse which led two young city girls to go alone into unsettled land, homesteading. Our people had been pioneers, always among those who pushed back the frontier. The Ammonses had come up from Tennessee into Illinois in the early days and cleared the timberland along the Mississippi Valley some forty miles out of St. Louis. They built their houses of the hand-hewn logs and became land

and stock owners. They were not sturdy pioneers, but they were tenacious.

Some of them went on into what Grandma Ammons called the Santa Fe Bottoms, a low marshy country along the river, where they became wealthy—or well-to-do, at least—by fattening droves of hogs on acorns. Generally speaking, my mother's family ran to professions, and my father's family to land. Though there was father's cousin, Jack Hunter, who had been west and when he came to visit us now and then told wild tales about the frontier to which my sister and I as little children listened wide-eyed. He wove glowing accounts of the range country where he was going to make a million dollars raising cattle. Cousin Jack always talked big.

It was from his highly colored yarns that we had learned all we knew of the West—and from the western magazines which pictured it as an exciting place where people were mostly engaged in shooting one another.

While Ida Mary and I were still very young our mother died, and after that we divided our time between our father's home— he had married again and had a second family to take care of—and the home of his sister. As a result my sister and I came to depend on ourselves and on each other more than two girls of our age usually do.

By the time we were old enough to see that things were not going well financially at home, we knew we must make our own way. Some of the girls we knew talked about "going homesteading" as a wild adventure. They boasted of friends or relatives who had gone to live on a claim as though they had gone lion-hunting in Africa or gold-hunting in Alaska. A homestead. At first thought the idea was absurd. We were both very young; both unusually slight, anything but hardy pioneers; and neither of us had the slightest knowledge of homesteading conditions, or experience extending beyond the conventional, sheltered life of the normal city girl in the first decade of the century.

We were wholly unfitted for the frontier. We had neither training nor physical stamina for roughing it. When I tried to explain to an uncle of mine that I wanted to go west, to make something of myself, he retorted that "it was a hell of a place to do it." In spite of the discussion which our decision occasioned, we made our plans, deciding to risk the hazards of a raw country alone, cutting ourselves off from the world of everyone and everything we had ever known. And with little money to provide against hardships and emergencies.

At that time the country was emerging from the era of straggling settlers. Immigration was moving west in a steady stream.

The tidal wave which swept the West from 1908 to the World War was almost upon us although we could not see it then. But, we thought, there would be new people, new interests, and in the end 160 acres of land for Ida Mary. Perhaps for me the health I had sought so unsuccessfully.

Primarily a quarter-section of land was the reason for almost everyone coming west. As people in the early pioneer days had talked of settling in Nebraska and Kansas and the eastern Dakotas, they now talked about the country lying farther on—the western Dakotas, Wyoming, Montana, Colorado. Over the Midwest the homestead idea was spreading rapidly to farm and hamlet and city. One heard a great deal about families leaving their farms and going west to get cheap land; of young college men who went out to prove up a quarter-section. The land would always be worth something, and the experience, even for a short time, was a fruitful one in many ways.

To the public, however, not so romantically inclined, the homesteaders were the peasantry of America. Through the early homesteading days folks who "picked up and set themselves down to grub on a piece of land" were not of the world or important to it. But the stream of immigration to the land was widening, flowing steadily on.

How did one go about homesteading? we asked. Well, all you had to do to get a deed to a quarter-section—160 acres of land—was to file on it at the nearest Land Office, live on it eight months, pay the government $1.25 an acre—and the land was yours. Easy as falling off a log!

The only improvement required by the government was some sort of abode as proof that one had made the land his bona-fide residence for the full eight months.

What would that cost? And the whole undertaking? It depended partly on what kind of shack one built and whether he did it himself or hired it done. A shack cost all the way from $25 to $100 or more. Some of those who had families and intended to stay, built cheap two- and three-room houses.

Of course, it cost women who had to hire things done more to homestead. But with grub, fuel and other necessities we figured it would cost not more than $500 all told.

Then we learned of this quarter-section with a shack already built, bunk and all. It had been filed on and the owner had left before proving-up time so that the claim, shack and all, had reverted to the government. We had about $300 saved up, and this was enough, we decided, to cover homesteading expenses, inasmuch as the shack was provided. So we had all but the final payment of $200 to the government, which would be due when we had "made proof."

We decided to let the money for that final payment take care of itself. The thing to do was to get hold of a piece of land before it was all gone. To hear people talk, it was the last day of grace to apply for a claim. They talked like that for ten years. We did not know there were several million acres lying out there between the Missouri and the Pacific waiting to be settled. We would have all winter to figure out how to prove up. And we found that one could get $1000 to $1500 for a raw claim after getting a deed to it.

The claim with the shack on it was in South Dakota, thirty miles from a town called Pierre. We looked that up in the geography to make sure it really existed. But when we tried to get detailed information, facts and figures to help us prepare for what was to come, we got only printed pamphlets of rules and regulations which were of no real help at all. Land Offices were so busy in those days that all they could do was to send out a package of printed information that no one could understand.

Armed with our meager array of facts, we talked to our father —as though the information we gave him so glibly had any real bearing on this precarious undertaking of his two young daughters. Whatever his doubts and hesitations, let us decide for ourselves; it was only when we boarded the old Bald Eagle at St. Louis one summer day in 1907, bound up the river, that he clung to our hands as though unable to let us go, saying, "I'm afraid you are making a mistake. Take care of yourselves."

"It will be all right," Ida Mary told him cheerfully. "It is only for eight months. Nothing can happen in eight months."

The first emergency arose almost at once. We started up the Mississippi in high spirits, but by the time we reached Moline, Illinois, I was taken from the boat on a stretcher—the aftermath of typhoid fever. It was bad enough to be ill, it was worse to have an unexpected drain on our funds, but worst of all was the fear that someone might file on the claim ahead of us. For a week or ten days I could not travel, but Ida Mary went ahead to attend to the land-filing and the buying of supplies so that we could start for the homestead as soon as I arrived.

The trip from Moline to Pierre I made by train. Ida Mary was at the depot to meet me, and at once we took a ferry across the river to Ft. Pierre. The river was low and the ever-shifting sandbars rose up to meet the skiffs. Ft. Pierre was a typical frontier town, unkempt and unfinished, its business buildings, hotel and stores, none of more than two stories, on the wide dirt road called Main Street. At one end of Main Street flowed the old

Missouri, at the other it branched off into trails that lost themselves in the prairie

Beyond Main Street the houses of the little town were scattered, looking raw and new and uncomfortable, most of them with small, sunburned, stunted gardens. But there was nothing apologetic about Ft. Pierre. "We've done mighty well with what we've had to work with," was its attitude.

Section 18, Range 77W—about thirty miles from Pierre. It seemed more real now. The hotel proprietor promised to find us a claim locator to whom that cryptic number made sense.

The next morning at sun-up we were on our way. At that hour the little homestead town of Ft. Pierre lay quiet. Other homesteaders were ready to start out: a farmer and his wife from Wisconsin, who were busy sandwiching their four children into a wagon already filled with immigrant goods, a cow and horse tied on behind.

At a long table in the fly-specked hotel dining room we ate flapjacks and fried potatoes and drank strong coffee in big heavy cups. Then, at long last, perched on the seat of the claim locator's high spring wagon, we jolted out of town, swerving to let a stagecoach loaded with passengers whip past us, waiting while a team of buffalo ambled past, and finally jogged along the beaten road through the bad lands outside of town.

Beyond the rough bad lands we came upon the prairie. We traveled for miles along a narrow, rutted road crossed now and then by dim trails leading nowhere, it seemed. Our own road dwindled to a rough trail, and the spring wagon lurched over it while we clung to the sides to ease the constant jolting, letting go to pull our hats over our eyes which ached with the glare, or over the back of our necks which were blistered from the sun.

Our frantic haste to arrive while the land lasted seemed absurd now. There was land enough for all who wanted it, and few enough to claim it. All that weary day we saw no people save in the distance a few homesteaders mowing strips of the short dry grass for hay. Now and then we passed a few head of horses and a cow grazing. Here and there over the hot, dusty plain we saw shacks and makeshift houses surrounded by patches of corn or flax or dried-up garden. Why were the houses so scattered, looking as though they had been thrown down at random? "They had to be set on the claims," our locator said dryly.

About noon we stopped at a deserted ranch house, surrounded by corrals—a camp, our driver explained, where some stockman held his cattle overnight in driving them to market. Here we ate a lunch and the locator fed and watered the team, refilling the jars from an old well with its long wooden water troughs.

There the trail ended. Now we struck out over a trackless land that grew rougher the farther we went. To look for a quarter-section here was like looking for a needle in a haystack. It was late summer and the sun beat down on the hot prairie grass and upon our heads. We had driven all day without sign of shade— and save for that brief interval at noon, without sight of water. Our faces and hands were blistered, our throats parched from the hot wind.

This was not the West as I had dreamed of it, not the West even of banditry and violent action. It was a desolate, forgotten land, without vegetation save for the dry, crackling grass, without visible tokens of fertility. Drab and gray and empty. Stubborn, resisting land. Heroics wouldn't count for much here. It would take slow, back-breaking labor, and time, and the action of the seasons to make the prairie bloom. People had said this was no place for two girls. It began to seem that they were right.

And this was the goal of our long journey—the tar-paper shack. We pushed the trunk over in front of the door which had no lock, piled the chairs and suitcases on top of the trunk; spread a comfort over the criss-cross rope bed and threw ourselves across it without undressing. We had no gun or other weapon for protection and were not brave enough to use one had we possessed it.

The little cellar windows which stood halfway between the low ceiling and the floor were nailed shut. But we needed neither window nor door, so far as air was concerned. It poured through the wide cracks like water through a sieve.

While we tossed, too tired and sick at heart to sleep, I asked: "What became of the young man who built this shack?"

"He lived here only a few weeks and abandoned it," Ida Mary explained. "The claim reverted to the government, shack, bunk and all. He couldn't stick it out."

The next morning we awoke to a world flooded with sunshine, and it was the surprise of our lives that we had lived to see it.

Ida started the oil stove and put on the coffee. Wearily I dragged myself out of bed. We fried bacon, made toast, unpacked our few dishes. Discovering that a hinged shelf on the wall was intended for a table, we put it up and set our breakfast on it. We found that we were really hungry.

Our determination to start back home was still unshaken, but we had reckoned without the prairies. We were marooned as on a desert island. And more pressing, even, than some way of getting back to Pierre—and home—was the need for water. We must get a jug of water somewhere. Water didn't come from a tap on the prairies. We began to wonder where it did come from; certainly there wasn't a drop to be found on Ida Mary's claim.

In the glaring morning sun which blazed on the earth, we saw a shack in the distance, the reflection of the sun on yellow boards. It was farther away than it appeared to be with the bright light against it.

This new home was larger than the regulation shack, and it had a gable—a low-pitched roof—which in itself was a symbol of permanence in contrast to the temporary huts that dotted the plains. It was made of tongue-and-groove drop-siding, which did away with the need of tar paper, and in the homestead country marked a man's prestige and solidity.

We were met at the open door by a pretty, plump young woman. A little girl of seven stood quietly at one side, and a little boy, perhaps five, at the other. As we stood there with the jug she broke into a pleasant laugh. "You've come for water! We have no well, but Huey hauled two barrels this morning from Crooks's, several miles away."

We were led into a large room, clean and cool. After one has been in a low, slant-roofed, tar-papered shack that becomes an oven when the sun shines on it, entering a house with a gable is almost like going into a refrigerator. There wasn't much in the room except beds and a sewing machine. The floor, on which a smaller child was playing, was bare except for a few rag rugs, but shining. An opening led into a small lean-to kitchen with a range in one corner; in the other a large square table spread with a checked tablecloth was set ready for the next meal, and covered with a mosquito bar. The home, the family, gave one a feeling of coming to anchor in a sea of grass and sky.

We learned that the name was Dunn and that they were dirt farmers from Iowa, but they had not come in time to do much farming that season. They had thrown up a makeshift barn as a temporary shelter for the horses and one cow until they could build a real barn—after they found out what the soil would do, Mrs. Dunn explained.

She hurried out to the kitchen, talking as she moved about, and came in with coffee and a plate of oatmeal cookies.

"I am so glad you are going to live here," she told us. "Neighbors within a mile and a half! I won't feel so much alone with neighbors close by to chat with."

We hadn't the courage to tell her that we weren't going to stay.

"You must have found the shack dirty," she said, with a glance at her spotless house. "A bachelor homesteader had it and they are always the worst. They wait until the floor is thick with dirt and grease and then spread newspapers over it to cover up the dirt. You'll have a time getting it fixed as you want it."

We wondered how anyone made a home of a tar-paper shack.

To hear Mrs. Dunn's casual remarks, one would think it no more of a problem than redecorating a city home.

As we started on the trek back, she called after us, "Huey will haul you over a keg of water tomorrow."

As soon as we were out of earshot I said, "We can hire Mr. Dunn to take us back to Pierre."

"That's an idea," Ida Mary agreed.

By the time we had walked back the mile and a half—which seemed five in the scorching heat—it was past noon and we were completely exhausted. So we did not get started back to Pierre that day. But we felt a little easier. There was a way to get out.

XVII

J. HYATT DOWNING

Born in 1888 in Granville, Iowa, Downing was raised in Blunt, S.D., where his father ran an elevator. His mother opened a boarding house in Vermillion later in order to put her two children through the University. Downing was captain of the football team while he was in school and also wrote two songs for the University.

Before Downing published his first novel, *A Prayer for Tomorrow,* at age fifty, he spent two years in the Southwest fighting TB, worked on a dairy farm, was employed by the Department of Internal Revenue in Aberdeen, served in the army during World War I, and was agency manager for Equitable Life of New York. Dissatisfied with these pursuits, he wrote his first novel while supported by his wife. The book was successful and was followed by four more novels in the next six years, including *Hope for Living,* 1939, and *Sioux City,* 1940.

With this encouragement he left for Hollywood, but in 1962 settled near his son in Shell Beach, California. He continued to write short stories for magazines and eventually published another novel, *Four on the Trail,* 1963, under the pseudonym of Mark Flood. He died in 1973.

The following selection is from the beginning of *A Prayer for Tomorrow.*

A PRAYER FOR TOMORROW

1

The rails said ruppity-rup, ruppity-rup. A shaft of sunlight like a bright golden sword lanced in through the little square window at the end of the car. It lay in buttery radiance over the small, heroic figure mounted on a mail-clad steed which served as the crowning ornament to the hard coal burner. The figure, to the boy who lay outstretched on the bale of hay near the partition which separated the saddle horses from the furniture end of the car, had always been a symbol of a gallant day which was gone from the earth and would never come back again. It held in its armored fist an upraised sword and leaned forward in the saddle as though in gay challenge to an unseen adversary.

The boy remembered vividly the first time he had consciously looked upon this brave little figure. It was while they were living in that little town in Iowa where, for a time, his father had made so much money in the lumber business. It was a windy day in April, and following a protracted period of warm weather, the fire in the base-burner had been allowed to die out. His mother had gone to church, but since he was very young, he had been left at home with his father. He remembered that, even then, he feared his father—his slightly bulging, cold blue eyes, his harsh voice, his heavy, bruising hands.

Except for the sound of the wind, tugging at the windows with insistent fingers and sobbing under the doors, the house was very still. His father was reading a newspaper, and now and then he turned a page with an impatient, slapping sound. Suddenly with the wind came the mournful tolling of church bells, deep, compelling, sad. They filled the room with their metallic clangor. They merged with the weeping wind into a wild tumult, freighted with fear and foretelling of doom. The boy raised his eyes to his father's face. It was hard, granitic, remote. Suddenly the child felt lost in a lonely, echoing world. He buried his face in his arms and began to cry.

His father glared at him over the top of his paper.

"Blast the brat. What are you crying for, Lynn?"

But the child, frightened at the menace of his father's voice, wept loudly. Through his tears he saw his father's eyes rove about the room searching for some object which momentarily might engage the child's attention. By chance his glance lit on the small figure of the embattled knight, and he rose and lifted it from the stove bracket where it was loosely fastened. He placed it in his son's hands.

"Here, take this and stop blubbering."

Lynn accepted the little figure doubtfully. His chubby finger explored the outlines of the horse, felt the sharpness of the poised sword. Suddenly a picture formed in his mind, a picture his mother had showed him in a book. A man was mounted on a horse exactly like this one; and in one hand he held a sword; in the other, a flag. The horse was running wildly, and there was an exultant smile on the rider's face as he led others mounted similarly on leaping, plunging steeds.

Lynn held the knight close to the floor and swept him forward in a desperate charge.

"Zoom," he cried happily.

The next hour, until his mother returned, passed in a haze of clashing lances, the drumming of flying feet, and the wild, tumultuous music of blaring bugles.

The shaft of sunlight sank lower over the barrels of dishes; the bulging, shapeless outlines of dressers and commodes wrapped in old quilts; washtubs packed with wadded paper which separated jars of preserves. The air of the immigrant car was heavy with the smell of manure and the pungent, sweetish odor which came from several crates where chickens murmured and fretted restlessly in their close confinement.

Lynn rose and moved to the wide door of the swaying car, resting his hand on the warm metal strip which protected the frame. During the day the country had been changing rapidly. The fat, black-soiled farms of Iowa had given place to the wide prairie reaches of Dakota. The houses, squatting so disconsolately on the broad face of the land, were lonely in their unpainted bleakness. Occasionally a plowed field flashed by, lying like a dark blemish on the prairie. But these Lynn's eye passed over quickly. It was the land, the country, the shining, rolling miles of grass which gripped and held his mind.

In Huron that morning, a friendly brakeman had paused beside the car door and rolled a leisurely cigarette.

"So you're goin' to Rudge, huh?"

"Yes. That's *cattle* country, isn't it?"

"Is now, but won't be long."

"Why?" A chill foreboding filled Lynn's mind.

"Plows, son, farmers with plows." He drew deeply on his cigarette, then made a sweeping motion with his hand. "There she is—the greatest cattle country that ever laid outdoors. I've seen trainloads of steers, a mile long, roll over this road. But these farmers'll fix it soon."

"But there aren't any farmers here now."

"Oh, yes, they is—a few, and more comin' every day. See that buffalo grass? Won't be much of that left when the farmers stick their plows into it."

But looking over the vast, shining plain, Lynn was completely unable to imagine enough plows to harm it. Land! Oceans of grass-covered land, brilliant in the sunlight, rolling westward and westward until somewhere it must slide smoothly into the ocean like the flat blade of a knife. Unconsciously his eye scanned the far horizons to see if he could discern the white flags of flying antelope. And then, with a little sigh, he realized that they like the glamorous beings represented by the knight on the base-burner were gone and could be found only in the dead pages of books.

The flat, rich shaft of sunlight was gone when Lynn turned back to his charges, the horses and chickens. He fed them and then from a battered suit case took the last of the fried chicken and thick, buttered slices of bread which his mother had given him when she kissed him good-by in Clarendon. She and his father would follow on the passenger train the next day. As he ate his cold supper, he stared through the open doorway of the car where dusk, like soft blue smoke, was falling. He wondered if he could ever get his fill of just looking. Here was romance, mystery, adventure, all the things he had read about and dreamed of back in the tight little Iowa town where he had spent the major portion of his growing years.

Presently he stretched the hammock, which his father had bought for his bed, between the two doors and, limiting his undressing to taking off his shoes, he lay down. Through the open car door he could see the stars shining. The rails chuckled softly beneath the spinning wheels. The hammock swayed gently. The horses made soft, crunching noises at their hay. He slept.

2

Lynn's first sensation on wakening was the startling absence of motion and the complete quiet which hung over the car. He leaped from his hammock and rushed to the door. The car had been "spotted" before the chute of a stock pen. He found the cleated boards which served as a bridge between car and platform and led the two horses, Don and Molly into the first empty pen he saw. Don, who in his younger days had been a race horse and still believed he was one, snorted wildly and threw up his head. Molly, sedate, dependable, minced daintily down the narrow chute and rewarded Lynn with a soft nicker when he threw the last of the baled hay into the low feed rack.

"You won't be here long, old girl. You're going to be a cow pony, do you know that?" he said happily.

Then he filled a water pail at a hydrant, sprinkled the backs of the chickens liberally "to give the darned things something to worry about," poured some into their shallow feed pans, and washed his face and hands vigorously with the water that was left. These tasks attended to, he went out and around the stock pens toward the depot which stood like a huge red packing case beside the shining rails of the track. He resolutely refused to look toward the town until he was in a position of vantage where his glance could take in the whole of Main Street.

When he had reached the station, he turned, facing the north, and opened his eyes wide. In that instant his heart sank. Rudge appeared to be an exact duplicate of all the other shrunken, gaunt, dreary little places he had viewed from the car since leaving Huron. At its northern edge low hills crept down to the straggling residential section and seemed to brood somberly over the ugliness of the unpainted, wooden buildings. The false fronts of the business section reared shamelessly into the brilliant clarity of the sunlight which searched out every broken window and sagging wooden canopy. The street was punctuated at intervals by gaping cellar holes where merchants had prudently accepted their fire insurance and moved away to more fruitful fields.

Lynn knew a moment of thankfulness at the thought that at least he wouldn't *live* in the place. There was, he felt, something vaguely sinister about the dusty street seemingly bereft of people. Filled with loneliness, he walked up the rickety wooden sidewalk, the loose boards clattering beneath his feet. He was hungry and in a sudden panic shot his hand into a pocket to make certain that the five dollar bill which his father had given him was still safe. A sigh of relief escaped him when his fingers found it neatly folded into a small square in a watchpocket just below the belt line. He quickened his steps.

Somewhere in the two blocks which comprised the business section of the town there would be a restaurant where he could get fried eggs and pancakes. There was nothing in the world so wholly delicious, at that time of Lynn's life, as two feather-light pancakes crowned by eggs fried with their "eyes open."

So absorbed was he in contemplation of this delectable breakfast that he failed to observe a tall man, wearing a dilapidated felt hat, approaching him with short, brisk steps, the high heels of his rider's boots coming down sharply on the boards of the sidewalk. Lynn jerked his head up quickly when he heard a slow, drawling voice. The man's eyes were smiling as was his wide mouth beneath his heavy black mustache.

"Hello, there. I don't think I've saw *you* before."

"No, sir. I just came."

"That so? What's your name, son?"

"Lynn McVeigh."

"Oh, now I reckon I know about you. Dad here yet?"

"No, sir. I think he'll be in today on the passenger."

"Had breakfast?"

Lynn explained that he was in search of a restaurant.

"Well, Lynn, I'll tell you. They is a restaurant, but I don't know's you'd find it just right. Miz Gunnison is used to cookin' for boiler-plated cow hands and them banjo-bellied drummers; and I don't guess she'd have what you'd want, ready to serve up, that is. I tell you what: S'pose you and me go up to my house and see what the old woman's got fit for a young feller like you. I ain't et yet, neither. I was just takin' a run over to the deepo to see if them damn shacks put off some freight for me I been lookin' for."

Lynn began to protest, filled with embarrassment and a little wonder, when the tall man wheeled him about.

"We'll just sashay back and find out about the freight and then head for home."

A moment later Lynn heard the voice of his new friend issuing from the room marked "Men."

"I ain't askin' yu. I'm *tellin'* yu. Get busy with that ticker toy of yours; and if that freight shipment ain't here by Saturday, there'll be hell poppin' an' no pitch hot. I'm goin' to take your hide off personally and hang it up to dry."

Soon the speaker issued forth smiling with complete serenity.

"Don't ever trust no railroader, Lynn. They're like what one of these phrenologist fellers said to a friend of mine one time. 'Mister,' he said, 'the truth's in you, but it won't never come out.' You pretty hungry, Lynn?"

The boy nodded mutely.

"Well, I reckon we'll soon fix that. That's my house over there. That little yaller one. My brother, Clem Hayward, lives in that fussy outfit just down the street. That's his wife's fault. She seen something in a magazine once; the *House Beautiful,* I reckon it was, and then she got *ideas.* She knows *beauty.* Clem don't give a cuss. He just wants some place where he can take his shoes off at night when he comes home from the store."

3

The Hayward house was a boiling center of activity. Leona Hayward, broad, full-breasted, and strong, smiled at Lynn from behind thick-lensed glasses. Her movements were quick, decisive, forceful. But with the touch of her hand Lynn knew instantly that she was a friend. She made no effort to make him feel comfortable or at ease. She merely assumed that he *was* comfortable and went on with her preparations for breakfast, talking at the same time, almost without pause, to her children of whom there seemed to be no end.

A little girl of four, completely naked, stood before Lynn gravely inspecting him as she sucked a thumb whitened by many insertions into her small mouth. Lynn flushed to the roots of his hair and studiously gazed through a window. Hayward laughed softly as he gathered her in his arms and carried her into an adjoining room. The air was rich with the tantalizing aroma of coffee, frying eggs, and bacon.

Presently Lee Hayward said, "Well, Lynn, I reckon we'd better come and get it, or she's goin' to throw it away."

Lynn thought he had never seen so many fried eggs on one

platter. They winked their golden eyes through a thicket of crisp bacon.

The children, ranging in age from a baby in its high chair to a boy two or three years Lynn's junior, grouped about the table while their father gravely gave thanks. A moment of utter quiet hung over the small room, blue with the smoke of cooking, as the short prayer was concluded. Then, as though a signal had been given, the family raised their heads, and pandemonium broke over the table.

Hayward dished up eggs, bacon, and admonitions. Once he laid down his great serving spoon and glanced in resignation at his wife.

"I swear, Leona, ain't you got no control over your family?"

But Mrs. Hayward only smiled as she tucked a napkin about the chin of her youngest in the high chair.

To Lynn, whose meals at home under the bleak eye of his father were ordeals to be gotten through as quickly as possible, this breakfast at the Hayward table was a new and altogether charming experience. He found himself answering questions which Hayward contrived to fashion in an interested, friendly manner.

No, his father had never been a cattleman before. He had always, as long as Lynn remembered, been engaged in the lumber business. He didn't know why he had suddenly decided to go ranching. He guessed he wanted a change. His father was always wanting to change from one town to another, one house to another. He didn't know if his mother would like Dakota or not. He hoped she would. Yes, he, Lynn, liked the prairies. He expected to be able to handle a rope and maybe a six shooter. How large was a regular ranch? Five thousand cattle? His father had only three hundred. But that would be only a temporary condition. They were all heifers, he had heard his father tell his mother; and the herd should double in a year. Lynn caught a quick look between Hayward and his wife.

"Not quite *that* fast, Lynn. You see, they's some that just won't drop a calf and some die of anthrax and black leg and some winter kill. But don't you worry," he added quickly as he saw the look of anxiety stamp itself on the boy's face, "you'll get a herd together. Sure you will. Things will be all right in this country for the cattlemen if the farmers don't move in too fast."

It was the second time Lynn had heard the voicing of that fear.

"But, Mr. Hayward, are there many farmers coming in now?"

"They's a few, son. You see, the Government says that any jasper that wants to move out here can have a quarter section of buffalo grassland if he'll just go on it, put up some kind of a shack, plow so many acres, and stay there five years. If he wants to shorten the period, he can commute it after six months by paying a dollar and a quarter an acre, and the land's his. But I can tell 'em one thing: if they ever plow up this grass, they'll be destroyin' a better crop than they can plant. Once they plow her up, she won't come back. She's gone."

Breakfast over, Lynn walked with Hayward to the store. Mrs. Hayward had followed them to the door laying her hand kindly on Lynn's shoulder.

"You come back with Lee for dinner, Lynn. Will your ma and pa be here today?"

"Yes, ma'am. At five o'clock, I think."

"Oh, on the five o'clock. Well, you'll find something to do to kill time, I guess, until then. Lee, don't you tell him any stories about this country."

Walking through the brilliant white sunlight over the rattling board sidewalk, Hayward chuckled quietly.

"My wife thinks I'm the damndest liar. But she knows I don't lie to her."

The Hayward brothers' hardware store was a long, dark cavern, lighted only by two front windows. The bare rafters were festooned with sets of harness, horse collars, scythes, whips, washtubs, boilers, sheets of tin roofing, coils of lariat rope, galvanized iron pipes, and pumps. The show cases had not been dusted, Lynn was sure, since they were installed. In them was a heterogeneous collection of every conceivable article a rancher might use for personal adornment, from silver-mounted, handsomely chased spurs to intricately stamped leather cuffs.

A small, dark man came dusting his hands from the gloomy regions of the back of the building. He scowled at Lee.

"Well, by God, Mr. Hayward, good afternoon. I'm sure glad you're so as to be around. Did you have a good time on your vacation, and where in hell is that No. 10 cycle bar for that old McCormick mower Haaken Neilson was askin' about?"

"Is your legs broke? How in hell should I know? Look for it," Lee replied pleasantly. "Clem, this is Lynn McVeigh. His pa is going to start ranching on the old Levy place. Lynn, you just poke around here and kinda make out for yourself. They's a lot of rifles and shotguns and such truck you might want to look at. I got to help my poor wore-down brother a little bit."

The store fascinated Lynn. Goods were piled everywhere: on the floor, on sagging shelves, suspended from hooks and nails. There was no attempt at any kind of order. Yet the brothers Hayward never for a moment seemed at a loss as to where a given article might be found. If a woman customer asked for a top on a special kind of fruit jar which had not been manufactured for several years, Clem, politely murmuring, delved into the recesses of a pile of miscellaneous debris and came up triumphantly with the article requested. If teeth for an out-moded threshing machine cylinder were wanted, Clem or Lee found them. They kept up a continuous banter with customers or swore pleasantly and with entire lack of rancor at each other. Their violent bickering often drew spectators from the street, a fact which they both thoroughly enjoyed.

Lynn was certain, however, that a deep bond of affection existed between them.

This opinion was confirmed when Lee said confidentially, "Don't listen to Clem. He don't mean nothin' he says when he acts mad all the time. They don't grow no finer than Clem."

And later Clem approached the boy, glancing about to see that he was not overheard. "Don't pay no attention to that brother of mine. He's God's worst liar. But outside of that and that damned mustache there ain't a thing wrong with him. Only don't let him tell you stories about side-hill gougers and hydrophobia skunks and snow snakes and tough fellers that sit around town waitin' to shoot your heels off just to see you dance."

Lynn promised that he would be prepared for the mendacious Lee. He found the Hayward brothers altogether to his liking. And, while the store and its customers throughout the long day did not cease to delight him, his deeper interest was held by the Haywards themselves. Lee, tall, loose, soft in speech and tone, darkly handsome, was the complete antithesis of his small, delicately made, saturnine brother. Lee greeted everyone who came into the store with a cheery and often unprintable salutation, his red lips curling under his darkly luxuriant mustache. Clem snapped and snarled at his customers.

At noon Lynn was ready for the boiled beef, boiled potatoes and onions, thick slices of bread, and tall, cool glasses of milk which awaited them. Leona Hayward hovered about the table and seemed delighted at the vast quantities of food consumed. Lee's speech to her, often rough though humorous, was warm with a quiet, deep affection; and Lynn noticed that when their glances met, they smiled.

For a moment he knew bitter loneliness. There had never been such an atmosphere, so alive with sympathy and understanding, in his home. He always felt a sense of relief when his father was absent at meal time. Then there was no strained tension, and he and his mother could talk naturally and without fear. Meals in the McVeigh house were wordless affairs. Lynn could not remember when he knew anything but dread with his father present. His mother's face always tightened; and one of Lynn's earliest memories was his mother saying, "Hush, your father's home."

But in this friendly house there seemed no room for fear or suspicion. The children ate noisily, lifting their voices above each other's clamor. Lee's eye roved up and down the table in pleased regard of his hearty brood or occasionally winked at some sally from one of the children which he considered especially witty.

The meal finished, Lynn left for the stock pens to care for his charges, Don, Molly, and the crates of chickens. As he walked through the street, he could not escape the feeling that the gaunt, wooden buildings sighed with weariness as they leaned against the strong wind which swept in from the open country. Before a saloon cow ponies drooped with sagging hips, awaiting the masters whose voices came noisily through the open door. Occasional riders moved up and down in swirls of dust, their spurs jingling musically, their bodies stiffly upright in the stirrups, moving rhythmically with the shuffling trot of their horses.

His tasks finished, Lynn walked to the edge of town where the grassland swept up like the tide of an ocean. Buffalo grass! It was brown, closely-curling, and matted, soft as a carpet, springy beneath his feet. On this, countless thousands had grazed in the days before the hunters came with their long Sharps rifles—perhaps in this very place before the blemishing blot of towns had marred the serenity of the prairie. He closed his eyes, and for a fleeting instant the dun-colored, hump-backed beasts stampeded over the rocking earth. And after the buffalo came cattle, millions of them, subsisting through the screeching blizzards, fattening for shipment during the long, hot summers, on this same grass. Riders, lonely figures on the vast panorama of the land, their sun-bleached eyes searching far horizons, came down from the hills. They were tall, lean, hard men who spoke little and then quietly. They, the cattle, the sweeping miles of land, the men who lived there and gave it all meaning were the West, the country of his dreams.

But the brakeman at Huron had said that this picture was to be changed, was, in fact, already changing. Men with plows were coming to do this. They would rip this soft grass into black ribbons of sod and with fences they would shut the cattle away from the creeks and water holes.

Lynn's eyes reached out to the hills. Beyond them for hundreds of miles was nothing but grass. What could a few farmers with plows do against that limitless expanse of prairie? The man was wrong. Sometime, perhaps when people crowded each other too much back in Iowa, Minnesota, and Wisconsin, more of the farmers would come. But not now. Not for years and years. Today it was cattle land, quiet, vast, serene.

The sun was slanting down the long bright planes of the sky

when Lynn turned back to the town. It would soon be train time. His father would be there with his hard, questioning eyes. As always when he thought of his father, a shadow fell across his mind. Quickly he ran over the list of duties with which he had been charged: The horses had been properly cared for. None of the chickens had died. The car stood ready for unloading. He had not spent the money which his father had given him to be used in case of emergency. He could think of nothing which he had left undone.

But as he approached the little station where a knot of people had begun to gather in anticipation of one of the principal events of the day, the arrival of the passenger train, he was conscious of the old shadowy feeling of guilt, a bleak conviction that in some manner his father would find reasons for criticism. And with that certainty a cold spot of dread lodged in his heart.

4

Lynn never forgot that long, tortuous journey to the ranch which John McVeigh had leased for his venture. His parents rode in the buggy. To the rear axle of this vehicle was attached the tongue of a mowing machine, bought at a farm auction in Iowa, and to the mower, in turn, was hitched a hayrake upon the leaping spring seat of which Lynn rode. The furniture had gone ahead in a huge hayrack driven by a polite hand from the livery stable in Rudge.

But something had been wrong, terribly wrong. Lynn felt it in the amused smiles of the few idlers who gathered to watch the unloading of the household furniture. Perhaps it was the boots his father wore, so obviously new, so high; and, contrary to the custom of the country, his trouser legs were *tucked in*. Perhaps it was the somewhat ridiculous team that Don and Molly made. Don, ex-race horse, had arched his neck, thrown his rump out against the tugs, and snorted in fancied alarm. Molly, solid little person that she was, immediately got down to business and started pulling on the heavy drag. Don lunged, stopped, lunged again. John McVeigh sawed on the reins, seized the whip, and lashed the horse savagely. Don, tossing his head wildly now, in a real panic, leaped more frantically and uselessly.

At last, by dint of the steady pulling of Molly, the procession— it was literally that—got under way; "hell bent for nowhere" Lynn heard a tall cowman whisper audibly to another interested spectator. As the high iron wheels of the hayrack struck upon the rails of the track crossing, Lynn glanced back at Rudge, squatting sourly upon the clean face of the prairie, and prayed that he would not soon see it again. He wanted to forget the squalid little town as nearly as possible.

They had spent the night at the Dickman House, and the rooms, hot, close, unventilated boxes, were as sound-proof as a tent. Once during the night Lynn was awakened and heard his mother weeping softly in an adjoining room. Then the heavy, harsh voice of his father, "Oh, for God's sake, Martha. Just because I came to a new country which seems strange to you to try to make an honest dollar, you have to snivel all night. It's enough to drive a man crazy."

After a while the crying ceased, and Lynn lay long, staring into the hot darkness of the room. He knew, now, the meaning of the look of terror on his mother's face as she alighted from the train that afternoon. It was the country. It was alien, unfriendly, and sinister to her. It was utterly desolate and terrifying. His mother was not of the stuff of which pioneers are made, he realized. While Dakota was not actually more than a day's journey by train from scenes which were familiar and dear to her, it might as well have been at the ends of the earth. But she smiled at him the next morning at breakfast and often, as they went slowly over the road which ran like a wild thing before them, she glanced back; and the corners of her sweet mouth lifted in a smile.

Slowly the country unrolled like a vast scroll. To the west reared the huge bulk of Medicine Butte, flat-topped, treeless, its tawny immensity shouldering out of the level floor of the prairie. Once they passed a new pine shanty; and a woman in bare feet and a soiled Mother Hubbard came to the door, a baby in her arms, and stared at them with dull eyes. Lynn saw his father point at the peculiarly hideous dwelling and say something quickly to his mother. A little further on where the land dropped into a shallow swale, they came upon a man behind a breaking plow, drawn by four horses driven abreast. The plowman stopped his team in answer to John McVeigh's raised whip. Lynn thought suddenly that it was characteristic of his father to halt people in that fashion, by raising his arm in command.

He lifted his voice above the hard soughing of the wind. "Plowing, I see?"

The man dropped his glance; let it rove over the thin flanks of his horses, out over the sweep of land, and back to McVeigh. A slight, ironic smile twitched at the corners of his lips.

"Well, I ain't gatherin' flowers and I ain't pickin' up cow chips."

"Are you farming this land?" McVeigh asked, ignoring the oblique reply, his lips tight and color flushing his cheeks.

"Well, Mister, what do *you* think? I ain't aimin' to raise cattle nor sheep with a breakin' plow."

McVeigh threw his answer against the man in a flat hard challenge. "This isn't *farming* country. It's *cattle* country."

"That's what you think. Uncle Sam says I can have a hundred and sixty acres of this land if I want it. Well, I want it. Look at that soil." He pointed his finger at the deep shaving of black earth turned up by the plow. "That's where wheat and corn comes from, Mister."

The taunt of McVeigh's harsh, brittle laugh came back with the wind.

"All right, farm and be damned. The dry summers'll take care of you and all the rest who think they can spoil this country with crops. You'll all starve out in a year at the outside."

"Maybe, but durin' that year, keep your cattle off this land, Mister."

In late afternoon they came to the ranch, the tall, two-story frame house rearing its ugliness against the gray background of the prairie. The house stood on a graveled knoll, and a windmill complained dryly in a nearby draw where pole corrals traced their pale skeletons in the rich light of the westering sun. Further down the draw was a hut, its roof a thatch of dead hay, its weathered siding stained with rain-washed manure which had been flecked against it by the churning feet of cattle. South of the house stood a lonely shed in one end of which were some roosts for chickens and in the other a long litter-strewn workbench where in past days machinery repairing had been done. It was now a dry, windy emptiness, its loose shingles rattling disconsolately in the rushing, heated air.

John McVeigh climbed stiffly from the buggy and helped his wife to alight. The hand from the livery stable was waiting to help unload the furniture. He rose politely from his haunches, restraining with difficulty the grin which pulled at his lips, and crushed out a cigarette as the strange procession approached.

At that moment Lynn's glance fell on his mother's face. Never, he thought, had he seen such bleak despair. Then she turned and walked resolutely into the kitchen door.

The following days were a period of feverish activity to Lynn. There were a thousand tasks, all demanding immediate attention. The leather valves in the pump had gone dry from disuse and must be replaced. There was the house to be settled, the corral fence to be repaired, the shed roof to be patched, the horse pasture to be made secure. The cattle had arrived, having been driven in a long, slow queue, over which hung a powdery veil of dust, from Rudge. The first duty was to provide them with water; and Lynn worked late with his father whose temper, frayed by unaccustomed labor, flared forth with increasing frequency. But when the metal wheel began to spin with the strong wind, and water from the deep-driven well spouted into the wooden tank, Lynn felt pride of accomplishment. The corral gate was left open; and the cattle, having drunk their fill, spread out on the nearby prairie, their multi-colored hides vivid against the tawny grass.

"Keep them close for a few days until they become used to heading in for water. After that we shouldn't have to watch them so much," his father said.

Lynn saddled the restive Don and pointed the herd out toward the range lying just to the westward. Don threw up his head, arched his neck, and pranced on dancing feet. Here was an unlimited race track upon which to run; and he pulled and tugged at the bit, flecks of foam spotting his black neck. At noon the cattle, having eaten their fill, lay down contentedly chewing their cuds, and Lynn rode the curvetting exhibitionist Don in for dinner.

The Levy ranch had originally been owned by a man who had managed to save, out of thirty years of railroading, enough money to buy a quarter section of land and five hundred head of heifers at the Chicago stockyards, and, with the money which remained, to build a house. It was a rapidly disintegrating example of bad planning and hurried construction. Only one of the rooms was ceiled; in the others nail points protruded from bare pine boards. Rafters arched overhead in warped dryness.

The second story was one large room beneath a steeply pitched roof upon which the wind drummed with tireless fingers. Here Lynn was to sleep. The heat hung in pools, trapped by the thin roof. Lynn was thankful for two small windows at either end of the large room which let in the fresh, clean smell of the land, dispelling old dead odors, which lay like dark thoughts under the sloping eaves. It was from one of these rafters, so the cheerful hand from the livery stable had said, that a neighboring rancher had found hanging the body of Levy, following the death of most of his cattle from anthrax, a periodic scourge of the range land.

On still nights when the wind had momentarily ceased, Lynn was often to lie staring into the thick darkness wondering from which of the ten rafters, stretching across the barren emptiness of the attic, the tragic Levy had suspended himself.

Once a thought, terrifying in its logical clarity, brought him upright in bed. "Why, we're doing just what he tried to do. What will happen to us?"

There seemed to hover in that dead room a brooding, sinister presence. Lynn heard it in the yielding creaking of the sun-dried timbers, in the metallic whine of the windmill as it stirred to a tugging current of superheated air.

But fifteen does not long harbor presentiments, and there was much to occupy Lynn's attention. First of the seasonal work was branding. John McVeigh had registered his brand, a coupled combination of J. H. M., at Pierre. In the work of branding they were assisted by Henry Davis, a rancher who, some years previously, had likewise come from the "East," as all states east of the Missouri River were then known. Davis' ranch lay five miles southwest of the Levy place. In the years which followed the suicide of its original owner, the ranch was never known by any other name than the "Levy place." Thus does tragedy isolate people and houses.

Davis was a small man of great wiry strength. He seemed to know the precise method to be followed in constructing a branding chute.

"They do it on the range with a rope and a running iron. We haven't got time to fool with them fancy doin's," he said.

His smile was reassuring, and his capable hands, covered with red bristles of hair, were firm and friendly.

It was Lynn's duty to keep the several irons at exactly the right heat. The cattle squirmed and bawled as the branding tool seared their flesh. The smell of the burning hair and hide nauseated Lynn at first. But he had little time for self-concern. Davis' darting glance constantly found new things for him to do.

"Here, Lynn, grab that heifer. *Grab* her. She ain't goin' to hurt you. There, drop the gate and turn her loose. You'll make a hand yet, boy."

Almost as pressing in necessity as branding was the putting up of hay against the coming of winter. With a reasonably open season the herd should come through to spring on one ton of hay to the head. Since it was now early July, there was no time to be lost in getting mowers into the swales and valleys where the lush, salt grass grew abundantly. It became necessary to hire men with teams and machines to assist, and John McVeigh complained bitterly at the wages he was forced to pay. Henry Davis smiled quietly and observed that he could take chances on coming through the winter without hay if he chose to gamble.

That summer was a period of endless toil for Lynn. Very little riding was required since the cattle grazed within a radius of two or three miles from the ranch, returning in late afternoon for their fill of water at the tank which the windmill kept replenished. If ranching in Dakota was less picturesque than he imagined it would be, he did not find his tasks unpleasant. Throughout July and August he rode a mower, drawn by Molly and Don, alternating with the hayrake in the afternoons when he bunched the grass which had been left in long windrows by rakes attached to the cycle bars of the machines. When several acres of hay had been cut and bunched, it was loaded into racks and hauled to the ranch where long, smooth stacks were constructed about the corrals. Thus it could be conveniently fed the cattle in the winter months when the open range was too deep in snow to permit grazing.

During haying, Lynn's father repaired fences and attended to the innumerable small tasks which demanded attention about the ranch buildings. Occasionally he walked out across the prairie to the place where Lynn was mowing and drove the team for an hour. He knew nothing of horses and managed them with a tight rein and threatening whip, exhausting both the team and himself. He was always in a towering temper when he relinquished the machine to Lynn and never failed to warn him to "keep moving." Everyone, he declared, appeared to think he was made of money.

Often on the long summer evenings when the sunset splashed planes of gold across the painted sky, Lynn sat with his mother on a bench beside the kitchen door. There she told him tales of her girlhood in England and of the field of Waterloo, which she had once visited with her grandfather, a veteran of that tragic battle. Or she would sing him old French songs, songs with a curious booming joyousness in them.

Once, after a little silence had fallen between them, she said suddenly, "It won't last, Lynn."

"What won't last, Mother?" he asked, though intuitively he understood the thought in her mind.

"This ranching episode. It is simply a phase in your father's life. He's a very emotional person, Lynn, and he loves to dramatize himself."

"Well, I can't see how he can get much fun out of it. He doesn't like ranch life, really."

"Of course he doesn't. But he caught a vision of himself once, heaven only knows how or why, dressed in a wide hat and high-heeled boots and possibly even chaps, mounted on a coal-black steed, viewing a vast herd of cattle, spread all over the prairie. I think that's the reason he bought that useless Don. The horse, being black and spirited, somehow completed the picture which he had conjured up of himself." Martha McVeigh laughed quietly. "You mustn't think I'm making sport of your father, Lynn. Life hasn't given him much of the thing he would really like to have. I know he's actually romantic, though he would be the last person in the world to admit it."

"You mean he likes adventure and things like that?"

"Yes, I think he would love to live dangerously. You see, Son, when he was a boy, he had a very hard time of it. His father—I

understand from the little things he has let drop—was a hard, ruthless man who believed that to spare the rod was to spoil the child.
I've heard your father say that he would be promised a whipping
on Monday to be given the following Saturday night. He gave his
son all week to think of his coming punishment. When he was still
quite young, he was bound out, as they used to call it, to a carpenter. That was almost like slavery. The master had full control
of his apprentices and could beat them and do with them just as
he chose. Once he ran away but was caught and punished terribly.

"When he was about your age, he managed to make his escape
and went to Chicago where he all but starved to death. But Chicago was booming then; and since he knew something of carpentry,
he finally got a job. He was large for his age, just as you are. And
I think he must have looked like you. He made good wages. Later
he went back to his home to visit his mother, and his father attempted to send him back to the man from whom he escaped.
Your father ran away again, and that was the last time he ever
saw his father.

"You see, Lynn, he never knew kindness in his boyhood; and I
know it made him hard. That is why I want you to try to understand him. He doesn't mean to be unjust. He was raised in a
hard school; and because he survived, he thinks it developed
strength and self-reliance. He doesn't really know tenderness—
he can't accept it. But I believe, Lynn, he would like to if he
could. He just can't."

"Is that why he takes it out on me?"

"He doesn't think he's taking it out on you, Son, as you call it.
He thinks he's helping you learn lessons which will come in handy
when you are older."

"Well, I'd just as soon learn some of it a little later. I don't think
he's thinking of what he can teach me, Mother. I think he's just
got to find some way of letting out his bad nature. He can't fool
me. He doesn't like me and never has."

"I wish you wouldn't feel that way, Lynn. It makes it so hard
for me."

"All right, Mother, I won't say it. I'll just try not to notice."

But in his heart Lynn knew that between him and his father lay
a chasm too wide to bridge; that neither time nor the best intentions could heal a rupture which had occurred far back in his
childhood.

5

Winter comes down savagely on the prairies. The soft haze of
late Indian summer vanishes like smoke. Pale, cumulous clouds

suddenly appear on the horizon, and then the wind sweeps bitterly over the gray floor of the land. Life congeals. Cattle, their backs humped against the piercing cold, hunt draws and breaks for protection; hides roughen; and their summer sleekness is gone. Snow collects in the coulees and gullies, but on the level reaches it goes spiraling with the wind. Later a heavy snow follows a period of mild weather. Then the prairie is a flashing, beautiful expanse of utter loneliness.

It was decided that Lynn would not attend high school in Rudge that year. John McVeigh declared shortly that he would be needed in feeding and caring for the cattle. The next year, perhaps. There was plenty of time. He, himself, had never gone beyond the sixth grade in school. He considered most of the furor for education mere balderdash. Made more fools than anything else. Lynn was content at this decision. It would give him a chance to ride and hunt rabbits on the wide prairie.

During the summer Henry Davis had given him a collie pup; and the boy found it an ardent companion in his gallops over the level range land, armed with his twenty-two caliber rifle which he had brought from Clarendon. The pup, named Rowdy because of his complete lack of regard for any form of controlled behavior, was wholly convinced of his ability to catch a pack rabbit. Though he always returned to his master with a shamefaced expression after each futile pursuit, he investigated each lodged tumbleweed where his long-legged quarry lurked. When one was flushed, he bounded after it joyfully as ever, his excited yelps floating back with the wind.

Once as Lynn described these undiscouraged but useless efforts to his mother, his father glanced up from a book he was reading, his lips a thin, sneering line.

"At least he tires hard. That's more than I can say for you."

A quick flush mounted the boy's cheeks, and a hot retort was on his tongue when he felt his mother's eyes in their frightened appeal. He stared a moment at his father; their eyes locked; then Lynn turned and went over to his mother, who was preparing supper. She touched his face fleetingly with her hand, and Lynn felt the gratitude and love in the gesture. He rarely, now, sat about the living-room reading lamp if his father were there, offering as an excuse that it was warmer by the kitchen stove.

The winter proved a long monotony of heavy tugging at reluctant and settled stacks, heading the cattle out to graze on fair days, and watching them closely that they might not stray and become lost in one of the quick, furious blizzards which periodically swept over the country. Only an occasional hunt for rabbits broke the boredom of his days. The long evenings beside the glowing kitchen stove were his great reward. The one thing in the McVeigh home in which Lynn found real content was the well-stocked shelf of books. John McVeigh was a voracious reader. He found in the written thoughts of other minds an escape from a life which, Lynn knew, had been somehow unsatisfactory.

Spring came rushing out of the south early that year, and suddenly the prairie was a lush, green beckoning. After sundown gray mists hung over the ground, and the air was a strong enchantment. The cattle grazed greedily, following the draws where the grass was thickest. Lynn had great difficulty in keeping them together. Most of the young heifers were heavy with calf, and Lynn was forced to watch them closely that they might not wander away to bring forth their calves alone and unattended.

But the days passed more swiftly; and he found endless amusement in watching the youngsters, as soon as they had discovered their legs, running about beside their mothers in awkward attempts at playfulness. It always interested him to observe the mothers' tender regard for their offspring. No calf could be lost so long that its mother did not recognize it when found. This puzzled him a great deal since they all looked exactly alike.

It was in the early days of spring, almost before the frost was out of the ground, that Lynn saw the first covered wagon crawling slowly over the prairie. He was out on Don searching for a young heifer which had strayed away from the herd. The wagon approached slowly over the twisting, deeply washed prairie road. It was drawn by two large, well-conditioned, farm horses. The huge, high, boxed vehicle was new. Behind the wagon trailed three milk cows driven by a youth of about his own age. The farmer stopped his team.

"How fer is it to Rudge, Bub?' '

"It's about fifteen miles straight down this road."

"Thanks, giddap."

"Are you coming out here to farm?"

"Yup. That's right."

"But this isn't a farming country. It's a cow country."

"You mean it *was* a cow country. Listen, Bub. Before the summer's over you'll see families scattered all over this prairie. I'm coming in early so's I can get my pick of the land. But they's lots more. They're coming in wagons, on horseback, and on the trains. I came this way 'cause it's cheaper. I'll git my outfit after I git my land. Giddap!" He shook his reins and rolled slowly down the road.

Lynn watched him for a moment doubtfully. This, then, was what the brakeman meant at Huron that day. The farmers *were* coming with their plows. They would tear off the shining grass into ugly patches of sod and build their raw, bleak, little houses all over the land. Fences would shut off the waterholes, and the free range would be gone. Anger surged quickly through his mind. He hated farmers, their wagons, and their plows; hated the stolid look of their heavy, unshaved faces, their graceless, bulky bodies, their sallow-faced, taffy-haired children, their work-driven, unlovely wives. They lived in the ground like moles, pushing up wheat and corn and oats. They brayed loudly at their own senseless humor and gobbled their meals at oilcloth-covered tables. These were the people who were coming to ruin the beauty and glamor of the grassland and take it away from its rightful owners —the cattlemen.

As Lynn turned his pony homeward, a cold, reasoning voice intruded itself upon his consciousness.

"Why should you care. Have you been happy on the ranch?"

"No, but that isn't the fault of the country."

"Don't you understand that this is progress? The cattlemen must give way to the farmer. It's been that way wherever land would produce crops. An acre of land growing wheat is worth a lot more money than an acre of land growing grass."

"But the farmers will change the whole country. It won't be interesting or beautiful any more."

"That depends on what you call interesting. The land will support a great many more people than it does now. Isn't that interesting?"

"Yes, but I hate farmers."

"But if they come, everyone will make more money. Your father could make a great deal of money if he invested in this cheap land. He could, probably, become rich."

Rich! The word rang like a bell in Lynn's mind. Maybe then if his father had all the money he needed, he would be pleasant and amiable; and there wouldn't be that atmosphere of strained reticence in his home which had shadowed his entire life.

He let Don have his head then; his mind filled with a wild hope. He'd better tell his father of this new way of getting rich, he thought, before the whole country found out about it.

He found his father standing before the windmill, eyeing it venomously.

"The infernal thing squeaks until I'm nearly crazy. Climb up on the tower and see if you can find where it needs oil."

Lynn clambered up the narrow ladder, oiled the wheel, and in a few moments was back on the ground.

"I saw a homesteader coming in on the Rudge road," he said. "I talked to him. He said there were lots more coming for the land the Government will let them file on this summer. He said there would be a family on every quarter section by fall."

A curiously weary expression stamped itself for a moment on his father's face.

"Yes, I know," he said quietly. "They're filing on land at Pierre at the rate of one hundred and fifty a day. The cattlemen have been buying up relinquishments, but they haven't money enough to buy off all the homesteaders. Cattle are finished here."

"Wouldn't a person—I mean, isn't there lots of money in buying and selling land?"

"I don't know anything about the real estate business. I know lumber. It begins to seem that lumber is all I do know."

He turned away. There was a definite droop to his shoulders and slowness in his step that Lynn had never before observed. He realized suddenly that his father would soon be an old man, an old and defeated man.

6

Summer bloomed; and with it came more and more homesteaders, by rail, wagon, and even horseback. Word had traveled swiftly over Iowa, Minnesota, and Wisconsin that in South Dakota was a free farm for the taking and land where flax, sown on freshly broken sod, literally poured from the ground. The main street of Rudge was choked with farm wagons, and Sven Peterson's general store was thronged with settlers and their wives. Sven, a portly, jovial Swede, threw up his hand to Clem Hayward.

"Yesus Christ. Aye tank aye go cracy."

By early September John McVeigh's settled look of apathy had given place to a curious liveliness and expectancy. He made frequent trips to town and came back smelling strongly of whiskey and willing to talk at the supper table.

"The town's filling up," he said one evening. "Real estate men as thick as fleas. The Acme Lumber Company is swamped. The man's a fool. He's giving credit, and these newcomers all have *some* cash. There's room for another good yard in Rudge."

Martha McVeigh lifted her eyes quickly.

"Why don't you take the opportunity, John? You know lumber. There is nothing here. The free range is going, and it will never be fit for cattle again. I think most of the smaller cattlemen will be forced to sell out. The bigger ones will migrate to Montana or Wyoming. What hope is there for us?"

It was a daring speech for Martha McVeigh, and Lynn knew that only a great sense of urgency and conviction would have spurred her into it. John smiled thinly.

"Well, you may be right. I've already looked over a site for a yard near the tracks. Right now I can get it on a five-year lease, longer if I want it, or buy it at about my own price."

The following morning Lynn, much to his surprise, was invited to drive into town with his father. As they went slowly over the looping two-path road, he thought of the first time he had come that way. A year had passed, and already the ranching venture was, or soon would be, over.

All his life he could remember such mercurial, kaleidoscopic changes in the life of the family. There had never been a sense of permanency. It always seemed when they moved to a new town or into a new house that they were merely camping there awhile. Soon they would go on to some other place, into a different house, among strange people. No sooner did Lynn form friendships than they were broken. His school work had suffered. He was more than one full year behind where he should have been. This had developed, at last, a fear of strangers, a deepening sense of inferiority.

It was characteristic of his father that as he contemplated a new venture, his spirits rose; and he became talkative and almost genial. He turned to his son as he pointed toward an immigrant wagon which was crawling over the road two or three miles distant.

"All those fellows are bringing some money with them. A good lumberyard should do well. I suppose you'd be glad to live in town again?"

"No, sir. I don't like Rudge."

"Don't like it? Why not?" he asked sharply.

"I didn't like it when I first saw it," Lynn replied, knowing that his words would irritate his father. "Rudge doesn't seem to be really a town. I don't think there are many boys there."

"I suppose that you aren't interested in whether or not we make any money?"

But Lynn's lips shut in a straight, repressed line. He felt his father's harsh glance upon him and knew that the remainder of the trip would be completed in silence.

It had been several months since Lynn had seen Rudge, and he was not prepared for the changes which met his glance when they turned out of the country road and crossed the tracks into Main Street. A pall of dust hung over the narrow thoroughfare. Farmers' wagons moved up and down, and the sidewalks were filled with people. There was a great sound of hammering in the air, and Sven Peterson's store was having its first bath of fresh paint in many years. Offices had sprung up on every side, their windows bright with legends of choice land, invitations to the prospective settler to come in and be given free advice as to the best filing locations still available. There was a noticeable absence of cow ponies before the saloon. Now farm teams were hitched there. Lynn heard his father talking with the banker, Colonel Winterslip.

"It doesn't seem possible that most of these people have come here within the last year, Mr. McVeigh," the Colonel said. "But they have, nearly all of them. Most astonishing thing. In one year we've seen a whole country do a right-about-face. When you moved here with your little bunch of cattle, I'd have said it was ten years off. But we already had a few farmers even when you came. They found out that land could be had, almost for the asking, that would produce thirty and forty bushels of wheat to the acre. There's the story. You couldn't stop them with a shotgun after that kind of news got around. Why, it's been like a gold strike."

The town did, indeed, resemble a boom camp. Lynn saw few women, and most of these were in the wagons of farmers, sitting stolidly on the spring seats, babies at their breasts, while their men bought supplies in the stores. A feverish, restless energy poured up and down the street. It was reflected in the quick, decisive gestures of men talking in groups on a corner, in the hurried, intent impatience of farmers waiting before the counter in Hayward's hardware store. The town was in the grip of a strong, pressing excitement.

Lynn went with his father to inspect the site of the proposed lumberyard. It was relatively near the railroad tracks. Only a short haul would be required to transport lumber from the cars. John McVeigh paced about, stepping off the boundaries of the yard-to-be, decided on the location where the office should stand. It developed that he already had taken an option on the ground. He stood quite still, at last, his head thrown back and hands in his pockets. Lynn observed suddenly that it had been some time since he had seen his father wearing the prized, high-heeled boots of which he was so obviously proud when he began his ranching experiment. If, Lynn thought, there were some insignia, some badge, of the lumber business that he could put on, he'd be wearing it now.

Presently his father nodded, and they walked back up the clogged street and into the bank. There he and Colonel Winterslip disappeared into a small room at the back where most of the bank's real estate transactions were made. Lynn remained in the crowded customers' space. Real estate men hurried in and out, their eyes intent, their hands full of abstracts and deeds. He gazed through the large plate window and watched the steady procession of wagons coming into town and going out on the roads leading to the prairie. He could not comprehend the change which had taken place in the little town in the short space of time which had elapsed since he had last seen it. He had left it a nondescript, characterless, little hodgepodge of drab, weathered buildings, dozing in the sun. He found it buzzing with activity, tremendously alive, enveloped in an atmosphere of straining haste.

When at last his father came out of the small room with the Colonel, there was a look of excitement in his eyes; and his manner was brusque. Coloney Winterslip appeared to be congratulating him.

"Very wise, Mr. McVeigh, very wise indeed," Lynn heard him murmur. "We need your type of business man in Rudge. The town has a great future, sire, a great future. Land will be selling for thirty dollars an acre in two years, mark my word. Yes, yes, certainly, you'll do very well in the lumber business here."

"Are we going to move to Rudge?" Lynn asked after groceries had been loaded into the back of the buggy, and they were out once more upon the road to the ranch.

"Yes, we're going to move to Rudge. My God, how glad I'll be to get away from those infernal cattle."

Lynn did not reply. In a year or two he'll be just as anxious to get out of Rudge, he thought.

Even though he recognized a deep restlessness in his father, a restlessness which found expression in his invariably futile attempts to establish a home where he could find some measure of happiness. And young as he was, Lynn knew that happiness would never be known by his father.

7

The following week John McVeigh stood at the corral gate, tally pad in hand, and checked out his herd to a representative of a commission firm in Sioux City. There was a quick liveliness in his manner, almost a jovial quality in his voice. The commission man had a bottle in his pocket; and they made several trips to the barn carefully shutting the gate each time and returning to take up the count where they had left off.

To Lynn, during the past year, the cattle had become individuals. He knew their eccentricities and peculiar markings. There was a two-year-old heifer that could go through any fence which had been devised. This one was playful and always in better condition than the others. That one was a jug-head—too dumb to hunt for grass if it happened to be covered by a dust of snow. There was Spot, one of the few old cows of the herd, frantically concerned over a calf which insisted on wandering out of her sight. How many times had he milked old Spot! She always came to the fence, waiting for him to come with his stool and pail, anxious to be relieved of the pressure in her udder. There was Skin-tail, a perverse creature who could and would, if given an opportunity, kick the hat off your head; old Bess, who always moved her hind quarters so obligingly when told to "heist." She was quiet and docile and never flicked his eyes with her tail even in fly time.

One by one he watched them go out the gate. A wave of depression swept over him. He was always saying good-by to friends, to places he loved, preparing for new homes in progressively smaller and more dismal towns. And Rudge was the smallest, dreariest of them all. He felt a hand on his arm and looked up to see his mother standing at his side.

"Don't feel too badly, Son. Maybe this is the last move we'll make for a long time. I hope so. You'll find friends in Rudge. Your father says new people are moving in every day. He's so enthusiastic about the opportunity he believes he has there. Oh, I hope he won't be disappointed."

"He was enthusiastic about coming out here on the ranch, wasn't he?"

"Yes, but do you know, Lynn, I believe he understood the day after he reached here that ranching could never be his business. He has been very unhappy, I know. Do try to understand him a little better, Lynn. I'll be much happier if you will."

"Sure, Mother," Lynn replied, turning his face away. "I'll try. But it won't be any use. He just doesn't like me."

"Please don't say that, Lynn. He does, I'm sure. But he can't permit himself to show it. But if you'll help as much as you can, everything will be better."

On Saturday a hayrack drove out from Rudge, and the household furniture was loaded into it. Don and Molly had been sold to the livery stable owner, Gus Littlesmith. Lynn's eyes misted over as he saw Molly led away to become a livery stable hack, abused and maltreated by unfeeling traveling men. He found himself wishing she could have died before this fate overtook her. Molly was a staunch little person, always giving all she had, her courageous heart always greater than her strength. She would not last long in livery work, he told himself.

The house which John McVeigh found for his family was a green-painted, story-and-a-half cottage surrounded by a wide, brown lawn. Two tall cottonwood trees stood before the front door. Their waxy leaves made a continuous murmuring in the wind. Back of the house was a plot of ground which was used by its former occupants as a garden. The rear boundary joined the grounds of the house where Lynn had eaten his first meal in Rudge—Lee Hayward's.

As he was inspecting the outbuildings, the small chicken house, the wood and coal shed adjoining, the privy with its Montgomery Ward catalogue suspended from a nail, Lynn heard the slow drawl of a voice he remembered. He had seen Lee Hayward but twice in the period, slightly more than a year, that he had lived on the ranch. Hayward had always been interested and friendly, humor ever lurking in his eyes and slow speech.

"Heard you was movin' in, Lynn. Well, your old man ain't no different from a lot of others I've seen. A good many land in Rudge when they come out to this country to go farmin' or ranchin'."

Lynn smiled dutifully, as he knew he was expected to smile.

"Yes, I guess all roads out in this country lead to Rudge, don't they?"

"That's right. Rudge is gettin' to be plumb populous. Seen it since you come in? Guess you'll like it pretty well now."

"No, I don't like it. I don't think I ever will like it."

"Well, hell, you hadn't orta feel that way. You're a queer kind of a kid. What's the matter with this town?"

"I guess there isn't anything," Lynn replied quickly, sure that he had given Lee Hayward a bad impression. "I can't get over the first feeling I had about Rudge the day I landed here."

"Well, you want to forget that. This town's goin' to be a hummer. Your dad will make a potful of money if he sets up a good yard and gets along with the farmers. Everyone will make money if the farmers do, and it looks like they think they will, at least. You see, Lynn, it works this way: the farmers are goin' to rob the land, and we're goin' to rob the farmers. Pretty, ain't it?"

The first two weeks of their residence in Rudge passed, and John McVeigh fumed at the slowness of the railroad in delivering his carload shipment of lumber. The yard was laid out, and daily he went to the station and sent telegrams, tracers, and frantic demands to Minneapolis. He was burning to get into the swing of business before winter shut down. His temper, which always lurked just back of his prominent, pale blue eyes, flared at every provocation. Unable to face inaction he drank heavily. The sight of farm wagons coming out of the Acme Lumberyard gate drove him almost to a frenzy. Lynn knew that his father hated every one of those farmers with a personal, venomous hatred, but he hated Wagner, the manager of the lumber concern, even more.

"He's a grinning ape," he complained to his wife. "Every time he goes past my yard where I'm working, he looks at me; and his ugly face splits wide open. When my yard is open, I'll drive him out of town."

One afternoon Wagner came unexpectedly into the yard.

"Just as well let me loan you some material, Mr. McVeigh.

You can pay me back when you get yours. It'll save you time. You can get your platforms and your office built."

John McVeigh looked at him, his jaw sagging with surprise.

"Well, all right," he said at last, ungraciously, "I'll see that you get as good or better lumber than you let me have."

"Oh, that's all right. Glad to oblige you. Maybe you can do me a good turn sometime."

McVeigh recounted the incident that night at home. "There's a trick in it somewhere," he said. "People aren't going around *looking* for a chance to do favors. He'll probably want me to ease up on competition. Well, I won't."

Martha McVeigh looked at him with musing eyes.

"Why don't you try getting along with people, John?" she asked. "It is so much easier than fighting."

"I've tried it. Don't work. From now on people can try to get along with me."

When Lynn went to the rival yard with a list of the lumber which would be immediately needed, Wagner grinned.

"Your old man's a stiff-necked, old coot, ain't he? Hell, you'd a thought he was doin' *me* a favor."

"Oh, he doesn't mean to be that way. It's just a way he has," Lynn replied quickly.

"Well, it don't weigh a hell-of-a-lot with me. After this you an' me will do business. I don't want no more of *him*."

The following week Lynn spent in helping the carpenters construct a long shed which would house the better grades of material, such as siding and milled products, and constructing bases upon which the piles of rough lumber were to rest in the open. The yard was carefully planned. A wagon could drive through the wide gate; make a complete circle; and come out loaded, posts and shingles being last. Later, McVeigh planned to build a weather-tight shed where would be housed cement, lime, and door frames.

He supervised the work of the two carpenters with a watchful eye, and they grumbled a good deal between themselves. Yet they worked rapidly, using all their skill to save material, knowing that their employer was as familiar with the job to be done as they. But they did not disguise their resentment at being driven.

One noon, as Lynn and his father returned home for dinner, they were surprised to observe that Mrs. McVeigh had a visitor. There had been no callers since the McVeighs had moved to town, much to the satisfaction of John. He hated people "trooping," as he described it, through his house. The caller was on the point of leaving when Lynn and his father entered the house.

"I know this isn't the time to call, but I was down town and I just wanted to see Mrs. McVeigh," she said in a singularly clear, pleasing voice.

Lynn's mother made the required introductions, and Mrs. Carr —Lynn knew that she must be the wife of Clarence Carr, cashier of the First State Bank of Rudge—held out her hand in a quick, friendly gesture.

As Lynn took it in his own, he raised his eyes to the loveliest face he had ever seen. She was a young woman, not more than twenty-five or six; and there was a bright vivacity in her smile that emphasized the warm, deep brown of her eyes. Her hair, very black and shining with life, was parted at one side of her small head and caught up in a loose knot at the back. Her mouth was wide and generous; and when she smiled, her teeth showed strong and white.

With a start of surprise Lynn heard his father speaking in a voice he could barely recognize. "This is *very* pleasant, Mrs. Carr. I have met your husband. Colonel Winterslip introduced us. He has great belief in the future of agriculture in this country."

"That is one thing in which I do not agree with my husband nor Colonel Winterslip. Haven't they tried this same experiment, making a farming region out of arid or semi-arid lands in Canada and other places?"

"Why, yes, I think it has been tried," John McVeigh answered with a slight frown.

He never could abide being questioned by a woman, Lynn thought.

"Of course, the methods have improved. We know something about dust blankets and subsoil which they didn't know in previous attempts. Besides, Mrs. Carr, it really rains in this country. I've seen it."

"Oh, yes," she said with a little laugh, "but there is another thing. Why destroy one industry to build another—especially when the one you're building may not be so profitable as the one torn down?"

"Well, if land will produce forty bushels of wheat to the acre, it is too valuable for grass crops. Don't you think so?"

"I suppose so. But it seems terrible to plow up all this fine buffalo grass which is as rich, I understand, as grain. It's so beautiful."

"Ah, there your heart speaks. You are concerned about the beauty of the country. But I'm afraid it can't stand up against the dollar sign. And I know of none more appreciative of money than beautiful women." He bowed slightly and a sardonic glint came in his eye.

Mrs. Carr flushed slightly and laughed.

"All right. You men can make it here, but we women will go to some happier place to spend it, won't we, Mrs. McVeigh? Now I really must go. What I wanted to ask was this: Can you and your husband come to our house next Thursday evening? There will be a few people there—I'm sure Mr. McVeigh has met all the men—and it's going to be very informal. Just a little music and cards."

Martha McVeigh glanced questioningly at her husband, and he replied at once. "I'm sure it will be splendid. It is thoughtful of you to ask us." He walked with her to the door, his head deferentially inclined; and when he came back into the dining room where his wife was putting dinner on the table, his face was curiously animated and lively.

"I wouldn't be surprised if she's right," he said abruptly. "A very smart as well as attractive woman I should say. If they ever plow up all this buffalo grass, it will be gone. It doesn't reseed itself, I'm told. Well, it's their funeral."

Lynn spent his evenings watching the show of the town. It really was a show to him. Real estate men talked feverishly on street corners. The sidewalks thronged with people: farmers with their wives and children, a few ranchers viewing the crowd with a thoughtful eye, new residents who like the McVeighs had but recently arrived. Lynn saw the red-headed Wagner moving busily about, shaking hands and laughing.

Once before the pool hall, Lynn observed a rider leaning negligently against a corner of the building. His blue overalls were carefully pulled down over his stitched and patterned boots, his wide hat pushed back exposing sun-bleached hair. Some impulse prompted Lynn to stop beside him.

"This town seems to be changed, doesn't it?" he asked hesitantly.

The rider dusted a few flakes of tobacco into a wisp of paper and lighted it, drawing in a deep lungful of smoke.

"The whole damn country's changed. I don't like her—none of her. I'm driftin'."

"Where will you go?"

"I'm goin' somewhere away from farmers an' I'm goin' now."

He spun his cigarette into the air between thumb and forefinger, and it made a bright arch in the gathering dusk. Then he walked to his pony, tied to a hitching rail, and swung lightly into the saddle.

"So long," he said, gathering the reins in his hand. The pony broke into a trot.

For as long as he could discern him in the gathering gloom, Lynn kept his eyes fixed on the fading, upright figure. The thought crossed his mind that with the rider's departure something was going out of Dakota that it would not know again, something which had made it colorful and interesting. It seemed as definite as the end of a tale that is told.

XVIII

J. C. LINDBERG

Born in Denmark, Mr. Lindberg came to South Dakota from Nebraska in 1905. For many years he taught at Northern State Teachers College in Aberdeen. He was the first editor of *Pasque Petals* and was president of the South Dakota Poetry Society.

THE PRAIRIE SPEAKS

I am the Prairie Singer—
The ghost of the days that were;
I am the voice of the long-forgotten past,
I am the cry since time began.

I sing the chaos before creation was
When mists blew vagrantly across the deep;
Primordial life whose fossil prints remain,
Uncovered from ten thousand years of sleep.

Primeval days I sing, when dinosaurs
And wilder beasts fought for supremacy—
When glaciers, like snow, creeping monsters, crawled
Across the plains and buried all within
Their cold embrace.

I sing the untold stretch of centuries—
Not yet so far away but echoes bound
    Across wide, troubled spaces,
    From legendary places—
The golden age of buffalo and deer,
The stern, idyllic days of tepee loves
And hates, of tribal wars—these, too, I sing.

I sing forgotten trails of pioneers—
A silent memory of those who heard
The first, far call of virgin promises;
The broken wheel, the porous, whitening bones—
The ghostly relics of a day now gone.

Unnumbered miles of waving grain, I sing;
Sleek cattle grazing on a thousand hills,
Broad-streeted cities, busy thoroughfares—
And over all a benediction reigns.
Old orders change, new systems take their place—
These, too, I sing.

TO A RATTLE SNAKE READY TO STRIKE

Fork-tongued, furtive charmer!
I fear your poisoned fangs;
I tremble when I see you coil
In self defense.
Your warning rattle
Strikes frozen terror to the heart
Of man and beast.
I hate you, loathe you, for your deadly sting.
And yet . . .
I stand in reverent awe
Before your all-compelling charms—
Your firm-poised head,
Your jet-black eyes,
Your graceful coil on coil which holds
Your fatal thrust,
The perfect symmetry
That marks your tawny coat,
The tantalizing, nervous tail;
You are, when all is said,
But one of God's consummate creatures
Whom He pronounced as "good."

And so . . .
I must absolve you from your ancient guilt
And cruel, primal curse.

XIX

RUDOLF G. RUSTE

Mr. Ruste was born in North Dakota in 1892, son of a Lutheran minister who for reasons of health gave up the ministry in 1901 and moved to a farm near Montrose, South Dakota. It was here that Ruste wrote "Last of the Virgin Sod" in 1912. While a student at Northern State Teachers College he offered to set type for a poetry magazine if his teacher, J. C. Lindberg, would finance the venture. And so a small four-page folder, *Pasque Petals,* Volume 1, Number 1, appeared in May, 1926.

After graduation in 1924, Ruste did graduate work in California and then taught in South Dakota, California, and Michigan, retiring from teaching in 1954.

His poem, "Last of the Virgin Sod," has been reprinted a number of times and made into a poster for the Farm Bureau and Conservation Department of the state of Missouri. Mr. Ruste has written one book, *American Heritage: Prognosis 2,000 A.D.,* published in 1967. He lives in Stone Mountain, Georgia.

LAST OF THE VIRGIN SOD

We broke today on the homestead
The last of the virgin sod,
And a haunting feeling oppressed me
That we marred a work of God.

A fragrance rose from the furrow,
A fragrance both fresh and old,
It was fresh with the dew of the morning,
Yet aged with time untold.

The creak of leather and clevis,
The rip of the coulter blade,
And we wrecked what God with the labor
Of countless years has made.

I thought while laying the last land,
Of the tropical sun and rains,
Of jungles, glaciers and oceans
Which had helped to make these plains;

Of monsters, horrid and fearful,
Which reigned in the land we plow,
And it seemed to me so presumptuous
Of man to claim it now.

So when today on the homestead
We finished the virgin sod,
Is it strange I almost regretted
To have marred that work of God?

SHARP KNIFE

"—and so the soldiers came
And rounded them up like cattle
And took them to reservations."

An old buck, wizened and grey and toothless,
Had listened in stoic silence.
Now he took the pipe from his gums
And spoke: "Sharp Knife, he did not go."

The salesman winked and placed
A finger against his forehead.

"Sharp Knife," I asked. "Who was Sharp Knife?"

"He great arrow maker."

"And where is Sharp Knife?"

"Sharp Knife still live in the Bad Lands."

Bad Lands—strata and talus and faults.
The strident rattler sleeps
On the dinosaur's petrified tarsus.
And look, a badger digging his den
Has unearthed the bones of a pterodactyl.
Bones, petrified bones of monsters;
Bones, of cattle and horses;
Bones, ah bones—Homo sapiens.

Shot, evidently—half inch hole in the skull,
Half inch hole in the scapula.
Indian. Arrow maker, by the heap of stone chips.
A shell—two shells—
Brazen and gangrenous green,
Wide-mouthed forty-five-nineties.

Moonlight on butte and mesa,
Shadows in weird arroyos.
Do the bones of the dinosaur sense
The eerie wail of the coyote?
Are the dead more dead than the living,
Or the living more live than the dead?
Was the toothless old Indian right—
Does Sharp Knife still live in the Bad Lands?

XX

CHARLES BADGER CLARK

Badger Clark, as he was known, lived a simple life filled with a passion for nature and an interest in archaeology and geology. He often lived alone and never married. Born in Iowa on January 1, 1883, he was in Dakota Territory three months later when his father was forced to move for reasons of health. The family lived in Mitchell at first, and Badger attended Dakota Wesleyan for one year but either dropped out or was asked to leave because of his poor record. Two years of adventuring in Cuba left him with paludic fever, and so he returned to Dakota where his parents were now living in Deadwood. A year later he contracted tuberculosis, the disease which had caused the death of his brother. Badger immediately left for Arizona where he stayed with a friend on a ranch near Tombstone. It was here that he began to write verses, sending them home in letters. His stepmother sent one poem to a publisher and Badger decided to be a writer.

In 1910 he returned to Hot Springs to take care of his aging parents. Fifteen years later he retired to his cabin at Legion Lake where he spent the rest of his life reading, writing, and wandering through the Black Hills. He once described his hobbies as "solitude, silence, and nature."

Over a period of forty years he published five books of poems and became known as a cowboy poet. For approximately the last twenty years of his life he was the first Poet Laureate of South Dakota. Death came on September 26, 1957, from lung cancer.

The following poems are from his first book, *Sun and Saddle Leather*, 1915.

A COWBOY'S PRAYER

(Written for Mother)

Oh Lord, I've never lived where churches grow.
    I love creation better as it stood
That day You finished it so long ago
    And looked upon Your work and called it good.
I know that others find You in the light
    That's sifted down through tinted window panes,
And yet I seem to feel You near tonight
    In this dim, quiet starlight on the plains.

I thank You, Lord, that I am placed so well,
    That You have made my freedom so complete;
That I'm no slave of whistle, clock or bell,
    Nor weak-eyed prisoner of wall and street.
Just let me live my life as I've begun
    And give me work that's open to the sky;
Make me a pardner of the wind and sun,
    And I won't ask a life that's soft or high.

Let me be easy on the man that's down;
    Let me be square and generous with all.
I'm careless sometimes, Lord, when I'm in town,
    But never let 'em say I'm mean or small!
Make me as big and open as the plains,
    As honest as the hawse between my knees,
Clean as the wind that blows behind the rains,
    Free as the hawk that circles down the breeze!

Forgive me, Lord, if sometimes I forget.
    You know about the reasons that are hid.
You understand the things that gall and fret;
    You know me better than my mother did.
Just keep an eye on all that's done and said
    And right me, sometimes, when I turn aside,
And guide me on the long, dim trail ahead
    That stretches upward toward the Great Divide.

BACON

You're salty and greasy and smoky as sin
    But of all grub we love you the best.
You stuck to us closer than nighest of kin
    And helped us win out in the West;
You froze with us up on the Laramie trail;
    You sweat with us down at Tucson;
When Injun was painted and white man was pale
You nerved us to grip our last chance by the trail
    And load up our Colts and hang on.

You've sizzled by mountain and mesa and plain
    Over campfires of sagebrush and oak;
The breezes that blow from the Platte to the main
    Have carried your savory smoke.

You're friendly to miner or puncher or priest;
  You're as good in December as May;
You always came in when the fresh meat had ceased
And the rough course of empire to westward was greased
  By the bacon we fried on the way.

We've said that you weren't fit for white men to eat
  And your virtues we often forget.
We've called you by names that I darsn't repeat,
  But we love you and swear by you yet.
Here's to you, old bacon, fat, lean streak and rin',
  All the westerners join in the toast,
From mesquite and yucca to sagebrush and pine,
From Canada down to the Mexican Line,
  From Omaha out to the coast!

THE PLAINSMEN

Men of the older, gentler soil,
  Loving the things that their fathers wrought—
Worn old fields of their fathers' toil,
  Scarred old hills where their fathers fought—
Loving their land for each ancient trace,
Like a mother dear for her wrinkled face,
  Such as they never can understand
  The way we have loved you, young, young land!

Born of a free, world-wandering race,
  Little we yearned o'er an oft-turned sod.
What did we care for the fathers' place,
  Having ours fresh from the hand of God?
Who feared the strangeness or wiles of you
When from the unreckoned miles of you,
  Thrilling the wind with a sweet command,
  Youth unto youth called, young, young land?

North, where the hurrying seasons changed
  Over great gray plains where the trails lay long,
Free as the sweeping Chinook we ranged,
  Setting our days to a saddle song.
Through the icy challenge you flung to us,
Through your shy Spring kisses that clung to us,
  Following far as the rainbow spanned,
  Fiercely we wooed you, young, young land!

South, where the sullen black mountains guard
　　Limitless, shimmering lands of the sun,
Over blinding trails where the hoofs rang hard,
　　Laughing or cursing, we rode and won.
Drunk with the virgin white fire of you,
Hotter than thirst was desire of you;
　　Straight in our faces you burned your brand,
　　Marking your chosen ones, young, young land.

When did we long for the sheltered gloom
　　Of the older game with its cautious odds?
Gloried we always in sun and room,
　　Spending our strength like the younger gods.
By the wild sweet ardor that ran in us,
By the pain that tested the man in us,
　　By the shadowy springs and the glaring sand,
　　You were our true-love, young, young land.

When the last free trail is a prime, fenced lane
　　And our graves grow weeds through forgetful Mays,
Richer and statelier then you'll reign,
　　Mother of men whom the world will praise.
And your sons will love you and sigh for you,
Labor and battle and die for you,
　　But never the fondest will understand
　　The way we have loved you, young, young land.

THE WESTERNER

My fathers sleep on the sunrise plains,
　　And each one sleeps alone.
Their trails may dim to the grass and rains,
　　For I choose to make my own.
I lay proud claim to their blood and name,
　　But I lean on no dead kin;
My name is mine, for the praise or scorn,
And the world began when I was born
　　And the world is mine to win.

They built high towns on their old log sills,
　　Where the great, slow rivers gleamed,
But with new, live rock from the savage hills
　　I'll build as they only dreamed.

The smoke scarce dies where the trail camp lies,
  Till the rails glint down the pass;
The desert springs into fruit and wheat
And I lay the stones of a solid street
  Over yesterday's untrod grass.

I waste no thought on my neighbor's birth
  Or the way he makes his prayer.
I grant him a white man's room on earth
  If his game is only square.
While he plays it straight I'll call him mate;
  If he cheats I drop him flat.
Old class and rank are a wornout lie,
For all clean men are as good as I,
  And a king is only that.

I dream no dreams of a nurse-maid state
  That will spoon me out my food.
A stout heart sings in the fray with fate
  And the shock and sweat are good.
From noon to noon all the earthly boon
  That I ask my God to spare
Is a little daily bread in store,
With the room to fight the strong for more,
  And the weak shall get their share.

The sunrise plains are a tender haze
  And the sunset seas are gray,
But I stand here, where the bright skies blaze
  Over me and the big today.
What good to me is a vague "maybe"
  Or a mournful "might have been,"
For the sun wheels swift from morn to morn
And the world began when I was born
  And the world is mine to win.

HALF-BREED

Fathers with eyes of ancient ire,
  Old eagles shorn of flight,
Forget the breed of my blue-eyed sire
While I sit this hour by the council fire,
  All red in the fire's red light.

293

Chant me the day of the war-steed's prance
    And the signal fires on the buttes,
Of the Cheyenne scalps on the lifted lance,
Of the women raped from the Pawnee dance
    And the wild death trail of the Utes.

Sing me the song of the buffalo run
    To the edge of the canyon snare,
With the roaring plunge when the meat was won
And the flash of knives in the low red sun
    And the good blood smell in the air.

Chant me the might of the Manitou—
    But the old song drags and dies.
Old things have drifted the sunset through
Till the very God of the land comes new
    From the rim where the young stars rise!

Fathers, red men, the red flame falls,
    And over the dim dawn lands
My white soul hunts me again and calls
To the lanes of law and the shadow of walls
    And a women with soft white hands.

THE BAD LANDS

No fresh green things in the Bad Lands bide;
    It is all stark red and gray,
And strewn with bones that had lived and died
    Ere the first man saw the day.
When the sharp crests dream in the sunset gleam
    And the bat through the canyon veers,
You will sometimes catch, if you listen long,
The tones of the Bad Lands' mystic song,
    A song of a million years.
The place is as dry as a crater cup,
    Yet you hear, as the stars shine free,
From the barren gulches sounding up,
    The lap of a spawning sea,
A breeze that cries where the great ferns rise
    From the pools on a new-made shore,
With the whip and whir of batlike wings
And the snarl of slimy, fighting things
    And the tread of the dinosaur.

Then the sea voice ebbs through untold morns,
   And the jungle voices reign—
The hunting howl and the clash of horns
   And the screech of rage and pain.
Harsh and grim is the old earth hymn
   In that far brute paradise,
And as ages drift the rough strains fall
To a single note more grim than all,
   The crack of the glacial ice.

So the song runs on, with shift and change,
   Through the years that have no name,
And the late notes soar to a higher range,
   But the theme is still the same.
Man's battle-cry and the guns' reply
   Blend in with the old, old rhyme
That was traced in the score of the strata marks
While Millenniums winked like campfire sparks
   Down the winds of unguessed time.

There's a finer fight than of tooth and claw,
   More clean than of blade and gun,
But, fair or foul, by the Great Bard's law
   'Twill be fight till the song is done.
Not mine to sigh for the song's deep "why,"
   Which only the Great Bard hears.
My soul steps out to the martial swing
Of the brave old song that the Bad Lands sing,
   The song of a million years.

XXI

ARCHER B. GILFILLAN

Born on an Indian reservation in Minnesota in 1887, Gilfillan attended Amherst University, graduated with honors from the University of Pennsylvania, and then went to Harding County in South Dakota to homestead in 1910, speculating in sheep. Forced out of the business by financial problems, he continued to herd sheep for other people who owned flocks, living in a sheep wagon.

His sister suggested to him in 1926 that he write about his experiences as a sheepherder. The book (from which "Sheep Herder and Cowboy" is taken) was published in 1929 with the simple title, *Sheep,* and became a best seller. In 1933 illness forced him to abandon sheepherding and to retire to a log cabin near Spearfish. However, he could not settle down after years of outdoor work, and so he became a roving reporter and wrote a weekly column called "Reflections of a Sheepherder" for a South Dakota newspaper. With wit, humor, and common sense he commented on a variety of subjects and people. The columns formed the nucleus of two books, *A Shepherd's Holiday,* 1936, and *A Goat's Eye View of the Black Hills,* 1953. Gilfillan died in 1955.

Archer Gilfillan, like others in his family, was an independent spirit, wanting to live a life of his own, and not afraid to turn from a college degree in the East to sheepherding in South Dakota. In some respects he became the state's Mark Twain.

SHEEP HERDER AND COWBOY

One really ought to remove the hat in the presence of the cowboy, for undoubtedly he is dead. Every once in a while some noted author, living in the East, tries to apply a literary pulmotor to him. But the poor cowboy is beyond the aid of a pulmotor. Nothing short of a major miracle could be of any benefit to him. Confidentially and between friends, what the cowboy really needs is the friendly offices of an undertaker. So we should be free to honor his memory without the embarrassment of entertaining his unburied corpse.

For there are still men walking around in raiment which they claim is an authentic reproduction of "What the Well-Dressed Cowboy Will Wear," although the oldest living cowboys deny knowledge of any such costume. There is a real distinction between the old-time cowhands and the modern chap wearers. One of the former, who was attending a rodeo, said, "I looked around and saw what was wearing big hats, and then went and bought myself a cap." The old-time cowboys are now much more interested in how many miles they can get out of a gallon than in how many jumps they can get out of bronc. I think we must admit that the fellow who rides around in chaps all day and then in the evening drives his car into town to the pool hall is not a cowboy in the generally accepted sense of the term.

It is amusing to watch the evolution of the modern cowboy. We see a boy going to school year after year, dressed like the rest of us in work shirt and overalls; and then one day he blossoms out in full cowboy regalia, no detail missing, and another cowboy is born. Clothes may not make the man, but strip a cowboy of his big hat, his chaps, and his spurs, and it would take a whole detective agency to tell him from a hired man.

Granted without argument that it takes nerve, and lots of it, to mount a bronc that is likely to pitch. It takes still more nerve to be an aviator or a structural-ironworker. But, unlike the cowboy, the aviator and the ironworker do not on this account arrogate to themselves all the other virtues, together with a few of the more attractive vices.

Is there any intrinsic reason why the man who takes care of cattle should be a romantic, half-mythical figure, while the man who takes care of sheep is either a joke or anathema? Let us consider the two occupations a moment. The herder is in sole charge of fifteen to twenty thousand dollars' worth of property, and the safety and well-being of the sheep are largely dependent on his faithfulness and good judgment. The cowboy is not in actual charge of anything, but handles the stock from day to day as he is directed. The herder is his own boss a large part of the time, and plans his own work. The cowboy may be able to carry more than one day's orders in his head, but he seldom has the opportunity of proving it. The herder's wages run from ten to twenty dollars a month higher than the cowboy's in summer and are almost double the latter's in winter. But in spite of this, there is no denying the fact that every kid in the range country looks forward to the day when he can get hold of a pair of hair pants, a ten-gallon hat, a Miles City saddle, and a pair of big spurs, and then cultivate a bow-legged walk and hire out to a cattleman. If he ever has ambitions to grow up to be a herder, his family will never know it unless he talks in his sleep.

There is, perhaps, no truer illustration of the old copy-book aphorism which says that "men are only boys grown tall" than the celerity with which figures of national and even international importance, not any particular one, but numbers of them, no sooner touch the fringes of the cow country than they deck themselves out in full cowboy regalia, get in front of a camera, and look tough. Naturally the toggery does not make the celebrity a cowboy any more than a fringe of grass around his waist would make him a hula dancer, but a pleasing illusion to the contrary doubtless exists.

Speaking of toughness, years ago there was a certain saloon keeper in Bellefourche who had a Pintsch light out in front of his saloon at a time when such lights were a novelty, and consequently he was very proud of it. There was a certain young fellow in town who had been around the cows only a few days, and therefore was extremely tough and anxious to prove it. He wished to shoot out the lights in true cowboy fashion, but he believed he knew the ethics governing the situation. He entered the saloon and, swaggering up to the bar, asked the proprietor, "How much will it cost me to shoot that light out?" The old saloon keeper drew a sawed-off shotgun from beneath the bar and patted the stock affectionately. "Go right ahead," he invited cordially. "It won't cost you a cent!"

There is an almost universal belief that a cowboy's work is romantic. It may have been once; but in the modern scheme of running cattle feed plays a very important part. In the old days cattle had to depend on what they could rustle themselves the year round. If the winter was an open one, they came through in fine shape. If it was a long winter with deep snow, they died by thousands. But modern competition is too keen to tolerate a waste like that, and nowadays the possibly once romantic cowboy gets very heavy on one end of a pitchfork. He puts up hay for a couple of months during the summer and he feeds it for many a long month during the winter. In fact he puts in from six to eight months a year handling hay in one form or another, and then another month or two handling the inevitable results. If this be romance, make the most of it.

Those who still insist, however, that the cowboy's work is romantic may gesture in the direction of Hollywood and maintain that the cowboys there are simply reënacting their former lives before the camera. If they spent their real cowboy days in rescuing satin-skinned heroines and riding good horses to death, they probably are; but the chances are all against it.

The movie horse is a fearful and wonderful animal. Where the ordinary horse is content to extract oats from a nose bag, the movie horse prefers to extract the cube root of an unknown number in the mind of his rider, and then polish off the performance with a lecture on the fourth dimension. The movie horse cannot walk, he cannot trot, he cannot even lope decently. He knows nothing but a senseless and headlong run. And this pace, which would burst an ordinary horse wide open in a mile or two, the movie horse can keep up indefinitely, up hill and down. With equal facility he charges up slopes that would make a Rocky Mountain goat dizzy, and he slides down precipices that an even ordinarily cautious housefly wouldn't attempt without chains. The movie horse leaves Jersey City one hour late, and he overtakes the west-bound limited just as it is slowing down to two miles an hour to pass through Philadelphia. The movie horse has not yet beaten an airplane in a straight-away, but give him time, give him time.

In the range country, if you see a distant horsebacker traveling at a lope, it is an entirely safe bet that the rider is either a woman or a kid. A kid's business is always important and, besides, he doesn't know any better, and women actually, as well as proverbially, have very little mercy on a horse. A man rider realizes that his horse, like himself, has just so much strength to give; and that if it is wasted when there is no need, it will not be there to draw upon when need comes. Therefore he proceeds no faster than a trot, a pace which is hard on him, but easiest for the horse.

Consider for a moment the two outstanding cowboys, the one of life, the other of literature, Will Rogers and the hero of *The Virginian*. The latter received his early training and the full impress of his character in Virginia. This fully formed character and his Southern accent he took to the West. His chaps and his guns were accidental and incidental. In his essence he was and remained simply a transplanted Virginian. In like manner Will Rogers is uniquely and inimitably Will Rogers, the darling of the gods and the delight of mankind, and millions have laughed at his wit who never had a chance to laugh at his chaps. Both of these men possessed remarkable personalities, and both would have been equally remarkable if they had never even seen a cow and had never learned how to hog-tie a steer or throw the bull.

When we consider the position of the sheep herder in literature, we find that he fares no better there than he does in life. He is apparently limited to two rôles. He either serves as an animated target for the drunken and high-spirited cowboy or, himself drunk, serves as a foil for the virtuous, noble, and high-minded cowboy. Once, in an O. Henry story, we find a herder who is apparently on the road to being the hero, but he turns out to be an escaped convict, still on the down grade.

The herder really yearns for higher things. He would like to follow the cowboy's example as the latter rides in concentric circles around the schoolhouse, looking for the locoed heifer that was last seen in that vicinity three years before. But, alas! the herder has a standing engagement with the sheep thirty-one days out of the month. He would like to rescue the schoolma'am from a fate worse than death, but the chances are that the schoolma'am would prefer even that fate to the ignominy of being rescued by a herder. But when the ignorant herder sees the cowboy risk his neck in breaking a bronc for five dollars, he comes to the conclusion that either the cowboy's neck is worth only five dollars or that his brains are located in that portion of his anatomy which clings most closely to the saddle. It is the novelists, later aided and abetted by the scenario writers, who have elevated the cowboy to his present position somewhere between heaven and earth, who have crowned his noble brow with all the laurel and bays there are, and who have arranged all the spokes and felloes in his halo; and until the novelists experience a change of heart, or until someone punctures their hero's gas bag, the attitude of the herder toward his ancient rival must be as that of one looking up.

Throughout a large part of the West to-day, cowboy stuff is merely a phase which boys pass through, like playing Indians or soldiers, only some of them never grow up. There will probably always be in the West a certain type of young fellow who cannot go out and drive in the milk cows without buckling on chaps and spurs. But with the present stringent laws against murder, there is probably nothing that can be done about this. It is all a part of life in the great open spaces, where cowboys will be cowboys and where *The Virginian* is still widely read—as a book of etiquette.

The good old days when the cowman and his cowboys used to tie the herder to the wheels of his wagon and club his sheep to death by the hundreds or drive them over a cutbank—those days are gone forever. To-day each rancher, whether sheepman or cattleman, uses and pays for his own grass as a rule, and range quarrels are no longer carried on over a wide front "from the Alps to the sea," but are local and individual affairs.

Every cattleman knows that sheep ruin the range for cattle, and that cattle dislike to graze where sheep have been—refuse to, in fact. Every cowman knows this and makes no secret of it, but proclaims it in season and out. The only trouble is that the cowmen haven't taken their herds into their confidence, and the result is that the cattle, never having been informed of their inhibitions, graze wherever they think the grazing is good, and they show a particular fondness for the grass that grows rich and rank on old sheep bed grounds. According to information in the hands of the cattlemen, they ought to shun spots like this as a beauty-contest winner would a smallpox sign.

No one wishes that this theory of the cattlemen were true any more fervently than does the sheepman. If it were true, he would be saved many a long ride chasing stray stock off his range, and his grass would go to market entirely surrounded by wool, instead of going to swell the commissariat of his neighbors' wandering herds.

"It cost me five hundred dollars to be a neighbor to that man," remarked a cattleman of his neighbor, a sheepman. What he really meant was that the sheepman had insisted that he keep track of his cattle, just as the sheepman kept track of his own stock. In other words, the sheepman pays one thousand dollars a year, the amount of his herder's board and wages, for the privilege of knowing where his stock is at all times. It is not unreasonable for him to insist that the cattleman make some effort to acquire a similar knowledge with regard to his own stock. The only apparent solution is a line fence. But since the sheepman still has to employ a herder as before, and since the cattleman's fence is in effect a herder hired once for all and paid in full, it is evident that the cattleman still has far the better of it as far as expense goes. And in this he is lucky, for his income is decidedly less than that of the sheepman in proportion to invested capital.

It would be an interesting psychological problem to determine why the average farmer or cattleman can view with apparent equanimity the presence of strange cattle or horses on his range, and yet at the sight of sheep on the same range be reduced to a state bordering on apoplexy, complicated further by homicidal tendencies. There somehow seems to be a strong, deep, and unreasoning prejudice against sheep on the part of practically everyone who does not own them. There seems to be no middle ground with regard to them. You are either for or against, whole-heartedly and completely.

Upon retiring at night the pious sheepman puts up a petition that his herder knows here all his sheep are—safe on the bed ground. About the same time the cattleman is praying fervently that nobody but himself knows where his cattle are—on his neighbors' grass. Ordinarily the cattleman when confronted with the evidence falls back on his one cast-iron alibi: "I didn't know they were there; I'll send over and get them." Usually this is considered good for three hundred and sixty-five days in the year, but in leap year it will be used three hundred and sixty-six times. When the herder is caught across the line with his whole bunch, about the only really effective alibi he has is to utter a plaintive blat, drop on his knees, and start cropping grass.

Both cattle and sheep are subject to wide fluctuations in price. For the past several years and up to a recent date, cattle have been in a prolonged slump. In many places it has been the sheepman's money that has kept the banks going. As one sheepman rather undiplomatically remarked, "We sheepmen have been tailing you cattlemen up for the last three years." It is the truth that hurts, they say, and when the cattleman realizes the strong economic position of his despised rival, and especially the latter's better standing at the bank, then the cattleman experiences a sharp and shooting pain between the small of his back and the cantle of his saddle.

A sheriff in a Western town, zealous for prohibition enforcement, arrested a sheepman who had a suspicious bulge on his hip. It turned out that the bulge was the money the sheepman had left over after paying his bills. The sheriff apologized publicly for having arrested him, but at the same time he announced that any cattleman displaying a similar bulge would be forthwith thrown into the calaboose without even being searched.

There is somewhere in the West a cattleman whose wife some years ago went into sheep on her own account and with her own money. For the last three years it has been her sheep money that has bought feed for her husband's cattle. The strangest part of this true story is that the couple in question are still living a happy married life. If matrimony as an institution can come unscathed through a test like that, surely it is destined to endure forever.

Sheep are somewhat more expensive to run than cattle, but they produce two money crops a year, the lambs and the wool. These two crops are marketed several months apart, the wool in the spring and the lambs in the fall. So the sheepman has ready money twice a year, whereas the cattleman has but one harvest. If the cattleman could skin his entire bunch every spring at a trifling cost and sell the hides for a fourth of what the cattle themselves were worth; if the cattle would then walk about happily and grow more hides for next year's skinning; if he could sell his calves every fall for about two thirds of what their mothers were worth—if he could do all this in place of his present system of marketing his stuff, then the cattleman could hold up his head and take his place with the sheepman.

XXII

VINE V. DELORIA, SR.

Vine Deloria was born in 1901 at the St. Elizabeth Mission in Wakpala and lived on the Standing Rock Reservation for twenty-five years. Then followed schooling at Kearney Military Academy in Nebraska and St. Stephen's College in New York, work in a Colorado coal mine, coaching at the Fort Sill Indian School, and finally more studies at the General Seminary in New York City. For thirty-nine years Father Deloria was a clergyman missionary for the Episcopal Church, including eighteen years on the Pine Ridge Reservation. Brother of Ella Deloria, noted for her writing and research in the Dakota language, and father of three well-known sons, Vine, Sr. has labored long and well for his people and is one of South Dakota's distinguished citizens. He lives in Pierre.

THE STANDING ROCK RESERVATION: A PERSONAL REMINISCENCE

The Standing Rock Reservation began around the year 1885. My father was already there as a young thirty-one-year-old missionary. In size, the reservation was about eighty-five miles north and south, and about seventy-five miles east and west. It was completely fenced in and was patrolled by mounted Indian police. (In 1912 we saw part of the fence still standing as we journeyed to the Cheyenne River Reservation to visit the family of Henry Hotchiss, my father's longtime friend who gave us a horse every time we went to visit them.)

The Standing Rock had three rivers: The Missouri, which was also our eastern boundary; the Cannonball and the Grand, which flowed east into the Missouri. Between the Cannonball and the Grand, about six creeks emptied into the Grand or directly into the Missouri. Between the streams and rivers were prairie plateaus of varying widths, from a mile to fifteen miles. The plateaus were not always flat. There were lone buttes or groups of them of different sizes and heights. The pride of the Standing Rock was *Paha Hanskaska,* or Long Buttes, called by the white man Chain Buttes, perhaps a more apt name. The formation began a little south and west of Fort Yates, the reservation Agency.

Our people lived all over the reservation but usually near the rivers or creeks. In those early days, the older people lived pretty much the same way as they did for thousands of years, in the Tipi. They moved about a great deal, enjoying the freedom of camping. They had wagons, saddles, and other traveling equipment. They did a little hunting both with arrows and with guns. The government gave them rations of coffee, baking powder, flour, and meat, most of which was cut thin and sun-dried. I loved that dried meat, especially with early small potatoes in their jackets and a little seasoning salt pork.

I have always been most grateful to the Great Spirit that our older people were able to live a life so much like their aboriginal way, and they died that way—happily. The Great Spirit's corp of engineers kept our creeks full of good clean water almost the year round. I mean the beavers. Our old people never knew the word "contamination" as the rest of us have come to hear about it.

The younger people, those up to the age of fifty, were urged to settle somewhere on the reservation, to build log houses, stables, corrals, and to fence in plots of ground from about ten to forty acres. The government sent expert log house builders, carpenters, gardeners, and stockmen to teach our people knowledge of these things. In the subagencies we also had ice houses, blacksmiths, cobblers, and wagon and harness makers. In time, many of our Indians became expert in these things.

We were really in the stock raising industry, cattle and horses. Big roundups were held in the spring and fall, in spring to brand new calves and colts, and in the fall to ship stock to market. At this time in history, the Standing Rock people were happy. There was minimal government supervision. Nevertheless, we were acquainted with our chief agent at Fort Yates and his assistants, called Assistant Farmers, in the several Indian communities such as Wakpala, Bull Head, Little Eagle, Cannon Ball. The chief agent went around on horseback or in a buggy to visit in the homes of the people around Fort Yates. Subagents also visited people in their respective areas.

Order was kept by the Indian police, who also patrolled the reservation fence. They used the Indian system of obedience, customary and powerful in the Lakota society, and based on the kinship system. When you broke the white man's law, an Indian policeman was sent to arrest you. He did not come and say to you, "You are under arrest." He was more likely to say, "Cousin (or brother, or father), I have been asked to come after you. It has been reported that you done such and such a thing which is not customary according to the white man's laws under which we now have to live." The offender then went with the officer voluntarily.

There is a little of this marvelous respect still left among the Indians. About twenty years ago Guy Lambert, Special Indian Police, was told by the tribal council to drive to one of the subagency areas and arrest a man. Just as Guy was leaving, a very serious incident in Mandan, North Dakota, was reported to him by telephone. It was obvious that Guy had to go to Mandan instead of the subagency. He tried to find another policeman to help him, but none was available. Finally he called the subagency, got his prisoner on the phone, and said, "Cousin, I was just about to come to see you about some custom you broke, and to bring you back here to Fort Yates. But, Cousin, I got a more serious call from Mandan and I have to go up there right away. Would you do me the favor of bringing yourself up here in the meantime?" "Sure, Cousin, I'll be up there before sundown. I'll wait for you in your office until you get back. How about supper?" Guy: "By the time you get here, there will be some police in my office. Ask them to take you to the cafe, and also get you some cigarettes and a newspaper, if you want them." Prisoner: "Thanks, Cousin. I'll be there." Guy returned from Mandan at midnight and found his prisoner fast asleep in his office, at the desk.

The Old Indian life said that it is customary to be polite, kind, patient, generous, honest, thoughtful, brave, and unselfish. Columbus saw this life and praised it, saying that "The Indians are gentle beings, souls of hospitality, curious and happy, faithful and truthful, walking in beauty, and possessors of a spiritual religion." Were the people violent in the country from which he came? Did they have a mechanized religion? If not, then why did he make such a comparison? George Catlin's Creed on the American Indian is another good one.

One time a Bishop said to me, "I did not know the Indians had compassion. But while I was preaching, a wasp was buzzing around the window, and an Indian sitting nearby gently caught the wasp, opened the window, and let him fly away."

The government hospital for the Indians was at Fort Yates. Some of our people had to travel 100 miles on horseback, or in a horse-drawn wagon. Doctors and nurses did make visitations all over the reservation, but they did their work mostly in the subagency areas. However, there were never any serious epidemics until the flu of 1918, and even then, strangely, most of the Standing Rock people escaped it. Some of the other reservations in South Dakota were hit very hard. One reservation lost 600 people.

Education on the Standing Rock was mostly the Boarding School. The Catholics had one at Kenel, South Dakota, and the

Episcopalians at St. Elizabeth's. The government had a boarding school at Fort Yates and another one at Little Eagle. Many of the children and young people were sent away to non-reservation schools like Rapid City, Pierre, Flandreau, and other places farther away like Carlisle, Hampton, Va., and Haskell at Lawrence, Kansas.

Children attending boarding schools were the best persons in communicating new knowledge to their parents, especially those from non-reservation schools. They explained their learnings, useful to their home folk, in the native tongue. Very few ever finished and graduated from the non-reservation schools. Those who did were free to stay on in white society, but most of them returned to the reservations. Of course, athletes like Jim Thorpe, Chief Bender, (famous pitcher for the Baltimore Orioles) and others with splendid education in some form of business stayed away. But there were not many. And many with equal skills simply preferred to return to their own people.

The work of the missionaries was admirable. Both men and women were known for their dedication to the Indian people. They traveled in buggies or by horseback and it took them weeks to cover their respective fields in all kinds of weather. A considerable number of them learned the Lakota or Dakota language and spoke it fluently, such as Dr. Riggs of the Congregational Church, Williamson of the Presbyterian Church, Ashley, Clark, and Flockhart of the Episcopal Church. In those days, I was too young to know who of the Catholics knew the language, but I am sure they had their Lakota speaking missionaries too. In those early days, most of those missionaries rarely took vacations. To be sure, the native ministers rarely enjoyed vacations. I know my father did not. Towards the close of his forty-five or so years on the Standing Rock, the Bishop gave him a six-month sabbatical.

One unfortunate situation brought about by the work of the missionaries was denominationalism which created aloofness in religion. They were friendly enough toward one another, but when the subject of religion came up there was no discussion such as we are enjoying today. Another difficulty created in religion was the complexity of St. Paul and the simplicity of Jesus. The Indians observed that it was so easy to understand Jesus but not St. Paul. Finally, the doctrinal statements of the Churches simply had to be assented to. Otherwise, it was too much for the Lakotas really to understand. They just had to believe by being taught over and over again. Finally, one noticeable effect was this True-Church business, each denominational group believing that their particular faith was the really true one. It caused enough divisions to start what has been known as the Brotherhood of Christian Unity.

This was started on the Yankton reservation by three young Yankton Indians, ages nineteen, twenty, and twenty-one, all of them already members of one of the Christian Churches among the Dakotas. It had started before 1873 as a farming society. Later, it adopted the name just mentioned for the purpose of keeping Dakota unity. Young men from the four denominations, then, banded together to express brotherhood. This is a sign of the power of the kinship system which I do not believe will ever die out as long as there are Plains Indians still living upon the earth.

At this point, I should perhaps mention also the religious Indianness which must be the power back of the kinship system. That is, was it the original Indian religious convictions which expressed themselves in the kinship system, and which in turn made customs more important than laws? Maybe. I should say: Religion, then custom, then kinship, and finally the social structure which took shape.

At any rate, the Plains Indians seemed to have been Sun Worshippers, and yet they believed in the Great Spirit which was held unquestionably greater than all tangible things. The Great Spirit was addressed as Grandfather because He had made all things. As the Maker of all the stars, sun, and the moon, and the earth, He was the father to them. However, as the Earth gave birth to all living things on it and man is one of them, the Great Spirit is Grandfather. The Earth is the daughter of the Great Spirit. The whole universe is a great big happy family, each part related to all the other parts. Why should not the Indian in church send out the wasp, trying to find his way out? A relative needed help.

The Plains Indians' worship with the peace pipe shows the basics of their religion. The pipe stem of wood is usually flat with four notches on each side. Whether you were right-handed or left-handed, you had four notches conveniently on your side on which to put your fingers. The first notch is for the Great Spirit, the second for Mother Earth, the third for other people, and the fourth for yourself. You lit the pipe, got it going good, and then pointed it skyward for the Great Spirit, groundward for the Earth, and four directions for other people, and finally the stem touching your chest, for yourself. All kinds of prayers are said. For example: "Great Spirit, help me never to try to deceive you, deceive Mother Earth, deceive other people, and never to deceive myself."

The American Indian, living close to Mother Earth, made patterns in terms of fours: Four seasons, four directions, four colors —black for the West (black thunder clouds), white for the North (the white snow), red for the East (red so often at dawn), and yellow for the South (the day a yellowish tinge at high noon).

The Bible says things like the Earth being the Lord's, but no-where is there anything telling people that you should respect it because you are a part of the Earth and the whole universe for that matter. If there are passages as strong about the network of life, and that you are part of the grand relay race of the universe, that you are part of life's circulation throughout the immense expanse, and with exhortations as vigorous as we were raised on, I have not been able to find such verses in the Bible. What does emerge from the Bible is love God, love neighbor, and behave yourself. Where is Mother Earth in this structure?

Of course, there were boys and men who disregarded the proper reverence and respect but, believe me, they were such a minority that anyone with such a mind at least had great fear about getting caught in a contrary act. I shall never forget the day when I shot some young wild ducks with a .410 shot gun. My father raked me over and told me that in the old days I would have had to banish myself because the power of social censor which had an efficient clout would compel me to leave. To this day, my stomach churns whenever a friend tries to get me to admire the head of a bear, or a moose, or a buffalo he has hanging from the wall, which he shot in Alaska or the Rockies. Also, the way fish are put in some sort of frames.

The Indian who trapped an eagle for his beautiful feathers cried, literally wept, before killing the majestic bird. The man chosen to cut down the tree for the Sun Dance Pole also literally cried for taking the life of that tree. The tree, all trimmed, was solemnly carried to the center of the circle where the dance was going to be held, and when set up became a *Can Wakan,* or Sacred Pole. They never killed for the sport of killing. They killed for the need for the life of man. Even then, it was difficult to hoard anything.

Such were the ways of the old Indian way of life. They adapted themselves to nature, not nature to themselves. In so doing, they learned the ways of the Great Spirit, the Sun, the Moon, the movement of the stars, and above all the ways of Mother Earth. It seems to me that if the world of today fails to leave enough of the ways of Mother Earth in her natural state, mankind will annihilate itself. Man, especially in the developed, advanced, progressive areas in meddling with Mother Earth, is already stark crazy.

With this background, the Dakotas came into the Christian Church, because the Episcopal Church, about 100 years ago, with the coming of William Hobart Hare of Philadelphia, made bishops to work among the Dakotas. I want to tell about this missionary work briefly. The Episcopal story may be pretty much the story of the three other denominations working among our people.

When Bishop Hare was elected bishop to work among the Sioux, the Americans in many quarters thought it was a great mistake to send such a splendid, well-educated and refined young man to the wild, bloodthirsty, cruel, ignorant savages of the West. He began his work in 1873, and by 1905 he had 10,000 of the Dakotas in 100 chapels over the ten Dakota reservations, with a native ministry of sixteen ordained men. How did the wild, ignorant, bloodthirsty, cruel savages make such a drastic change in only thirty-two years? It was a drastic change. The answer is that they were given those uncomplimentary names because they did fight furiously to try to stem the never ceasing encroachment of the white man upon his ever shrinking lands. As George Catlin says, in his Creed of the American Indians, "They only fought the white man on their (the Indian's) land." Another point I wish to mention is that the Dakotas, and the other American Indians for that matter, were already of some spiritual stature in their own right when Christianity came to them.

Today, adherence to Christianity has slumped fantastically throughout the world, but this need not have happened among the American Indians except for one reason. Christianity does not seem to have that skill of motivating her adherents to desire experience of the realm of the Great Spirit, which I shall call the third dimension. The old Indian religion possessed this marvelous faculty. So, the Dakotas came into Christianity with their own native, inherited, spirited stockpile which had been steadying them, but at long last it seems to be alarmingly dissipated today. They made the Church go because they already had what it takes, during most of the past 100 years.

What is the matter with the American Indians today? What is the matter with the Plains States area? What is the matter with the Dakotas? What is the matter with the Standing Rock? I think I can name the big trouble of the Standing Rock.

In 1887, the Dawes Alotment Act was passed by the Congress as another measure to aid in the white man's efforts to make the Indians over into the image of the white man, a shrewd act over those who might have had a genuine concern for the welfare of the Indians. Their shrewdness lay in the fact that the Act was a means, also, of further dispossessing the Red Man of his lands by declaring unalloted reservation lands as surplus land to be opened up to white settlers.

This law finally caught up with our people, the Hunkpapayas, the people of Sitting Bull and Gall, in 1906. Our people resisted it as long as they could, wanting to own the reservation tribally, but coercion and threats finally forced us to accept alotment. This was the beginning of the end of the good life on the Standing Rock. Our people had been doing well selling horses and cattle annually.

However, the reservation looked about the same as ever in my teens and on into my early twenties. Our people were slow in fencing their lands, now privately owned. You could still go to Fort Yates from Wakpala, forty miles, without worrying about fences. You could ride toward the south for another forty miles and still find no fences in your way. There were many horses and cattle grazing at will all over the reservation, generally. Little did I realize as a boy of fourteen that our stock economy was waning badly. From the early twenties I did become aware of the fact that land-selling seemed to be increasing, but I was not alarmed until a white man settled between St. Elizabeth's Mission and Grandma Lulu White Eagle's place to which I used to ride straight across for about four miles. I found that I had to take longer because the white settler had completely enclosed himself on his land and forced me to ride longer to go around his holding.

I once discussed this matter with my father and he told me that from about 1915 on, land-selling had already reached alarming proportions. According to the adult Indians, land alotment and inconsistent and inadequate government economic programs were also undermining the well-being of our people. All in all, father said that it was the Indianness of our people that was a great factor in the ultimate dislike of the whites. He felt that whites must feel insulted that we did not eagerly respond to their white American ways. I remember how our language and simple innocent customs were not only frowned upon but the Churches and the Government, for at least two decades, maybe three, also barred the use of our own tongue and condemned our customs, or tried to shame us away from them by mimicking and mocking us. One of the reasons why I do not like the word Pow Wow is that I strongly believe it is one of the products of mimicking Indian singing at Indian dances. These days, when the young whites in the Universities, and many educated people, are far more sensible, understanding, and sympathetic, I hope this word Pow Wow will get out of use. Why don't they say Indian *Wacipi,* or Indian Dancing, instead.

By the mid-twenties things must have been pretty bad with the American Indians, for the Government conducted a survey on Indian Administration and the result was the Merriam Report. I wonder if, in the report, the surveyors said that alotment and expropriation of surplus reservation land away from the Indians was a tremendously large factor in the breaking of the backbone of Indian economy and welfare.

To my knowledge the only bright spot in my life of any duration was the Indian Reorganization Act of John Collier, Commissioner of Indian Affairs, with Interior Secretary Harold Eckes in full support behind Mr. Collier.

Mr. Collier must have envisioned the Indians' desire to progress on their reservations, basing the economy mainly on cattle and encouraging the raising of Morgan horses, for the time being, for use in the working of their ranches. All in all, he was encouraging "rural economy" or raising fowls, pigs, owning a few milk cows, and he tried to develop an excellent skill in gardening. Canning, both white and Indian methods, was also encouraged. Land purchasing to consolidate and enlarge the reservations went very well during his twelve years as Commissioner.

Education was improved and standards and grades were raised for higher education. Attention was given to health facilities, Indian cultural recovery, and the restoration of self-government through the tribal council. $10,000,000 was set aside from which Indians borrowed for their many enterprises. During the twelve years of the Indian Reorganization Act, the Indians had borrowed over $200,000,000 and at the end the Indian owed only $54,000— a repayment schedule which no foreign nation, aided by the U. S., could match. In other words, the Indians were the best risk, and yet today, with the Indian Reorganization Act ignored, the Indians' efforts to get money have been nearly impossible.

I hope for the Tribal Councils of the Dakotas to consolidate their reservations, develop rural economy on smaller acreages of land to make sure that if worst comes to worst they could always have canned or dried foods to keep alive. Politicians keep preaching that Indians must leave their reservations for lack of space. True. No longer can each Indian family have 640 acres. However, each family can easily live on from twenty to forty acres and practice rural economy, plus figuring out some way to buy things it cannot raise at the home place. I once visited a man near Manning, Iowa, on only eight acres plus being a janitor at the high school in town for seventy-five dollars a month to make it all right. All that is needed is the ability and characters of a few of the Indians themselves to live this style of life. People they look up to could demonstrate what rural economy can become. I believe those whom they respect and admire by their performance can make such enterprises attractive.

To me, American society and life style is about as fragile as a cobweb. Very efficient, but it cannot stand hard knocks. Several years ago, about one-fifth of the U. S. had a blackout through power failure for thirty-six hours. As usual, the Americans praised themselves on how well they behaved and how their finest characters came out. But what if that blackout had knocked out half the U.S. and lasted thirty-six days in the winter time? Everything, especially transportation, would soon come to a standstill and people would be walking in packs through the woods in search of farms, to eat up the harvest and stock.

Today, whenever I visit the Standing Rock reservation area, memories of my boyhood return so vividly that I am occupied with that past for a few days afterwards. The life of a happy Indian boy began when he had a saddle horse of his own. With most boys, the age was between eight and ten. I did not start until I was twelve. My father, an Indian minister on a salary of $50 a month, and with a family of six, could not afford to buy me a horse, saddle, boots, hat, etc. But finally a happy day came into my life when Uncle Joe Claymore married the wonderful daughter of Mad Bear. Uncle Joe was about sixty and my aunt was forty, a maid formerly. On their way home from their wedding, they stopped at our home for dinner. My mother wanted to honor her new sister-in-law.

She took a liking to me and asked me several questions in a general way, and then she said: "In a few days, you will see eighty head of horses being driven right past St. Elizabeth's here, and among them there will be a dandy gray horse for you. They will be bringing them from my father's place near Kenel to your uncle's place where I am going to live from now on. You have your parents bring you over the day after those horses go by here." Right away, one of my older sisters, home for the summer from her teaching position in some college, told me that she was going to order the boys' saddle in the E. C. Cogshell Saddle Co. of Miles City, Montana, and boots.

So we made the visit and I saw my first saddle horse, three years old, but it was unbroken. Father asked a cousin of mine who was also an Indian policeman, Protus Yellow, to break the horse for me. He got the horse, broke it, and was about to bring him to me when my dandy three-year-old horse disappeared. Indian police were alerted all over the reservation, all 6,000 square miles of it, but all in vain. I mourned for my horse. But about a month later, my aunt, Mrs. Claymore, came with a ten-year-old buckskin horse and gave him to me. It belonged to their famous cowboy and foreman of the Joe Claymore ranch who died in an accident in Mobridge. (It was rainy, and the slippery street caused the buckskin to fall and kill James Skinner, the foreman.) He was a wonderful horse. He really needed no bridle. Lean forward in the saddle and he would break into a run. Lean backward and he would quickly come to a stop with a few jumps. Lean to your right or left and he would turn as if you so indicated with the rein.

I rode that horse all winter, and then on Easter Day in April, the most wonderful thing happened. I was all dressed up and about to leave for church when my mother called me: "Vine, look. Protus Yellow is coming into the yard leading your gray horse." Some Indian police had found him unexpectedly among a herd of horses about fifty miles from Yellow's place. So, I quickly became the owner of two saddle horses.

I belonged to a group of boys: Sammy Cadotte, Jimmy McLaughlin, Ambrose Shields, and I were the mix-blood members of the gang; Chester Powell was the white boy in the bunch. He understood Dakota but could not speak it. Always answered in English. Oliver White Face, Isaac Raw Hide, and Harry Bone Club were the full Indians. We did not always ride around together—usually by two's, three's, and four's until there was a church meeting or a dance in Wakpala. Then we sometimes all rode together. Respectively we all had our home chores to do, such as watering and feeding horses or cattle, helping with hauling water and burning garbage, and haying and harvesting. Any fun? Indeed.

In smaller groups, we would ride yearling calves for the enjoyment of having them buck us off. We rarely put ropes around their bodies to hold on to, because what if an emergency arose and we did not have time to take the rope off—emergency in the form of the owner of a herd coming and we had time only to escape unseen. We usually worked a herd into the woods to some bare, open spot and there did our riding.

One day, Oliver White Face and I did this with the St. Elizabeth's School herd. We caught a black two-year-old with a white face which for bucking had them all beat. We did put a rope on her because we had my sister, Susie, standing at the edge of the woods to watch the hired man of the School. Even with a rope, Oliver simply could not stay on the hard-bucking young cow for more than two or three jumps. She would send him easily three feet into the air, and how I would squint my eyes just before Oliver hit the ground. After about six tries he finally gave up, and I thought he had exhausted his ambition for riding for the day.

That same night at about 10 p.m., with a nearly full moon, he wanted to ride Calf Calf, the name we gave to the two-year-old, with a saddle. The herd was pasturing in a small four-acre lot back of the huge school barn, but all of them conveniently standing, bunched together against the northwest corner of the fence, farthest away from the barn and therefore farthest away from the main school buildings where Deaconess Baker, the School principal, and Mr. Scarlett lived. But Oliver figured they certainly must be fast asleep at 10 p.m. So, we rode out, in a round about way, got to the north of the school barn, and approached the herd.

On the whole, the twenty or so cows were fairly gentle, especially Calf Calf, being so accustomed to being ridden. I fully expected Oliver to use his own saddle because it was a much lighter saddle, about twenty pounds. Mine was about thirty, possibly thirty-five, because of the fifteen inch taperdores I had over the stirrups. But he wanted to use mine because the taperdores would be more glamorous, making slapping noises each time Calf Calf landed from a jump. My father had built the high six-strand wire fence. I told Oliver it would be easier to throw his light saddle over the fence in case of emergency. He persisted, saying that he would run with my saddle and I could take off the rope around the cow's horns.

Oliver talked me into his plan. One by one we let the cows slip away, but little did we realize that they were headed for the barn and on out into the school yard proper. Somebody had forgotten to close the four-acre pasture area by the barn.

I reminded Oliver of our respective duties to perform in case of trouble. The rope around the cow's horns was my forty-foot hard twist rope. I was going to run alongside, letting out the rope as Calf Calf went too fast for me to keep up with her with boots on over a field just returning to soil and thus rather soft. "Oliver, when she gets through bucking, you take the saddle off, if there is trouble, and run with it. I'll take care of the rope. Are you ready?" I was holding the cow by the head to keep her calm. "No wait a minute," said Oliver. Instead, he was admiring himself, sitting in the saddle with his hat in his hand to fan the cow with. He further said: "Each time she lands, those taperdores will slap that sweet noise on each side, won't it?" I said: "Yes. But let's get going."

Finally, he took off. It was a pretty ride. Oliver was so limber from the waist up you would think he were double-jointed. Swaying over the cow one time, and the next time the back of his head would almost hit the rump of the cow. Just then, out of the corner of my left eye, I caught sight of Deaconess Baker, coming by the barn with her toes out, scraping and spraying some pebbles that were there as she walked fast. As Calf Calf jumped into the air for her next buck, I dug my heels into the soft soil, putting my end of the rope half way around my body. Calf Calf, consequently, turned in the air while Oliver flew into the air with all ten fingers spread out.

I stood by the cow to take the rope off. Oliver, with an incessant "what's the matter?" was trying to take the saddle off on the wrong side. I kept whispering: This side, this side. Finally I handed him the rope, took the saddle off, and we started to run for the fence, I carrying the saddle. By this time Deaconess was about twenty yards behind us, also running. She kept saying, "Stop running, boys. I know who you are. Stop it this instant." I kept going because I did not believe she knew us. Had she said; "Oliver and Vine, stop," I would have stopped. Since she was a woman of about fifty we finally outran her. Oliver got to that six-stranded wire and went through it. How? I would never know. He hopped on his horse and was going full speed from the scene of our crime. I was all in when I got to the fence, but with all the energy I could rally, I tossed the saddle as high as I could. The cinch became ensnarled on a couple of the wires. Then I also went through those six strands. I don't know how, to this day.

She impounded my saddle but Mr. Scarlett tipped me off as to its whereabouts in the school building when I went over to get some milk for my father, who was ill at the time. I returned with the milk, skipped breakfast, and crept up a slope in front of the school, and lay waiting and wondering whether to make a run for it or not. But what if Deaconess was in that part of the building? Just then, I heard her calling chickens outside on the other side of the main school building. Chick, chick, chick, chick. You would think she had said, "Vince, come get your saddle."

For the rest of the summer, I sat behind her in church every Sunday, as she was the organist, and left during the last hymn. By September, I returned to Kearney Military Academy, Kearney, Nebraska. Before I returned for summer vacation, the next year, Deaconess had retired and was gone. The next time I saw her was in Cincinnati, Ohio, during the General Convention about fifteen years later. (I, then, was an ordained clergyman for about five years.) She suddenly came up behind me and said: "Why, Vine Deloria, my dear boy, I always knew you were going to be a leader of men." She was somewhat affluent and so took me to lunch and brought up the subject that she knew who we were. I disagreed, and so in spite of a very pleasant lunch, we had to argue over the matter, but we managed to say very nice things to each other and parted as friends, dropping the subject for all time.

So we spent our early teens. I must mention also how we used to swim in ponds and creeks and would dive for turtles to give to the old people. They loved it and would often suggest in various ways that we go turtle hunting again. We also used to shoot prairie dogs for the old people, like Grandpa Iron Ribs, White Soldier, Brown Elk, and several others near whose homes we must have done a great deal of our riding. We chased coyotes too. Once four of us formed such a strategy that one coyote was really cornered by us. He finally quit and lay down. We felt sorry for him and let him go. I think he knew it. He got up after awhile and slowly walked away.

Whenever there were gatherings we were there—church, Fourth of July, some big Indian Dancing. We fought prairie fires, and there were some bad ones in those days. One started a few miles south of Fort Yates and spread as it burned until by the time it was put out it was only eight miles from Wakpala. It was fun watching more and more Indians, police, and white ranchers and their cowboys arriving to help in fighting the fire. They would shoot a steer and two riders would drag it over the high flames, followed by men on foot with gunny sacks to put out the flames, before they rose back up high. The riders pulling the steer wet their bandannas and tied them over their faces.

I was gainfully employed by my brother-in-law, Fred Lane, during the summers of 1915 and 1916. Fred was an Englishman who worked his way to America, starting at the age of fourteen, working on a cattle boat across the Atlantic. For two years he was stalled in New York City and he and another boy ate out of garbage pails back of restaurants. Finally, he rode the freight and got out to Montana where he and Harry Sherwood staked a claim on 160 acres of land as homesteaders for a couple of years, considerably improved the property, sold it and returned to South Dakota.

While in Wakpala they learned that Miss Mary S. Francis, principal of St. Elizabeth's School, was looking for a couple of young men to paint all the school buildings. They walked the two miles to the Mission and offered their services. They got the job, and Miss Francis was so well pleased not only with their painting job but also with their splendid courtesy and manners that she hired them to be caretakers at the school, managing the dairy, the cattle herd, horses, poultry, and other farm items of the school, and directing the annual huge gardening program with the students of the school. They were all-round men as carpenters, blacksmiths, cobblers, etc., in which things they gave instructions to the thirty or forty boys of the school.

It was through this position that Fred and my sister, Lyma, met and married in 1910. They moved to Uncle Herbert Welsh's ranch by the Missouri River and there they operated a very successful small ranch of about 200 head of cattle.

During the years of 1915 and 1916, a British buyer of horses (for use in World War I) came to Fred and asked him to buy horses for him. This is where I came in. Fred hired me to go all over the reservation as an interpreter and to drive a herd, when it reached thirty head, back to his place. I closed them up in a pasture, changed saddle horses, and caught up with Fred as he moved along from community to community and Indian home to Indian home.

One day we rode into the ranch of Patrick Shields at just about noon. Mrs. Shields, one of the prettiest women this world has ever seen, was home and came to the door to talk with us. She could understand English rather well but was too bashful, or felt awkward about it, to speak it. Consequently, I did the interpreting. Fred asked her where Pat was. Mrs. Shields: "I am very sorry but he has gone to Timber Lake and will not be home until tomorrow evening." Fred: "Tell him that we'll be back next week on this day and will be glad to have him show me the Harry Holy Medicine herd of horses."

Then Mrs. Shields said, "It is noon and I would invite you and your brother-in-law for dinner, but I have only Indian food of dried meat (*pahpah*), turnips, garden onions, and wild rice with baked biscuits, *wojapi,* and tea." I paused for a moment and said, "Yes, maybe he will not be used to eating our Indian food." Right at this point, Fred cut me off and said to Mrs. Shields, "Mrs. Shields, did you invite us for dinner?" She said, "Yes" (this time in English). Fred got right off his horse and said to Mrs. Shields, "You bet, Mrs. Shields, *Miye* (I) *lila* (very) *locin* (hungry). Let him go on his way," motioning with his mouth towards me.

On our way from Pat Shields' place, my brother-in-law lectured to me about food. "Never belittle food, boy. I learned my lesson in New York City for two years. Besides, any white man that looks up his nose at Mrs. Shields' cooking ought to be horse whipped." In other words, I admired my brother-in-law, immensely. However, I had a good notion to send Fred on his next horse-buying trip alone. Shucks, he could give a good account of himself in the Sioux language when he had to, I found out.

In my early twenties, I continued to love reservation life. College and its allied influences could never win me over to urban living or the Euro-American culture. It was a bore to me to have to know English literature, German music, and the like. I could not get very interested in what was so foreign to me. I liked Ancient and European history because they were explaining what man across the water was like.

How often I have wished since those reservation days that the population of the U. S. had been somehow stabilized and kept at about 100 million. At such a figure, humanity on this continent would continue to be the tail, wagged by the Continent. As it is going, we are at over 200 million, reaching the stage where we shall be wagging the Continent, and the signs that this is not going to be good are already prominently before our eyes, but we are too unrealistic and unimaginative to realize them.

During my early twenties, our people were still living on their own lands, still had a few horses and cattle, and cared for fruitful and useful gardens, for the most part. The railroad had come and laid its tracks the length of the reservation around 1906, and this was a good thing. We had small towns and stock yards, handy for shipping stock instead of ferrying or swimming them across the Missouri River. Trains were romantic, especially sixteen-car passenger and six-car locals. We had coast trains 15 and 17 to the Pacific and 16 and 18 to the East. The two locals also caused excitement as they came to each town. How we loved to watch the fast trains pick up mail on the dead run! Now and then, for some special reason, one of the coast trains would stop at Wakpala. I loved to see the several brakemen and conductors step off, just as the train stopped, carrying their little milking stools for people to step down on. Then, they were always sure to look at their watches, pulling them out of their vest pockets. The shout of "Board!" was sweet to us Indian boys as on horse back we would watch this frequent drama.

Or else, I have been frustrated with the government and the churches for being so nearsighted or indifferent to what was happening to the American Indians, after they were short changed by the expropriation of their reservation lands, for instance. That is, obviously our people had to have something else in the place of the stock raising industry to make up for the tremendous acreage loss. There was nothing adequate or consistent, which our people with confidence could take hold of, offered by the government. At long last, John Collier came along and he did last for twelve years, but with the change of administration, the program was simply ignored and instead Termination, to end the life of the American Indian, was promoted, barely stayed by our few able white friends who sacrificed much to take the story of the threat to the American people.

Okinawa has just been returned to the Japanese. If only the American Indians numbered 80 millions, maybe the government would not mind returning the W.W. II gunnery range on the Pine Ridge (which they borrowed) back to the Pine Ridge Oglalas. They might have gone around the home of the Senecas, instead of flooding the reservation of that tribe, putting in the Kinzua Peridy Dam. They might go to bat to help the Indians of the Northwest and their treaty fishing rights. The contemptuous indifference of the government in her acts towards a weak people, the American Indians, makes a list which only plants despair in the American Indian to think about. We, the American Indians, are "the least of these" America's brothers, and yet the government can't treat us fair. Why? Because America bullies the weak instead of going to bat for them. This is one of the great, great differences between Indian culture and white culture. We remembered the weak, the sick, the stranger, etc., long before the diluted, distorted religion was brought here in the name of Jesus who would not recognize this religion preached in his name, if he were here today. When the cry rang out in old Indian life, *Ohunke sni kin wicakiksuyapo!* (Remember the weak!) even the feeblest, wayward Indian of those days, nothing like feebleness and waywardness of today, rose to his finest to defend the weak. I cannot help being Indian, and with the explanation of this, I'll close my story.

When I was three years old, my father took the loss of my brother so hard that one day he was found on the reservation prairies, completely out, lying on the ground. Some men haying about half a mile away noticed a team and buggy standing still for a long time. They rode over and found my father in this condition. The doctor told him it was caused by a near non-functioning liver, in turn caused by his grief. It took him five years to recover. Consequently, from the time I was six years old, my mother travelled with him. I was then baby-sat by Grandpa and Grandma Brown Elk while they were gone for sometimes ten days.

These old Indian people would come into our yard and pitch their tipi and I would be their guest. Many times, mother would invite them to live in our house, but Grandma Brown Elk always refused, saying that she did not know how to keep house like a white man, although mother was one-fourth Indian. But I loved living with my grandparents, because they lived according to the kinship system.

Nearly every evening, Grandma would cook a big meal and about supper time four to ten of our old people, living down below and around the Mission nearby, would come and join us for a dandy social gathering afterwards. Grandpas—Iron Ribs, Walks in the Wind, Wind Soldier, Red Bird, Blue Cloud, Carrier—even Joe Claymore, younger, about sixty, would come. His name in Indian I love: Counter-Attacking Bear. *Mato Iglamna.*

I was supposed to go to sleep but I would stay awake and listen to the most exciting stories, songs, philosophies from those who lived according to the physical and moral laws of Mother Earth. I knew I was hearing all these things which must have gone back to the great grandfathers of these men. Stories, by now, which must go back 200 years. I know twenty songs which have not been sung for the past 150 years. I sing them now, only when I am all alone.

I was baby-sat until I was fourteen, when my mother died and I was sent away to a military school only two weeks after her funeral. By this age, I must have absorbed a culture that was never going to leave me. I am just a good actor in seeming to be perfectly at home in American white society. There is constantly a slight strain in my associations with white people. From time to time, I have to go off by myself and relive that early culture to get refueled, so to speak, for refreshment, recalling the ways of the Standing Rock people of sixty years ago. Especially helpful to me has been the glimpse of the art of the Plains Indians in the way to enter into the realm of the Great Spirit, or the Third Dimension, so to speak. Had I gone on the stage as an actor, I think I could have made out rather well because I know I can act, pretending to be something else, something I am really not, and I think I have been getting away with it most of the time. I repeat: the only way I can tell that I have never really crossed over is the strain I am sure to feel after being in the white world without any recreation for some time. Attending conferences, seminars, etc., especially wear me down.

When I left the reservation at the age of fourteen, as I recall now, our people, the Hunkpapayas, were like the Columbian Indians, "gentle, full of hospitality, curious and happy, faithful and truthful, walking in beauty, and the possessors of a spiritual religion." I returned as an ordained minister when I was thirty, and my heart was broken. My people were different. They had slumped badly—physically, mentally, spiritually, morally, socially, and economically. Could not the Government and the Christian Church have noticed this, or didn't they care? I know one Bishop told me: "Time will solve all things."

When I die, I want to be cremated and have Ed McGaa fly over the Chain Buttes of the Standing Rock reservation and let my ashes float down on to the land of Sitting Bull and Gall, where I was born.

XXIII

BENJAMIN BLACK ELK

Born in 1899, son of the famous Black Elk who was cousin to Crazy Horse and participated in the Battle of the Little Big Horn, Ben also became famous in his own way. He was probably best known as the "fifth face on Mt. Rushmore." Dressed as a Sioux chief, he posed for tourists and photographers at the foot of the Mt. Rushmore National Monument, sometimes photographed as many as 5,000 times in a single day. It is possible that he was the most photographed man who ever lived.

Ben was also a successful rancher, appeared in motion pictures, and often lectured on the Dakota traditions in which he strongly believed. Following the production of *How the West Was Won,* in which he appeared, he traveled through Europe to give publicity to the film. Ben died in 1973.

The following "poem" has been arranged by the editor from a tape recording of Ben's rhythmic speech. (Recorded by Wayne Knutson.)

RED IS THE KNOWLEDGE

My people have came a long ways,
with the sky our father,
the earth our mother;
we have come a long ways to this land,
guided by the Great Spirit.
Our history has been written on four winds,
only to be captured by our wise men
such as Red Cloud, Crazy Horse,
Spotted Tail, and my father.

I am Black Elk, and I came from a family
that was not too well known,
not great chiefs.
My great, great, great, great, great-grandfather,
his name was Black Elk.

We always wonder how an Indian gets his name.
It's by deed or by—on the warpath—some great deed,
or bravery, or by an unusual, or by a vision.
My name was unusual, 'cause my great, great, great, great
great-grandfather killed an elk
that was blacker than ace of spades.
The name was handed down to seven generations
and I am the seventh one.

My grandfather was at the Fort Philip Kearney fight.
He got wounded there.
At that time Crazy Horse was young
and he led the warriors with Red Cloud.
My grandfather, he's the brother of Crazy Horse's father,
so my father and Crazy Horse are cousins.
My father was a sort of lieutenant to Crazy Horse.
My father witnessed the death of Crazy Horse.
That is the background of my story, of myself.

Everything that we do in our lives,
the Indian, he has a prayer.
We send a voice to the Great Spirit,
through a tree, through the rocks.
Everything was made by the Great Spirit for us to use,
that we should ask them to help us.

The sweat bath, the keeping of the spirit,
and the making of relatives, and the throwing of the ball,
the sun dance, all that, it came about by visions
of our people as we came along.
So, that is the Indian religion.

We have four corners of the universe,
that control the universe.
We have colors for them.
The black, or the dark blue, stands for the West.
And the white stands for the North.
The red is East, and yellow is South.
And turquoise blue is heaven,
and the green is earth.
Each one has a meaning.
From the West we get our rain,
the thunderbirds—water is life.

When they comes, they're terrible;
they create a commotion, they destroy,
they'll kill. But yet they makes the earth
so green and fresh after the rain.
The white is snow, where the giant lives.
And the West is where the sun goes down,
and North is where the giant lives,
and then we get our cleansing power from the North,
the spirit that controls that corner.
And we get knowledge from the East—it's red.
Red is the knowledge.
It's a dangerous signal for the white
but we, we get knowledge from men.
And, yellow stands for the South
which means source of life.
In other words, you the white man,
mourns with black. When he mourns
he uses black. But the Indian uses that
for joy. Black is for joy.
And yellow reminds of our death,
because yellow stands for source of life;
that's where we come from, from Mother Earth,
and when we die that's where we're going back.
And turquoise blue stands for heaven—
that's the happy hunting grounds.
Green for earth.

So the medicine man uses symbols to . . .
directs all this to the proper places . . .
in order he makes his medicine, he uses a pipe.
First pinch (of tobacco) is for the West,
second for the North—he puffs the pipe—
then East comes next and South,
then one pinch for Mother Earth,
then one for the wingéds of the universe,
and then one for the four-leggeds,
and then one for anything that's moveable
in this universe.
And lastly, the two-legged.
Then he seals the pipe,
And thus he loads the whole universe in the pipe.
Then he prays to the Great Spirit,
to take care of all of us.
So, that's the medicine man's power,
and, I don't know, a lot of us believe that

a lot of them died with this secret.
We know, for a fact.

Now this is pretty hard to do
because the white buffalo woman that
established this religion, with regulations,
strictly, that we do not dare to now.
We are supposed to be civilized
and yet we're not civilized at this time.
Our people at that time were more civilized
than what we are today.
So, things have happened.

Our prayers is essential.

Our history, our prayers, and our songs.

XXIV

JOHN R. MILTON

Born in Minnesota in 1924, Milton has lived in South Dakota since 1963. Professor of English at the University, and editor of the *South Dakota Review,* Milton is a poet (five books) as well as a writer of fiction. "The Inheritance of Emmy One Horse" appeared in *Best American Short Stories,* 1969, was translated into Chinese for broadcast over the Voice of America, and has been published in England and The Netherlands.

THE INHERITANCE OF EMMY ONE HORSE

I

And the water of life flowed past his door.

He pushed the short stick into the sand between his bare feet. He drew a circle around it with his forefinger, and added several wiggly lines, apparently aimless in direction, each one ending at the circle. From the pouch at his waist he withdrew a tuft of hair—lynx or bobcat, he thought, although the memory was dim— and carefully placed the hair on top of the stick, not pushing this time but letting it rest easily and precariously. He was ready again. He would get five more before sundown.

He heard the car bearing down upon the approach to the bridge, then speeding across, and as the car was directly above him he muttered the words and hit sharply at his stick with the tuft of hair on it and sent it all flying into the river. The car sped off into the distance. No matter—it would crash at the next bridge and fall into the water. All of its occupants would drown. He chuckled. In the past years—he did not know how many—he must have killed over a thousand white people. The spell was infallible.

What more could he ask.

Crazy, they called him, and cast him out from the tribe. He could not remember how long he had lived under the bridge. Or how long ago it was that Samuel Big Medicine had become Samuel Talks-in-Circles. Or just Sam TIC. The young braves in their beat-up Fords and Chevvies laughed at him, and the women turned their eyes away as though he had been forever expelled from the Yanktonnais. So he had. No longer shaman, no longer powerful, no longer useful—so they said. A judge— white—came to the reservation and ordered him taken to a big house. Sam refused to go. His people honored his request and took matters into their own hands, into tradition, into the old way which said that a tribe member no longer useful must be sent away to die by himself.

He survived.

Stumbling across the prairie, walking blindly into fences that cut him and angered him, avoiding towns except once when he did not expect to find a town out in the middle of nowhere, he fell, exhausted, down an embankment at the end of a bridge and rolled into the water. Had it been deep at that point he would have drowned, gladly. But his head remained on the sand, and he raised it as proudly as he could and took command of the territory, a small place, under a highway bridge.

He slept all night with his body partly in the water, rising the next morning with wrinkled skin, shivering in the early chill of dawn, noticing driftwood along the river bank. Without moving his lips he smiled at the thought of making a fire without the white man's matches. He knew of no Indian who could still do it.

At this point in his life, Sam TIC decided to wage war upon the whites again, as his people had done successfully generations ago, being defeated ultimately only through the numbers and weapons brought to bear against them. He was still shaman. He had established his territory; like holding a pass against the invaders in the old days, he would now hold the bridge. They would not see him. He would work his magic, alone, unseen, and all would die.

Deep under the bridge he lived.

A foray into the nearest town—it became necessary—yielded matches and several cans of beans. He got away unseen. From the driftwood along the river he selected those pieces which could be propped against each other and the bridge support to make a shelter. Other pieces he burned, for heat and for cooking the beans.

They had said he was crazy: formerly revered, formerly respected in the inner circles of the tribe, a member of the council, now outcast, now isolated from two civilizations. He had taken his old hunting knife with him. Its new use was inglorious—cutting into the tin cans of beans. He dreamed at night of sprinting across the prairie and through the brush along the river, knife in hand, upraised, needing only a swift strike to bring down a deer. But, in the daytime, awake, prowling up and down the river, Sam saw no deer, no rabbits, no game of any kind.

Crazy. A hermit. He liked it, more than he would admit to himself. He became a scavenger, invading the town with all the stealth of a Sioux warrior, returning with a board, a few bent nails, a piece of tar paper, and soon he had a respectable and portable shack built and set upon two runners. When he needed sunshine in the winter, he pulled the shack out into the open. When he wanted shade in the summer, he pulled it back under the bridge.

He was tolerated, after they found him there, because he did no harm.

Little did they know, the palefaces, that he was the power which was destroying them, one by one, as their cars went off the highway in fatal accidents, either at the next curve or at the next bridge. Twice he had literal proof of the strength of his medicine. A car full of noisy young whites failed to make the turn at the other approach to the bridge—the one Sam could see across the river from him—and careened into the river. There was much excitement then, and much wailing and mourning for the lost young people, but no one suspected that it was Sam's particular talent which had dealt the blow. Again, after yellow signs with crosses on them were erected at the curve, a car came speeding at the bridge and went through the rail and into water deep enough to cover all traces of the accident. Only Sam saw that one.

It was no accident.

Let it be said that Sam was no murderer. He was engaged in legitimate warfare; other than that, he was—at least in his own sight—a good and responsible man. He even acquired an odd kind of love for the bridge itself, after seven or eight years of living under it. He loved the bridge in the way that a man loves a woman, seeing her always as she was when first she became part of his life. The bridge grew old, and Sam did not notice. It was wrinkled and stiff and had more than one aching joint—all unnoticed, because Sam took the bridge for granted, as a man does his wife.

Others had noticed—civil engineers of the highway department.

In town, those people (all of them) who did not know that Sam TIC had caused the highway deaths through his making of medicine, who, indeed, had never heard of Sam, complained to the state highway department, to the governor, that six yellow cross signs at the old bridge were quite enough. A new bridge, with new approaches, was needed. And, the old bridge was getting dangerous for other reasons also—it might fall into the river.

And so one day some strange men came and prowled around the bridge, poking at it, looking at it, and talking constantly in numbers and formulas. Sam did not understand what was taking place, and he simply told the men to quit, to move away, to get out of there. Damn it.

They did not go, until toward evening. Sam found his knife, opened a can of beans, and contemplated what kind of spell he would cast upon the men if they ever returned.

He had almost forgotten them when they came back. This time they were followed by a swarm of trucks and machines and gadgets which Sam had never seen before, and there were many more men. Every one of them marched to the edge of the bridge, stood hesitantly above the river, and looked down at Sam. He decided that the best thing was to ignore them. At that very moment he was jarred by the loudest voice he had ever heard, from a giant in a leather jacket: "Hey, old man," the voice roared, "you'll have to pull out of there!"

Sam slowly turned his head in the direction of the voice and peered wonderingly but a little belligerently at the giant. "I ain't go-un anyplace."

The giant did not move, but his roar increased: "Oh yes you are! Get out! Scram! Vamoose! We got work to do, redskin, and you're in the way."

"Work?" Sam could hardly utter the word. "There ain't no work to do here. I am here eight years and no work." He thought for a moment. "Go away. You must be crazy."

A small man, with glasses pushed up on his forehead, stepped in front of the big man and told Sam that he must at least move his shack out from under the bridge. It was dangerous to remain under the bridge, he said.

Sam tried to think about the little man, but he could not comprehend the necessity of moving his shack. It was early summer, he guessed, very warm, and he wanted to be in the shade. He would move the shack later on, perhaps in October.

The men did not talk any longer. Four of them half slid down the embankment from the bridge, walked in a group to the shack —as though afraid to act individually—took hold of the ropes which Sam used to move the shack, and pulled it to the edge of the river. The very edge. Sam looked at the men and said nothing. Two men got behind the shack and pushed, tipping it on its side into the water. In less than a minute the current got hold of the boards and they drifted down the river, a rough, weather-beaten, flimsy box with the open door gaping blackly like a mouth open in protest.

Sam did not protest. If he could have known that the old bridge would not be demolished until the new one was completed, he might have stayed awhile longer—but he did not know and he did not stay. He still had his knife and his personal totem bag. He still had a firm belief in his powers as shaman.

Samuel Big Medicine walked slowly, head up, toward the little town upriver.

II

"You ain't got all of your head!"

The little brown devils were buzzing around her, coming at her and yet not coming. They made her head spin and her heart beat too fast. She thought she was crying out "stop it!" but she could not hear her words. Something was wrong again.

"Emmy is crazy, Emmy is crazy, Emmy is crazy!"

The little brown devils (or were they red? or copper?) changed color and swirled about as leaves do in a stiff autumn wind. Colored leaves—brown, yellow, blue—but leaves were not blue. Always something was wrong. Blue leaves fluttering in her face, but leaves could not be blue, and they could not strike out at her as these blue things did.

"Go home, Emmy One Horse, and find the rest of your head!"

"Let me alone."

"Yah, yah, Emmy's crazy!"

She stumbled, and the blue leaves (only now they were definitely dark red) retreated from her. The wind must have changed, because now she could hear her voice, her own voice, far away yet, but she heard it. "Let me alone," the voice cried. "Go away and let me alone."

She swung her arms up to defend herself and beat wildly at her tormentors. "I hate you!" she screamed. "I'll kill you!" And the brown devils which weren't really brown at all fell back and hesitated and fell back again. The red and black and blue became blurred and mixed up as the colors on little boys' jackets do when the little boys are crowded together and pushing each other in their haste to get away from something they suddenly fear. And Emmy began to remember now, and she turned and ran away from the boys.

As she ran, the fresh new air streamed into her lungs and her eyes and worked itself down into her legs so that she ran faster; and as she ran her head cleared and she realized that she was running toward the big white house at the end of the street. And in the house, the white frame house, she knew that she was running up the stairs toward the big white room at the back, the room with the sunshine flooding through the windows and the sturdy door was there and she could shut it against the devils no matter what color they were.

Here she was safe.

"You're crazy, Emmy."

She leaned from the bed and flung open the door. The hall was empty. "I hate you!" she screamed. "I'll kill you!" She ran to the closet, pushing aside the dresses, dumping the hatboxes to the floor. No one was there. She fell to the floor, landing too hard on one knee, and searched under the bed. Only dust and a bit of lint. One canvas shoe with the lace missing. She wondered what had happened to the shoelace, and then her knee hurt and she looked at it to find blood seeping through the scraped skin.

Emmy watched as the blood oozed, red across the brown skin, dark red because of the brown underneath, oozing, then moving slowly down the leg and over the little bumps she had gotten during the morning from the brown devils. The bumps had not killed her but the blood might—if enough came out. If her blood ran all over the floor until it dripped, pluht, pluht, pluht, down the stairs and out the front door—then the brown devils would see that she could no longer be bothered. No more devils if the red water flowed fast enough and far enough.

It stopped.

She went outdoors again. The blood had not even reached her ankle. There was perhaps enough for the boys to smell it. They would go away.

She was safe.

It was good to be lazy in the April sun, late April. Fluffy white clouds chased each other across a pale blue sky that was picking up a little more color, a deeper blue, each day. There were no black or brown or copper-red clouds. No devils in the sky. That was where Emmy wanted to live, in the sky, in white clouds, in whiteness like when a woman went to live with a man, or a lake froze peacefully in the winter, or the popcorn was heaped for the children in the park. But Emmy did not dare go to the park anymore, and ice made her cold, and she was an Indian.

Partly at least.

She heard her father call, voice muffled from the kitchen, and she stretched out on the steps and stayed where she was. Her eyes closed to the afternoon sun as she waited for energy, for purpose. It did not come. The boys were gone and Emmy suddenly felt lazy, not exactly lazy either, just more peaceful than anything else. Her head had stopped spinning.

Finally.

Why had Bill and Les and the Riley boys wanted her to go fishing with them? She had gone with them before, but only as a child, when she was some kind of toy or curiosity to them. That was long ago. She didn't always remember because sometimes her head felt fluffy like the clouds only not white but brown and black and sometimes red and green and yellow and brown. She remembered that the boys had asked her to go fishing this morning.

"I'm too old to play with boys."

"Aw c'mon Emmy," pleaded Les.

"No."

"What's the matter?" asked one of the Riley boys, and she could not remember which one it was, but they were Rileys.

"Nothing's the matter," she answered. "I don't want to go fishing." Then she had arrived at the inspiration of the young lady who is superior to her tormentors: "Nice ladies don't do that."

Bill threw his head back so hard that his cap fell off; he guffawed and hollered and pranced around, then doubled over and held his stomach as though he had cramps—laughing all the time. The Riley boys stared first at Emmy and then at Bill, as though they could believe neither one. But it was Les who stood sullenly off to the side and said so quietly that no one heard it for a moment, "Nice lady, hell. Your old man's an Injun, or had you forgotten?"

"My mother was white," she screamed back at him, and her head began to pound again. "White! White! Do you understand?"

"Yeah." Les continued to speak softly, as though to keep anyone else from hearing. "But she's gone. And you're old enough to come down to the river with us now. Get what I mean?" The boys all stood quietly now, facing Emmy expectantly, not certain that they had said the right thing but wanting to find out.

She fled. It was not clear to her now, but she must have run, because the only visual image remaining was the line of boys advancing upon her, and the only sound was the chant that followed her from an earlier year,

Half-a-head Emmy
Can't think worth a penny,

and the rest was mixed up with the colored but mostly brown things that buzzed around her and frightened her.

She was on the porch.

Had she gone to the river? She could not remember.

III

Samuel (Big Medicine) Talks-in-Circles and Emmy One Horse sat together on a grassy knoll seven feet above the swirling brown water. The river current was strong at this point and had deposited a tangle of driftwood below the bank. The bare rooted end of a tree lying in the water looked like a horse's head.

We are the last two, Sam said.
My mother was white, Emmy insisted.
I have killed many whites.
You should not do that. I think you have not done it.
See my totems.
There is only some hair in there (fur?), and a few sticks.
You know nothing of the old ways. You listened too much to your mother.
She was white.
I know. That was her trouble.
How could you know about her?
I know.
Don't you have any troubles, old man?
No, no, only with the bridge.
Yes, you told me that. You were foolish.
Don't say that.
I just said that you were . . .
No. I ain't crazy.
I didn't say that.
You think. You no say. You think.
Talk straight. Maybe you are crazy after all.
We are all crazy.

Not me.
No. You ain't crazy.
I mean it.
We are the last two, Sam said.
What shall we do? Emmy asked.
They will put us in the big house now.
I won't go. My father can stop them.
He is Inyan.
Yes, but my mother was . . .   ·
. . . white. I know.
It makes a difference.
Make-un you crazy is what it did.
No, I only have headaches. They go away.
Inyans go away too. All go away. None left.
They're on the reservation.
They go away. None left. Only whites.

But my mother . . .
. . . was white. I know. Too bad.
What shall we do? Emmy asked.
Make medicine, Sam said.
The sticks?
And the hair of the cat.
Will it work on me, too, because I'm white?
You Inyan.
Are you that sure?
Sure.
Will it kill many?
Watch. All the hair left, on all the sticks. Big totem. We kill all the whites in the land, keep land for Inyans, everything will die except our people, and our land.
I'm afraid.

Sam emptied his medicine bag on the grass. He pushed the sticks into the ground and capped each one with a piece of fur. He took more time than usual to utter his words, his incantation, his final work of magic. He was the big shaman of the Sioux and would return to his tribe in honor as soon as he kicked the sticks into the river. He became excited at the thought, and he jumped to his feet as quickly as his stiff legs would allow, drawing back his right foot—the kicking foot—and lashing out with all his remaining vigor at the hair-topped sticks. He kicked too hard and lost his balance. He fell over the edge of the bank and dropped heavily into the river. Emmy started for the edge and drew back when she saw that Sam had hit his head on the wood which looked like a horse and was floating unconscious, drifting rapidly downstream as the current caught him and took him away from her.

There was nothing she could do except return to the big white house.

For a while her headaches increased as she wondered if Sam TIC had killed her mother on the old bridge. She went back to the grassy knoll one day and kicked tentatively at one of Sam's sticks, still there. Nothing happened. She kicked one stick so hard that it flew into the river, but there were no accidents that day either.

By October, when the leaves were blowing across the town—almost all of them were yellow this time—the new bridge had been built and dedicated and the old one demolished. Some of the pieces floated down the river. Emmy's headaches were less frequent, and she was able to talk to the Riley boys without upsetting either them or herself. The boys found the rest of the sticks, with their hairlike caps, and Emmy persuaded them to set the sticks gently in the river and let them float downstream. The act was performed with reverence, and the procession moved on the water with dignity.

And the water of life flowed past, as it always had.

XXV

JOSEPH HANSEN

Joseph Hansen was born in Aberdeen in 1923, lived in South Dakota for ten years, Minnesota from 1933 to 1936, and since then has resided in Southern California. A novelist, he has published fourteen books. In 1974-75 he was awarded a fellowship grant by the National Endowment for the Arts, in creative writing. His three most recent novels are *Fadeout* (1970), *Death Claims* (1973), and *Troublemaker* (1975).

MOURNER

A few weeks after Briggs Nelson's mother was bolted inside a shiny metal coffin and buried in the dry, dustbowl earth of the cemetery at Stander, South Dakota, a parade straggled up Main Street, trying to be gay. Rodeo horses reared and shied between the flat, sun-bleached faces of the buildings. The old tomato-red fire engine coughed. The Legion drum and bugle corps marched in powder blue uniforms and nickle-plated helmets. Sweating aldermen waved from open Packards on which bunting flapped.

But all Briggs noticed were the Indians.

They wore beaded jackets, fringed leather pants, paint, feather bonnets and bear claw necklaces. The men straddled spotted ponies. Their squaws walked behind, round-faced, stoical, with eyes black and glassy as basalt, braids down their backs and, one or two of the young ones, with papooses in slings. Briggs had seen Indians before. There were big reservations near Stander. He had watched Indians in many parades and remained reasonable.

But not this time.

This time he broke away from his father and ran along beside them. He ran block after block—not fast, of course, but at a steady trot—until his legs ached and his mouth was dry. He didn't yell out loud, but inside his chest, where his heart beat like a tom-tom, he was yelling all the time. And when the parade broke up, and the Indians disappeared into the armory, he sat down on the hot tin fender of a parked Model T and almost bawled. Which was unreasonable too, and unsettling, because he was eleven years old and never cried any more. He hadn't even cried when his mother died.

But he couldn't get the Indians off his mind.

The next morning he went to the public library and lugged home all the books about Indians he was allowed. And all afternoon, and after supper, and then late into the night in his hot, slope-ceilinged little room—while his father, on the other side of the wall, walked forlornly up and down in his stocking feet, creaking the floorboards—Briggs read of how the noble savages were tricked and sold out, decimated by the rifle bullet and the white man's diseases, and finally herded on to reservations in bitter and inhospitable lands where they shivered, starved and died.

What he read disturbed him. He wanted to do something, to get to the reservations somehow and to rouse the chiefs and braves, to set them on the warpath again, to avenge what had been done to them, to right their wrongs. But all he did in fact was to start a neighborhood enthusiasm for playing Indian. Along the alleys frequented by youngsters he knew, or in the scrubby clump of wind-bent oaks dying near the high school on the fringe of town, or farther out, in the abandoned gravel pit, bows and arrows displaced cap pistols. Pheasant feathers were rummaged out of cellar corners where they had blown the previous fall, when dads had brought home gunny sacks bulging with the big, limp birds, rainbow bright and full of buckshot. Headbands to hold the feathers were stitched by harassed mothers; Mrs. Horst, the lady downstairs, sewed Briggs'. Realism was what he mainly sought in the games he contrived, pictorial realism. The farther off from home the games were played, the more nearly naked everybody got. But no one was burned at the stake or pinioned to the earth to be devoured by ants.

Briggs didn't see the Indian that way.

Two other sad things had happened around the time Briggs' mother died. His father's shoe store had failed. And their new house had to be given back to the bank. After the funeral, the Nelson furniture had been moved into these four stuffy rooms on the top floor at the Horst's, and Briggs' father had taken work— it was The Depression, and jobs were scarce—traveling as a shirt salesman through the Dakotas, Montana and Wyoming. He was able to return home nights when his trips didn't take him too far.

When they did, he arranged for Briggs to stay with friends.

Twice he stayed with the Eamses, who had three kids, and twice with the Melgards, who had two. But he wanted to stay with the Meisners because Mr. Lou Meisner was Sheriff of Stander County, and the Meisner house was over the jail. It was a big, red brick place that stood high on a mound of brown lawn that was like an enormous grave. And in the basement, in the grave, were the cells. Briggs knew they were there but his mother had never permitted him to see them. He'd had to imagine them, as in the Buck Jones and Tim McCoy movies—grimy, black barred, crowded with sulky gunslingers. And the sight of Sheriff Meisner, large and heavy bellied, a big, brown revolver strapped to his thick thigh, lent conviction to these imaginings.

So Briggs was pleased when, six or eight weeks after the parade, by which time he had exhausted the library's stock of Indian lore, and had been sunburned so brown that he doubted, hopefully, that he would ever bleach back to his normal Scandinavian pallor, his father sent him to spend a week at the Meisner's. At night he shared the bed of Johnny, who was his own age and whose principal merit, so far as Briggs was concerned, was that he talked very little. Briggs liked to talk, and since it was too hot to sleep, he lay in the dry darkness beside Johnny and lectured him about Indians. He talked fast and indignantly, so that it was some time before Johnny could interrupt. When he did, it was very quietly.

"Dad's got an Indian in jail," he said.

Briggs sat up. "Right now? You mean downstairs? Locked up?"

"Sure. Name's Charlie Two Horses." Johnny yawned and turned on his side. "I'll take you to see him tomorrow."

"But what's he in jail for?" Briggs was shocked that the genial sheriff would treat one of his red brothers that way. "What did he do?"

"I don't know. But he's a good guy." Johnny's voice faded sleepily. "Knows a lot of great cowboy songs . . ."

The jail surprised Briggs by being bright and clean. The pale gray paint was fresh, the cell bars naked, gleaming steel. Except for Charlie Two Horses, the place was empty. And, being below ground, it was a lot cooler and more comfortable than the house upstairs. Briggs leaned his face against the cold, shiny bars and stared worriedly and with pity at the prisoner in the cell.

He was a brown, underfed young man in dirty work clothes. His stiff hair needed combing and there was grime under his fingernails. Briggs supposed the narrow eyes and hawk nose looked savage, all right, but because of his grin, which showed teeth white as the porcelain toilet at the back of his cell, it was easy to forget that his father had likely scalped some soldier of Custer's. Seated on the bunk, Charlie hunched his shoulders and made his guitar jangle and twang as if it was alive with mice. He tilted his head back and shut his eyes, trying to think of a song to sing.

" 'Whuppy Ti Yi Yay,' Charlie," Johnny said.

Charlie kept his eyes shut for a second longer, hunting up the words and tune. Then he let out an experimental yup-yup, and began:

" 'As I was out walkin' one mornin' fer pleasure . . .' "

Briggs had always agreed with his mother when she'd called this kind of music trashy. They had both preferred the Walter Damrosch symphony broadcasts and records like "The Two Grenadiers." But, listening to Charlie's easy, drawling voice, watching his hands on the strings, his foot tapping in its ragged tennis shoe, Briggs guessed there was something to be said for it, even for "Pretty Redwing."

Charlie slid the guitar under the bunk. "Okay, that's all the songs today, kids. Now, you do me a favor. I'm out of makin's." He pulled a greasy calfskin pouch out of his shirt and took a dime from it. "Can you catch, Briggs?"

"I can," Johnny said.

"He asked me," Briggs said. "Sure, Charlie."

"Right." Charlie flipped the coin, spinning, in a high arc. It cleared the bars neatly, but when Briggs grabbed for it he missed and knocked it rolling. It tinkled across the cement floor into the cell opposite and flattened out under the bunk inside.

"Some catcher," Johnny said.

"I'll get it." Briggs ran to the door of the empty cell and tugged. He felt his face turn red. "It's locked."

"That's all right," Charlie said. "Johnny knows where the keys are." He winked at the Sheriff's son.

"Sure." Beside the door to the upstairs stood a big rolltop desk. Johnny pulled open its central drawer and brought out a shiny key ring. "Keys are all numbered," he told Briggs, "to match the cell doors they fit. See, here's six." He fitted the large key into the large keyhole, turned it, and swung the door open on its oiled hinges.

"Let me get it." Briggs felt urgent about this. He dodged in and slid on his knees to reach the dime under the cot, then stood up with his heart beating hard, and walked back to the door. "There's the dime," he said to Johnny. "Now lock it."

Johnny turned his freckled face half away and looked at Briggs out of the corners of his eyes. "What?"

Across from them, Charlie said, "Get out of there, Briggs. If Johnny's dad come and found you in there, he'd be sore."

"You don't have to really lock it," Briggs pleaded. "Just shut the door. Only for a minute. I just want to see what it's like to be—locked up under ground. Please."

"You're crazy," Johnny said. "Come on. I've got to put the keys back."

Briggs felt like yelling at him, but his father had told him to be polite because the Meisners were doing him a kindness, having him stay, so he came out. But, standing staring into the empty cell, while Johnny locked the door and put the keys away, Briggs ached in his chest. Behind him, Johnny's voice had a lost, sad sound, echoing off the bare walls, asking Charlie:

"Bull Durham?"

"Yeah, and get it back here, will you? I'm clean out. Musta smoked all night." He flapped an empty sack at them, a scrap of soiled cloth with a black paper label. "So don't horse around, huh?"

"We won't." Johnny ran to the barred door that shut the jail off from the upstairs. He halted. "Come on, Briggs. What the heck's wrong with you?"

Briggs sighed. "Let's go."

When they came back, Charlie was asleep, sprawled face down on his bunk, the back of his shirt dark with sweat.

"Watch me wake him up," Johnny said, and raised the pudgy new tobacco sack to throw it.

Briggs caught his arm. "Don't. What do you want to wake him up for? He was awake all night. He was suffering. It's wrong to lock Indians up. They get sick and die, longing for the sky and the prairie."

Johnny looked at him sideways again. But he didn't throw the bag of Bull Durham. He laid it quietly on the crossbar of Charlie's cell door. Then they went upstairs and hung the key to the jail door on the hook at the top.

Briggs took that key down again in the middle of the night. Barefoot, pajamaed, he groped after it in the dark. It was pretty high up, and his fingers trembled and were slippery with sweat so the key refused to unhook itself at first. But finally he got it. His knees acted wobbly and he kept hold of the railing going down the cold stairs to the jail. The stairway jogged. He halted. Below, a light showed. He stood for a long time, heart banging, and wondered about that light. But he seemed to recall from some movie that prisons were often kept lighted at night. So he went on down the rest of the steps, but very cautiously, as if there were broken glass on each one.

At the bottom, he squinted between the bars of the door. The jail looked grim at night. The light fell bleakly from a caged bulb in the ceiling. He couldn't see Charlie Two Horses, but he could hear him breathe. He pushed the key into the lock. It turned noisily and the hard walls rattled back its noise. He flinched, but nobody seemed to have heard. He swung the door out, went quickly to the desk for the keyring, ran with it to Charlie's cell, fumbled for the number five key, and opened the door.

Charlie ought to have been sitting miserably on his bunk, smoking, and yearning with vacant, haunted eyes for the great outdoors, or maybe pacing restlessly, like a caged coyote. Instead he was asleep, on his back this time, arms flung out, mouth slack. He slept as if there were an arrow through him, as if he were dead.

"Charlie." The name came out weakly because Briggs felt small and scared suddenly, which shamed him. "Charlie," he said again, louder, but still from the doorway. The Indian only sighed. It wouldn't work. Briggs would have to move. He forced himself to cross the cell to the bunk. "Wake up, Charlie. Come on, wake up." Briggs was suddenly annoyed. He grabbed the Indian's shoulder and shook it. "Come on. You can get out, now, you can get out."

"Huh?" Charlie opened his eyes and stared. Then he sat up so fast he nearly knocked Briggs over. "What the hell are you doing here?"

"I came to let you out. Look, the door's open. Both doors. You can leave, Charlie. You have to go quiet through the house, but you can leave. Everybody's asleep."

"You crazy kid," Charlie said, "you'll get in bad trouble." But just the same, he got off the bunk and walked, in his sleep-twisted shirt and pants, to the door. He swung it a little, maybe just to show himself it was really open. "Bad trouble," he repeated, only this time he was absent minded about the meaning and he grinned to himself. "Jeez." He wiped his hand down over his face, walked into the open area between the cells, turned around twice, came back and looked at Briggs. He shook his head and laughed. "You're a crazy kid, but you're all right. All right." He squeezed Briggs' shoulder, then pulled his shoes and guitar from under the bunk. "Come on, let's go."

"No, I'm staying here." Briggs held out the key ring to the Indian. "Here. Lock me in."

"What? Listen, kid, forget that." Sweat shone on Charlie's forehead. "Come on. We've got to get out of here before the Sheriff comes down." He moved to the door.

"No," Briggs said, "I'm staying. Lock it up, Charlie. And here's the key to the door down there. It hangs on the hook at the top of the stairs. Put it back."

"Look, come on, Briggs," Charlie pleaded. "This ain't no game." He kept moving out of the cell and coming back while he talked. "No time for horsin' around. You're gonna do this kind of thing, you can't play games."

"I'm not," Briggs said. "I want to stay here. I'm breaking the law anyway. Besides, Charlie, a white man doesn't mind. Red men mind jail. But a white man doesn't. Anyway, not so much."

"Oh?" Charlie stopped moving and blinked thoughtfully at Briggs for a moment. Then he shrugged. "Okay, okay, kid. Thanks." And he locked the door while Briggs stood inside.

"Goodbye, Charlie," Briggs said.

"So long, kid." The Indian dropped the key ring on top of the desk, and he didn't bother to lock the stair door. But that didn't matter a lot. Briggs went to the bunk that was still warm from Charlie's sleep. He lay down. The light glared in his eyes, and his heart was pounding so from excitement that he thought he never would, but after a long time he did fall asleep.

Mrs. Meisner found him there at six the next morning when she came down with the prisoner's breakfast on a tray. "Briggs Nelson!" she gasped. "Briggs Nelson!" Her bony face got red as a chicken's. She squawked like a chicken. She flapped to the stair door. "Lou! You better get on down here, right now!"

The Sheriff came, buckling on his gunbelt around his night-shirt. He was still nine-tenths asleep, and when his spindly wife pointed at the cell where Briggs stood in his pajamas, all he could manage at first was a grunt. The rest of the Meisners came down behind him, wide-eyed girls in pale flannel bathrobes and with curl-papers in their hair, and last of all Johnny, looking white under his freckles.

"What the hell?" the Sheriff finally managed to choke out. He clattered the key ring and scraped four or five keys around on the steel plate of the lock until he got the right one at last and could pull the door open and yank Briggs out. "What in all con-solidated Hell you done? Where's the Indian?"

"Gone," Briggs said loudly. "Back to the wide prairies and the open skies."

It wasn't a hard speech to make. He had practiced it. But he hadn't practiced any other speeches, so that when the Sheriff and his wife sat him down upstairs in the roller-shade darkened parlor and asked him questions about why he had set Charlie Two Horses free, and what kind of a way was this to act in somebody else's house, and what would his father say, he couldn't answer.

Somehow, they got his father back. He looked pale to Briggs, and strange, standing beside the big, sunburned Sheriff, apologizing in his thin, quiet voice. The Sheriff seemed ready to laugh about what had happened now. But Briggs' father never laughed any more. The best he could manage was a wan, crooked little smile.

"All right, Lou, if you say so, we'll forget it. You understand— it's just that he's—well, losing his mother, her being gone, he—"

"Sure, Henry, I know," the Sheriff said. "But I gotta answer to the County. Oh, hell, I can get Charlie Two Horses back easy enough. That's not it. He'll be drunk someplace by sundown. Just pick him up and dump him in the car. But supposin' it'd been some killer, for instance—"

"I understand, Lou." His father nodded tiredly. "Anyway, thanks." The two men shook hands and then stared at Briggs. His father sighed and tried the smile again that didn't work. "All right, son. Got your suitcase?"

And they went.

"What we'll do," his father said that night, "is go to Minneapolis. To your Aunt Christine's. All right with you? Nothing left for us here—not even the car, now. When I got back today, after Lou called me, Reardon's had a man waiting. See, it wasn't quite paid for. God knows what good it'll do them. Can't sell anybody a car today. Anyway, I sure can't travel for Hi-Style without it. There'll be a better job for me in Minneapolis. Well, some kind of job. Anyway, there'll be a home for you, with a woman in it. You like your Aunt Christine."

"Sure," Briggs said.

"If we sell the furniture," his father said, "we'll have enough for train fare to Minneapolis, and some left over to keep us till I get work."

After the furniture was gone, they didn't linger in the blank, brown-papered rooms above Horst's. They carried their suitcases through the rusty iron gates of the cemetery and up the long, curving cinder drive inside. They stood side by side staring down at the dry-grass-covered mound that was his mother's grave, and then his father cleared his throat and said:

"We can come back to her, come back to Stander sometime. Things won't always be this bad. Minneapolis isn't so far away. We can come to visit."

Briggs had never ridden on a train before. But it wasn't exciting. There was nothing to look at except flat land that the

…n was burning up and from which the wind was all the time raking the topsoil. Dead cows lay in the fields, bloated sometimes, sometimes only skeletons. Farm houses stood vacant, windows and doors boarded up, paint peeling. Barns leaned with the wind. Silos had fallen over.

The wheels of the train made sounds as if they were biting off sections of rail in even lengths and spitting them out. But all they were really doing, of course, was rolling, carrying him farther and farther from the dead grass on the mound in the cemetery, the shiny metal coffin down under it, away down, his mother lying prim and strange on her back inside. Briggs looked at his father.

"Some Indians," he said, "bury their dead at the tops of trees."

Then, for some reason, he cried.

XXVI

HARRY W. PAIGE

A native of New York (born in Syracuse in 1922), Harry Paige has spent several summers on the Rosebud Reservation in South Dakota. From his research has come *Songs of the Teton Sioux,* 1970, plus a number of short stories, including "The Summer of the Sweet Return."

Paige, who has also published poetry and articles in many magazines, is a professor of humanities at Clarkson College, Potsdam, New York.

THE SUMMER OF THE SWEET RETURN

By August it was known by the Indians as *CaN WakaN KiN,* the holy tree. Ruben Black Bear, the one to see the vision, became a celebrity in the tiny community of White Thunder. And he had stopped drinking overnight! The more skeptical among the Indians who had looked into the giant Cottonwood and had seen nothing, found Ruben's abstinence the real miracle, if indeed there *was* any miracle.

"He's been drunk since the War," his brother-in-law, Noah Hawkman told Father Bates one day as they stood near the holy tree. "And suddenly he stops! How do you explain that, Father?"

The young Jesuit, fresh from graduate study in the East, shrugged his narrow shoulders and gazed abstractly into the summer foliage. "I don't know," he answered, twisting his head to one side to gain a new perspective. "I just don't know."

Noah Hawkman shook his head slowly in disbelief. "Practically a drunk for over twenty years an' suddenly he won't touch a drop. Sure beats me, Father."

"The Lord works in mysterious ways . . ." The young priest smiled. "That's what they say, Noah."

The Indian grinned a broken-toothed grin. "Then we need more of them 'mysterious ways' around the reservation, Father," he observed.

By the middle of August an average of ten people a day were coming to the tree. Tony Good Voice was seen pushing the battered wheel chair of his sister, Jessica, over the stubbled prairie to a position from which the crippled girl could place her hands on the trunk and cry out in the shrill keening of the Sioux women: *"WakaNtaNka, uNshimala ye!* Great Spirit, have pity on me!" Before she left the tree she made her brother cut off one of its smaller branches and this she placed beside the plastic statue of the Virgin that stood on an upturned orange crate beside her bed. Others came—the curious, the skeptical, the hopeful and the frightened. Now there were tire tracks leading up to within twenty feet of the holy tree although the nearest road was over a mile away. Someone had placed sage and sweet grass in the lower branches as an offering.

"They're going to set the prairie on fire with their tobacco offerings and cigarette butts," Father Duggan complained.

"It's gone far enough," Father Juniper agreed.

"It approaches paganism, idolatry," Sister Angeline protested with passion.

Ruben Black Bear, sober now, with a new light in his dark eyes, quietly denied all this. "The Sioux have always had their sacred trees," he told them. "Like the tree used as the Sun Dance pole. Anything can be sacred to the Indian people—a bird, an animal, the sky, a stone. Why not a tree?"

"Why not *God?*" Sister Angeline huffed.

Ruben Black Bear smiled graciously into the pale face that seemed to tremble like a candle flame in a breeze. "Why not?" he returned simply.

Frank High Pine, a medicine man who lived by himself on a butte overlooking the holy tree, became a self-appointed devil's advocate for the traditional Indian community. He smoked the pipe with Ruben Black Bear and questioned him. "Were you drunk that day?" he asked, looking away. "I do not like to ask in this way, but I must know."

"I was on my way to town," Ruben Black Bear admitted. "I had money for wine. But I never got there. I passed by the holy tree. It was noon and the leaves were all silvery, turning in the wind. I heard the rustling and heard the tree talking to me. 'Look up into my branches' it said. I looked and saw a woman where the biggest branches spread out - - -"

"An Indian woman or a white woman?" the medicine man interrupted.

"Truly, I do not know, my cousin."

"Did she speak to you?"

"Yes, my cousin. She spoke to me in our language. I never

forget her words. 'Do what is right. Believe in me and the people shall live!' That is what she said. Only that."

For ten minutes Frank High Pine smoked in silent meditation. "It could have been a vision of the White Buffalo Woman as well as the Blessed Virgin," he decided.

"Hecetu. It is so, my cousin. Truly it could have been the woman who first made us one people. I do not know."

After more than two hours of questioning and a visit to the holy tree, Frank High Pine pronounced the vision to be a true one. He told the Lady of the Vision's words to all he met. *Do what is right. Believe in me and the people shall live!* He told it in the language of his people. Her words spread through the community of two hundred in a single day.

When Ruben Black Bear went to the holy tree again he was followed by a crowd of fifteen people. At the end of the processional came Tony Good Voice, pushing his sister's wheel chair. The young priest, Father Bates, walked by the side of Ruben Black Bear.

As soon as the Indian looked into the tree, his face shone in recognition. *"WiNyaN waste, uNshimala ye!* Good Woman, have pity on me!" he intoned, falling on his knees. Father Bates whispered "Amen!" and gripped his crucifix with whitened hands. The other Indians stood still, their dark faces holding wonder like mahogany bowls.

The reservation became split into two camps—those who believed and those who did not. There was a further division—those who believed that the woman in the holy tree was the Virgin and those who believed that she was the White Buffalo Woman. There were also those who believed none of it, except that men who drink most of their lives are not the stuff that visionaries are made of.

Lyle Thomas, the Superintendent of the Agency, referred impatiently and derisively to the whole episode as "that vision business." He concluded, in consultation with Tribal Chairman Tony Shangreaux, that such nonsense introduced a devisive element into Indian-white relations.

"This kind of thing should be stopped," he told Shangreaux. "You know that it doesn't take much to rile the long-hairs in these full-blood communities." "Besides," he mused, an ominous and prophetic note in his voice, "it won't be long before some outsider comes in here yellin' about freedom of worship or somethin'. Raise a big stink over it. Make it a real issue. An' we jus' quieted down that shootin' out by Eagle Butte a few weeks ago."

Shangreaux chewed on the end of a pencil. "What's there to

do?" he asked in quiet resignation.

The Superintendent looked out of his window and across the waves of prairie grass and the shimmering ghosts of heat that danced above it. "I don't know—yet. But I'll think of somethin'—even if I haf'ta chip that damn tree down myself. The tourist season will last another two, three weeks. I don't want 'em to get the idea we're a bunch of superstitious fools out here—."

He was interrupted when the door opened and a young Indian girl entered. "Father Duggan would like to see you, Mister Thomas."

The Superintendent shot an I-know-what's-coming look at Shangreaux. Then he said: "Alright, Linda. Show him in."

The priest entered wearing a sport shirt and tennis shoes. He was puffing heavily on a dirty pipe. "Got a few minutes, Lyle?" he asked.

The Superintendent nodded. "Sure, Father. But I bet I know what's on your mind. You had only around thirty people at Mass yesterday."

The priest raised his shaggy eyebrows in surprise. "Twenty-six," he corrected. "How'd you know?"

The Superintendent smiled. "Same with the Episcopal mission out at Horse Creek. Sixteen out'a thirty-seven. I haven't heard from the others."

Father Duggan shook his head. "It's bad enough when we've got the Peyote and *Yuwipi* Cults to put up with. Now, it's a holy tree—"

"We know all about it, Father," Shangreaux injected.

"And do you know," the priest went on, "that there were nearly a hundred souls gathered around that tree yesterday? On Sunday! Did you know *that?*"

Shangreaux nodded. *"That* too, Father."

"It's crazy," the priest said, shrugging helplessly.

"It's Indians," Shangreaux corrected.

The Superintendent rose from his swivel chair and began pacing the floor. "Twenty-four years workin' with the Bureau." He looked up at the ceiling with a martyred expression. "I don't think I'll ever understand these damned—" He shot an apologetic look at the Tribal Chairman. "I mean the long-hairs," he corrected himself. "People like you—well, we see eye to eye, Tony."

Shangreaux bit on the pencil again. "What can we do about it, Father?" he asked, ignoring the Superintendent's observation. "Why don't you go out there to the tree and talk to them? Tell them it's the Blessed Virgin—"

"I can't say *that,"* the priest complained, his voice rising to a whine of protest. "How could I ever explain that to the Bishop?

347

You expect me to take the word of an alcoholic—"

"Ruben Black Bear is one of your parishioners, Father. An' besides, he's off the stuff now. He hasn't had a drink since—"

"Why don't you have a talk with him, Father?" the Superintendent asked. "Explain it to him psychologically or somethin'. Tell him he's made a mistake. Tell him it's like a sin to go around seein' the Mother of God in trees."

"Ruben didn't say it *was* the Blessed Virgin," Shangreaux reminded him. "It could have been the White Buffalo Woman."

"White Buffalo Woman!" the Superintendent mocked. "That's even worse! Over a hundred years of missionaries an' Christianity an' now the White Buffalo Woman! Back to the beginning again! It'll be worse than the Sun Dance. They'll be wearin' feathers an' blankets next." He turned away in disgust.

Shangreaux rose to speak. "Look," he said to the two men, "I think we're makin' too much out'a this whole thing. Too big a deal. We'll get an over-reaction from them if we try to discourage it. Jus' let it run its course—like a fever. When nobody else sees this vision, the whole thing'll die out." He turned to the priest. "You remember a couple of years ago, Father? When the Indian Messiah was supposedly born on Christmas Eve? North of Wounded Knee. There was a lot of talk for a couple of weeks an' then it was all forgot jus' as fast."

The Superintendent nodded. "Maybe you've got a point, Tony." He shrugged. "Besides, I don't see where we got any other choice right now."

The priest sighed heavily. "No other choice," he repeated, as though it were a part of a liturgy. "Except perhaps to pray that it all passes—like a dark cloud."

But the cloud did not pass. Nor did the Indian people consider it dark. It was for them the red road across the sky, the path that led the way to things old and sacred. Attendance continued to fall off at mission churches. The *Yuwipi* Cult flourished, its shamans predicting the return of an Indian millennium, complete with the epiphany of the White Buffalo Woman. The drum and the rattle were heard from behind covered windows, their driving rhythms breaking into the early hours of the morning. Reports of miracles swept the community of White Thunder into a tide of religious fervor. It was reported that Jessica Good Voice had left her wheel chair long enough to walk the last twenty yards to the holy tree. Danny White Feather reappeared, six months after his death had been reported. Joe One Bull returned to his wife and children, leaving a red-headed woman stranded in an Omaha hotel room. Jack Cloud reported seeing a white buffalo northwest of his home near Vetal. Corporal Roy High

Eagle won the Bronze Star in Vietnam.

"Truly, it is good to be a Lakota!" Frank High Pine exulted. And the other Indians who were listening broke in with a guttural chorus of *Haus.*

Ruben Black Bear came to be regarded as a Holy Man in the traditional Indian community. The people listened to the former derelict as to a prophet inspired. More and more pressure was put on him to reveal whether his visions in the holy tree had been of the Virgin or the White Buffalo Woman.

"Truly I do not know," he repeated to his inquisitors in an agony of doubt. "Perhaps if she appears again . . ." His voice trailed off into a thoughtful silence.

Old Nellie Stands, unofficial keeper of tribal lore for more than forty years, called it the Summer of the Sweet Return and drew pictographs in the old Indian way showing a woman in white buckskins standing in a V of summer foliage. The woman wore a crown of sage and carried a pipe in her outstretched hands.

September came and Ruben Black Bear had not seen the vision again although he had continued to make his daily pilgrimage to the holy tree. Banners of colored cloth—red, green, blue and white—trailed from the holy tree, streaming in the wind that now bore a hint of autumn. The singing and the dancing began in early September. Frank High Pine revealed that a song had come to him in a dream of the Woman in the holy tree. Each day he went to the tree to sing his song as she had commanded him in his dream. In his high, trembling quaver he sang in the Indian language:

> This holy tree
> I see before me.
> Believe in me
> And the people shall live!

He sang the song over and over again, expanding the four lines into a ritual of several hours. Then, suddenly, the hoarse and croaking voice stalled to silence and he gazed into the softly rustling Cottonwood until he became as one in a trance. The same day that he introduced his song, Old Nellie Stands began to dance around the tree to the drumming of her oldest son. She wore her ceremonial white buckskins and a black shawl thrown around her thin shoulders. She danced, bending stiff knees and circling in the direction of the sun. The chanting of Frank High Pine and the heavy rhythms of the drum pulse were carried on the wind. Slowly, a few at a time, the Indians made their silent appearance, as though they had sprouted from the ground. The older people were the first to arrive and before long they were joined by their children—and then their grandchildren. Soon, the holy tree was ringed by a flurry of feathered dancers and the strident cries of the singers as they picked up the song from Frank High Pine and added to its dimension, each in his own way.

"A carnival of emotionalism," Father Duggan called it, driving by in the mission's battered station wagon. His companion, young Father Bates, craned his neck to watch the dancers. "I don't know," he muttered aloud. "Sometimes I wish—" He swallowed his words in deference to the opinion of the older priest. As they slowed down to allow a pick-up truck filled with Indians to cut across their path, the young priest felt his pulse stir to the primitive rhythms of the drums and the shrill, piercing cries of the dancers. "I hope it is the Holy Mother," he said to the older priest. "In that way it'll be like a native re-enforcement of the mystical elements in the Church. It'll be their own contribution."

Father Duggan smiled at the tolerance of the younger man's analysis and didn't say anything.

"They're good Christians, but they're also Indians," the young priest continued, interpreting the smile as an encouragement. "Seems to me such passion shouldn't be discouraged—" He stopped, surprised at his own boldness. "Of course, I'm new to all this," he added hastily, with a sweeping, inclusive gesture. Then he grinned. "I guess I've got a lot to learn."

Father Duggan didn't hear him. He was blasting his horn at a pack of lean and snarling dogs that blocked his path.

In a week they were coming from other reservations, informed about the holy tree through the moccasin grapevine. They came from the Rosebud and Cheyenne River Agencies to the East and from Standing Rock to the North. A small group of Cheyennes had made the pilgrimage from their homes in Wyoming, lured by stories of miracles and the stimulation of cultural renewal. A few Omahas made the trip from Nebraska on horseback. An assortment of academics, laden with cameras and recording equipment, descended on White Thunder on week ends but they left, a few at a time, when it became clear that the Indians would not talk about sacred things. Nor would the Indians permit them to film or record the spontaneous rituals that had evolved from Ruben Black Bear's vision. Even the Christian missionaries on the reservation were forced to watch their own parishioners singing and dancing in the new and mysterious ritual. "It is not good to talk of things wakaN," Frank High Pine explained patiently. "Too much talk is bad medicine." But generously, he invited the whites to dance with them to celebrate the holy thing that was happening.

It all came to an end on the twenty-first of September as dramatically as it had begun. The weather turned hot and muggy by early afternoon. Thunderheads boiled up in the West. The wind raked the prairie and tossed the trees wildly at the sky. Lightning jabbed a flaming finger at the earth, cracking a static whip. The prairie dwellers ran for cover.

White Thunder received the full fury of the storm. Rain drove into the ground, breaking in an explosion of silver nipples. The only dirt road through the community churned into muddy ruts. The lightning interrupted the thunder—a quick stitching of light to darkness.

When the storm finally rumbled past White Thunder and down the canyon, Frank High Pine came out of his prairie shack to feel the clean wash of air and the smell the fresh rain smells. As he let the cool air bathe over him, a sudden trembling shook his thin frame. Something was wrong! His failing eyes ran over the matted prairie grass to where a rainbow arched the distance. Beneath the arch, where the holy tree should have been framed in color, there was nothing! A tight fist closed on his heart! He stumbled down the side of the butte, sliding in the mud and wet. Two thirds of the way down, he stopped. Where the holy tree had been there stood only a shattered trunk sealed with the marks of burning. Splintered branches, still heavy with foilage, were strewn around the base of the tree in a careless pattern of destruction.

"The holy tree's been lightning struck!" he cried aloud, his voice breaking on the words.

From the direction of the Trading Post he could see a small group making its way toward the fallen tree. With stiff joints protesting, he hurried to meet them. As they drew nearer he could hear the confusion of sounds that followed them, sounds punctuated by the shrill keening of the women. Some were waving their arms wildly and pointing toward the splintered tree.

By the time they gathered about the remains they were rain-drenched and splattered with mud. They milled about, probing the ruins of their dream, their eyes dull with sorrow. Sobs were choked down to rattle in their throats. Finally, Ruben Black Bear spoke: *"Le wana henala,"* he said softly. "Now it is over." He seemed to age, even as he spoke the words. His shoulders slumped forward and he gazed at the muddy ground where only yesterday a hundred feet had worn a dancing path. Without another word he left the group of mourners and slowly walked toward the road. On the way he met Old Nellie Stands who was walking in the direction of the tree, an umbrella over her head and mud-caked winter overshoes on her feet.

"TiyaNka! Toka hwo?" she called to him. "Hold on! What's

the matter?"

The bent figure of Ruben Black Bear went on. The old woman repeated her question, *"Wamatuka,"* he said, sighing heavily. "I am tired." Then he added under his breath: tired way into tomorrow.

In twenty minutes he approached the road that led to town. A station wagon had slid off the muddy road and appeared to be stuck. Coming closer, he found that it was Father Duggan and his young assistant, Father Bates.

"How about a hand?" Father Duggan called out in recognition.

The Indian nodded. "Sure, Father." Then he asked: "Can I get a ride to town with you?"

"You bet," the older priest exclaimed as he slid behind the wheel. The young priest and the Indian pushed as the wheels spun mud all over them. In a few minutes they were back on the road heading for town, the older priest guiding the wagon skillfully in the worn ruts.

"We heard what happened," Father Bates told the Indian. "I'm sorry."

Ruben Black Bear nodded his acknowledgement and gazed out of the window.

"It's probably for the best, Ruben," Father Duggan said. "It may not seem that way to you right now—but when you look back on it, you'll see it was for the best."

The Indian continued to stare abstractly at the familiar scenery giving no indication that he heard.

"It may be God's way of telling us something," the older priest went on.

"WakiNyaN," the Indian corrected. "The Thunder Beings. They are the ones who use the lightning."

When they got to town Ruban Black Bear got out at the Post Office. *"Pilamiye,"* he thanked them. He watched until the wagon passed out of sight.

Inside the Post Office Ramon Shangreaux, brother of the Tribal Chairman, handed him his mail—a seed catalog and a letter from an anthropologist at the State University wanting to know more about ". . . the new revitalization movement which might fit into the complex of Pan-Indianism." He threw the mail into the waste basket and went out.

There weren't many Indians in town, he noticed. Probably because of the muddy roads. From across the street the neon sign above Larry's Cafe pulsed, shooting a stabbing arrow through the gathering dusk of the after-storm. Ruben Black Bear shook his head sadly, as though in answer to some secret question, sighed heavily and crossed the street toward the frail transfusion of light.

XXVII

E. R. ZIETLOW

Born at Presho, South Dakota in 1932, Zietlow lived on a ranch until he went to college, Dakota Wesleyan. After service in the army he did graduate work at Boston University and the University of Washington. In addition to short stories and poems, he has published one novel, *These Same Hills,* 1960, set in the western part of South Dakota. He is a professor of English at the University of Victoria, in British Columbia.

WINTER WHEAT

Bud was eleven and his Uncle Art had promised to let him drive the pickup when the custom combiners arrived. They would have a truck and Uncle Art would let them haul the wheat directly to the elevator in Pinnacle. Bud could drive the half-ton pickup and haul what it held to Uncle Art's granary. It was the first summer that Bud would get to work with the combiners. They had self-propelled machines—Massey-Harris, Farmall, International. They came from Texas, and they followed the harvest north, way up into Canada. One day they appeared and when the fields were cut, they were gone. Bud had tried to imagine their journeys; what kind of roads they went down and what kind of country they saw. But it was hard for him, because he had never been outside South Dakota. He had always lived on his dad's farm.

His dad did not plant wheat. He said that this was not wheat country. He planted cane and millet to feed the sheep. Bud often had to herd the sheep in order to keep them on a rented pasture his dad didn't want to fence. While herding, Bud watched the trucks on the highway and the tractors in neighbouring fields. During harvest time, he watched the combines and thrashing rigs. Finally, this summer, his Uncle Art had asked his dad if Bud could drive the pickup for him. His dad had consented, but at home he said: "He's looking for some free help. I don't know that he's ever come down here and given me a hand with anything." He told Bud: "You ought to ask him how much he's going to pay you." Then he gave a little laugh which Bud knew had nothing to do with things being funny, although Bud always smiled at his dad when his dad gave that laugh. But he did not ask Uncle Art how much he was going to get paid. For what if Uncle Art should change his mind?

It was hard to do nothing but herd the sheep while he waited for the day the combines would arrive. He stuck a lath into the ground and put a dead thistle on top of it and sat in the shade—it was terribly hot—and dreamt. His uncle would introduce him: "This is Bud. He drives the pickup." He would shake hands with the man who drove the big self-propelled combine and with the man who drove the truck. Maybe the combine would break down. And he would be the one to fix it. "It's this chain here. We'll fix it with my belt buckle. Just fits!" Or the grasshoppers would be moving in like an army and he would say: "Cut in front of them. Don't go around the field. They move too fast. Got to go back and forth in front of them." And the wheat would be saved.

When the combiners came, his mother would have to watch the sheep or put them in a fenced pasture. He would be doing the important thing, and she would be looking after his chore. "How long do you think it will be before they get here?" he asked her.

"Oh, four, five days," she told him. "Don't get excited. They'll come when they come."

And his dad said: "If that damned Art had bound that grain he would have it all down now. With this heat we're liable to get hail. He don't know nothing. If he was smart he wouldn't even plant wheat. He'd get a bunch of sheep and plant some cane."

Bud knew what Uncle Art would have answered. "Bind, hell! Then you go around the country thrashing for a month. I want the stuff combined. One day, that's it."

Bud was glad. There was nothing as wonderful as a self-propelled combine. Someday he would own one somehow. He would drive it. Maybe he would be a custom combiner, or maybe he would plant his own big fields of wheat.

When, three days later, Bud saw a truck on a side road hauling a self-propelled combine, he left the sheep and ran almost half a mile to tell his mother. "The combiners are here! I saw them!"

"Well, they're going to Stinson's first. Then they have a half a day at Haug's. Don't get in a rush. You better hustle back there and watch them sheep."

It seemed twice as hot walking back to the sheep as it had seemed running to the house. In the afternoon, Bud watched thunderheads poking up in the west. He wished they would come over the sun so that it would be cool. But then he thought about what his dad had said about hail. "Don't hail. Don't hail," he said to the sky. Later he could hear the thunder and see the lightening in the distance, but the clouds never covered the sun.

Two days later, Uncle Art came over at dinner time—he was a bachelor and liked to stop in at dinner time. He was a small man, and very thin and bony. "Them combiners are broke down over at Haug's," he said. "Looks like they ain't going to get to my wheat tomorrow after all."

Bud's dad said: "You should have bound that wheat. You can't depend on other people."

Uncle Art said: "Well, a man's binder could break down too. Anyway, next year I'm going to have me a combine. It's a good crop this year. I'll get me one of them little self-propels, and Bud can drive the pickup. We'll do her ourselves."

Bud sat up straight and twisted a little in his seat and grinned.

"Oh, that's damn foolish," his dad said. "You don't get one crop in three years. The damned machine will just set around and rust." Uncle Art, having no family, had always spent his money on machinery. His farm was cluttered with rusted-out machines he had bought new but used very little.

Bud said, "Maybe we could go out custom combining."

Uncle Art said: "I thought of that. If I make enough money, I'll buy another section. Then I'll get a big combine and a big truck. How'd you like that, Bud?"

"I could learn to drive the combine when I get a little older," Bud said.

His uncle nodded.

"Ten years ago you was going to buy another eighty," said Bud's dad. "You ain't been able to buy one acre in ten years, so how do you figure on buying another section next year?"

"I only need one good crop," said Uncle Art. "I'm going to have a good crop this year, and I bet I'll have one next year."

Uncle Art left, saying he would come back to get Bud when the combiners arrived.

Bud could hardly sleep that night. Next day, he kept watching for Uncle Art to come down the road. At noon he drove the sheep to the water hole and went in to eat. He asked his mother whether Uncle Art had been there. Why hadn't the combiners fixed the combine yet? When would they come?

"Keep your shirt on," his mother told him. "They'll come."

That day passed and then the next. The day after that it hailed.

Bud had driven the sheep in as the storm approached. He watched with his mother and dad as the hail stones beat the house and the lone apple tree and the hollyhocks. "Damn good thing that I got a lot of feed left from last year," his dad said.

After the storm, his dad drove with him to Uncle Art's. They didn't know whether the hail had struck Art's field or not. But they found out that it had. The tall wheat was broken down to a wet hash.

His dad looked over the field and shook his head. "Damn fool!" he said. "If he'd bound that grain he'd have it now. You see? You see how he is? He fools around with them combiners and this is what he gets."

Then they went up to the house, where they found Uncle Art tinkering with a part from the engine of his pickup. "Well, that was some storm, wasn't it?" he remarked, grinning.

"Did you see what it did to your wheatfield?" Bud's father asked.

"I ain't been out there yet," said Uncle Art. "Had a little trouble starting the pickup and thought I better try and get the bugs out of it before the combiners came."

"Well, you won't have to worry about that anymore," said Bud's dad. "Come on. Get in my car. I'll drive you out."

The three of them drove back to the field. They got out and walked through the battered wheat.

Bud's dad said: "What have I always been telling you? This is no country for trying to make your living off grain. Get some sheep. They're the thing."

"Hell," said Uncle Art, "I don't want no damn sheep. You have to lamb them and sheer them and dip them and feed them. Baby them all year around. Walk through their manure."

"You afraid of work?" asked Bud's dad. "I sure don't see you making no fortune this way."

Uncle Art had walked on. Bud's dad followed, and Bud trailed behind. He didn't want them to look at him. He didn't want them to see his eyes.

Uncle Art stopped walking and stood with his hands on his hips, the thumbs forward, the fingers on his back. He stood very still, with his head cocked ever so slightly to the right, and he looked across the field for quite a long time. Bud and his dad stood nearby and looked at him.

Finally Art spoke to them. "This fall I'm going to put in winter wheat. Winter wheat matures earlier. Next year I'll have a good crop and get it out of the field early. Then if I can get me some more land and a combine, I can raise a bigger crop the year after. Keep on building up like that. Winter wheat's the thing. I should have planted it for years. I'm going to start getting the tractor in shape right now. Then I'll see about a loan for some seed. I'll plow this stuff under and keep the ground worked up so the weeds don't get a start. Come fall I'll be ready to put her in to winter wheat."

On the way home, Bud's dad kept shaking his head and muttering: "Goddamnfool! I've never seen the beat!"

Next day Bud was out with the sheep. He stuck a lath in the ground and put a thistle on it and sat in the shade. Across the prairie, rippling in sun, he pictured endless fields of winter wheat. And into it he drove with a great red combine. Massey-Harris, Farmall, International—it bore one of those magic names. It moved along like the electric clipper on the back of his neck when he went to the barber shop, and it sheered the prairie of thousands of bushels of wheat.

XXVIII

FAITH GILLESPIE

Born in Pollack, South Dakota in 1931, Ms. Gillespie went to college at Gustavus Adolphus in Minnesota and the University of Michigan. The mother of seven children, she has lived in London, among other places, where she has done some writing for BBC and has translated poetry from the Portuguese. She has also been involved in international women's movements.

DAUGHTERS OF THE AMERICAN REVOLUTION

Mine was a thoroughly modern
Mother. Out of the Black
Hills and Deadwood wilderness,
Offshoot of Boone and after
Calamity, through the Irish
Rebellion coupled with Abolition,
Laughing she came.

Was a flapper, scandalous,
Bare-kneed and beaded, paraded
For the Franchise, organized
Demonstrations for emancipated
Pay, trampled juniper
Berries in bathtubs.
(Or was it Prohibition
She marched for? No matter.)

Was a painter of riotous
Mother Goose murals on barren
Walls of prairie schoolrooms
For bread and soul and W.
P. A. She said, "All men are
Brothers, and so, by God,
Are women."

Was cheerfully married in black
Lace and red roses to Father,
Whose father had fled from
Conscription in Europe, who
Crewed on a section of Soo Line.
They had me, in hunger, at home,
With no anesthetic but hope.

Was a natural protestant
All of her life, laughing, and
Leaving to me the wholehearted
Gift that lets me accept
Without panic, my daughters,
Your protest.

XXIX

MARIE DAVIDSON REANEY

Ree Reaney (her writing name) has lived in California since 1939 although she was born in Waubay, South Dakota in 1915 and lived also in Pierre, Watertown, and Sioux Falls before leaving the state. She took college classes at Long Beach City College, Cerritos College, and U.C.L.A. but did not aim for a degree. She has written articles, fiction, and poetry. As the following "portrait" will show, Mrs. Reaney still considers herself a South Dakotan.

PORTRAIT OF PAPA

"But Papa , I've never *tried* to skate . ." I wailed, as he buckled skate straps over my hightop shoes. Bundled to the ears against clear biting cold on a Midwest winter day, I had trouble walking, let alone skating. What would happen when I tried to stand on oversized hand-me-down skates?

"You'll never know till you try," said Papa, and the words were so familiar they penetrated no further than the outer layers of my substantial woolen stocking cap.

Papa went first. He always did. With graceful strokes, his skates took him to the center of the frozen 'pond' that was our back yard. Carefully, he tried his weight in the center, then assured that March winds had frozen the prematurely melted snow to a depth that eliminated the fascinating 'rubbery-ice' he beckoned to me. Just yesterday, the rubbery ice had treacherously dunked my brothers. Their wet socks still dried near the furnace. But now the prairie cold had turned a weaving crust to solid thick ice, and Papa painstakingly pushed his fledgling across it.

I didn't learn that day, to master the hand-me-down skates. I was only six. But I *tried,* before Papa gave up, and sure enough, discovered it to be less frightening, less formidable, just as Papa had predicted.

Papa was willing to try anything. One later day, April's pale sun began to melt our 'pond', and Papa, really a kid at heart, 'didn't know till he tried' that the waving undulating ice which stretched and delighted his sons, would snap and break under Papa's greater weight. Sheepishly, he pulled himself out of jagged broken ice and freezing water, drenched for his daring and courting pneumonia.

Papa was not a big man, but he was tall and muscular, with enough weight to hold his own among men, the daring to do so if need be, and the placid quiet charm which usually made it unnecessary. He had thick black hair that he wore parted in the center and waved to each side, just matching the mustache he wore in younger days with handsome results.

Results were always Papa's aim. He loved the old fiddle he sawed away at, until he made it whistle and sing and tug at our dancing feet. From the strenuous "Irish Washerwoman" to slow sweet strains of "Traumeri," Papa plucked gay staccato or brought muted melody from its strings—until the day the fragile instrument snapped. He'd encouraged one of the boys to try. Ludicrous sounds led to disastrous horseplay.

"Try," he'd said. Far from tragedy, the broken violin became a challenge to Papa. An old encyclopedia with worn covers and loosened pages yielded some information, the local music store more. Even the man in the hardware store became a cog in repair machinery, when Papa set about fixing it.

The old violin, splinted, strapped, clutched with clamps, was glued with a special glue that Papa mixed with the loving care of a scientist. It was 'hospitalized' in our attic, and through our musical patient was to have no small visitors, all of us peeked, and touched and marveled at Papa's ingenuity.

"Papa can do anything," we said in awe, when music came again from the mended violin. And Papa's smile grew. Once more we tapped our shoes and Mama's workworn hands sturdily pounded out accompanying chords on the old piano.

"Try again, Ray," Papa said, handing over the repaired instrument. Sure enough, though smooth sounds and lighthearted melodies eluded young Ray for years, Papa's pushing, his praise, paid off. At last, he was as adept as Papa!

Mamma couldn't read notes. She played "The Old Rugged Cross" 'by ear.' And dreamed of the day when her only daughter could play the beloved hymns she sang in her sweet quavery voice as she went about her work.

When I was ten, I was to 'take lessons.' But the novelty of 'lessons' wore off even before I accustomed myself to the deep nononsense voice of the local music teacher. Though I could pound out 1-2-3-4-5 in time, hitting the right notes as long as I glued both hands to starting position, Mamma still had to 'chord' for Papa.

Never given to waste, Mamma and Pappa stopped the 'lessons'. But Papa didn't give up. He had other tricks up his bow-swinging sleeve. He brought home sheet music for a popular song. This, in itself, was no mean feat. Our local music store featured only dust-encrusted instruments and a yellowing stack of music. Nothing in that pile was newer than Sweet Adeline, and mostly it contained instrumental arrangements for impossible parts: a nine-stringed clavichord with separate obligatto for percussion, or some far-fetched and improbable instrumental duet.

I'll never know how he produced sheet music. But I'll never forget that song: "Sometime." I suppose no one later than Bobby Breen ever recorded it.

The music fascinated me. Right or wrong-fingered, I picked out the melody by suppertime. My 'lessons' hadn't prepared me for 'left-hand music' but Papa thoughtfully searched out my discarded (and hated) lesson book.

Patient Papa. It was weeks before we played it 'together.' But every noontime, we *tried*. I'd play until I hit the first wrong note (sometimes two or three bars, sometimes two or three notes) and then, shaking my head and saying "No!", I'd sigh and start again.

"Don't say 'No,' Little No-No," he'd smile gently. "Just go on. We'll be making music instead of noise. ."

"But Papa, I can't. . ."

"You never know till you try. . ."

With lessons, I faltered, stumbled, stopped. With Papa's encouragement, I persisted, trying over and over and over, until Mamma must nearly have lost her mind. I didn't really notice that Mamma had taken over my chores, while I plinked and planked: and finally *played*.

Papa lovingly pushed us into much more than recreation or play. I was a very little girl when first we heard of a 'wireless' radio that brought sound waves from far away to our very ears. Papa read about it first. "Maybe we could find out more about it," he said. "You never know. . ."

Ours was the first receiver set in our small town. Papa and my oldest brother, never knowing till they tried, built a receiving set, then a sending set, raised a tall tower, and soon OUR sounds were going halfway across the state and then the nation, bringing back fascinating conversations with fellow-enthusiasts who chatted and challenged and charmed our whole family. While we learned by *trying*, Science was taking giant strides and soon Papa and my big brother were feeling frustrated and far behind.

Papa found a correspondence course. "Here," he said. "we can learn together. I'm no longer young, but *you* are. You could be an electrician, you could learn about radio—learn the secrets of the great world of sound. . ." and under his breath, the old familiar phrase: "you never know till you try. . ."

They tried. Sid became an electrician and a good one. One of the best in his line. And Papa repaired all of the townspeople's radios, and later all of the electric appliances in a town that eagerly accepted innovations unknown in Papa's youth.

One day, Papa had a neighbor's radio in his shop for repair. Papa'd repaired it before. He knew it worked properly. Still, the neighbor kept returning it, complaining of lack of volume. Papa repeatedly demonstrated its volume in our basement workshop.

Then, with a secret smile, he mounted the small radio precariously on a corner of our roof, hooked it to a long dropcord and called the neighbor on the telephone.

"Mrs. Brown," (that wasn't really her name) "can you come to your kitchen door?"

"Sure, John . . why?"

"Just want you to hear something," he said, and climbed to the roof. When the neighbor stepped out her door, a block away, he turned up the volume. It blasted, echoed and reverberated.

She laughed, clapped her hands over her ears. The radio was never returned for repair.

"How did you know it would be loud enough for her to hear, Papa?" little John asked.

"You *know*," said Ray, scathingly. "You *try*."

Papa's indomitable courage stood him in good stead on a terrible evening when they brought us news of an accident. We were deep in a family rug-making project. All except Sid, the oldest, who was then fifteen. He'd gone to spend the night with a friend who lived on the edge of town. The boys walked in the balmy spring evening.

I remember the doors and windows were open, to let in the sweet-scented air, heavy with the smell of apple blossoms. The younger children rolled strips of carpet rags, the older ones cut even strips and Mamma sorted worn-out clothing to be cut. Papa helped everywhere, and kept all of us at our work with jokes and stories and fiddle music. Great-Grandma's big loom had been set up in our 'front room' turning it into a workshop during her stay with us.

Mamma was the one who heard 'rapping' at the door. (Doorbells came much later than this.) Guests called 'Yoo-hoo!' and walked in. Or, more formally, cleared their throats and 'rapped' with bare knuckles on the outer door.

We knew by the absence of the 'yoo-hoo' that it wasn't a casual caller.

Mamma smoothed her apron and patted the puffs of her pretty brown hair (her secret pride, with never a strand of gray, for all her six babies and days of hardship and hard work).

"It's the Marshal!" she whispered. Papa put aside the fiddle and they stepped together into the darkness to talk in low urgent tones. Suddenly, Great-Grandma and a grown-up cousin seemed to be in charge of our workshop and Mamma and Papa had slipped quietly away with the Marshal, a man who somehow struck fear and awe in our hearts, because he represented the Law. We thought of the word as capitalized in those days. He was the only law officer in our area. We couldn't conceive of his mission here, but we knew it to be awesome. Childish fears mounted, the more so because the grown-ups seemed so bent on convincing us there was no cause for alarm.

Great-Grandma cooked our breakfast next morning, an unbelievable circumstance. Mamma brooked no interference in her kitchen and guarded well her reputation of Cook, par excellence, so this was unprecedented. We were delighted with extra thick-spread toast and unbelievably generous dollups of jam. (Mamma believed in temperance in all things, and that included what she called being 'piggish' at table. Her reproving, "Sah, now!" was enough to dissuade our over-indulgence.)

We were glorying in a forbidden jam spree when Mamma, red-eyed and stiff-backed, but head held high, came in with Papa. He cleared his throat and Mamma turned away, so the little ones couldn't see her quick-starting tears.

"We've got some news for you," Papa started nervously.

"They don't know. . ." whispered Great-grandma.

"Oh." said Papa. He turned to Mamma, whose shoulders twitched, though no sound of crying reached us.

"Mary," he directed, "bring the bottle of brandy."

It was the first time we had ever seen it opened, though we'd seen it glisten goldenly from the top cupboard shelf as long as any of us could remember. Solemnly, he measured and administered a teaspoon to each of us. It tasted like sweet thin cough syrup, and each of us wrinkled our noses, but swallowed the fiery driplet without questioning why it was given.

Then Papa told us the story. There'd been an accident. Walking along the gravelled highway, Sid and his friend had seen wavering headlights coming toward them. They stepped quickly into the deep ditch for safety, but relentlessly the unsteady lights advanced. Sid had been crushed beneath the wheels of a car with a drunken driver!

The Marshal, who had brought the bad news, believed Sid had only moments to live. The doctor working over him agreed.

Papa and Mamma, we learned later, had entered the doctor's office to find him working desperately to stem the flow of blood from one leg broken in two places, the bone protruding through torn flesh.

Moans came from Sid's lips, but they were almost inaudible and growing weaker. His chest had been crushed. Efforts to save his life seemed hopeless at that moment.

Months later, Mamma told us that Papa, feeling faint, swallowed often and breathed deeply to bolster his courage, steady his hands. Then he bravely helped to splint and bandage and stem bleeding.

Mama, drawing strength from her infinite belief in God's goodness, cleansed wounds, sterilized instruments, followed instructions and prayed. All night, the three worked over an almost lifeless body.

But, "He's alive this morning! He's sleeping. He's come through the first night. . ."

It was the first of many nights. There were no steel pins to help ambulate in those days. There was danger of pneumonia to Sid's crushed chest. There were endless days and nights, trays and bedpans, pain and pills, bruises and bandages, tears and prayers. Quietly Mamma became full time nurse, keeping vigil at his bedside, in the only downstairs bedroom, and continuing her other roles as well.

And Papa, joking, fiddling and clowning more than ever, kept up the spirits of the wounded, the overworked, and the too-young-to-know-the-seriousness.

Months later, the long-bed-ridden boy tried his weight on the injured leg.

For once, Papa was less than confident. "It may be too soon," he worried. But then, "You never know till you try. We've got to follow the doctor's advice. . ."

Sid stood uncertainly, then toppled back on the bed in a dead faint. It had been too soon. The break was not healed!

Frightening doctor's visits, re-splinting, endless inactivity began again. Day followed endless day, until once again it was time to try his weight, to remove splints and heavy cast.

This time, the mis-shapen bone had knit. It held. He tried and found it healed. Slowly, the use of it returned, the crutches were cast aside, though the crooked bone that resulted frightened and fascinated and held us spellbound as long as he lived.

And live he did. Less hardy souls would have given up on that long-ago night of horror. But Papa, never knowing till he tried, and Mamma, believing implicitly in Papa's creed, had taught their son well: he could not let courage fail.

There were some failures, however. No one escapes them all. There was pneumonia that struck swiftly and left an empty place at our table and an ache in our hearts when our happy-go-luckiest brother died. And later, Earl lost his life. A knee-injury in his teens contributed to a succession of illness that finally resulted in death. Sid, too, was gone from our family circle, when at 40, surgery to correct conditions caused by the terrible accident at *15*, resulted in death. Grief turned Mamma's smooth cheek to one softly criss-crossed with lines, her smooth brow saddened into a gentle network of furrows. But her red-brown hair stayed bright, her blue eyes clear, and she continued to hold her head high.

As Papa aged, and Life dealt sadly with him, his hair thinned and whitened, his moustache was replaced by a smooth-shaven upper-upper lip. Later still, he grew an amazingly luxuriant white beard and his sharply chiseled features took on a softness that can only be described as an 'Abe Lincoln gentleness.'

Mamma and Papa outlived three of their brood of six, and each loss made them stand a bit straighter, and somehow love mankind a bit more. They seemed symbolic of the tall straight South Dakota trees that withstood rugged winters, withering summers, winds of Nature; and they became stronger for the struggle. Troubles were the tools that God used to fashion Mamma and Papa, to strengthen and sustain them.

"You never know what Life will deal out as your fair share," Papa said often. "You don't know, sometimes, how you can stand the troubles Life brings. . ."

But then, as he always finished, "You never know what you can do until you try. . ."

Papa's words were the sum of a man. Sometimes they seemed lost in the rush of living. But in the final analysis, they remained. In his simple lifetime, he tried much. And in the trying, he left honest impressions on those who knew him best. He never knew what he could do until he tried, but Papa tried.

No man does more.

XXX

GRETCHEN GALL (SHOEMAKER)

Ms. Gall was born in Wessington Springs, South Dakota in 1914. She has degrees from Morningside College and the University of South Dakota, and she has taught in public schools in Moorhead, Iowa and in Yankton. Although she has travelled extensively (including Colombia, South America, Mexico, and Spain), her poetry is centered almost entirely on South Dakota. Her most recent of four books of poems is *Touch Earth,* 1973, from which the following poems are taken. Ms. Gall is an English instructor at the University of South Dakota.

QUESTION

In everything I read there's talk of doom
reports of rampage   threats that really jar
late summer sloth   disputes in Zanzibar
or southern Cal   dread words plus TV zoom.
True   all about Dakota earth's in bloom
corn dries below a sky without a mar
warm winds tell tales of sweetning plums not far
away   yet wind-dropped flowers remind of doom.

Question

To mind the passing beauty of the earth
or tend the ills convulsing man from birth?

Perhaps such either / or is hardly real
assuming choice displays a childish zeal
for beauteous and bad seem intertwined
inseparable   perforce I work in kind.

FIDDLE A LITTLE

Come   come.   Fiddle a little tho Rome burns.
Be gay a bit.   Admit the flesh is weak.
Be glad the earth in usual habit turns
the year and grows wild roses by the creek.
Dismiss what youthful wish it is that yearns
to set the world aright and straight.   Come   tweak
the nose of time.   Maybe the wise man learns
to look and then he turns the other cheek.
It's true   as we've been warned at verbal length
that man's affairs are in great roil and rile
but roses have not been so pink in years
while any year is full of blows and tears.
Let some one else bear trouble for a while
Come   look with me.   Touch earth again for strength.

XXXI

MERIAL SCOTT

Although most of Mrs. Scott's published work has been in the juvenile field, she has also written articles and poems for adults, such as the poem included here. "EKG" shows not only her attachment to the land, but also an objectivity achieved by seeing her native South Dakota through the maturity of experience. She was born in Hot Springs in 1922, lived also in Nebraska, in Brooklyn, and in Rapid City for many years before moving to Lead in 1972. She was educated at Nebraska Wesleyan University.

EKG

dust
sifts up unnoticed through
the pain inside his chest
compounded in his head
of eight to five
obstacle courses
hurdles shaped like
paperwork with
incandescent lighting and
the curled lip
of his son
his wife's
menopausal no

forgotten dust
that suffocated hollyhock rows
in the thirties
refusing a penny sucker and
obliterating the movie marquee

dust
with silicone points
honed to agony
by a pursuing wind
across a forty-year-long prairie
scooping fear out of its plowed-up pockets
dropping grain by grain
its burden
on his chest.

XXXII

MARY HEDIN

Professor of English at the College of Marin, Mrs. Hedin was born in Minneapolis in 1924, attended the University of Minnesota, moved to California in 1950, and attended the University of California at San Francisco. A mother of four, she has, in addition to her teaching, established herself as a poet and fiction writer. She has vacationed in South Dakota but has also crossed the state many times on her way to Minnesota. The poem "Odyssey: Travelling Home" is included here because it places South Dakota in the perspective of several other states, with the poet's choice of images intended to convey a brief set of impressions of each of the states involved in the journey home.

ODYSSEY: TRAVELLING HOME

1.
Outside Reno
poplar trees

      solitary

      as cowboys.

On the iron sky their leaves
like nickels
      spin.

My mouth is a pocket
      turned
      out
for the nickel slots.

In the tall night
I listen to white leaves

      counting.

2.

In Nevada: between Elko and Winnemuka
   the land
   flat as a dish.

   Too much light
   splinters
   down

   cracks back
   to hard sky.

   Colors die:
      earth: bone white
      brush: grey
      far ranges: heaps of ash

   No one lives here.
   No cattle graze.

   Behind the rocks
   in thin shadow
   the snakes:
      lean and efficient.

   And between the humps of sage
   swift
   over their lurching shadows:
   the mad
   rabbits!

3.

Idaho: the mountains
   send signals
   from huge gods.

   Down splintery slopes,
   across broad valleys:
   the Snake

pours itself
500 miles
    silver
    and curling blue

becomes the staff:

all the green leaning!

4.
Wyoming:

whatever it is in us that reaches
for distance
perceives here a sound
like thunder
rolling beyond the ear's
wide range:
and plunges
wild as the spinning
wings

pursuing.

5.
Nebraska: homely, treeless.

On dry plains
cattle huddle together.

Among them,
pale and peaceful,
antelope:
refugees
on their own place
one color with the ripe field.

This is hunter's country.

Autumns,
men with guns at their shoulders
ride in Lincolns
the barrels braced
on the metal frames:
65 miles an hour.

In the season of fire
the antelope:

on the long
flatness

run

run

6.
North Dakota: we drive
into 8 p.m.

Plains open as napkins:
    siloes like thumbs over barnyards;
    cattle lean against a red sun;
    combines fling grain high, bounty
    of kings: lavish!

A pheasant

cuts across the road:
we veer!
Safe in the weeds.
His wild beauty!

We settle our fears,
hurtle
toward the long
dark.

7.
South Dakota: an empty box.
The small towns: Kadoka, Wall,
    Okaton, Murdo, Kennebec, Draper
    Reliance, Pukwan.

Or Huron, 14180
    Mitchell, 12555
    Brookings, 10558
    Watertown, 14077

Main streets broad enough
        for buffalo herds
        lined with gambles, peeneys, Sears
        & Roebucks, the Puritan Cafe,
        The Regency Hotel
        the Roxie Theatre
        six gas stations.

The radio sings hymns.

In the cafe at breakfast at 8 a.m.:
        the jeweller
        the barber
        the pharmacist
        the oculist
        the station manager
shirtsleeved, drink four cups of coffee, trade
jokes.

Why do I believe they are lonely?

8.
Minnesota: the domestic fields:
        corn like crowds
        of townfolk: orderly.

        The common wires
        carry civilized
        messages and doves
        like gloved popes:
        fat.

        The water: everywhere!
                lakes
                streams
                rivers
                ponds
        return any image
        the sky gives.

        Even the shaggy oaks
        are tame.

        In the wheat, the blue
        corn, quietness
        gathers:

listen!

Is there
anywhere
any note
of wildness
here?

An Indian
in the lean darkness
waits.

9.
A plunge through
the tunnel
of sound.

The baggage comes behind us.

The world is changed.

avenues narrow
houses blister
trees wrinkle into dark.

Home is a museum.

everyone's face
is a portrait of someone
I ought to know.

I turn to open my suitcase.
Will I find the someone
I was before
I left?

No one is there.

XXXIII

BYRON FRANZEN

The contrast in this poem is between the old man who stays on the Dakota farm and the young man who escapes, to venture out into a larger world. The escape, attempted by many young people, is never quite complete.

Byron Franzen was born on a farm in South Dakota, went to college in Minnesota and Canada, and became an expatriate, living in Amsterdam, where he has been a free-lance journalist and part-time editor.

GRANDFATHER

Jet-aged, bound
for Hong Kong,
I strain to see the field recede,
encompassed still by roamings
in a Midwest nursing home.
The brain gone dry,
in memory concedes,
identities
get mixed. I make
excursions toward a long-
gone working day.

That wheat field fence line
might have been a dike
or moat, banked as it was in loam.
Each time your spade shoved in
and caught the bottom strand
I felt a tide release.
Mine was the better back.
I yanked the woven wire up,
loosing past

associations, as you told
how places I had never seen
had sent their soil there thirty
years before in storms.

Great clouds of specks as
roiled as locust swarms
merging at random
blocked the sun
and settled down at last
to leave that South Dakota fence
knee-deep in Kansas, Oklahoma . . . .

Expended there
you also spoke of men,
fantastic nicknamed drifters riding north
to man the threshing teams.
You never told the same tale
twice the same—
but, chaffed through every change,
forever would that city slicker
harness horses backwards,
a hundred times Crabapple Slim
get crocked with Arkansas
and almost burn
the barn down in his glee.
Assuming I'd get rich
you didn't dream I'd be
suspended too, intoxicated on
the airways of the world.

The compass swings. The left wing
dips toward Himalaya peaks.
Swept up in this great roar,
the pockets inside out,
the brain cannot
keep track
of what is left behind.
I'm banking on
the wind, Old Man,
make me content.
One-half this world away I float,
a random dust mote in your mind.

XXXIV

JAMES HEYNEN

James Heynen spent the first eighteen years of his life in Sioux County in Iowa, where he was born in a farmhouse in 1940. He has also lived in Grand Rapids, Michigan; Hull, Iowa; Iowa City; Flint, Michigan; Custer, South Dakota; Eugene, Oregon; Anchorage, Alaska; and Boise, Idaho. He is an editor, a college instructor, and a coordinator for the Artists-in-the-Schools program. He has been learning the Sioux language in order to translate the songs of the Sioux into English.

Mr. Heynen's first book of poems was *Maedra Poems,* 1974, followed by *Notes From Custer* in 1976.

AFTER READING *BLACK ELK SPEAKS* AND CLIMBING HARNEY PEAK

"Then I was standing on the highest mountain of them all, and round about beneath me was the whole hoop of the world." Black Elk, His Vision

A little cloud came out for Black Elk
at this point in his last climb;
a sacred touch, a little rain.

Today there's only South Dakota's
clear dry sky,
but the view is good:
the arrogant granite spires,
and farther, Custer City
reduced to an amber stain
on the dark blanket of pine.

I read the ledger left in the army
look-out tower, testimonies
of a thousand Americans
struck by the grandeur of God.
The view *is* good:
I sign my name.

A wild goat comes toward me,
looking up: what for—an apple,
an open hand? Tame-eyed
demon, who sent you?
Not even your fleece is wet.

Perhaps this is how it will be:
a wild goat and I
discussing the nature of God
and the future of man. But I
who have drunk from all
the fountains of disbelief,
empty enough to hope,
only forget the question.

The goat leaves, quietly
down the steep slope.
I look around wondering
if I've spit in the eye of vision,
missed its one quick glance.
Goat, was it you?

Coming down, I get another chance:
a new-born fawn on the slope, innocent,
pure as an ancient offering.
I stroke the slimy hair, and then
remember too late: my odor, my
fatal touch. The doe is wise, I know,
will never return. More
dry bones, dry bones, in the
old man's dream of his nation.

XXXV

WILLIAM E. RYAN

W. E. Ryan was born in Chicago in 1943 and lived there for twenty-four years. He has also lived in New York City and San Francisco for one year each and in South Dakota for six years (Mission, Pierre, and Vermillion). He is a poet, an artist, a photographer, and brings these talents together, along with other concerns, in the field of communications. With James Minor, he is the author of *Reflections in a Circus Mirror*.

PEYOTE CEREMONY

you began lynx-eyed
& held one sudden
  swirl of sickness
  between fire & drum
  a splash of flame
  climbing
vision turned inside
out
slits across marble
  oklahoma to south
  dakota: a northern ceremony
  bonehigh & boneshirt
  body like stick
  in the warmth of campfire
  on seasons of snow
  with
  animal robes covering you
  in a land of dreams
  as a she-dog clinging to her pups

                the earth & sky
                are enough
in your night
                later
you ask a drum to be placed
                upon your breast
                to travois your gentle
                dying song
                as a silver mist
                threading priestly pine
                & become
                a spider's web
                to drape yourself carelessly
                across the void that is time
in your dawn
extinction lurks
                everwaiting museumed headdress
                catches your spirit
                a blur
                with the once buffalo
                while the dance slows to suntake
                & new-beaded morning

                the awl gone
                you make a laughing bowl
                to wash the hand
                that touched
                your bow of body

HEADED WEST

this farmhouse leads me
        down a highway
        to pass a dead fox:
                freshkill
                littered
                across old pavement

my sudden presence scatters scavengers
        of the moment,
                rousting
                the winged wake
                in a no passing
                        zone

I drive straight ahead
    watching the world
    through a rear view mirror:
        remembering that we all
        somehow
        end up empty
        in the same waiting room
        &
with our lives flowing two directions
we break circuit with the fox
attempting hollow answers
for desperate questions

forgetting patience
with aphoric sight
    we break step
    in weathered shoes
    to criss-cross highways,
forgetting maps & familiar signs,
    &
    run out of road

carrying the images of ghostfox
    my vision yellows
    past a hitchhiker
    at sixty miles an hour
into the sun

XXXVI

JAMES MINOR

A resident of South Dakota since 1972, Minor was born in Aurora, Illinois in 1942 and lived in Wheaton and DeKalb before moving west. As Byron Franzen is an example of the young people leaving the state, so Jim Minor (like W. E. Ryan) represents a new reverse trend, that of people from densely populated states seeking a quieter life with more freedom in an essentially rural state.

The Minor-Ryan book of poems, *Reflections in a Circus Mirror,* 1970, won the book publication award sponsored by the National Federation of State Poetry Societies.

SMITH FALLS

Early afternoon
beneath a South Dakota sun
had been
a warm one

walking field
& stretching wire fence
wide enough
for passage.

There you led me,
both of us children,
directing my sight
away from the falls,

the walk,
steep & rooted
rounded, straightened
into an almost full view
of sound,

you stood,
cautioning me
before the final bend
to follow
blinded until
I stood
where sight
& sound
became at once
one.

There Smith Falls
like the talon
of a hawk
cut deep into headstone

& we stood
in the peaceful spray
of angels,
motionless,

talking
as if one could retrace
the footsteps of time
in an hour.

Afternoon at Smith Falls
had been
a heady one,

remembering Fritz
        (whose shoes
        seemed sewed
        to his feet
        & never did
        come off).

MISSION, SOUTH DAKOTA

At abourezk's the sioux
are old wood,
autumn skin weathered
and dry of paint,

on benches they sit,
head bent, awning
in the sun,
lakota tongue running deep
and fresh as wellspring,

by 5 p.m. a thunderbird
rises in the west,
driving wind across
the bone and
feathered plain,

here tipi ring
like prayer circle
is broken, black road
from the east
darker to travel.

WINTER & SOUTH DAKOTA

Oh my love why
are you barren
in this time I
love you best.

XXXVII

FREYA MANFRED

A native of Minnesota (born in Minneapolis, November 1944), Freya Manfred graduated from Macalester College in St. Paul and then received the M.A. from Stanford University in 1968. She has been associated with the University of South Dakota, with the Poets-in-the-Schools program, and for the 1975-1976 school year was a Radcliffe Scholar in Cambridge. Although her father is a novelist, Freya has concentrated on poetry. Her first book was published in 1971—*A Goldenrod Will Grow*.

VERMILLION WEST

A walk in the dark
cold prairie at night
held back at the ankles
by tangled grass.
The sunset was rooster feather red and yellow;
now smoke is in my hair;
the fire set it there.
As I leap a low bush,
a male duck hawks in the swamp below.

You need not take my arm.
I'll walk by myself.

There's a sun glint barely left
on the edge out there.
Coyotes sound like loons
inside a house—not here.
One rounds his shoulders
on a wind-ice hump top,
leans forward to stretch back legs.

If my arms would stretch
straight out a mile flat,
I'd touch him—
Straight the other way a mile,
his mate.
Their blood through mine,
I think, could come on a center.
Heart, my heart pumps full,
warm in the body —
Body warm in the night's belly.

XXXVIII

DAVID ALLAN EVANS

David Evans was born in Sioux City, Iowa and lived there from 1940 to 1962. After two years in Alamosa, Colorado and two more in Iowa City he went to Brookings where he is an associate professor of English at South Dakota State University. His degrees are from Morningside College, the University of Iowa, and the University of Arkansas. Evans has been active in the area of poetry in South Dakota, through writing, teaching, editing, and poetry readings. His books are *Among Athletes,* 1971, and *Train Windows,* 1976.

WINTER-KILL

Ears aim upwind.
December sun is
frozen in his eye.
He is hunched in the
last north acre
of the final field
where little game trails
cross and cross.

Someone is moving near
crouched goggled
full tilt in the
Polar Cat—

He whirls to go
but the Cat
is *here above him*
with him silvering
over blurring stubble
until his breath
bursts like a torch
and he runs down slow inside
giving a face to snow
giving into
it.

POEM WITHOUT A METAPHOR

for father, dead seven springs

    the seventh robin
    lights on the thumb
    of my son

    my lilac bush
    is doing its
    white explosions

    a south breeze
    stirs my unnamed tree

    the Missouri
    swells far from the
    bluff of your grave

    a Dakota farmer
    inverts a corn field

    a rock
    will soon go skimming
    the perfectly round
    pond of childhood:

    seven springs
    and still I lack
    the metaphor
    of your death

SUNSET

Before I left my spot
on a bridge over the Sioux
watching the sun go down,
I heaved a single handful
of gravel that, when it

met the silent current
burst into applause

XXXIX

DENNIS SAMPSON

A native of South Dakota, Dennis Sampson graduated from South Dakota State University, spent a semester studying contemporary poetry at the University of South Dakota, and after working at a packing plant in Sioux City was admitted into the writing program at the University of Iowa, 1974.

DAKOTA LOVE POEM

Monday and all alone and I am brave
enough to investigate the sound like rubbing
on the outer wall of the farm—the door
opens and is the mouth of darkness as
    I enter into it.
    The darkness wraps me round.

I flee into the thicketed regions,
I am happy to be wind. I see the cities
lighting up the sky, the bones of the living,
the bones of the dead. All around me are the stars.
    A dog sleeps under a tree.
    A fire burns in on itself.

I go into the mind of a child.
I am the unidentified man in his deepest dreams.
Waking he will forget me, I vanish fast.
I attend the dying, the almost dead.
I let a cry go out for the homeless,
the nameless, the lost of the world.
The moon listens to me and is silent.
I see the moon go down like a hand
into the empty pocket of the sky.
The sun rises round like a new face.
I watch secretly old men refilling old pipes

with their stubs of fingers, saying, "If it
doesn't rain today it will rain tomorrow."
The Missouri river powerfully pushes a rotted
log. A farmer cups his rough hands into water.
I hear swallows singing and step closer to
understand how they make such happiness.
I breathe the rank odor the split carcass
of the lamb exudes. I rub a dull stone.
The coyote hears me and the heavy fur of his
back stands up. A child shinnys up a tree.
The shelterbelts are shining in the light
of a long rain. The pool halls are opening.
A skinny hoodlum is flirting with the eight ball.

But finally I remember who I am. I remember
the ashtray tilted like a hat on the carpet,
the fly trying to escape through its wall
of air, the sour odor of my body.
I remember my muscular forearms,
my naked, my somber face.

I look over my shoulder.
The door closes. Click.

THE FARMHOUSE

Summer is deep with evening,
The night is mild
With hidden crickets
By all the lighted window sills.

I am only a small way
From the Farmhouse porch,
Where mom and dad are chuckling
Over gin rummy and a light red wine.

I would be with them tonight,
But the moon blushes so well
And rushes behind the clouds
That I like to watch it, here,
With my back against an oak.

No one moves this land
Or shakes this tree
Or tells us that we must desert
The wooden house, a rocking chair,
Or plow the earth a certain way.

XL

LYNN SHOEMAKER

The son of Gretchen Gall Shoemaker, Lynn was born in Racine, Wisconsin in 1939. He lived in Yankton for many years, then spent eight years in California where for a while he was associated with the publication, *Beyond Baroque*. Since 1970 he has been in Ithaca, New York. Besides writing poetry he teaches woodshop to youngsters in an alternate elementary school.

Following his college work at Harvard, the University of South Dakota, and the University of California, Lynn worked in the peace movement for six years. He has one daughter and has written one book of poems, *Coming Home*.

SAND

beachcomber

 old man
 pulling a wire-mesh cradle
 dragging your eyes along the ground
 sucking your chin
 down into your chest
 a last breath
 arms and ten fingers
 an outreaching and some far point
 between your shoulders
 pull
 but you sink foot by foot
 into the sand

prophecy

 in South Dakota
 near the Missouri or
 in the rich bottom lands

of the Jim
a few oldtimers still keep plow-teams
post-industrial era seldom use them
sweat still turns to white salt
and flies
under a hard sun

the plow
I put my face close to it
it was shiny
it could cut my face turn
my face around
it could cut the earth
turn fertility
over
it was dark and red
and shiny

International-Harvester
John Deere   Massey-Harris   Ferguson
combines
finding in their own sound
and fury kernels
of the same old idiot's voice
the sun in sand
sand in sun

beachcomber

what do you hope to find
old man
the old and new mother is
spread out at your feet
near her warm
near the water
you have uncovered the voluptuous
neck of a whiskey bottle
nothing in it

can you put it close
up to your eye and see
more than rocking horses from Kentucky
rocking cradles and chairs
nailed to the sand
and ocean floor

can you see her she's
waiting for you
to throw off your spotted
trenchcoat three sizes too small
run and rip hell
out of your small-step
black Chaplin-of-the-caves pants
and feel the whirlwind inside
your red cracker throat

your breath is not made of laughs
old man   your clothes are devouring you
when I look back your
flesh is gone
a piling driven
into the ground with your
shoes laced on so tight you'll never
spread your toes
spine limbless leafless
the rain drips off the end
of your despair

prophecy

the Oglala Sioux believe
a tree grows out of the sun
its limbs spread
through the gaps of a dream
its leaves fall one by one
into a dark cave

Black Elk their eldest Shaman speaks
of a day when
the abyss will be filled
and overflowing will feed all
the earth's skeletons
the buffalo will rise and roam
trampling even the voice
of the sand